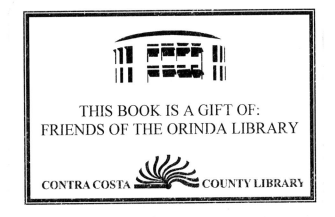

Scottsboro and Its Legacy

Recent Titles in
Crime, Media, and Popular Culture

Scottsboro and Its Legacy

The Cases that Challenged American Legal and Social Justice

James R. Acker

Crime, Media, and Popular Culture
Frankie Y. Bailey and Steven Chermak, Series Editors

PRAEGER

Westport, Connecticut
London

Library of Congress Cataloging-in-Publication Data

Acker, James R., 1951–
    Scottsboro and its legacy : the cases that challenged American legal and social justice / James R. Acker.
      p. cm. — (Crime, media, and popular culture, ISSN 1549–196X)
    Includes bibliographical references and index.
    ISBN-13: 978–0–275–99083–1 (alk. paper)
1. Scottsboro Trial, Scottsboro, Ala., 1931. 2. Scottsboro Trial, Scottsboro, Ala., 1931—Press
coverage. 3. Southern States—Social conditions. 4. Criminal justice, Administration of—Social aspects
—United States. 5. Social justice. I. Title.
KF224.S34A25 2008
345.761′9502523—dc22   2007039689

British Library Cataloguing in Publication Data is available.

Library of Congress Catalog Card Number: 2007039689
ISBN-13: 978–0–275–99083–1
ISSN: 1549–196X

First published in 2008

Praeger Publishers, 88 Post Road West, Westport, CT 06881
An imprint of Greenwood Publishing Group, Inc.
www.praeger.com

Printed in the United States of America

The paper used in this book complies with the
Permanent Paper Standard issued by the National
Information Standards Organization (Z39.48–1984).

10 9 8 7 6 5 4 3 2 1

To Jenny, Elizabeth, and Anna.
And to the Scottsboro Boys—Olen Montgomery, Clarence Norris, Haywood Patterson, Ozie Powell, Willie Roberson, Charlie Weems, Eugene Williams, Andy Wright, and Roy Wright—and to those who have fought to correct legal and social injustices in their cases and others.

Contents

Series Foreword

This volume is part of an interdisciplinary series on Crime, Media, and Popular Culture from Praeger Publishers. Because of the pervasiveness of media in our lives and the salience of crime and criminal justice issues, we feel it is especially important to provide a home for scholars who are engaged in innovative and thoughtful research on important crime and mass media issues. The books in the series touch on many broad themes in the study of crime and mass media, including process issues such as the social construction of crime and moral panics; presentation issues such as the images of victims, offenders, and criminal justice figures in the news and popular culture; and effects such as the influence of the media on criminal behavior and criminal justice administration.

During the summer of 2007, as this book was going to press, several events that illustrate the interactions of mass media, popular culture, and crime were in the news. The critically acclaimed and immensely popular HBO series, *The Sopranos,* broadcast its last first-run episode. This was covered by the media with interviews of the cast and creators of the show and with discussion of the series as a cultural phenomenon. Another matter in the news involved The Church of England and Sony, the manufacturer of the PlayStation video game "Resistance: Fall of Man." BBC News reported that the Church is considering legal action against Sony because the company did not obtain permission to use the interior of the Manchester Cathedral as the setting for a scene in the video game in which hundred of combatants are killed. The Church and concerned citizens of Manchester assert that the company has been irresponsible in locating the video game in a city that has been plagued by real-life gun violence and has been struggling to deal with the problem. In the most recent media event, Atlanta Falcons quarterback Michael Vick was indicted on federal charges alleging that he had sponsored dog fights and traveled across state lines to participate in such fights. The extensive media coverage of the allegations included images of animal-rights groups protesting as they demanded that Vick be fired by the Falcons, comments from politicians and others about the brutality of dog fighting, and "man-on-the-street comments" from African Americans who questioned the rush to judgment that seemed to be denying Vick his day in court.

The media coverage of these events—the end of a television crime drama about New Jersey mobsters that became a part of American culture, the response of the Church of England and citizens of Manchester to the use of a real setting in a violent fantasy game, and the commencement of yet another "media trial" (see Surette 2006) of a celebrity alleged to have engaged in violent behavior (against canine victims in this case)—illustrates the involvement of the media in the social construction of images of crime, criminals, and the criminal justice system. In this series, scholars present research on issues central to the complex nature of our relationship with media. Peter Berger and Thomas Luckman coined the phrase "the social construction of reality" to describe the process by which we acquire knowledge about our environment. They and others have argued that reality is a mediated experience. We acquire what Emile Durkheim described as "social facts" through a several-pronged process of personal experience, interaction with others, academic education, and, yes, the mass media. With regard to crime and the criminal justice system, many people acquire much of their information from the news and from entertainment media. The issues raised by *The Sopranos* phenomenon and the use of the Manchester Cathedral by Sony in a video game illustrate not only the blurring of the line between make-believe and reality but more generally the impact of what we consume—what we read, watch, see, play, and hear—on our lives. The Michael Vick coverage illustrates the manner in which a criminal case can blur the boundaries between news (for example, the federal investigation of an illegal sport) and entertainment (that is, the coverage of major league sports and athletes).

The interactions of crime and mass media/popular culture that we now observe have evolved over a period of time. In fact, print media in the nineteenth century assumed its modern form at the same historical moment when criminal justice agencies were being created. With the birth of the "penny press," newspapers became inexpensive enough for the working man. The editors of these newspapers quickly realized that they could sell more papers by not only introducing regular "police beats" in their pages, but by reporting on sensational crimes. In New York City, the birthplace of the penny press, reporting of two such crimes increased circulation in 1836 and 1841, respectively: the trial of a young clerk for the murder of a stylish brothel prostitute named Helen Jewett and the

mysterious death of Mary Rogers, "the beautiful cigar girl" who was found float-
ing in the Hudson River.

By the end of the nineteenth century, the idea of journalistic professionalism
had emerged. At the same time, the newspaper wars between the Pulitzer and
Hearst newspapers had given rise to the sensational reporting that came to be
called "yellow journalism." This was followed by the "jazz age" reporting of the
1920s. But during and in the aftermath of World War I, the media were also giving attention to the "Red Scare" inspired by the Bolshevik Revolution and the
Russian Civil War. The concern about antigovernment conspiracies in the
United States was further fueled by a bomb scare that led to a series of raids in
1919, ordered by U.S. Attorney General A. Mitchell Palmer and coordinated
by J. Edgar Hoover, Assistant Director of the Bureau of Investigation (later
renamed the Federal Bureau of Investigation). The raids involved the roundup
of socialists, communists, and other alleged conspirators. Thus, in the 1920s,
Americans were aware of the Communist Party, and many had come to perceive
those who allied themselves with the communist movement as dangerous
radicals.

In this volume, James R. Acker examines the media coverage of the Scottsboro
Boys case. This case attracted international attention because of the involvement
of the International Labor Defense (ILD), the legal arm of the Communist Party.
Nine young black men were accused of the gang rapes of two young white
women while all were hitching a ride on a slow-moving Alabama train. The case
is fascinating not only because of the spotlight it shines on Southern justice,
regional conflicts, and gender issues, but because of the social and political issues
highlighted in the battle between the National Association for the Advancement
of Colored People (NAACP) and the ILD over who would represent the young
men, known as the "Scottsboro Boys," in court.

In the first trial the defendants were reluctantly defended by local attorneys
appointed by the court. Eight defendants were convicted and sentenced to death.
The ILD gained permission from the Boys' families to find them more effective
legal representation. The ILD persuaded Samuel Leibowitz, one of best criminal
defense attorneys in the United States, to take the case. Leibowitz was Jewish and
from New York City. His religion and the fact that he was a Northerner became
important factors in the series of trials that followed. The Scottsboro Boys saga
would eventually yield two Supreme Court decisions about the rights of the
accused. But for the defendants the ordeal would drag on for years.

In this outstanding addition to the series, Professor Acker provides a fascinating account of the case that lives on in cultural memory. The Scottsboro Boys
case is "one of the essentials" for those readers seeking to understand the interaction of American social and cultural history with criminal justice. In 1931, as the
Scottsboro Boys trials were underway, a state militia unit stood guard outside the

courtroom to ensure that the nine young black men would not be taken out and lynched by a mob. Almost 60 years later, in 1989–1990, the mainstream media in New York City reported on the alleged rape of a young, white, investment banker by a gang of young black and Hispanic teenagers in what became known as "the Central Park Jogger case." The negative stereotypes used in describing the young men led the *Amsterdam News* (a black newspaper in the City) and some white journalists to question whether the young men could/did receive a fair trial (see Benedict 1992). As recently as 2003, when Kobe Bryant, a black National Basketball Association (NBA) player, was accused of the rape of a young white female hotel employee, discussion again turned to the impact of media coverage on the outcome of the case. This time one of the questions was whether the alleged victim was being negatively portrayed in the media, including the release of information about her on Internet sites. Again, the media were castigated by some scholars for perpetuating "rape myths." Other observers raised the specter of a "racial hoax" similar to the Scottsboro Boys case. The collision of race, class, and gender issues played out in front of media audiences and in "water cooler" conversations inspired by media coverage.

In the Scottsboro Boys case, we see an early twentieth century example of the collision of these issues that still plague us. The Scottsboro Boys story offers a window on American crime and justice. As Professor Acker shows us, it is also the story of an American tragedy.

Frankie Y. Bailey and Steven Chermak,
Series Editors

REFERENCES

Benedict, Helen. 1992. *Virgin or Vamp: How the Press Covers Sex Crimes.* New York: Oxford University Press.

Surette, Ray. 2007. *Media, Crime, and Crime Justice,* 3rd ed. Belmont, California: Thomson Learning.

Preface

Much can be learned from studying criminal trials. The people in them, as in all walks of life, are venal and courageous, fragile and strong, peevish and righteous, ambitious and humble, myopic and enlightened—and possess all of those qualities at once and in different measure depending on some peculiar mix of fate, fortune, and life circumstances. Trial issues spring from facts. The facts are often ambiguous and disputed. They involve the accuser and the accused but also transcend them, embracing witnesses and social context. They demand resolution. Yet their resolution can be uncertain, and invoke issues beyond the competence and control of the involved parties. Criminal trials are designed to ascribe guilt and proclaim innocence within a system of justice. The decisions are weighty and made with high expectations. Criminal trials sharpen our focus about what is right and wrong and how we arrive at those answers. The courtroom, sometimes, is a metaphor, and the verdicts there reached speak beyond the actors in them to illuminate larger social truths and visions of justice.

The trials of the Scottsboro Boys—nine black youths accused of raping two white women on an Alabama train in 1931—offer this much and more to those willing to become immersed in them. They open a window on a time and place where social norms weighed so heavily on principles of law that the law buckled, resisted, and then buckled again in uneasy dialogue between lawyers and judges and juries, and between the courts of Alabama and the U.S. Supreme Court. They generated enormous local, regional, national, and international interest that alternatively worked to the benefit and the detriment of the nine young men. They brought social and legal issues to light that demanded attention then and compel our attention now.

In telling a part of the Scottsboro Boys' story and exploring some of the timeless issues associated with their trials, I owe much to two earlier writers who compiled detailed and fascinating histories of the cases. Readers interested in gaining their perspectives should consult Dan T. Carter, *Scottsboro: A Tragedy of the American South* (Baton Rouge, Louisiana: Louisiana State University Press, rev. ed. 1979) and James Goodman, *Stories of Scottsboro* (New York: Vintage Books 1994). Professor Douglas Linder's informative "Famous Trials" Web site also should be consulted (http://www.law.umkc.edu/faculty/projects/FTrials/scottsboro/scottsb.htm) for a wealth of background material about the cases. The rich 2001 PBS documentary, *Scottsboro: An American Tragedy,* produced by Daniel Anker and Barak Goodman, is well worth viewing.

My own work, which relates in part to the media's important role in reporting on and helping give definition to the Scottsboro cases, relies heavily on contemporaneous newspaper and magazine coverage. I could not have begun to assemble my research materials without the heroic help of the interlibrary loan department at the University at Albany Library, and the similar assistance I received from reference librarians at the Cornell Law School Library. I am indebted to Qing Wei for her invaluable assistance in acquiring microfilm and other newspaper records, printing them, and organizing her work so I could take advantage of it. I thank Michelle Storm for performing similar duties. Giza Rodick very generously shared her own research about the Scottsboro Boys with me. I benefited immensely from my collaboration with Elizabeth Brown and Christine Englebrecht on a chapter that we coauthored about these cases in Frankie Y. Bailey and Steven Chermak, eds., *Famous American Crimes and Trials* (Westport, Connecticut: Praeger Publishers 2004). I also thank Frankie Bailey and Steve Chermak for their help with this volume, and Suzanne Staszak-Silva for her immense patience and guidance in seeing this book through. Errors and shortcomings are entirely my own.

Introduction

Few events are as mesmerizing as a criminal trial born of events that transcend the parties and particulars of a local courtroom and that, redolent with symbolism, compels the nation to confront fundamental questions of social justice. Trials embodying these qualities serve a function reminiscent of the public morality plays of a bygone era.[1] Through their presentation and resolution of case-specific facts and issues, they give meaning to and reaffirm the value of fundamental abstract principles. Yet unlike oft-staged dramas that enable audiences to witness them firsthand, court proceedings (at least prior to the advent of Court TV and its ilk) are one-time events that occur erratically and have limited seating. Most people have little direct contact with the criminal justice system and necessarily rely on published accounts of trials as a substitute for what they cannot personally witness.[2] Consequently, what is portrayed in the media, and how those accounts are presented, not only inform but also help shape public perceptions and attitudes about crime and justice.[3]

Few sagas combine the transcendent significance of a criminal trial and the news media's representation and construction of the social meaning of the events giving rise to it with the power and poignancy of the Scottsboro Boys[4] cases. This epic legal drama began near Scottsboro, Alabama in the midst of the Great Depression. Nine young black men were put on trial for their lives after being accused of raping two white women. The immediate disputes of fact and law were never far removed from issues of race and social class. On trial, in addition to the defendants, was the tenor of Southern justice. The Communist Party embraced the case as a *cause celebre* as did, shortly thereafter, the NAACP and other organizations committed to racial equality. One of the country's leading criminal defense attorneys waged battle against not only local prosecutors, but also capricious judges, regional prejudices, and overt anti-Semitism. The proceedings were conducted within the brooding dark shadow of Alabama's electric chair. The U.S. Supreme Court twice issued decisions granting the defendants new trials, and in the process announced magisterial rules of constitutional law that foretold dramatic changes in federal court oversight of state systems of criminal justice.

Although the Scottsboro Boys cases date back to the 1930s, their defining issues are starkly familiar to contemporary criminal justice. The death penalty remains in effect throughout much of the United States, although no longer for rape[5] or for juveniles.[6] The high stakes of capital cases continue to focus attention on problems that mar the administration of justice today, including claims of racial bias, ill-prepared and inadequately funded defense counsel, unrepresentative juries, prejudicial publicity, and wrongful convictions—all of which are vividly reminiscent of the Scottsboro trials. Controversy still swirls about the rules of evidence that govern rape prosecutions, including the proper boundaries for cross-examining complaining witnesses, an issue that hovered over the allegations involving the Scottsboro Boys.

The nine young men accused of rape in Alabama, indelibly labeled by the news media as "the Scottsboro Boys," are with us no more. Nor are their accusers, the lawyers who represented and prosecuted them, the jurors who sat in judgment of them, the judges who presided over their trials and appeals, and the newspaper reporters and editors who reported on them to the nation and the world. Still, the legal and societal issues linked so closely to this case endure with discouraging persistence. The case is a prism that helps make visible the interrelated social forces that shape the administration of the criminal law. And it also is a window on the media influences that sustain and give content to public perceptions of justice, in both historical and contemporary context.

The stories told in the ensuing pages are based in part on trial transcripts and other court records, but primarily on the contemporaneous newspaper and other media accounts of the cases and the perspectives of social commentators who offered their interpretations about them. As such, the narratives are not presented as an unbiased historical record of the events as they unfolded but rather as a story that reveals as much about the storytellers and their milieu as the cases and case participants. This is a tale of the Scottsboro Boys and the events in which they were immersed, as molded and defined by the media and the enveloping social context of the times.

Arrest and Accusation

On "Black Thursday," October 24, 1929, panic had besieged the New York Stock Exchange during Herbert Hoover's presidency. Stock prices temporarily stabilized but then plummeted. "Black Monday" gave way to "Black Tuesday," and within three years the average price of a share of stock had fallen by 80 percent.[1] In 1931 Americans were on the move, leaving their homes, looking for work, struggling to make ends meet. By year's end, more than 11 million people would be unemployed, double the number of the prior year. A drought began that would turn major sections of the Midwest and South into a dust bowl. Farmers abandoned parched fields, in search of a way to support their families. Others took to the rails, knowing that even if prospects for work were not better in the next town, they could not be worse than in the previous one. The United States was mired in the second year of the Great Depression. On March 25, 1931, Ida B. Wells-Barnett, an African American anti-lynching activist and journalist who had been forcibly removed from a Memphis train in 1884 because she refused to ride in the "blacks-only" car, died in Chicago.[2]

At 10:20 A.M., Wednesday, March 25, 1931, somewhat behind schedule, a Southern Railroad freight train left Chattanooga, Tennessee, bound for Memphis. Between the engine and caboose of the half-mile long train were tank cars, flat cars, boxcars, and gondolas—sturdy, low-sided cars without roofs that commonly were used to haul heavy loads of coal and gravel. Scattered about the cars were several riders who were "hoboing," having hopped the rail in search of employment or simply to move on to wherever the train would take them. Among the illicit passengers were Victoria Price and Ruby Bates, who were returning home to Huntsville, Alabama after failing to find work in Chattanooga's textile mills. Price was 21 years old, and Bates 17. Each was white. Four friends who lived in Chattanooga also had scrambled onto the train: 18-year-old Haywood Patterson; brothers Andy (age 19) and Roy (13) Wright; and Eugene Williams (13). They did not know five other young men from Georgia who were on board, nor were those five acquainted with each other. Charlie Weems, the oldest, was 20. Clarence Norris was 18; Olen Montgomery 17; Willie Roberson 15; and Ozie Powell 15.[3] The nine youths—soon to be known as the Scottsboro Boys—were all black.

Although Memphis was due west, the train would meander through northern Alabama and then slice through part of Mississippi before reaching its destination. Shortly after departing Chattanooga it entered Alabama's Jackson County, which borders Georgia to the east, and Tennessee to the north. A number of white youths also were on board the train, riding the rails. Trouble began shortly after the locomotive emerged from the tunnel that burrowed through Lookout Mountain. A white boy stepped on Haywood Patterson's hand as Patterson clung to the side of a tank car. An exchange of words gave way to rock throwing.[4] The train pulled in to the station in Stevenson, Alabama, some 45 miles removed from Chattanooga and another 20 miles away from Scottsboro, a town of 3,500 and the county seat. The confrontation resumed when the train continued its westward journey. A fight broke out pitting a group of the white boys against several blacks.[5] The black youths got the better of the whites, all but one of whom either jumped or were thrown off the slow-moving train. Orville Gilley, spared ejection because he risked serious injury or death if he hit the ground after the train had picked up speed, was the lone white combatant remaining on board as the locomotive rumbled toward Scottsboro.[6]

The deposed whites were none too pleased. They made their way back to Stevenson and reported to the stationmaster that they had been assaulted and thrown off the train by a "bunch of Negroes," and that they wanted to press charges.[7] Although they had been illegally on board the train themselves, they undoubtedly (and correctly) perceived that the authorities would consider their treatment at the hands of the black youths as the more serious affront to Alabama law and thus had no inhibitions about lodging their complaint. By the time they made their report, the train had already passed through Scottsboro. The Jackson County Sheriff, M.L. Wann, telephoned a deputy who lived near Paint Rock, the train's next scheduled stop, roughly 20 miles beyond Scottsboro. The sheriff gave instructions to "capture every negro on the train," and to deputize as many citizens as could be found to carry out this order.[8] When the train arrived in Paint Rock just before 2:00 P.M., it was greeted by dozens of armed white men, who immediately fanned throughout the train's 42 cars in search of black riders. They found Olen Montgomery alone in a tank car near the caboose. Willie Roberson occupied an otherwise empty boxcar. Ozie Powell was in a nearby gondola.[9] They and the other six black youths who were dispersed throughout the train were rounded up at gunpoint, tied together with a plow rope, and marched to the back of a flatbed truck where they awaited transportation to the Scottsboro jail. A deputy told Haywood Patterson that they were being charged with assault and attempted murder,[10] an apparent reference to the claims made by the white boys in Stevenson.

The search of the train revealed more than the nine young blacks. Also uncovered were Victoria Price and Ruby Bates, whose unanticipated presence surprised members of the posse but did not command their immediate attention. Some 20 minutes later the accusation first surfaced that would come to define the Scottsboro Boys case and soon cascade over the Alabama countryside, and then the nation and the world. One of the young women, perhaps Ruby Bates, either volunteered or else responded affirmatively to a sheriff deputy's question that they both had been raped by the gang of blacks while the train made its passage.[11]

The nine youths taken into custody did not learn of this accusation until several hours later, when they were led from behind bars at the Scottsboro jail and lined up so they could be confronted with the two white women.[12] In the interim, the women had been examined by two local physicians, Dr. R. R. Bridges and Dr. Marvin Lynch. News of the alleged rapes spread like wildfire through the community, first by word of mouth originating with the deputies in Paint Rock, and then later that afternoon in the local newspapers. Headlines in one of Scottsboro's newspapers blared, "Nine Negro Men Rape Two White Girls," and denounced the "black fiends" who had "committed [this] revolting crime."[13] The *Huntsville Daily Times,* the hometown newspaper of Price and Bates, ran a front-page story on the afternoon of March 25, in which the "accused ravishing" was "described as one of the most brutal attacks in the history of the Tennessee Valley."[14] A mob of several hundred gathered outside of the jail, threatening to storm the facility if the boys were not turned over to them.[15] The prospect of a lynching could not be dismissed. Although in decline by the 1930s, more than 2,800 lynchings had been documented in the country over the past half century, frequently involving southern white mobs acting against blacks suspected of raping white women.[16]

Sheriff Wann placed an urgent telephone call to Montgomery, imploring Governor Benjamin Meeks Miller for assistance. The governor responded promptly. He ordered armed National Guard troops dispatched to Scottsboro from the closest armory, approximately 20 miles away.[17] Order was maintained and after the immediate crisis subsided the boys were transferred to a sturdier jail in Gadsden, in nearby Etowah County.[18] The *New York Times'* first report on the case appeared on March 26 under the caption, "Jail Head Asks Troops as

Mob Seeks Negroes; Riot Feared in Scottsboro, Ala., After Arrest of Nine, Held for Attacking Girls."[19] A prominent Alabama paper, the *Birmingham News,* conversely proclaimed on its front page on the same day: "Town Reported Quiet After National Guard Arrives to Watch Prison." The story noted that "the negroes...slept soundly during the night while the soldiers protected them from any mob violence."[20]

The different newspaper renditions of events in the immediate aftermath of the two women's rape claims harbingered a dramatic and intensifying competition involving the media, interest groups, and courtroom actors to give meaning to the Scottsboro Boys case. At least formally, what happened on that Southern Railway train after it left the Stevenson station and prior to its arrival in Paint Rock would be determined in a court of law. For courts are where factual disputes of this nature are meant to be resolved, through legal procedures that have been refined over centuries to best elicit the truth. But courthouse walls are not impermeable. The law, in operation, is subject to social influences that find no recognition in rules of evidence or procedure. The deeper meaning of the Scottsboro Boys case is only revealed through understanding the social context and the pervading extralegal factors that left their imprint on the courtroom evidence.

More was on trial than the nine young men, who risked capital punishment if convicted. Also at issue was whether justice dispensed in an Alabama rape trial in the 1930s could be impervious to the deeply ingrained social taboo, especially inviolate in the South, against black men engaging in sexual relations with white women. At the same time, the economic and social unrest occasioned by the Great Depression had provided a catalyst for the Communist Party to recruit disaffected workers. The Communists perceived the Scottsboro Boys case as a vehicle for making inroads in the South, particularly among blacks. The legal issues thus became infused with politics and social class, in addition to having sectional and racial dimensions.

Fundamental questions of law intersected with the cultural currents of the Scottsboro trials. The nine youths were poor, uneducated, and far from home when arrested. On trial for their lives, they lacked the resources and skills to defend themselves against the rape accusations. They were dependent initially on the State of Alabama to provide them with the essential ingredients of due process of law, including competent legal representation, impartial jurors, and fair-minded judges. If the state courts failed in their obligation, they would have to persuade the federal courts to intervene. Difficult evidentiary issues stalked the rape prosecutions, and those issues became especially challenging as information emerged about the backgrounds and reputations of the accusing witnesses. Few of the legal questions would be resolved easily, and many endure in contemporary criminal trials.

Jackson County officials moved swiftly in the face of the unrest following the Boys' arrest to press charges and bring the cases to trial. Indeed, it was understood that quick legal action could be instrumental and perhaps essential to help quell community agitation and avert a lynching.[21] The *Montgomery Advertiser* lauded the decisive action taken by Sheriff Wann and the governor. It editorialized:

Ordinarily it would be next to impossible to restrain the mob spirit in such circumstances....

Governor Miller acted promptly and in the best Alabama tradition in sending National Guardsmen to Scottsboro. This was a wise precautionary measure.

The courts are acting promptly in arranging for a grand jury investigation of the crime.

In other words, in face of extreme provocation, Alabamians have again shown that they are willing to let the law have its way.[22]

Circuit Judge Alfred E. Hawkins conferred with the circuit solicitor, H.G. Bailey, and Sheriff Wann, and announced within 24 hours of the Boys' arrests that he would travel to Scottsboro to convene a grand jury. According to the *Birmingham News,* the officials would proceed "immediately to indict the nine negroes. A prompt trial...also was indicated."[23] Solicitor Bailey declared that "he would demand the death penalty in every case."[24] Meanwhile, the youths remained in the Gadsden Jail.

The Jackson County Grand Jury met in Scottsboro on Monday, March 30, to hear evidence in the case.[25] True bills of indictment were returned the following day, formally charging each of the nine prisoners with rape. The young men were charged jointly in two indictments, one of which named Victoria Price as the victim and the other naming Ruby Bates.[26] The indictment listing Price as the victim read:

The grand jury of [Jackson C]ounty charge that before the finding of this indictment Haywood Patterson, Eugene Williams, Charlie Weems, Roy Wright, alias Ray Wright, Ozie Powell, Willie Roberson, Andy Wright, Olen Montgomery and Clarence Norris, alias Clarence Morris, whose names to the grand jury are otherwise unknown than as stated forcibly ravished Victoria Price, a woman, against the peace and dignity of the state of Alabama.[27]

Less than a week had passed between the return of the indictment and the day the boys boarded the train and were placed under arrest. Under Alabama law, trial juries were given the discretion to impose sentence ranging anywhere between 10 years imprisonment and death upon a conviction for rape.[28]

The boys were transported from the Gadsden jail to Scottsboro on the morning of March 31, the day the indictments were returned, still under the watchful eye of scores of armed National Guardsmen.[29] They were arraigned that afternoon. Judge Hawkins presided. Alabama law provided for the appointment of counsel in capital cases for defendants too poor to hire their own lawyers.[30] The accused stood before Judge Hawkins, indigent and without legal representation. A day earlier, a Chattanooga lawyer, Stephen Roddy, who had been retained with offerings collected by a church group from that same city, had driven to Scottsboro with a promise to resist any efforts that might be made to "railroad" the youths. However, Roddy had already returned to Tennessee before the indictments were delivered and did not appear in court for the arraignment.[31] Peering down at the nine young men who now stood charged with rape, Judge Hawkins "'appointed all members of the local bar'" to represent them "for the limited 'purpose of arraigning the defendants.'"[32] Seven lawyers comprised the local bar. None stepped forward in the ensuing days to act on the Boys' behalf, and three were soon hired to assist the prosecution.[33]

Among the observers attending court to witness the arraignment were two members of the Communist Party. These Party workers lived in Chattanooga and had heard news of the Boys' arrest and the subsequent gathering of a mob outside of the Scottsboro jail. They relayed this information to the New York City office of the International Labor Defense (ILD) and warned of a possible lynching.[34] The ILD served as the legal arm of the Communist Party USA and although it was not an official Party organ, it was commonly regarded as functioning in that capacity. The ILD had participated in the defense of Sacco and Vanzetti and was actively involved in civil rights and anti-lynching activities, mindful of opportunities to help recruit Party supporters.[35] Its interest in the developing events in Scottsboro thus was not unusual, although its prescience in identifying the Boys' case as a potential rallying cause at this early date was unusually keen.

The first account of the developing case in the *Daily Worker*, the New York City-based newspaper published by the Communist Party USA, was reported on page 1 of the April 2, 1931, edition, just two days following the arraignment. The story began:

Intensifying their campaign of terror against the Negro workers in an effort to smash the growing unity of white and Negro workers as expressed in the growing resistance of the working class to the persecution of the Negro and foreign born workers, the local bosses and courts are rushing through the frame-up of nine Negro workers who were taken off a freight train a few days ago and thrown into jail on the usual lynch-terror inciting charge of "attacking white women."

The report warned of "[t]he danger of a mass lynching" and fumed that "[l]ipsticked girls and their business men escorts drove up in fine cars to be in at the killing." It concluded by exhorting: "Only the nationwide protest of the working class started immediately and expressing in mass protest meetings, resolutions and telegrams to the governor of Alabama and the officials of this town can save these workers from a mass lynching."[36]

Early depictions of the case in other newspapers could not have differed more significantly. The Boys' guilt was largely presumed upon their arrest in many Alabama periodicals. The *Montgomery Advertiser* attributed to Sheriff Wann the revelation "that all nine negroes had confessed assaulting the two girls,"[37] an assertion that later proved to lack corroboration. The *Jackson County Sentinel* reported that "some of the negroes held the two white girls [while] others of the fiends raped them, holding knives at their throats and beating them when they struggled."[38] The Scottsboro *Progressive Age* warned that the "details of the crime coming from the lips of the two girls, Victoria Price and Ruby Bates, are too revolting to be printed and they are being treated by local physicians for injuries sustained when attacked and assaulted by these negroes."[39] The *Huntsville Daily Times,* however, was not similarly restrained about what it printed. It characterized "[t]he crime [as] one of the most horrible ever perpetrated in the United States," and gave a detailed account of what occurred, as described to its reporter by Price, Bates, and "Orville Gillie" [*sic*], the white boy who had remained on the train.[40] It was similarly unforgiving in its characterization of the accused black youths. "And as the story was being unfolded, the negroes were telling jokes in another part of the bastile. Nasty jokes, unafraid, denying to outsiders they were guilty, laughing, laughing, joking, joking, unafraid of the consequences, beasts unfit to be called human."[41]

Just as the accused boys were jailed immediately following their arrest, so too were their accusers. Price, Bates, and the several white boys who had been on the train and had fought with the blacks, were all held in the Scottsboro jail as material witnesses. The *Huntsville Daily Times* ran progressively sympathetic accounts of the two young women as its news coverage continued. The paper's initial description of the "Huntsville girls," on March 25, the day of the alleged attack, was that they "were hoboing with male companions on [a] freight car," and that after having been "made captive[]" and "ravish[ed]" by "[a]ll nine of the negroes," both were "considered in a most serious condition."[42] The following day's story provided a richer portrait of the reputed victims.

Both girls are daughters of Huntsville widows. Both are in poor financial circumstances and had caught a "free" ride to Chattanooga the day before hoping to obtain employment of some nature in the larger city.

Unsuccessful in getting work they were forced to take the same type of transportation back home. They climbed aboard the train, an oil tanker, and there ran across the seven white boys. Victoria Price, 21, one of the girls, recognized O'Dell Gladwell of Houston, Texas, as a half-brother she had not seen for several years. It was a happy reunion and after introductions were made, the group jumped off and climbed aboard a coal car where they soon were deep in conversation. . . .

Here's the story of the attack both [Orville] Gillie and the girls told Sheriff Wann and a reporter of this newspaper.

"We were dressed in overalls. We started to climb over the car when a big negro grabbed us and pulled us back on the gravel pile. He had a big knife in his hands.

"Another man tore our overalls from our bodies and with five men holding each of us, one with an open knife in his hands, they committed the crime.

"Near Paint Rock they attempted a second attack and were only stopped when we declared they could take our lives." . . .

The Price girl said she resided on Arm street and Ruby Baites [sic] on Winston street. The older girl is a blonde, rather heavy set. The younger is a slim girl of a brunette type, frail in physique and apparently unaccustomed to hardships.[43]

The March 30 edition of the paper ran a "Special" column featuring a highly personal account of Victoria Price's plight under the heading, "Cannot Come Back Home."

"I can never go back home now after this awful thing."

Victoria Price, 21, one of the two girls alleged to have been attacked by 12 negroes aboard a Southern freight train last Wednesday near Stevenson, explained why she will seek in other cities for employment when the cases against her assailants are disposed of.

She had just finished reading a letter from her mother, a poor Huntsville widow. Crying bitterly she turned to her companion, Ruby Baites, 17, for comfort.

"Mamma is so upset. I could never face her after this," she said. "I don't know what I am going to do. Oh why should I have been the one?"

Victoria said she had been almost the sole support of her mother since she was 12 years of age. She had always been employed in the cotton mills of Huntsville and knows of no other work for which she would be qualified.

Clad in clothing purchased at the request of officials of the Huntsville mill in which both were formerly employed, the girls are being looked after by Sheriff M. L. Wann of Jackson county while being held as material witnesses against the negroes who will face trial. . . . The extreme penalty will be demanded against the blacks.

"I don't know what I will do but it's certain I won't go back home," the girl said again.

Teh [sic] girls have requested authorities to stop the sale of their photographs on local streets and have asked for a private trial.[44]

The sympathetic portrayal of Price and Bates in Huntsville newspaper contrasted starkly with how the women were described in the *Daily Worker*. As the trial loomed, the Communist Party publication slammed "the fake charge" lodged against "the nine young Negro workers," of raping "two white girls 'bumming' a ride on a freight train." The article emphasized that a "prominent county official admitted to [an] investigator that the two girls supposed to have been attacked are notorious prostitutes."[45]

This preliminary skirmishing to give definition to Victoria Price and Ruby Bates was of deeper significance than first appears. It implicated much more than simple stylistic idiosyncrasies among competing newspapers. Under one construction, the particulars of the charged rapes struck at the heart of what traditional white Southern culture primevally feared and abhorred. Widespread apprehension existed among whites about the presumed insatiable sexual appetite of black men.[46] Compounding the threat associated with this perception was the revered station of Southern white women, who by custom were "elevated . . . to a pedestal and worshipped . . . as the symbol of virtue, honor, and chastity."[47] As described by W. F. Cash in *The Mind of the South*:

> To get at the ultimate secret of the Southern rape complex [involving black men and white women], we need to turn back and recall the central status that Southern woman had long ago taken up in Southern emotion—her identification with the very notion of the South itself. For, with this in view, it is obvious that the assault on the South would be felt as, in some true sense, an assault on her also, and that the South would inevitably translate its whole battle into terms of her defense.[48]

At still another level, "[t]he rape of white women by blacks provoked . . . profound rage among southern white men because they viewed female sexuality as property that they owned, like slaves, and protection of this property was a key to preserving their position in society."[49] It was no coincidence that death was reserved as punishment for rape almost exclusively in the South, and that during the 1930s and ensuing decades executions for that crime disproportionately were carried out against blacks and confined almost without exception to cases in which white women were the identified victims.[50]

The symbolic representation of Price and Bates thus mattered. They could be popularly perceived as standard bearers for the "virtue, honor, and chastity" of white Southern women—women worthy of "protection" by men and law alike —or, alternatively, as fallen women with loose morals and tainted character. Even in a formal evidentiary sense, whether they were chaste or promiscuous, of unimpeachable standing or ill repute, arguably had implications reflecting on the veracity of their allegations.

In a report commissioned by the American Civil Liberties Union, Hollace Ransdall offered an insightful assessment of the two women who claimed that they had been raped. Ransdall's journalistic skills and her knowledge of economics shine throughout the lengthy report, which she completed in late May 1931, just two months after the boys were taken off the train in Paint Rock and charged with the crimes. She based her conclusions on ten days spent in northern Alabama and Tennessee interviewing an array of community members and people with knowledge about the case, including Price and Bates. Her observations speak volumes about matters that are essential to understanding the Scottsboro Boys trials, involving not only two of the principals, but broader social issues as well.

REPORT ON THE SCOTTSBORO, ALA. CASE
made by
Miss Hollace Ransdall
representing the
American Civil Liberties Union
May 27, 1931

HISTORY OF THE CASE

Two Huntsville Mill Girls Hobo to Chattanooga

On March 24, 1931, two mill girls from Huntsville in Madison County, northern Alabama, dressed up in overalls and hoboed their way by freight train to Chattanooga, Tenn., about 97 miles away. The older of the two, Victoria Price, who said she was born in Fayetteville, Tenn. and gave her age as 21, planned the trip, urging the younger one, Ruby Bates, 17 years old, to go with her...

[Ransdall interviewed "the two girls separately several weeks after the trial ..."]

The talk with Victoria Price, particularly, convinced me that she was the type who welcomes attention and publicity at any price. The price in this case meant little to her, as she has no notions of shame connected with sexual intercourse in any form and was quite unbothered in alleging that she went through such an experience as the charges against the nine Negro lads imply. Having been in direct contact from the cradle with the institution of prostitution as a side-line necessary to make the meager wages of a mill worker pay the rent and buy the groceries, she has no feeling of revulsion against promiscuous sexual intercourse such as women of easier lives might suffer. It is very much a matter of the ordinary routine of life to her, known in both Huntsville and Chattanooga as a prostitute herself.

The younger girl, Ruby Bates, found herself from the beginning pushed into the background by the more bubbling, pert personality of Victoria. She was given little chance to do anything but follow the lead of Victoria, so much quicker and garrulous. When I talked with her alone she showed resentment against the position into which Victoria had forced her, but did not seem to know what to do except to keep silent and let Victoria do the talking.

Why the Two Girls Made the Charge?

The first of these questions can be answered only by some knowledge of the conditions of life in the mill town of Huntsville, as it affected the lives and development of the two young mill workers, Victoria Price and Ruby Bates.

Huntsville, the town seat of Madison County in northern Alabama, has within its city limits, some 12,000 inhabitants. Taking in the four mill villages which surround it, the population is about 32,000. There are seven cotton mills in and around Huntsville, the largest being the Lincoln mill made up of four units.... Then there are two old fashioned plants under the same management and owned by local capitalists—the Helen knitting mill and the Margaret spinning mill. It is in this last place, the Margaret Mill, that both Victoria and Ruby Bates worked before the trial and afterward.

Wages were always low and hours long in all the Huntsville Mills, but in the Margaret and Helen especially, working conditions are very bad. The workers had to bear the brunt of the competition with the modern mills, backed by outside capital and with outside connections to help them out, while the Margaret and Helen management was muddling along in the old way. Respectable citizens of Huntsville said that only the lowest type of mill worker would take a job in the Margaret and Helen Mills.

All the mills were running on short time during the period of the Scottsboro case, and had been for some months before. Most of them had cut down to two, three, and four days a week. The Margaret had its workers on shifts employed only every other week, from two to four days a week.

Mill workers found it a dreary, hopeless enough struggle making some sort of a living when times were good, so when the slump hit them, it did not take long for a large group to fall quickly below the self-sustaining line. Low standards of living were forced down still lower, and many were thrown upon the charity organizations. It is from the charity workers of Huntsville that one may get an appallingly truthful picture of what mill life in Huntsville in time of depression means to workers who are doggedly trying to live on the already meager and uncertain wages of "prosperity."

High standards of morality, of health, of sanitation, do not thrive under such conditions. It is a rare mill family that is not touched in some form by prostitution, disease, prison, insane asylum, and drunkenness. "That's the kind of thing these mill workers are mixed up with all the time," complained one social service worker. "I'm beginning to forget how decent people behave, I've been messing around with venereal disease and starvation and unemployment so long."

Under the strain of life in Huntsville, the institution of the family does not stand up very well. Charity workers grumble that too many men are deserting their families. "If they get laid off, and can't get another job they seem to think the best thing for them to do is to leave town, because then the charities will have to take care of their families," said one.

There was no father in evidence in either the families of Victoria Price or Ruby Bates.

Husbands come and go in many cases, with marriage ceremonies or without. A woman who takes in a male boarder to help out expenses is unquestionabl[y] assumed to share her bed as well as her board with him. The neighbors gossip about it, but with jealousy for her good luck in getting him, rather than from disapproval of her conduct. The distinction between wife and "whore," as the alternative is commonly known in Huntsville, is not strictly drawn. A mill woman is quite likely to be both if she gets the chance as living is too precarious and money too scarce to miss any kind of chance to get it. Promiscuity means little where economic oppression is great.

"These mill workers are as bad as the Niggers," said one social service worker with a mixture of contempt and understanding. "They haven't any sense of morality at all. Why, just lots of these women are nothing but prostitutes. They just about have to be, I reckon, for nobody could live on the wages they make, and that's the only other way of making money open to them."

It should perhaps be mentioned that there are undoubtedly very many mill families in Huntsville to whom these things just described do not apply, but is also true that there is a large group of workers to whom the conditions do apply, and Ruby Bates and Victoria, with whom this part of the report is concerned, come from this group.

Ruby Bates and Her Family

As has been said, it is from the most economically oppressed of the mill workers of Huntsville that the two girls in the Scottsboro case come. Ruby Bates, the younger of the two, has a better reputation among the social workers of Huntsville than Victoria. They say that she was quiet and well-behaved until she got into bad company with Victoria Price.

Ruby is only seventeen. She is a large, fresh, good-looking girl, shy, but a fluent enough talker when encouraged. She spits snuff juice on the floor continually while talking, holding one finger over half her mouth to keep the stream from missing aim. After each spurt she carefully wipes her mouth with her arm and looks up again with soft, melancholy eyes, as resigned and moving as those of a handsome truck horse.

Ruby lives in a bare but clean unpainted shack at 24 Depot Street, in a Negro section of town, with her mother, Mrs. Emma Bates. They are the only white family in the block. Of the five children in the family, two are married and three are living at home. Mr. Bates is separated from his wife and lives in Tennessee, according to the report of neighbors, who say that he comes occasionally to see his children.

The house in which the Bateses lived when I visited them on May 12, several weeks after the trial, had been vacated recently by a colored family. The social service worker who accompanied me on the visit sniffed when she came in and said to Mrs. Bates: "Niggers lived here before you, I smell them. You can't get rid of that Nigger smell." Mrs. Bates looked apologetic and murmured that she had scrubbed the place down with soap and water. The house looked clean and orderly to me. I smelled nothing, but then I have only a northern nose.

Out in front while we talked, the younger Bates children were playing with the neighboring Negro youngsters. Here was another one of those ironic touches which life, oblivious of man's ways, gives so often. If the nine youths on the freight car had been white, there would have been no Scottsboro case. The issue at stake was that of the inviolable separation of black men from white women. No chance to remind negroes in terrible fashion that white women are farther away from them than the stars must be allowed to slip past. The challenge flung to the Negro race in the Scottsboro case was Ruby Bates, and another like her. Ruby, a girl whom life had forced down to equality with Negroes in violation of all the upholders of white supremacy were shouting. As a symbol of the Untouchable White Woman, the Whites held high—Ruby. The Ruby who lived among the Negroes, whose family mixed with them; a daughter of what respectable Whites call "the lowest of the low," that is a White whom economic scarcity has forced across the great color barrier. All the things made the respectable people of Scottsboro insist that the Negro boys must die, had meant nothing in the life of Ruby Bates.

Yet here was Ruby saying earnestly, as she sat in a Negro house, surrounded by Negro families, while the younger members of her family played in the street with Negro children, that the Scottsboro authorities had promised her she could see the execution of the "Niggers"—the nine black lads who were to be killed merely for being Negroes.

Ruby's mother, Mrs. Emma Bates, clean and neat in a cheap cotton dress, talked with a mixture of embarrassment and off-handed disregard for her visitors' attitude toward her. She has worked in the mills for many years. She was employed by the Lincoln textile mill, the largest one in Huntsville, some time before the trial. When I saw her she was out of a job, but the neighbors reported that she had a "boarder" living with her, a man named Maynard. They also gossiped that she frequently got drunk, and took men for money whenever she got the chance.

Neither mother nor daughter showed signs of regarding the experience Ruby is alleged to have been through as anything to be deplored especially. They both discussed the case quite matter-of-factly, with no notion apparently, that it had marred or blighted Ruby's life at all. The publicity which the case has brought to them, however, has impressed them greatly. They humbly accept the opinion of respectable white people; it never occurs to them, of course to analyze the inconsistencies it makes with their own way of life. Accustomed to seeing Negroes all around them on equal status with themselves for all practical purposes, and looking upon sexual intercourse as part of the common and inescapable routine of life, they have no basis in their own lives for any intense feeling on the subject of intimate relations between whites and blacks. They have just fallen in with "respectable" opinion because that seems to be what is expected of them, and they want to do the proper thing. There are so few times when they can.

Victoria Price and Her Mother

Victoria Price was born in Fayetteville, Tennessee. She has been married but says she is separated from her husband. She left him because he "lay around on me drunk with canned heat," she said. She was known at the trial as Mrs. Price, though this is her mother's name, not her husband's. Her age was variously reported in Scottsboro as 19, 20, and 21. Her mother gave it as 24, and neighbors and social workers said she was 27.

Victoria lives in a little, unpainted shack at 313 Arms Street, Huntsville, with her old, decrepit mother, Mrs. Ella Price, for whom she insistently professes such flamboyant devotion, that one immediately distrusts her sincerity. This impression is strengthened by little side looks her mother gives her. Mrs. Price fell down the steps while washing clothes, and injured her arm, which is now stiff and of little use. Victoria says her mother is entirely dependent upon her for support.

Miss Price is a lively, talkative young woman, cocky in manner and not bad to look at. She appears to be in very good health. The attention which has come to her from the case has clearly delighted her. She talks of it with zest, slipping in many vivid and earthy phrases. Details spoken of in the local press as "unprintable" or "unspeakable" she gives off-hand in her usual chatty manner, quite unabashed by their significance. Like Ruby, Victoria spits snuff with wonderful aim.

Victoria and her mother, after some warm argument on the subject, agreed finally to the number of years that Victoria had worked in the mills as being ten. Eight of these years were spent doing night work, they said, on a twelve-hour shift. Victoria is a spinner, and used to run from 12 to 14 sides, she said with pride. "Yeh, I used to make good money. I've made as high as $2.25 a day workin' the night shift before hard times come." Now nobody is allowed to have more than 8 sides to run, and the average is 6, Victoria says. She gets 18 cents a side now, where she used to get 22 cents. "I make on an average of $1.20 a day now, workin' two, sometimes three days a week. Every other week we are laid off altogether. You know nobody can't live on wages like that."

Although Victoria with a sly eye on me to see if I had heard of her record and would scoff, assured me that in spite of her low wage she never made a cent outside the wall of the mill, her reputation as a prostitute is widely established in Huntsville, and according to the investigation of the International Labor Defense, also in Chattanooga. One of the social workers reported that Walter Sanders, chief deputy sheriff in Huntsville, said that he didn't bother Victoria, although he knew her trade, because she was a "quiet prostitute, and didn't go rarin' around cuttin' up in public and walkin' the streets solicitin' but just took men quiet-like."

Sheriff Giles, of Huntsville, said he had information that she was running a speak-easy on the side with a married man named Teller, who lived in the Lincoln mill village and had several small children, but was now running around with Mrs. Price and leaving his wife. The sheriff said he had been trying to catch them with liquor on them, but had not succeeded so far. He said that he had caught the Teller man in her house, however, and had given both of them a warning.

Mrs. Russell, a neighbor of the Prices, claims that Victoria is a "bad one" and has been in no end of scrapes with married men. She was reported to be the cause of the separation of a Mr. and Mrs. Luther Bentrum, and was rumoured to have received the attentions of a man named George Whitworth, until his wife threatened to kill her, and Victoria hurriedly moved out of the neighborhood. One morning after the Scottsboro trial, Mrs. Russell said she saw her lying drunk out in the back yard with a man asleep on her lap. Mrs. Russell is also authority for the statement that Victoria's mother was as notorious for her promiscuity in her day as Victoria is now.

These stories are typical of the sort that circulate continually among the mill workers of the group from which both Ruby and Victoria come. Whether true or exaggerated, they give some idea of the social background of both the plaintiffs in the Scottsboro case.[51]

Ransdall's May 1931 report perceptively captured the intensifying struggle to give definition to Victoria Price and Ruby Bates. The competition to cloak the alleged rape victims in the Scottsboro Boys trials with an encompassing cultural identity would rapidly escalate. It would be waged not only in the courtroom but, via the media, throughout the South, the North, and internationally. Would Price and Bates emerge as "a symbol of the Untouchable White Woman," evoking "the inviolable separation of black men from white women" or, less threatening to prevailing mores, as "nothing but prostitutes" who "respectable Whites call 'the lowest of the low,' that is a White whom economic scarcity has forced across the great color barrier"?

And what was known and reported about the accused beyond their youth and skin color? The local press already had branded them "fiends" and "brutes," a characterization countered by the *Daily Worker's* depiction of them as "the nine young Negro workers." Ransdall recounted that numerous "officials and citizens" in and around Scottsboro made their views "disconcertingly clear."

They said that all negroes were brutes and had to be held down by stern repressive measures or the number of rapes on white women would be larger than it is. Their point seemed to be that it was only by ruthless oppression of the Negro that any white woman was able to escape raping at Negro hands. Starting with this notion, it followed that they could not conceive that two white girls found riding with a crowd of Negroes could possibly have escaped raping. A Negro will always, in their opinion, rape a white woman if he gets the chance. These nine Negroes were riding alone with two white girls on a freight car. Therefore, there was no question that they raped them, or wanted to rape them, or were present while the other Negroes raped them—all of which amounts to very much the same thing in southern eyes—and calls for the immediate death of the Negroes regardless of these shades of difference. As one southerner in Scottsboro put it, "We white people just couldn't afford to let these Niggers get off because of the effect it would have on other Niggers."[52]

Newspaper accounts provided little specific information about the young men and their backgrounds beyond the focal point of their race. The initial *New York Times* report about the accusations offered neither their names nor ages, and referred to them simply as the "nine Negroes" and "the Negro tramps."[53] The *Birmingham News* printed the Boys' names and hometowns, and offered that "[t]he negroes...gave ages ranging from 15 to 20 but were apparently older."[54] In addition to identifying all of the boys by name and branding them as "fiends" and "beasts unfit to be called human," the *Huntsville Daily Times* charged that "Haywood Patterson and Eugene Williams [are] said to be the worst negro characters in Chattanoonga."[55]

Patterson, age 18 at the time of his arrest,[56] was born and spent his first nine years on a farm in Elberton, Georgia, where his father was a sharecropper. He was the fourth oldest among nine children. His parents "lived together as husband and wife for thirty-seven years, honest working people," who taught their many children "to respect the human being and the human form."[57] The Patterson family moved to Chattanooga in 1921, where Haywood's father found work in a steel plant. Haywood began hopping trains when he was 14, "finding rough young friends...also not afraid to see the world and make their way."[58] Patterson could not read or write when arrested, but "took up word studying" with the assistance of a Bible and a dictionary after he was locked up. He had made enough progress by Christmas 1931 to write a letter to his mother in his own hand.[59]

Patterson had boarded the Southern Railway train on March 25, 1931, with three friends from Chattanooga, Eugene Williams, Andy Wright, and Roy Wright. At age 13, Williams and Roy Wright were the two youngest Scottsboro Boys. Williams had worked previously in Chattanooga as a dishwasher and Roy had a job in a grocery store. The ill-fated train ride on March 25 was Roy's first trip from home. He clung to a copy of the Bible while incarcerated and was described as "the smartest" of the nine boys. Roy's older brother Andy was 19. Andy dropped out of school after the sixth grade, when the Wrights' father died and he sought work to help support his family. He began driving a truck for a Chattanooga produce distributor when he was just 12 years old.[60]

The other five boys, all from Georgia, had not known the four Chattanooga youths nor were they acquainted with one another before March 25. Charlie Weems was sent to live with an aunt in Riverdale, Georgia after his father became ill. Weems was the oldest of the Scottsboro Boys at age 20. His mother died when he was four, and six of his seven brothers and sisters had passed away during childhood. Weems quit school after completing the fifth grade and found work in a pharmacy.[61] Clarence Norris, 18, was born in Warm Springs, Georgia, one of 11 children. His father, who had been a slave during his own youth, was a sharecropper and the family moved frequently. Norris was put to work picking cotton at an early age and did not attend school beyond the second grade. He could not read or write. He clashed regularly with his father, who whipped and beat him as punishment. The last job he held before being arrested was digging a house foundation at the rate of 20 cents an hour.[62]

Seventeen year-old Olen Montgomery, from Monroe, Georgia, was nearly blind in one eye owing to a cataract. He also was so nearsighted that he could barely see without glasses. He was traveling to Memphis with the hope of finding work so he could afford to purchase a new pair of glasses. Ironically, the eye-glasses that he was wearing on the day of his arrest were broken and two years would pass before he acquired another pair. Although he completed only the fifth grade, he was the best writer among the nine boys.[63] Willie Roberson was born on the 4th of July in 1915. He was 15 years old when arrested. He, too, suffered from a physical infirmity: an advanced case of syphilis and gonorrhea that had caused painful sores and swelling of his genitals. He walked with difficulty and relied on a cane. He was en route to Memphis in search of a better job and medical treatment. His mother died when he was two, after his father had left the household. He had been living with his grandmother in Atlanta until her death in 1930. He had completed the seventh grade, but he could not read or write and may have been mentally retarded.[64] Ozie Powell left home when he was 14, working in sawmills and at other jobs and moving from town to town. He was born in rural Georgia, then moved to Atlanta at an early age with his mother after his parents separated. He had just one year of schooling and could only write his name when arrested, at age 15. Like Roberson, Powell may have been mentally retarded. His IQ was measured at 64.[65]

As the nine Scottsboro Boys stood for arraignment on March 31, 1931, in the Jackson County courthouse in Scottsboro, Judge Hawkins kept his pledge for a speedy resolution of the charges. He scheduled their trials to begin on Monday, April 6, less than a week away, and just twelve days after the Boys' arrest.

Scottsboro: Trials and Appeals

April 6, 1931, was the first Monday of the month. As such, it was "Fair Day" in Jackson County, an occasion for farmers and townspeople from surrounding communities to gather in the county seat to sell and barter goods and produce, and to socialize.[1] Even under ordinary circumstances Scottsboro would have been expected to swell that day from its normal population of approximately 3,500 citizens. The added lure of the beginning of the Scottsboro Boys trials attracted what a local newspaper editor described as "the largest crowd in the history of Scottsboro. There are five times as many automobiles in the streets than ever have been at any previous time."[2] Estimates of the crowd size ranged as high as 10,000 people.

Among those gathered in Scottsboro were five companies of National Guardsmen under the command of Major Joe Starnes, who had been dispatched by Governor Miller to maintain order during the trials. The Guardsmen arrived with machine gun encampments and carried rifles fashioned with "bayonets glistening in the sun."[3] The Communist Party's *Daily Worker* took a jaundiced view of the preparations. It charged that "[t]he trial was deliberately set for [April 6] because this is horse-swapping and fair day in this town." The scheduling was certain to attract a crowd and fuel the "mob spirit" in the "tense lynching atmosphere." The newspaper was openly cynical about the readiness of the troops. "Guardsmen with machine guns have been placed in front of the court house, but no one here entertains the idea that they would really shoot to protect the nine Negro workers against whom the bosses have been inciting the mob."[4]

Hundreds who sought entry to the courthouse on the trial's opening day were turned away as the courtroom quickly filled to capacity. Women and children were denied admission,[5] owing to the salacious nature of the charges. One hundred men reported to court for jury duty. Alabama law limited jury service to a county's "male citizens"[6] between 21 and 65 years of age. And although not expressly ordained by law, all of the potential jurors also were white. The nine accused youths would be the only blacks in the Jackson County courthouse. Haywood Patterson later recalled that "I didn't see a Negro face [in all of Scottsboro] except two farmers in jail for selling corn.... That courtroom was one big smiling white face."[7]

When Judge Alfred Hawkins called the docket, Solicitor H. G. Bailey announced that he was ready to proceed on behalf of the State. Stephen Roddy, the Chattanooga lawyer who had traveled to Scottsboro the prior week at the request of a ministers' group in anticipation of the Boys' arraignment, once again was present in court. Roddy had not previously entered a formal appearance in the case. He normally handled real estate matters, not criminal cases, and he was not licensed to practice law in Alabama.[8] He also had a drinking problem. A member of the prosecution team commented that Roddy was so "stewed" that morning that "he could scarcely walk straight."[9] Clarence Norris recalled that Roddy "had liquor on his breath and he was as scared as we were."[10]

Several local attorneys also were in attendance. One of them was Milo Moody, who was nearly 70 and whose better days as a practicing lawyer, by all accounts, were unquestionably behind him. Moody had the reputation of allowing the prospect of a fee to overcome any qualms he might have about his ability to handle a case. One person who knew Moody described him as "a doddering, extremely unreliable, senile individual who is losing whatever ability he once had."[11] Another, only slightly less uncharitably, called him "an ancient Scottsboro lawyer of low type and rare practice." [12] Haywood Patterson recalled him as "an oldish lawyer...[who] didn't do anything for us. Not a damned thing."[13]

As the trial for the Boys' lives was about to open, Judge Hawkins inquired about which lawyers had assumed responsibility for their defense. Roddy volunteered that "I am here but not as employed counsel for these defendants; but people who are interested in them have spoken to me about it.... I was here several days ago and appear again this morning, but not in the capacity of paid counsel." Judge Hawkins tartly interceded: "I am not interested in that; the only thing I want to know is whether or not you appear for these defendants." Roddy responded, "I would like to appear along with counsel that Your Honor has indicated you would appoint."[14] The following dialogue ensued as the judge tried to get an answer to the ostensibly straightforward question of who would be representing the defendants in the capital trials that were moments away from beginning.

The Court: If you appear for these defendants, then I will not appoint counsel; if local counsel are willing to appear and assist you under the circumstances all right, but I will not appoint them.

Mr. Roddy: Your Honor has appointed counsel, is that correct?

The Court: I appointed all members of the bar for the purpose of arraigning the defendants and then of course I anticipated them to continue to help them if no counsel appears.

Mr. Roddy: Then I don't appear then as counsel but I do want to stay in and not be ruled out in this case.

The Court: Of course I would not do that—

Mr. Roddy: I just appear here through the courtesy of Your Honor.

The Court: Of course I give you that right...[Then addressing all lawyers present:] Well are you willing to assist?

Mr. Moody: Your Honor appointed us all and we have been proceeding along every line we know about it under Your Honor's appointment.

The Court: The only thing I am trying to do is, if counsel appears for these defendants I don't want to impose on you all, but if you feel like counsel from Chattanooga—

Mr. Moody: I see his situation of course and I have not run out of anything yet. Of course, if Your Honor purposes to appoint us, Mr. Parks, I am willing to go on with it. Most of the bar have been down and conferred with these defendants in this case; they did not know what else to do.

The Court: The thing, I did not want to impose on the members of the bar if counsel unqualifiedly appears; if you all feel like Mr. Roddy is only interested in a limited way to assist, then I don't care to appoint—

Mr. Parks [another local attorney]: Your Honor, I don't feel like you ought to impose on any member of the local bar if the defendants are represented by counsel.

The Court: That is what I was trying to ascertain, Mr. Parks.

Mr. Parks: Of course if they have counsel, I don't see the necessity of the Court appointing anybody; if they haven't counsel, of course I think it is up to the Court to appoint counsel to represent them.

The Court: I think you are right about it Mr. Parks and that is the reason I was trying to get an expression from Mr. Roddy.

Mr. Roddy: I think Mr. Parks is entirely right about it, if I was paid down here and employed, it would be a different thing, but I have not prepared this case for trial and have only been called into it by people who are interested in these boys from Chattanooga. Now, they have not given me an opportunity to prepare the case and I am not familiar with the procedure in Alabama, but I merely came down here as a friend of the people who are interested and not as paid counsel, and certainly I haven't any money to pay them and nobody I am interested in had me to come down here has put up any fund of money to come down here and pay counsel. If they should do it, I would be glad to turn it over—a counsel but I am merely here at the solicitation of people who have become interested in this case without any payment of fee and without any preparation for trial and I think the boys would be better off if I step entirely out of the case according to my way of looking at it and according to my lack of preparation for it and not being familiar with the procedure in Alabama....If there is anything I can do to be of help to them, I will be glad to do it; I am interested to that extent.

The Court: Well gentlemen, if Mr. Roddy only appears as assistant that way, I think it is proper that I appoint members of this bar to represent them, I expect that is right.

If Mr. Roddy will appear, I wouldn't of course, I would not appoint anybody. I don't see, Mr. Roddy, how I can make a qualified appointment or a limited appointment. Of course, I don't mean to cut off your assistance in any way—Well gentlemen, I think you understand it.

Mr. Moody: I am willing to go ahead and help Mr. Roddy in anything I can do about it, under the circumstances.

The Court: All right, all the lawyers that will; of course I would not require a lawyer to appear if—

Mr. Moody: I am willing to do that for him as a member of the bar; I will go ahead and help do anything I can do.

The Court: All right.[15]

The appointment of defense counsel thus was resolved. Judge Hawkins granted a 25 minute recess to enable Roddy and Moody to confer with their clients. Although Moody had volunteered to Judge Hawkins that "[m]ost of the bar have been down and conferred with these defendants in this case," it is unlikely that his optimism was merited. The lawyers' conversation of less than a half hour with their clients on the morning the cases were called for trial was likely the first and only consultation that had taken place, and certainly was the first involving Roddy or Moody and the boys.[16] The attorneys' independent investigation of the case facts, it can be inferred, was likewise nonexistent.[17]

When court resumed following their conference, Roddy promptly moved for a change of venue. He argued that the inflamed community sentiment undermined any chance of his clients receiving a fair trial in Jackson County. Attached to his motion were copies of a few articles and editorials from three local newspapers, including the *Jackson County Sentinel*. Lacking other supporting evidence, Roddy called Jackson County Sheriff Wann and Major Starnes of the National Guard to testify about the size and nature of the crowds that had gathered following the Boys' arrest and at the trial. This strategy promptly backfired, as both law enforcement officers offered their opinion that the crowds were simply curious, and not hostile, and that Jackson County would provide a fair trial venue.[18] Judge Hawkins had no quarrel with the prosecution's argument that "the defendants would probably get as fair a trial in Scottsboro as at any other county seat in the state," and he denied the change of venue motion.[19]

The lawyers next grappled with whether the defendants would be tried individually or collectively. Alabama law entitled jointly indicted defendants to a severance, or individual trials, if they so requested. Solicitor Bailey nevertheless proposed to go forward by joining Charlie Weems, Clarence Norris, and Roy Wright for the first trial. His apparent motivation was to lead with the cases in which Victoria Price, his star witness, could provide the most damning testimony. Price was considered to be the shrewder of the two women and she possessed better verbal skills than Ruby Bates. Bates also remained vague about the identities of her alleged assailants. For reasons that never were made explicit, all of the trials would proceed pursuant to indictments that named only Price as a rape victim, even though the grand jury also had charged the boys with raping Bates.[20]

Roddy registered a single objection to the prosecution's plan to join Weems, Norris, and Roy Wright for the first trial. He argued that neither Roy Wright nor Eugene Williams had yet turned 16, and that their cases consequently should have originated in juvenile court instead of criminal court. Rather than spend time resolving a dispute about Roy Wright's age, Judge Hawkins pressed for the prosecution to proceed first only against Weems and Norris.[21] Solicitor Bailey agreed and determined that Haywood Patterson would be tried next. A third trial would involve Olen Montgomery, Ozie Powell, Willie Roberson, Eugene Williams, and Andy Wright. Finally, evidence would be presented against Roy Wright, the youngest of the defendants.

The first order of business was to impanel a jury for the trial of Norris and Weems. Although jury selection frequently consumes weeks in modern capital trials, when twelve jurors were not sworn to hear the case until 3:50 that same afternoon, newspapers reported that "[s]election of a jury...[had] moved forward slowly."[22] The chosen jurors included nine farmers who hailed from Scottsboro and the nearby towns of Bridgeport, Rash, Tupelo, Pisgah, Limerock, and Princeton; two merchants, one from Fross Springs and the other from Hollywood; and a mechanic from Bridgeport.[23]

Victoria Price was the prosecution's first witness. Under Solicitor Bailey's questioning, Price offered a harrowing account of the events of March 25, less than two weeks earlier. She described how she and Ruby Bates had boarded the freight train that morning in Chattanooga. They were riding in a gondola car that had been loaded to within two or three feet of the top with chert, or gravel, as the train traveled between Stevenson and Paint Rock, Alabama. Seven white boys were riding with them in the same car. Suddenly, twelve black youths jumped into the open car from an adjoining box car. She identified one of the attackers as Weems, who waved a .45 pistol and ordered the white boys to "unload" (in other words, get off the train). Norris, another of the invaders, demanded to know "if I was going to put out," and then pulled off the overalls she was wearing and ripped apart her "step-ins." Although she "struggled, hollered and screamed," Norris had intercourse with her while Weems held a knife at her throat and other of the assailants held her legs. When the train stopped in Paint Rock, she fixed her clothes and climbed out of the gondola.[24]

On cross-examination Price explained that she was married but that she had not seen her husband for a month or more and did not know his whereabouts. She testified that she and Ruby Bates had traveled from their hometown of Huntsville, Alabama to Chattanooga on Tuesday, March 24. They spent the night with Mrs. Callie Brochie, a friend of hers who lived in Chattanooga on Seventh Street. When their search for a mill job proved unfruitful, the two women hopped a freight train to return home shortly before noon on the 25th. They began their journey in an oil car but switched to a gondola when the train stopped in Stevenson. Seven white boys also were in the gondola when "[t]he colored boys came over and said 'All you sons-of-bitches unload.'" A fight ensued, and all of the white boys except one named Gilley were either thrown or jumped off the train. Six of the black youths raped her, she claimed, and six others—three of whom got away—raped Ruby. She screamed and resisted to the best of her ability, but she was overpowered. One of her attackers hit her in the head with a gun. Although she had snuff in her mouth, her assailants "wouldn't even let me up to spit." "When they got through with me they were still in there, telling us they were going to take us north and make us their women or kill us one." The rapes ended just five minutes before the train pulled into Paint Rock. She fell unconscious after leaving the train car and only "came to" while sitting in a grocery store. She was taken to Scottsboro and examined by two doctors about an hour or hour and a half after the train arrived in Paint Rock. She subsequently remained locked up in the Scottsboro jail.[25]

The two Scottsboro physicians who examined Price and Bates on the afternoon of March 25 were the next witnesses. Dr. R.R. Bridges described Price as being talkative in his office, and "not hysterical." He reported finding a few bruises on her lower back and the top of her hips and some minor scratches on one arm, but she was otherwise injury free. He observed no tearing or bruising about her genitals. Bridges retrieved semen from Price's vagina and upon examining it under a microscope ascertained that spermatozoa in the sample were "nonmotile," or not moving, thus supporting the inference that they might no longer be living. In response to the prosecutor's questioning, he confirmed that it "is possible" that six men could have had sexual intercourse with Price consistent with her condition at the time he examined her.[26]

On cross-examination, Dr. Bridges described Price's bruises as small, amounting only to "a few little blue spots on her back," and reiterated that she had no lacerations and was not bloody. He described Bates as having a bruise about the size of a nickel on either side of her groin and, like Price, as not being hysterical or otherwise displaying signs of injury. He also retrieved sperm from Bates's vagina. He explained that a man typically discharges one to two teaspoons of semen during sexual intercourse and that he had been able to secure a sample only from Price's cervix during the exam. Judge Hawkins sustained objections to defense counsel's questions about the women's prior sexual experiences, including whether they had admitted to being "in the habit of having sex," whether they suffered from syphilis or gonorrhea, and whether either was a virgin.[27]

Dr. M.H. Lynch largely confirmed Dr. Bridges's testimony. He reported finding about two spoonfuls of semen in Bates's vaginal canal. He detected less semen in Price, which he collected by taking a smear from the vaginal wall. This evidence, he opined, supported the conclusion that the women had engaged in sexual intercourse. In response to the prosecutor's question he explained, "I could not at all tell the difference in the spermatozoa of a negro and a white man." He acknowledged on cross-examination that he could not determine whether the sexual intercourse had occurred when the women were close to Paint Rock or earlier, nor how many men had engaged in intercourse with them. He conceded that the "girls were not hysterical," and that there was "nothing to indicate any violence about the vagina."[28] Court then adjourned for the day.

On the second day of the trial, "[t]he crowds that thronged Scottsboro...at the opening of the trial were absent....The court room was barely filled."[29] Testimony resumed with two members of the posse describing how they met the train when it arrived in Paint Rock on March 25. Tom Taylor Rousseau testified that he had seen most or all of the arrested boys get off the very gondola in which Price and Bates were riding, and that Price was carried off the train, unconscious. Jim Broadway recalled that Price "could hardly walk" when she got off the train. Bates, on the other hand, was "in good shape."[30]

Ruby Bates next took the witness stand. On direct examination she did little more than corroborate that she had seen several young black men, some of whom had guns, scramble over the top of a box car after the train left Stevenson and enter the gondola in which she and Price were riding. All of the white boys in the car except one left after they were ordered to "unload." Her brief testimony included no mention of either Price or herself being raped. However, not content to let matters rest there, defense counsel's cross-examination produced a much more detailed account. Bates explained how she had been "ravished" by six "negroes." One of her assailants held a knife against her and another brandished a gun, while a third had intercourse with her. Meanwhile, she stated, the other black youths were with Price. She confirmed Price's testimony that the two young women had spent the previous night at Mrs. Brochie's house on Seventh Street in Chattanooga and had sought jobs in a mill. She explained that she had never been married, that she lived with her mother and did not know her father, and that she had never before ridden on a freight train. Judge Hawkins sustained an objection to a question about whether she had previously engaged in sexual intercourse.[31]

The prosecution concluded its case by offering the testimony of three men from Stevenson who recalled seeing the train on March 25. Luther Morris witnessed between eight and ten blacks "put off" five white boys from the freight train and then "take charge of two girls." As the girls tried to jump off the train, Morris continued, "the negroes" grabbed them and pulled them back on.

T. L. Dobbins testified that he had seen "three darkies in a box car," and several others scuffling in a gondola. Lee Adams, the last witness, reported that he had seen a group of blacks "striking" at the white boys in the gondola, and that he later noticed several bloodied white youths going up the road toward Stevenson. With that, the State rested.[32]

Roddy and Moody opened their defense with Charlie Weems proclaiming his innocence. Weems explained that he had boarded the freight train in Chattanooga on March 25 and that a fight involving several white and "negro" boys broke out on a gondola after the train left Stevenson. He identified Haywood Patterson, who he did not previously know, as the leader and as having a pistol. Patterson, he said, threatened to shoot him if he did not "[c]ome on and help me get the white boys off." Weems denied participating in the fight, claiming that he did no more than tell the white boys to get off the train. He denied seeing either of the girls on the train, insisting that he first saw them after the train pulled in to Paint Rock. He maintained that "I had nothing to do with the girls at all." On cross-examination Weems identified Clarence Norris, Ozie Powell, Willie Roberson, and Olen Montgomery as having been in the gondola with Patterson, himself, and the white boys. He repeated that he had not seen either Price or Bates until after the train stopped at Paint Rock and that he "never saw anything done to the girls."[33]

Clarence Norris followed Weems to the witness stand. The attorneys' lack of preparation for the case soon became painfully, and disastrously, apparent. Norris's testimony began smoothly enough. He denied participating in the fight between the white and black youths on the train, or that he was even in the gondola where the fight had occurred. He nevertheless volunteered that he was able to see what had taken place in the gondola. Although he initially denied having seen Price and Bates and insisted that he had nothing to do with them, he then admitted that the boys had known that the girls were on the train. He also recounted how Haywood Patterson had vowed to run the white boys off the train and announced that he was "going to have something to do with them white girls." [34]

Norris completely fell apart on cross-examination. Still maintaining that he had never entered the gondola and only witnessed what had occurred there, he burst out, "I saw that negro in there with those girls. I seen every one of them have something to do with those girls after they put the white boys off the train. . . . I saw that negro just on the stand, Weems, rape one of those girls. I saw that myself. . . . They all raped her, every one of them." An attempt to rehabilitate Norris on redirect examination failed miserably. Not picking up on cues implicit in the questions he was asked, he denied that he had ever offered his lawyers a different account of what had happened. "I told Mr. Roddy I did not have anything to do with them and the rest of them did have something to do with them." He insisted that "all eight of" the others had something to do with the girls in the gondola, "but I did not." Finally, on the prosecution's re-cross examination Norris affirmed, "I am positive and I am swearing now. I hold up my right hand to tell the truth, and I am telling the truth. That negro Weems that was on the witness stand did ravish that girl. He was on her."[35]

In its same-day edition, the *Huntsville Daily Times* reported on the bombshell nature of Norris's testimony. "Clarence Norris, 19 year old negro youth on trial with Charles Weems...for attacking with seven other negroes two Huntsville girls on a Southern Railway freight train March 25, startled counsel for state as well as defense by admitting...that he had seen his companions outrage the girls."[36] Readers learned that "[d]efense counsel immediately asked for a recess until afternoon and during the recess are understood to have approached state's attorneys with a proposal to have all the defendants plead guilty and accept life terms. H.B. [*sic*] Bailey, state solicitor, declined, declaring the extreme penalty is to be exacted—death."[37]

The defense offered no additional evidence following Norris's devastating admissions. When the trial resumed after the noon recess, the State offered rebuttal evidence from Deputy Sheriff Arthur Woodall, who testified that "I searched all the darkies" after their arrest in Paint Rock. He stated that he had taken a knife from Clarence Norris, "that big lipped one."[38] Victoria Price then returned to the stand. She identified the knife that the sheriff had confiscated and claimed that Norris had taken it from her.[39] With Price's concluding testimony, both sides rested.

Roddy and Moody elected to make no closing arguments to the jury. They sat by while the prosecution summed up the cases against first Weems and then Norris. The *Huntsville Daily Times* reported that, "Attorneys for the state described the crime as the most horrible in the history of the state and added: 'If you don't give these men death sentences the electric chair might as well be abolished.'"[40] Judge Hawkins delivered his jury instructions and then dispatched the jurors to begin their deliberations. Meanwhile, another jury was impaneled for Haywood Patterson's trial.[41] Like the previous jury, it consisted of twelve white men.

As in the first trial, Victoria Price was the lead witness in the case against Haywood Patterson. She described how Patterson was among the twelve black youths who had come over the top of the train shortly after it left Stevenson and entered the gondola in which she, Bates, and seven white boys were riding. While ordering the white boys to unload, Patterson fired a shot from the .38 caliber pistol he was carrying and hit one of the boys with the gun. As others held her down, Patterson had sexual intercourse with her. She remembered him having a knife and cursing. Price concluded by describing how she passed out as she reached the bottom step of the gondola car when she exited the train in

Paint Rock. She complained of being raped, she said, after she came to in a store, and then was taken to Scottsboro for a medical examination.[42]

The cross-examination allowed Price to inform the jury that she fought against her assailants as three of them removed her clothing, and that six of the attackers had intercourse with her while six others violated Ruby Bates. As in the first trial, she described how she and Bates had traveled to Chattanooga in search of work and had spent the night with Mrs. Brochie on Seventh Street. Although Judge Hawkins sustained an objection to the defense's inquiring whether she had "ever practice[d] prostitution," Price nevertheless answered the question, first protesting that "I do not know what prostitution means" and then continuing that "I have not made it a practice to have intercourse with other men." Judge Hawkins also sustained an objection to the defense's follow-up question, "Never did?" Price nevertheless again insisted on answering. "I have not had intercourse with any other white man but my husband. I want you to distinctly understand that."[43]

As Price wrapped up her testimony, the jury in the case against Weems and Norris reached a verdict. An hour and fifty-five minutes had elapsed since they had begun their deliberations.[44] Patterson's jury was ushered out of the court-room to the jury room—some 20 feet away, with a partially open window above the transom[45]—while the first jury was led back in. The jury foreman handed the verdict forms to the clerk of court, who announced the results to the packed courtroom. Both Weems and Norris were guilty as charged. The sentencing verdict in each case was death. This announcement spawned a raucous celebration in the courtroom that quickly spilled into the street. "The cheers rose high above poundings for order and Judge J.A. [*sic*] Hawkins, presiding, who had threatened to clear the courtroom if a demonstration occurred, ordered guardsmen to restore order. Eight persons were ejected from the courtroom by guardsmen. As soon as the crowds outside the courtroom and on the streets learned the verdict they took up the cheering."[46] A band outside of the court-house burst into playing "Hail, Hail, the Gang's All Here," and "There'll be a Hot Time in the Old Town Tonight." The demonstration could not have been lost on the jurors for Patterson's trial, who were immediately returned to the courtroom to resume hearing evidence.

Patterson's trial continued with Ruby Bates's testimony. Solicitor Bailey's direct examination elicited a fuller account of the events from Bates than in the earlier trial. He established, for example, that some of the black youths who had stormed into the gondola had "ravished" Bates and that others, including Patterson, had sexually assaulted Price. Bates additionally corroborated that Price had lost consciousness upon exiting the train in Paint Rock. She was not seriously challenged on cross-examination, where she provided a few details of the young women's stay in Chattanooga, affirmed that two of the assailants were armed, one with a .38 caliber pistol and the other with a .45, and explained that three of the twelve blacks involved in the assault had left the train before its arrival in Paint Rock.[47]

The prosecution was content to rely on Dr. Bridges as its medical witness, dispensing with Dr. Lynch for Patterson's trial. The doctor's testimony was somewhat more conclusive than at the first trial. He described how the women's vaginas "were loaded with male semen, and the young girl [Bates] was probably a little more used than the other." He noted finding bruises about Bates's pelvic region and lower back, and small scratches and a bruised spot on Price's neck, although he remarked that neither woman appeared to be nervous or hysterical when he examined them. As opposed to labeling the spermatozoa that he examined microscopically as "nonmotile," as he had done at the earlier trial, he testified simply that he could not confirm whether they were alive or dead. On cross-examination he added that neither woman's genitals were torn or bleeding and characterized their bruises as "minor." However, in response to final questioning by Solicitor Bailey, Dr. Bridges stated, "In my judgment as a physician, six men could have had intercourse with these women, one right after the other, without producing lacerations or tears."[48]

The prosecution's case continued with two members of the posse who had met the train in Paint Rock on March 25, and two witnesses who had seen the train after it had passed through Stevenson that day. As he had done at Weems's and Norris's trial, Thomas Rousseau bolstered the State's case by explaining that in Paint Rock "the negroes" had departed the train from the same car in which Price and Bates had been riding. C.M. Latham confirmed this observation and reported that the women said, "We have been mistreated" as they left the gondola. Lee Adams described how he had seen a fight involving blacks on the gondola, followed closely by two white boys hurrying toward Stevenson. A new witness, Ory Dobbins,[49] offered details that the jury in the first trial had not heard. Dobbins owned a farm outside of Stevenson that adjoined the railroad tracks. He testified that, from his vantage point approximately one hundred yards from the train track, he had seen two women in the company of several blacks on the train and watched while one of "the colored men" grabbed a woman and threw her down.[50] Solicitor Bailey then rested the prosecution's case against Patterson.

Roddy and Moody opened their defense by calling Haywood Patterson to the witness stand. Patterson acknowledged that he had seen Price and Bates on the train after it had left Stevenson. However, he claimed that he was on a boxcar and never entered the gondola in which the women were riding. He denied having sex or otherwise laying hands on the women and denied having a knife or a pistol. On cross-examination his testimony became confused and inconsistent. Although Clarence Norris's damning testimony about witnessing Patterson and the other black youths rape the two women had been presented at his own trial, out of the presence of Patterson's jury, Solicitor Bailey nevertheless asked Patterson, without objection, whether he had heard Norris accuse him of raping the women. Patterson conceded that he had, but disputed Norris's claim. However, he then admitted that he had seen Charlie Weems participate in the rapes, and that "I saw all but three of these negroes ravish that girl." He claimed that he and his three friends from Chattanooga, Andy and Roy Wright and Eugene Williams, had remained on top of the boxcar and did not enter the gondola, which twelve other blacks had occupied. He then performed an abrupt about-face, claiming that he had seen "no scuffling" in the boxcar, that "I did not see any negroes on top of either one of those girls," and finally that "I did not see any girls...until we got to Paint Rock."[51]

Thirteen year-old Roy Wright supported Patterson's denial that he or the other friends from Chattanooga had anything to do with the girls on the train. His allegiance to his friend was obvious but in other respects his testimony substantiated the women's allegations. He volunteered on direct examination that, "There were nine negroes down there with the girls and all had intercourse with them. I saw all of them have intercourse; I saw that with my own eyes." On cross-examination he confirmed that a fight had taken place involving the black and white boys, asserted that Clarence Norris had a knife, and admitted that "I saw five of these men here rape the girl."[52] Court adjourned for the evening following his testimony. The second day of the trials had been eventful, with convictions secured against Weems and Norris, two death sentences returned, and the case against Patterson in progress.

Sometime during the afternoon, following the return of the verdicts against Weems and Norris and while testimony was being presented in Patterson's trial, the International Labor Defense sent a telegram to Judge Hawkins. The judge announced receipt of the telegram and released its contents. It read:

In names of masses white and negro workers we protest attempt legally lynch nine young negro workers Scottsboro on frameup assault charges. We demand immediate change venue, new trial, dismissal defense lawyers openly advocating quick execution. Imminent danger lynching. Mob, guardsmen open advocate lynching.
We hold you responsible for lives these nine workers.[53]

Alabama newspapers described the telegram as a "veiled threat"[54] against Judge Hawkins and reported that law enforcement had been requested to investigate.

The following day, Scottsboro officials responded publicly. The first *New York Times* account of the trials was captioned, "Deny Negroes' Trial is Legal Lynching." With reactions to the telegram being the focal point of the story, the ILD's interest in the Scottsboro trials and its perspectives about the cases commanded the attention of readers of the nation's leading newspaper. News of the verdicts and sentences thus far returned in the trials was buried much later in the article. "The trial judge, the prosecutor and defense counsel took exceptions today to charges of the International Labor Defense of New York, made in a telegram to the court, than nine Negroes being tried here for attacking two young white girls were subjected to attempts to 'legally lynch' them."[55] Judge Hawkins, the *Times* reported, labeled the charges "absurd," and explained that "I appointed able members of the Jackson County bar to represent them." Solicitor Bailey "called attention to the National Guard and augmented force of peace officers to preserve order and said: 'It is hardly time for any New York defense to claim the Negroes are being railroaded.'" Stephen Roddy, "[s]peaking for the six [*sic*] defense attorneys, . . . added: 'I do not see how any one can say that we are not striving to see that the defendants are getting the fairest trial.'"[56]

Patterson's trial resumed at 8:30 on Wednesday morning, April 8. Summoned to follow his brother Roy as the next defense witness, Andy Wright explained that he would be turning 19 on April 23. He described how he had boarded the freight train on March 25 in Chattanooga with Roy, Patterson, and Eugene Williams, and how the four of them had met up with several other "colored boys" in Stevenson. A fight involving the black and white youths started after a white boy almost knocked Patterson from an oil car. Andy denied seeing any girls on the train and maintained that he first saw Price and Bates after the train arrived at Paint Rock. He refused to be shaken from his story on cross-examination, insisting that he "never saw any negro have anything to do with girls in the gondola."[57]

Eugene Williams testified next. Stating that he was 14 years old, Williams, like Andy Wright, acknowledged that a fight had broken out between a group of black and white boys in a gondola, but he denied having anything to do with or even seeing any girls on the train.[58] The next defense witness, Olen Montgomery, claimed that he knew even less about the events of March 25. He testified that he had remained on an oil tank car toward the end of the train, that he knew nothing about a fight or what may have happened in the gondola car, and that he had nothing to do with any of the other boys on the train until his arrest in Paint Rock. On cross-examination, the nearly blind Montgomery explained that "something is wrong with my eyes; one is weak and one is out." He insisted that he "was by my lonesome," nowhere near the gondola, and that he neither ravished nor knew anything about the girls.[59]

Roddy and Moody then recalled Haywood Patterson to the witness stand to explain that he and his three Chattanooga companions had been riding on an oil tank car that was two cars away from the gondola where the fight had broken out. On cross-examination Patterson denied seeing Olen Montgomery on the train or knowing anything about him. He then offered his fullest account of how the fight began, stating that the white boys kept running back and forth across the oil tank car to which he was clinging, "and liked to have knocked me off, and I asked him to ask me when he wanted by and I would get up and let him by...and he asked me what was my part about it, what did I care about him running off, and he said he was going to put me off..." That initial altercation led to the bigger fracas on the gondola. Patterson again denied having seen Price and Bates in the gondola.[60]

Ozie Powell, the final defense witness, testified that he was in the gondola when the fight broke out, but denied participating in it. He maintained that he had not seen any girls in the gondola, did not know they were on the train until after it arrived in Paint Rock, and saw neither Patterson nor anyone else ravish the girls.[61] When the defense rested, the prosecution recalled Victoria Price, who disputed Powell's testimony by identifying him as being in the gondola car when Patterson raped her. She also insisted that both of the Wrights and Olen Montgomery were present in the gondola.[62] Following Judge Hawkins's instructions, the jurors retired to begin deliberating about Patterson's fate. It was not yet 10:00; less than 90 minutes had elapsed since court had opened that day.[63]

The whirlwind pace of the prosecutions continued as another round of jury selection began. Solicitor Bailey joined all of the remaining defendants for trial except Roy Wright. Although the defense argued that Eugene Williams, like the younger Wright, had not yet reached 16 and thus was entitled to have his case first considered in juvenile court, only Roy's trial was separated from the others. The lawyers had no proof of Williams's age and he did not have as youthful an appearance as Roy. Twelve jurors were chosen—each, once again, a white, male citizen of Jackson County between the ages of 21 and 65—and the trial of Olen Montgomery, Ozie Powell, Willie Roberson, Eugene Williams, and Andy Wright got underway. For the third time in as many days, Victoria Price was placed under oath to give her account of what had happened on March 25.

Price's testimony became increasingly detailed and graphic. She identified each of the five defendants on trial as among the twelve blacks who had come over the roof of the immediately adjacent boxcar and entered the gondola in which she, Bates, and seven white boys were riding. After knocking all of the white youths off the train except for one named Gilley, the blacks divided their attention between herself and Bates. Price pointed out Eugene Williams as holding a knife to her throat and threatening to come to the girls' houses and "hunt us up" if they told on the boys. Motioning toward Olen Montgomery, she exclaimed, "[T]he one sitting there with the sleepy eyes...he ravished me." The other boys exhorted Montgomery to "hurry up" because "they wanted their share." While Montgomery was having his way with her, another boy held her legs and "the others were going up by the side of the car, looking and keeping the white boys off, telling them that they would kill them, that it was their car and we were their women from then on." She accused each of the five on trial of wielding knives and affirmed that each was still in the gondola when the train arrived in Paint Rock. She concluded the direct examination by explaining how she had lost consciousness after stepping out of the train and how two doctors had examined her later that day in Scottsboro.[64]

On cross-examination, Price described how three boys had to gang up on her to remove her overalls. Six of the black youths had intercourse with her, she testified, and the rest had intercourse with Ruby Bates. Solicitor Bailey elicited on redirect examination that Olen Montgomery, Eugene Williams, and Andy Wright had all raped her. "While one was having intercourse with me the others were running up and down the car box, hallering [sic], 'Pour it to her, pour it to her.'" In the meantime, the white boy remaining on the train, Gilley, was being held with a knife to his throat.[65]

Court adjourned for its lunchtime recess and when it was called back into session at approximately 1:35 P.M., the jury from Haywood Patterson's trial had reached a verdict. Mindful of the uproar that had occurred the day before when the verdicts for the first trial were announced, Judge Hawkins admonished that, "'[I]f I hear a pin drop,' the persons guilty will be sent to jail. Twenty-five extra guardsmen were in the court room to check any demonstration. One spectator after the tension had relaxed, remarked 'I could even hear myself breathe.'" Amidst a dead quiet courtroom, the clerk read the verdict. As the *Huntsville Daily Times* reported, "The state scored for the third consecutive time today when a jury...returned a verdict of guilty in the case of Haywood Patterson... and sentenced him to death in the electric chair."[66] The *Montgomery Advertiser* headline blared, "Third Negro In Jackson [County] Attack Is Given Death."[67]

After the jurors from Patterson's trial were discharged, the case against Montgomery and the other four boys resumed. Ruby Bates confirmed that Montgomery, Powell, Roberson, Williams, and Andy Wright were among the twelve blacks who invaded the gondola and ordered the white boys to unload. Cross-examination allowed her to elaborate about how a "colored boy" had removed her overalls and how she had been ravished by six of the youths, and Price by the others. However, she was unable to identify her specific assailants. She explained why she and Price had been in Chattanooga, including how they had spent the night there with Mrs. Brochie.[68]

Bates was followed on the witness stand by Dr. Bridges, who again described examining "both girls" and the minor scratches and bruises his inspection revealed. He confirmed that each of the young women had engaged in sexual intercourse, although he told the jurors that he could not discern precisely when. He explained that their vaginas were "still loaded with secretions, and especially in the Bates girl; her vagina had more secretions than Mrs. Price; both had plenty of the semen in there, plenty of the male germ. In my judgment as a physician six negroes could have gone to these women without lacerating them or tearing their genital organs." On cross-examination the doctor reported that he detected no movement of spermatozoa on microscopic examination and accordingly that he could not swear "if they were dead or alive." Dr. Bridges acknowledged that he had examined Willie Roberson and explained that "He is diseased with syphilis and gonorrhea, a bad case of it. He is very sore. . . . I think it would be painful [for him to have intercourse] but not very painful. . . . It is possible for him to have intercourse. I have seen them that had it worse than he has." Defense counsel finally established through the doctor's testimony that neither Price nor Bates had recent lacerations about their genitals, and that Price had acknowledged having engaged in intercourse with her husband "and the other [Bates] said she had" previously engaged in sexual intercourse as well.[69]

The prosecution concluded with the testimony of two witnesses who reported observing the five defendants in the same gondola in which Price and Bates were riding when the train arrived in Paint Rock on March 25. Two other witnesses remembered seeing a scuffle taking place in a gondola shortly after the train left Stevenson that day.[70] Moody and Roddy then opened the case for the defense. Their strategy was to call each of the five boys on trial to the witness stand to maintain his innocence. This same tack of course had backfired miserably in earlier trials, when both Norris and Patterson reported witnessing other defendants raping the women while denying their own involvement. Nevertheless, they proceeded as planned, with considerably fewer problems. Each boy denied assaulting Price and Bates and also protested that he knew nothing about the alleged rapes.

As the first defense witness, Ozie Powell denied participating in the fight with the white youths or even being in the gondola. Although he admitted witnessing the fight while positioned between the gondola and a boxcar, he insisted that he never saw the girls and knew nothing about them being on the train until after it stopped in Paint Rock.[71] Willie Roberson followed Powell to the witness stand and professed having even less knowledge about the allegations. After climbing into an empty boxcar near the end of the train, he recounted how he simply "stayed put" until the train arrived in Paint Rock. Not only was he unaware that a fight had taken place on the train, but he insisted that it would have been impossible for him to have raped anyone. He explained that he had hopped the train to seek medical attention in Memphis after suffering from syphilis and gonorrhea for four months. "I have chancres. . . . It pains and hurts me all the time. I was sick on the train, lying down in the box car. There was something the matter with my privates down there; it was sore and swelled up. It hurt me to walk. I can not lift anything. I am not able to have sexual intercourse. I couldn't have."[72]

Andy Wright acknowledged having seen the fighting between "the colored and whites" on the train but stated that his only involvement was helping pull a white boy back onto the moving train to help him avoid injury. He claimed not to have seen the girls on the train and that he only learned about their presence after the train arrived in Paint Rock. He adamantly denied ravishing either woman and denied having said, "'Yes, you will have a baby after this.' I will stand on a stack of Bibles and say it."[73] Then, much like Willie Roberson before him, Olen Montgomery testified that he had remained by himself on a car near the end of the train and had neither seen nor taken part in anything having to do with the white boys or the women. "If I had seen them," he elaborated, "[I] would not have known whether they were men or women; I cannot see good." He had been en route to Memphis with the hope of finding a clinic or hospital where he could get help with his eyes. Montgomery's glasses were hopelessly inadequate and he would lose them altogether following his arrest.[74] The last of the defendants then on trial, Eugene Williams, admitted having observed the fight in the gondola but he also insisted that he had not seen the girls. Williams acknowledged that he had a knife in his possession on the train, but denied using it to help rape either of the girls.[75]

The jury then heard from several rebuttal witnesses, beginning with Victoria Price, who accused Eugene Williams of raping her while another of the boys held Williams's knife to her throat. Then, to refute Willie Roberson's claim that he was so disabled with venereal disease that it was painful for him to move, the prosecution called witnesses who recalled seeing Roberson run and jump from car to car after the train arrived in Paint Rock. The final witness was Orville Gilley, the one white boy who by all accounts had remained on the train at the conclusion of the fight and thus presumably could have corroborated Price's and Bates's claims at each of the trials. Gilley's testimony nevertheless established only that the five boys presently standing trial had been in the gondola with Price and Bates. He offered nothing to confirm that the women had been raped and he was asked no questions on cross-examination. The presentation of evidence concluded with Gilley's testimony.[76] As in the first trial, the defense declined to make closing arguments, thus leaving the prosecution's arguments unanswered. Judge Hawkins's charge instructed the jurors that any of the accused who aided and abetted in rape were guilty of that crime whether or not they personally engaged in sexual intercourse.[77] The jury was dispatched to begin deliberating at 4:20 P.M., or slightly more than six hours after the trial of the five boys had begun.[78]

The day's work was not yet completed. Roy Wright's case began with an agreement that because of the boy's age—he was understood to be just 14 years old—the prosecution would not seek the death penalty. With remarkable efficiency, owing to the principals' familiarity with their roles gained from the three previously completed trials, a jury was chosen, evidence (consisting only of the testimony of Victoria Price and Ruby Bates for the prosecution, and of Roy Wright for the defense) was presented, and the judge's instructions were delivered to the jury by shortly after 6:00. At 9:00 P.M., when the juries from both Roy's trial and the one involving his brother and the other four defendants were still deliberating, the jurors were sequestered for the night in anticipation of resuming their deliberations at 8:00 the following morning.[79] With verdicts from the cases begun earlier that day the only outstanding business, the four trials involving rape charges against the nine boys had spanned just three days.

In "a packed court room and amid strained silence," the jury from the third trial reported its verdicts at 9:00 A.M. on Thursday, April 9. Olen Montgomery, Ozie Powell, Willie Roberson, Eugene Williams, and Andy Wright were guilty as charged. Punishment for each was fixed at death.[80] Roy Wright's jury continued deliberating into the afternoon before reporting that it was hopelessly deadlocked. All jurors agreed that Roy was guilty but they could not agree on a sentence. Although the prosecution had not requested the death penalty, when the jurors were polled seven reported favoring capital punishment and five held out for life imprisonment.[81] The result was a mistrial, effectively nullifying the prosecution and requiring Roy to be retried.

The Associated Press described the scene in the courtroom as Judge Hawkins formally imposed sentence on the eight boys who had been convicted. "Stoically calm, eight negroes today were sentenced to die in the electric chair at Kilby prison on Friday, July 10, for an attack on two young Huntsville girls while they were 'bumming' their way home on a freight train.... While the negroes showed no emotion, Judge J.A. [sic] Hawkins's eyes were wet with tears as one after the other he pronounced the sentence. It was the first time the jurist had pronounced a death sentence in his five years on the bench."[82] The *New York Times* ran a shorter, more prosaic version of the AP report. The story, buried deep within the newspaper at page 52, noted in its lead paragraph that, "Eight hobo Negroes from Tennessee and Georgia were sentenced today to death in the electric chair by Judge J.A. [sic] Hawkins in Jackson Circuit Court for attacks on two young white girls of Huntsville, Alabama."[83] The Communist Party's *Daily Worker,* in contrast, described the complainants as "two notorious white prostitutes who are evidently advertising themselves by claiming that they were raped by the Negroes."[84] It denounced the proceedings as "state murder"[85] and a "lynch holiday"[86] and reported that, "When sentence of death was pronounced and the date of execution for eight of the young workers set for July 10, the judge asked the workers if they had anything to say. All are reported to have returned a contemptuous 'NO.'"[87]

The ILD renewed its strategy of verbally assailing trial officials through telegram transmissions, as it had done following the verdicts returned in the first trial. The *Montgomery Advertiser* printed the text of the telegrams as the lead paragraphs in its account of the sentencing proceeding.

The International Labor Defense today made public two telegrams officials said they had sent to Alabama.

One to Judge J.A. [*sic*] Hawkins said, "The Associated Press reports you 'will welcome an investigation of trial.' Accept offer to investigate. Sending attorney. Meantime we demand stay of execution and opportunity to investigate and prepare for new trial or appeal. We demand the right for our attorney to interview defendants and obtain formal approval as defense counsel. And above all, we demand absolute safety for defendants against lynching."

The other, to Gov. Miller, said, "International Labor Defense conducting investigation past ten days has facts of frameup against nine negro workers convicted to electric chair in 48 hours. Lawyers appointed by court only interested in catering to prejudices of mob. In the name of hundreds of thousands of workers we protest this legal lynching. Sending attorney to make motion for new trial or appeal. Demand stay of execution."[88]

The next day, Judge Hawkins responded. Referring to the ILD, he said, "Let them come on. I still say I will welcome any investigation of the trial they want to make. However, it seems to me that they are investigating at the wrong time. I wonder what interests they have in the case and whether the defendants are members of the organization?" The judge's opinion that the ILD's call for an investigation came "at the wrong time" is somewhat obscure, but he apparently was intimating that their interest in the cases should have been manifest before the verdicts instead of after them. Governor Miller declined comment other than to confirm receipt of the ILD telegram along with telegrams received from the League of Struggle for Negro Rights and the Anti-Imperialist League of the United States, two other New York organizations protesting against the trial proceedings.[89]

While newspapers were bandying about the trial results and the ILD was pressing forward to gain a foothold in the case, the boys were escorted from Scottsboro under the protection of National Guard units and were once again incarcerated in the Etowah County Jail in Gadsden. Soon after their arrival, the eight young men under sentence of death (because of his different status Roy Wright was locked in a different cell) staged what the *New York Times* and Alabama newspapers reported as a "riot."[90] The *Daily Worker* called the same events a demonstration of the Boys' "utmost militancy."[91] The outburst was reported to have originated with the Boys' demanding "special food" and involved their beating on the cell bars, destroying bedding, and hurling oaths "at the court, officers and white people generally." Sheriff T.L. Griffin enlisted the help of National Guard troops while jail guards entered the "'bull pen'... and subdued the negroes, handcuffing them in pairs."[92]

Clarence Norris later recalled that the boys had requested hot food instead of cold biscuits, although Haywood Patterson remembered a specific demand for pork chops. Each acknowledged that the Boys' frustration over their convictions and death sentences had helped trigger the fracas, and both charged that the guards' reaction extended well beyond simply "subduing" them. Norris claimed that, "They beat us damn near to death. They kicked, punched and stomped us till they got tired."[93] Patterson agreed. "They came in serious. The cell door banged open. They beat on us with their fists. They pushed us against the walls. They kicked and tramped about on our legs and feet."[94] As a security measure, all of the young men were swiftly transferred to the Jefferson County Jail in Birmingham.[95]

The Scottsboro Boys case by now had begun to emerge into national prominence. The Communist Party aggressively continued agitating to intervene. As early as April 11, the front page of the *Daily Worker* broadcast that "Protests Grow" over the Boys' scheduled July 10 executions[96] and announced that the ILD was sending an attorney to Scottsboro to offer representation. Two days later it reported that "mass meetings" were held in both Cleveland and New York City in support of the boys.[97] Within two weeks a demonstration in Harlem to "Smash the Scottsboro Frame-up" inspired a *New York Times* story headlined, "Police Clubs Rout 200 Defiant Reds Who Attacked 'Lynch Law' in Alabama."[98] On April 16 the *Daily Worker* ran a front-page photo of the "Negro Youngsters Being Railroaded to the Electric Chair." Beneath a headline reading "Start Nation-Wide Fight to Free Nine Negro Youths," it reprinted Haywood Patterson's plaintive letter:

My Dearest Sweet Mother and Father:

This is to let you know of my present life and worried to think that your poor son is going to die for nothing.

Do all you can to save me from being put to death for nothing. Mother, do what you can to save your son.

We did not get a fair trial, and you try to have it moved somewhere else if we get a new trial. Do you all try to come down here and try to get me a new trial or I will be put to death on July 10.

I am in jail for something I did not do. You know that it hurt me to my heart. I will be moved to Kilby Prison.

Good-bye and good luck.

HEYWOOD

April 8, Scottsboro, Ala.[99]

Sensitive about the negative publicity associated with the case, the *Jackson County Sentinel* published a testy apologia at the conclusion of the trials that was directed against critics. The *Sentinel's* remarks were reprinted, with editorial support, in the April 14 *Montgomery Advertiser*.

For the past two weeks, Jackson county [sic] has been bearing the heaviest cross ever imposed on a rural county in the State. It fell our lot to have to dispose of one of the worst cases in crime history and it was very costly in a financial as well as an adverse publicity way and strain upon our citizenry....

The greatest expense is that of carrying out the law as it should be carried out. These citizens of Jackson County summoned as jurors did not have an easy task: it is not easy to pass death sentence on a human being and not one of these jurors got any pleasure out of the task. But they did their duty as citizens.... Men like these are the men who build and hold civilization—those who do not shirk a duty because it is unpleasant.

The evidence in these cases was astounding in clearness and corroboration. Yet over the country there will be many people who cannot believe this and who will cary [sic] that prejudice ruled. This is not the truth; these negroes were given every protection and every right of the law for defense; their own evidence was so conflicting that the attorneys trying their best to defend their lives were almost helpless to aid them. Not even one intimidation of a prisoner or guardsman or officer was reported during the whole time from arrest to conviction. Jackson County wanted to do what was right; as a citizenry composed of people who hold inviolate its women, it offers no apology to the rest of the country for the penalty imposed upon these blacks who would, according to the evidence, be a dangerous menace to any section of any country in the world.

Our county will, in all probability, never live down the bad advertising this crime caused, because it is outstanding not only for our own country but for the whole civilized world....

Not only do we hope Jackson County will never again experience a case like this, but we hope no other county will have to take up a cross like this one.[100]

The editors of the *Montgomery Advertiser* dismissed the notion that the *Sentinel* may have owed anyone an apology for Jackson County's handling of the case. They instead showered praise on its neighbors 200 miles to the north.

The Advertiser does not agree at all with its valued contemporary that Jackson County "will never live down the bad advertising this crime caused."

Jackson's name has not been injured, but has been glorified. It will not soon be forgotten that the people of that county deported themselves sanely, honorably and bravely at a time when they were tempted to go on a rampage. Jackson has vindicated the dignity of law, under extraordinary circumstances. All honor to its name![101]

Just two months would pass before the obliquely defensive tone of the Alabama newspapers would be replaced by open hostility against critics. One of the distinguishing features of the Scottsboro Boys case, its propensity to cause interregional strife, had surfaced as explicitly as had the Communists' assault on the quality of justice in capitalist society. On June 21, 1931, the *New York Times* published John Temple Graves's commentary addressing the *Montgomery Advertiser's* editorial stance about the case. Graves, a *Times* correspondent then associated with the *Birmingham Age-Herald,* wrote a column appearing under the caption: "Alabama Resents Outside Agitation."

"Scottsboro," according to an Alabama editorial last Monday, "is significant of the whole task which lies before the South today: the task of preserving itself against the passions and misemployments of others, even as it cleanses itself of its own."

Alabamans in general feel that a prejudice as strong as any of which they themselves may have been guilty in the past has actuated some of the committees and individuals from outside the State who have concentrated funds and legal talent at Scottsboro in efforts to undo the death sentence passed upon eight Negroes convicted of criminal attack upon two white girls.

The crime charged against these Negroes is one which Southern law punishes with death and which Southern opinion holds the most serious in all the categories. Local opinion has considered the trial a fair one....

"There was no intimidation of the court and the jury from Jackson County people," [Grover Hall, editor of the *Montgomery Advertiser*] declared in an editorial last week. "The only attempt at intimidation came from New York, where [Theodore] Dreiser's idiotic committee is headquartered."

Another factor injected at Scottsboro which Alabamians resent is communism. They believe that the efforts of certain radical organizations to make the condemned Negroes appear as martyrs in a class struggle are vicious and assuredly misplaced.... [T]here is reason to believe that the outsiders, by their presence and activities, may be creating enough additional local hostility to the defense cause to impair any possibility of a commutation of the death sentences.[102]

Among the outsiders expressing interest in the Scottsboro Boys was Theodore Dreiser, the noted author of books including *An American Tragedy*. Dreiser had traveled in Russia during the 1920s and would join the Communist Party decades later, shortly before his death in 1945. As the case's notoriety grew, intellectuals including Upton Sinclair, Albert Einstein, Thomas Mann, and others would lend weight to criticisms of the Boys' trials.[103] In the meantime, in the weeks following the Boys' convictions and death sentences imposed in Jackson County, the struggle intensified over who would champion their cases in the courts.

In a 1930 policy statement, the Communist Party of the United States recognized that:

The building and the work of the party cannot be effective without a serious change in its attitude and practices in regard to the work among the Negro masses and the transformation of passivity and underestimation into active defense and leadership of the struggles of the Negro masses. The party must be made to express in energetic action its consciousness that a revolutionary struggle of the American workers for power is impossible without revolutionary unity of the Negro and white proletariat....

Negro workers and farmers persecuted on the basis of race discrimination must be accepted and treated as class-struggle victims....

The party must openly and unreservedly fight for the right of Negroes for self-determination in the South, where Negroes comprise a majority of the population....

Unless our Negro program is concretized and energetically pushed, the work of our party in winning the majority of the working class will be fruitless in the North as well as in the South.[104]

However, just as the Communists sought to advance the standing and interests of Southern blacks and in the process cultivate favor with them, so, too, did the National Association for the Advancement of Colored People (NAACP). By the time of the Scottsboro Boys trials, the NAACP already had established an impressive record of legal advocacy on behalf of blacks in criminal cases, including earning victory in an important 1923 U.S. Supreme Court decision, *Moore v. Dempsey*.[105] But in contrast to the Communists' early recognition of the significance of the Scottsboro cases and their immediate offer to represent the boys, the NAACP initially was reluctant to become involved. This hesitation may have owed in part to the financially strapped organization's concerns about taking on a case involving such serious charges when doubts existed about the Boys' innocence. The inaction alternatively may have resulted from a misapprehension that the boys already had able court-appointed counsel,[106] or the leadership simply may have made an error in judgment. Whatever the explanation, the ILD gained an early advantage in the rapidly escalating skirmish for control over the litigation.

After first being rebuffed by Stephen Roddy, and then failing to entice Clarence Darrow to join their efforts, the ILD retained Chattanooga attorney George Chamlee to assist Joseph Brodsky, the ILD's New York-based chief counsel, in an attempt to intervene and offer legal assistance to the boys.[107] Brodsky visited the boys in the Birmingham Jail on April 20. He impressed them with his concern for their welfare and quickly won their consent for the ILD to take over their cases. Because the boys were minors, gaining their parents' assent was important to solidifying the arrangements for their representation. In the ensuing bitter and increasingly public struggle to secure the right to represent the boys, the ILD embarrassed Walter White, the executive secretary of the NAACP, by publicizing comments he had made implying that the parents were ignorant: "It should be remembered," White had said, "that the boys and their parents are humble folk and have had few opportunities for knowledge."[108] The ILD also published on the front page of the *Daily Worker* an ill-advised letter written on NAACP letterhead by William Pickens, the NAACP's field secretary, hailing the ILD's efforts on behalf of the boys and noting the enclosure of "a small check for that cause."[109]

For its part, the NAACP accused the ILD of exploiting the case for propaganda purposes and being willing to make martyrs of the boys to advance its political agenda.[110] Walter White argued that Communist involvement in the case would alienate the Alabama courts and ultimately prejudice the Boys' chances of securing a new trial. He also worried that collaboration between the NAACP and the ILD lawyers would risk tainting his organization with the Communists' distasteful politics. White visited the boys in the middle of May and succeeded in wooing some of them away from the ILD and into the NAACP camp.[111] Months of wrangling and altering allegiances ensued. The boys were often bewildered.[112] Finally, after a last-ditch effort at negotiations broke down that involved Clarence Darrow and Arthur Garfield Hays on behalf of the NAACP, and Chamlee and Brodsky for the ILD, the NAACP bowed out of the case.[113]

The NAACP's ill-fated spat with the ILD for control of the Boys' appeals was more than a minor embarrassment. It raised more fundamental questions pitting the NAACP's tolerance for gradual social change in race relations against the Communists' radicalism, and its reliance on support from the black middle class in contrast to the Communists' wooing of working class blacks. Walter White's leadership was called into question and the NAACP publication *Crisis,* which was edited at the time by W. E. B. Du Bois, adopted a defensive, staunchly anti-Communist position regarding the cases while giving short shrift to their merits.[114] In one sense, the struggle between the two organizations "was not just for control over the case but for the 'hearts and minds of the black public.'"[115]

The NAACP incurred criticism from all but its most loyal supporters for its delayed interest in the cases and for its preoccupation with assailing the Communists while the Boys' lives hung in the balance. Among the several weekly black newspapers comprising "the Negro press" of this era,[116] the Pittsburgh *Courier* and the St. Louis *Liberator* remained loyal to the NAACP's anti-Communist stance, but several others, including the Chicago *Defender,* the Baltimore *Afro-American,* and the Oklahoma City *Black Dispatch,* openly questioned or criticized the NAACP's refusal to work cooperatively with the ILD on the Boys' behalves.[117] The black press generally had adopted a cautious style in reporting and editorializing about the Scottsboro trials. Some of the nation's black newspapers had ignored the proceedings altogether.[118] The Cleveland *Call and Post* relied on routine wire service coverage of the cases as it urged that city's black community to support the boys by donating gifts and writing them letters.[119] Others reprinted editorials from mainstream newspapers that expressed concerns about the prosecutions but studiously refrained from voicing their own misgivings.[120] At this early stage of the cases' history, with the facts developed in the rapidly conducted trials still awaiting fuller definition, the editors of the nation's black newspapers appeared reluctant to rush in to embrace the Scottsboro Boys' cause. Yet many of them had become frustrated with the NAACP's intransigence about working with the ILD to provide the boys with able legal representation and said as much in the pages of their newspapers.

In the midst of the turmoil surrounding their legal representation, the eight boys under sentence of death had been transferred to Kilby Prison on the outskirts of Montgomery. Roy Wright remained in jail in Birmingham. Kilby housed Alabama's electric chair. A stay pending appeal of the convictions to the Alabama Supreme Court had indefinitely postponed the scheduled July 10 executions, yet Haywood Patterson recalled learning about the stay just three days before that date arrived. Another convict, Will Stokes, was not as fortunate. His execution, also set for July 10, proceeded on schedule. It made a profound impression on Patterson.

If I live to be a hundred I will never forget that day...Him going and us staying made us feel how life can hang by a hair. You can't forget when a man tells you what night you're going to die.

When they turned on the juice for Stokes we could hear the z-z-z-z-z-z of the electric current outside in the death row. The buzz went several times. After the juice was squeezed into him a guard came out and gave us a report. "Stokes died hard. They stuck a needle through his head to make sure." I sweated my clothes wet.[121]

The attempt to stave off the Boys' execution began with unsuccessful motions for new trials before Judge Hawkins, followed by appeals to the Alabama Supreme Court. George Chamlee and Joseph Brodsky and another ILD lawyer, Irving Schwab, represented the boys on appeal, while Thomas E. Knight, Jr., the youthful Attorney General of Alabama, had taken charge on behalf of the State. Knight, a former prosecutor, had been elected Attorney General in 1930, at age 32. He was ambitious and affable, slim and dapper, and smart.[122] His father, Thomas Knight, Sr., was a member of the Alabama Supreme Court. No one, including the defense, apparently perceived this relationship as presenting a conflict of interest. The elder Knight not only would participate on the appeal, but he ultimately would write the majority opinion in the case. Although the appeal formally involved only the legal issues arising from record of the Boys' trials, like other aspects of the case it could not escape the increasingly encompassing broader social context.

While the lawyers prepared their briefs and readied for oral argument in the state high court, protests about the case erupted within the United States and beyond. In late June 1931, 1,500 marchers organized by the ILD and the League of Struggle for Negro Rights paraded through Harlem, carrying placards bearing slogans such as "Smash the legal lynching of the Scottsboro boys."[123] Double that number gathered at an NAACP rally in New York City, while other protest meetings were staged in Chicago and Boston.[124] Meanwhile, Communists declaiming the Scottsboro Boys as "victims of judicial murder" smashed windows of the American Consulate General in Berlin, and other protests were carried out in Havana and Geneva.[125] *Time* magazine announced, "Thus...did the case of eight blackamoors, condemned to death for rape, take on its first international aspect."[126]

The *New York Times* wrote that Alabama Governor Benjamin Meeks Miller was besieged by "[l]etters, telegrams, radiograms and cables from all parts of the world and from persons in all walks of life protesting in behalf of eight young negroes sentenced to death at Scottsboro."[127] In September, the *Times* reported, "A statement signed by H.G. Wells, thirty-three members of Parliament and other prominent Englishmen, in which the sentencing to death of eight Negro boys in Scottsboro is characterized as 'inhuman,' is being circulated in England. ...The statement deplores the court decision, which, it says, 'was apparently influenced by mob passion,' and urges a retrial or appeal."[128]

Nor was the Alabama Supreme Court spared petitions urging justice for the boys. On the day that oral arguments began for the appeal, January 21, 1932, the headline of the *Birmingham News* trumpeted, "Supreme Court Threatened." Chief Justice John C. Anderson opened the session by denouncing the "bombardment" of communications about the case that had descended on the court. It appeared that his principal concern involved improper attempts to influence the court rather than the "threatening" nature of the messages:

These letters and resolutions attempting to bulldoze and browbeat the court are highly improper....

I've been on the bench the greater part of my manhood, more than 30 years, and this is the first time in my judicial experience that attempts have been made to bring outside pressure on the courts.

I serve notice now to defense counsel and everybody else that those letters will have no more influence on this court than a drop of water on the back of a duck.

The court will confine itself strictly to the records in the cases. If they show a reversible error, the cases will be reversed, if there is no reversible error, the cases will be affirmed.[129]

After assuring the chief justice that defense counsel bore no responsibility for the messages, Chamlee, Brodsky, and Schwab pressed several grounds for reversal. They cited the prejudicial publicity and hostile atmosphere surrounding the trials, Judge Hawkins's failure to grant a change of venue, the exclusion of blacks from the grand and petit juries, and the celebration that followed the announcement of the verdicts in the first trial with its contaminating influence on Haywood Patterson's jury. They argued that trial counsel, impeded by their late appointment in the case, failed to prepare adequately or conduct an effective defense. They also maintained that the trial court had erred by excluding evidence of Victoria Price's and Ruby Bates's reputations and that new evidence undermined the integrity of the verdicts. They finally pressed that Eugene Williams's case was not properly before the Jackson County Circuit Court because Williams had not yet turned 16 at the time of the alleged crimes.

The oral arguments were closed to the public but were witnessed by several newspaper representatives. According to the *Birmingham News,* among those in attendance were "a negro reporter for the Associated Negro Press, and members of the press service of the International Labor Defense.... The negro representative...was declared to be the first negro reporter ever to cover proceedings in the Alabama Supreme Court. He was provided with a special table in an advantageous position." The paper also offered its assessment of the defense advocates. It described Chamlee as "Southern born, Southern in looks and actions and speech," and "a lawyer of much experience but a rather tiring speaker." Schwab was "young, Jewish looking, [and] obviously not accustomed to arguing before a Southern Supreme Court on a criminal matter of this sort..." Brodsky, on the other hand, was depicted as "brilliant, at once a keen analyst of the case and a superb orator..." The *News* assured its readers that, "From the outset of the hearing...it was evident that the Supreme Court would grant every courtesy to the defense attorneys in spite of what might be a natural resentment of the members of the tribunal against the attempts to intimidate them through threatening telegrams and messages."[130]

The *Daily Worker* offered a dramatically different interpretation of Chief Justice Anderson's declaration concerning the case-related messages that had inundated the court. The Communist Party newspaper began its coverage of the proceeding with the accusation, "Court Threatens Working Class." It continued: "The statement of the Chief Justice reflects the fear of the white ruling class in the face of the growing united front fight of white and Negro workers against the lynch terror." After describing the arguments presented by Chamlee and Schwab, the paper did, however, concur about the powerful oratory of the third defense advocate. "Those present in the court were electrified as [Brodsky] told how the boys were convicted while lynch gangs packed the court, paraded outside and cheered the first convictions."[131]

The arguments carried into a second day, when Attorney General Knight addressed the court and defended the verdicts in the cases. Knight was described as "boyish-looking" by the *Birmingham News* as "he pleaded with ease and fluency and occasionally a touch of humor, apparently not much disturbed by the fact that among the justices on the bench was his father." Taking his cue from the chief justice's admonition at the outset of the hearing, Knight expressed dismay about the attempts made to "browbeat" the court and denounced similar efforts directed against himself. He displayed "copies of radical newspapers," and their characterizations of Alabama justice, and then launched into a refutation of the arguments that had been advanced to overturn the convictions.[132] The *Daily Worker's* account of the oral arguments made no mention of Knight or the State's contentions.

Two months later, on March 24, 1932—just one day shy of the reported crimes' anniversary—the Alabama Supreme Court announced its decisions in the appeals. In the principal case, *Powell v. State,* the Attorney General's father, Thomas Knight, Sr., wrote the majority opinion affirming the convictions and death sentences of Ozie Powell, Willie Roberson, Andy Wright, and Olen Montgomery. Chief Justice Anderson, alone in dissent, maintained that the defendants had been denied fair trials. Eugene Williams's conviction, however, was overturned. The court ruled that the State had failed to negate the suggestion that Williams had not yet turned 16, thus depriving the criminal court of original jurisdiction over his case. [133] In separate opinions, by identical 6-1 votes, the state supreme court upheld the convictions and death sentences returned in the trials of Charlie Weems and Clarence Norris, [134] and Haywood Patterson. [135]

Justice Knight's majority opinion only briefly recited the evidence against Powell and his codefendants. "We have deemed it best not to rehearse the testimony in detail in this case, as in many respects it is too revolting, shocking, to admit of being here repeated." Lest there be any doubt about the judges' views: "If the two girls, Victoria Price and Ruby Bates, are to be believed, the defendants were guilty of a most foul and revolting crime, the atrocity of which was only equaled by the boldness with which it was perpetrated."[136] The opinion quickly dismissed objections involving the form of the indictment and joining the defendants for trial. It dealt at greater length with the claim that Scottsboro was an unfair trial venue before rejecting that argument as well.

The character of the crime was such as to arouse the indignation of the people, not only in Jackson and the adjoining counties, but everywhere where womanhood is revered, and the sanctity of their persons is respected. That many should have been attracted to Scottsboro during the days covered by the trial, and the preliminaries incident thereto is no small wonder, considering the character of the crime charged. . . . The alleged victims . . . were, if the testimony is to be believed, two young white women, unknown, and entirely defenseless. No matter whether their sins were as scarlet, it neither gave justification nor excuse to any man to lay a violent hand upon them, or to force them to submit against their will, to the violation of their persons. The record of facts in this case, notwithstanding the atrocity of the crime charged, does not disclose a single act done by the populace to show a disposition to take the law into its own hand. . . . To the contrary, considering the nature of the crime and its revolting features, the people seem to have conducted themselves with a commendable spirit and a desire to let the law take its due course.[137]

The majority opinion rejected the remainder of the defendants' claims for a new trial. It noted that the defense attorneys had failed to seek a continuance when the cases were called for trial, thus undermining their argument that they had insufficient time to prepare a defense. Similarly, the "exclusion of negroes" from the jury venire had not been raised prior to trial and accordingly could not be pursued on appeal. A new trial based on newly discovered evidence—specifically, that "Victoria Price had the reputation of being a common prostitute"—was rejected because the evidence was irrelevant. "This evidence could only be admissible as tending to show consent. The entire theory of defendants' case was that they had not touched the woman, and had no intercourse with her. The question of consent...was not therefore an issue in the case."[138] Nor was the rapid onset of the trial, conducted just two weeks after the alleged crime, reason to overturn the verdicts. Justice Knight observed that Leon Czolgosz had been tried and sentenced to death within ten days of his 1901 assassination of President McKinley, with his execution carried out roughly six weeks later.

True this Czolgosz verdict was rendered in a case where a human life had been taken in a most dastardly manner. But we are of the opinion that some things may happen to one worse than death, at the hands of an assassin, and, if the evidence is to be believed, one of those things happened to this defenseless woman, Victoria Price, on that ill-fated journey from Stevenson to Paint Rock, on March 25, 1931.[139]

The majority opinion concluded by approving of defense counsel's performance. The opinion pointed out that "Mr. Roddy...asked to appear not as employed counsel, but to aid local counsel appointed by the court, and was permitted to so appear. The defendants were represented...pursuant to appointment of the court by Hon. Milo Moody, an able member of the local bar of long and successful experience in the trial of criminal as well as civil cases." The lawyers made a "very rigorous and rigid cross-examination of...the alleged victims of rape," and it was "purely conjectural" whether presenting closing argument to the jury would have helped rather than hindered the defendants' cause. In short, Justice Knight concluded, "[w]e do not regard the representation of the accused by counsel as pro forma."[140]

Chief Justice Anderson's dissent did not dispute the majority opinion's characterization of the alleged crime; to the contrary, he noted that it "was of such a revolting character as to arouse any Caucasian county or community." This starting point, however, led him to a very different conclusion. The rapid progression from arrest to indictment to trial caused the legal proceedings to unfold "when the entire atmosphere was at fever heat." The presence of armed soldiers at the trial "was enough to have a coercive influence on the jury." The appointment and performance of trial counsel were additional cause for concern. "The court did not name or designate particular counsel, but appointed the entire Scottsboro bar, thus extending and enlarging the responsibility, and, in a sense, enabling each one to rely upon others." The defendants had been "confined in jail in another county...and local counsel had little opportunity to confer with them and prepare their defense." Moreover, "the record indicates that the appearance was rather pro forma than zealous and active and which is indicated by a declination on the part of counsel to argue the case." The imposition of death sentences on all eight defendants, "without discrimination whatsoever" based on "age, leadership, etc.," also indicated to the chief justice that "the juries that tried these cases were coerced by public feeling or sentiment or actuated through passion or prejudice." His insistence on procedural justice was unequivocal. "[W]hether or not these defendants are guilty is not a question of first importance, the real one being, Did they get a fair and impartial trial as contemplated by the bill of rights?" Answering the latter question in the negative, the chief justice concluded that the defendants were entitled to new trials.[141]

Reaction was rapid and widespread to the Alabama Supreme Court's affirmance of the convictions and death sentences of seven of the eight boys. The next day's headline in the *Daily Worker* read, "Alabama State Supreme Court Decrees the Burning of 7 Innocent Scottsboro Negro Boys!"[142] The ILD fired off a telegram to Governor Miller demanding the defendants' immediate release and pledging "to leave no stone unturned to free these boys." Roger Baldwin, director of the American Civil Liberties Union (ACLU), stated, "The Alabama Supreme Court runs true to Southern form in upholding the death verdict in the Scottsboro case. Considering the general attitude in the South toward any rape case, however disputed the facts, it was hardly to be expected that a new trial would be ordered."[143] The *Birmingham News* adopted a conciliatory tone in an editorial commenting on the decision, recognizing that, "Obviously, there is ground for divergence of opinions concerning these cases. The matter is something about which many persons have felt and will continue to feel doubtful, and about which no one, perhaps, should venture to feel absolutely certain." The one matter that was clear was that "[t]his affair has been a most unfortunate one for the people of Alabama, and particularly for the people of Jackson County."[144] Meanwhile, a German organization comprised of hundreds of intellectuals cabled President Hoover and Governor Miller "asking them 'in the name of humanity and justice' to pardon" the boys, and the governor's office was swamped with hundreds of additional telegrams over the next few days.[145] When insulting telegrams rained on the Alabama Supreme Court justices "from all parts of the world, Attorney General Knight went so far as to threaten Montgomery telegraph offices with contempt if deliveries were not stopped."[146]

Although the state supreme court had set May 13, 1932, as the new execution date for Montgomery, Norris, Patterson, Powell, Roberson, Weems, and Andy Wright, it subsequently granted a stay to enable the defendants to seek review in the U.S. Supreme Court. The ILD enlisted the services of Walter H. Pollak, a New York lawyer whose considerable experience before the Supreme Court included arguing important cases during the 1920s involving the First Amendment rights of radicals.[147] The petition requesting Supreme Court review was submitted on May 23, just a week after the *New York Times* reported that the justices had received "many letters...from Communists in different countries urging the court to intervene." For the first time in its history, "extra officers had been detailed to the court to forestall a reported Communist demonstration."[148] The justices announced on May 31 that they would hear the cases in October.[149] "Fearing that Communists might demonstrate if the court refused a review to the Negroes, more than 100 policemen and plainclothes detectives were stationed at the court and other strategic points, while motion picture wagons waited in the Capitol plaza for the expected 'Red parade.' When the court's action became known, the movie men drove away and the extra policemen withdrew. No Communists appeared."[150]

With the legal issues held in abeyance, extralegal forums continued to give attention to the Boys' plight. The Communist Party USA declared May 7, 1932, as International Scottsboro Day and encouraged worldwide protests.[151] Ada Wright, the mother of Andy and Roy, embarked with ILD General Secretary Louis Engdahl on a European speaking tour to gain support for the boys. Although she had never before set foot outside of the American South, she soon became a world traveler. Beginning in May 1932, Mrs. Wright addressed rallies in Germany, Austria, Switzerland, France, Belgium, and England. By year's end, Engdahl estimated that they had appeared before half a million people in 16 countries. They concluded their tour in Moscow's Red Square, where "tens of thousands of Russian workers crowded the streets with banners, calling for freedom for the sons of Ada Wright and the collapse of world imperial order."[152]

Oral arguments before the United State Supreme Court were presented on October 10, 1932. Walter Pollak represented the seven condemned youths and Attorney General Thomas Knight represented Alabama. Two days earlier, an estimated 3,500 "Communist sympathizers" had gathered in New York City's Union Square, where the Scottsboro cases were denounced as "part of a 'calculated policy of terror against the Negro masses'."[153] Security was tight at the Supreme Court in anticipation of similar demonstrations, although none ensued as the cases were argued. Protests nevertheless were carried out internationally to coincide with Supreme Court hearing.[154]

Pollak's challenge before the Supreme Court was not an easy one. Prevailing legal doctrine largely insulated state court criminal decisions from review under the federal Constitution. The Bill of Rights, the source of most safeguards in the U.S. Constitution for individuals charged with crimes, originally did not apply to state criminal trials. When those first ten amendments to the Constitution were ratified in 1791, two years after the first Congress submitted them to the states, the enshrined rights were understood as limiting only the power of the newly established federal government. As such, defendants in state criminal proceedings were left exclusively with whatever protections were provided in state constitutions and statutes. They could not complain to the U.S. Supreme Court that their federal constitutional rights had been violated.

However, the federal Constitution was amended at the conclusion of the Civil War to include rights that were enforceable against the states. The new provisions were added principally to ensure that black citizens freed from the bonds of slavery would not have to rely exclusively on potentially hostile state governments for legal protections. Thus, the Thirteenth Amendment, adopted in 1865, formally abolished slavery, and the Fifteenth Amendment, which became effective in 1870, guaranteed citizens the right to vote irrespective of race. Sandwiched in between those enactments, the Fourteenth Amendment, ratified in 1868, provided in relevant part that: "nor shall any State deprive any person of life, liberty, or property, without due process of law; nor deny to any person within its jurisdiction the equal protection of the laws." The due process and equal protection guarantees placed new constitutional obligations on the States but decades would pass before the nature of those obligations became clearer.

In 1923, just nine years before the Scottsboro Boys' case was argued, the Supreme Court for the first time relied on the Fourteenth Amendment's Due Process Clause to invalidate a state court criminal conviction. *Moore v. Dempsey*,[155] in common with the cases arising from Scottsboro, involved several black defendants sentenced to death in a southern state (Arkansas) for a crime (murder) committed against a white victim. The killing occurred amidst a race riot that erupted in Phillips County, Arkansas, in 1919, precipitated by white landowners' attempts to intimidate black sharecroppers from forming a tenants union.[156] Moore and several other blacks were arrested, spared from lynching only by the intervention of federal troops, and brought to trial four days following their indictment. Justice Holmes detailed the allegations they had raised in federal court seeking relief from their state convictions and death sentences.

[The defendants] were brought into Court, informed that a certain lawyer was appointed their counsel and were placed on trial before a white jury—blacks being systematically excluded from both grand and petit juries. The Court and neighborhood were thronged with an adverse crowd that threatened the most dangerous consequences to anyone interfering with the desired result. . . . The trial lasted about three-quarters of an hour and in less than five minutes the jury brought in a verdict of guilty of murder in the first degree. According to the allegations . . . there never was a chance for the [defendants] to be acquitted; no juryman could have voted for an acquittal and continued to live in Phillips County and if any prisoner by any chance had been acquitted by a jury he could not have escaped the mob.[157]

If substantiated, the Court ruled, those allegations represented a violation of the defendants' due process rights and entitled them to relief in federal court. Justice Holmes's opinion relied on the Court's earlier pronouncement in *Frank*

v. Mangum,[158] "that if in fact a trial is dominated by a mob so that there is an actual interference with the course of justice, there is a departure from due process of law." Leery of intruding too boldly on the states' administration of justice, the opinion was quick to point out that "mere mistakes of law" made in state criminal trials were not subject to federal correction. "But if the case is that the whole proceeding is a mask—that counsel, jury and judge were swept to the fatal end by an irresistible wave of public passion, and that the State Courts failed to correct the wrong," then the federal courts would enforce the defendants' Fourteenth Amendment due process rights.[159]

Striving to fit the Boys' convictions into this framework, Pollak contended that the Scottsboro trials had been conducted in an atmosphere of mob domination in violation of federal due process requirements. He raised two additional arguments in the nation's highest court. He charged that the boys had effectively been denied the right to counsel by the untimely and irregular appointment of Moody and Roddy, and by the lawyers' consequent woeful performance. The absence of properly functioning trial counsel, he asserted, represented a denial of due process of law. He also argued that blacks had systematically been excluded from jury service in Jackson County, contravening the Fourteenth Amendment's equal protection guarantee.[160] Attorney General Knight countered by contending that public "curiosity," and not mob domination, characterized community sentiment surrounding the trials. He relied heavily on the Alabama Supreme Court's ruling that the boys had been afforded a fair trial, including representation by able counsel, and he told the justices that he had "no apologies to make" for the verdicts in the cases.[161]

The Supreme Court's decision came less than a month later. On November 7, 1932, the eve of Franklin Roosevelt's election to his first term as president, the justices announced what immediately was hailed as a landmark ruling in Powell v. Alabama. By vote of 7–2, the Court invalidated the Boys' convictions and ordered new trials. Justice Sutherland's majority opinion considered only "whether the defendants were in substance denied the right of counsel, and if so, whether such denial infringes the due process clause of the Fourteenth Amendment."[162] In responding affirmatively to both of the identified issues, Justice Sutherland relied heavily on Chief Justice Anderson's dissenting opinion in the Alabama Supreme Court ruling.

To support the conclusion that the boys effectively had been denied trial counsel, Justice Sutherland quoted at length from the colloquy involving Judge Hawkins, Stephen Roddy, and Milo Moody at the outset of the first trial, when the judge made inquiry into the Boys' legal representation. The result, he concluded, of "this casual fashion" in which the appointment of counsel was resolved was that "until the very morning of the trial no lawyer had been named or definitely designated to represent the defendants." This untimely resolution was prejudicial because "during perhaps the most critical period of the proceedings against these defendants, that is to say, from the time of their arraignment until the beginning of their trial, when consultation, thorough-going investigation and preparation were vitally important, the defendants did not have the aid of counsel in any real sense, although they were as much entitled to such aid during that period as at the trial itself."[163] Under the carefully delineated circumstances specified in the majority opinion, the absence of counsel violated due process of law as guaranteed by the Fourteenth Amendment.

The right to be heard would be, in many cases, of little avail if it did not comprehend the right to be heard by counsel. Even the intelligent and educated layman has small and sometimes no skill in the science of law.... He lacks both the skill and knowledge adequately to prepare his defense, even though he have a perfect one. He requires the guiding hand of counsel at every step of the proceedings against him.... If that be true of men of intelligence, how much more true is it of the ignorant and illiterate, or those of feeble intellect....

   In the light of the facts [already] outlined...—the ignorance and illiteracy of the defendants, their youth, the circumstances of public hostility, the imprisonment and the close surveillance of the defendants by the military forces, the fact that their friends and families were all in other states and communication with them necessarily difficult, and above all that they stood in deadly peril of their lives—we think the failure of the trial court to give them reasonable time and opportunity to secure counsel was a clear denial of due process.

   But... even if opportunity had been given to employ counsel,... we are of the opinion that, under the circumstances just stated, the necessity of counsel was so vital and imperative that the failure of the trial court to make an effective appointment of counsel was likewise a denial of due process within the meaning of the Fourteenth Amendment. Whether this would be so in other criminal prosecutions, or under other circumstances, we need not determine. All that it is necessary now to decide, as we do decide, is that in a capital case, where the defendant is unable to employ counsel, and is incapable adequately of making his own defense because of ignorance, feeble-mindedness, illiteracy, or the like it is the duty of the court, whether requested or not to assign counsel for him as a necessary requisite of due process of law.[164]

   In a testament to the significance of the Supreme Court's ruling, the *New York Times* reprinted the opinion in its entirety in its November 8 edition.[165] Its front page story contrasted the "stormy scene" outside of the Court, where just before the decision was announced the police had used tear gas and clubs to disperse a crowd of "100 Communists and other radicals," with the Court's inner chamber, where "[n]ot a whisper disturbed the solemnity."[166] Walter White was "elated" about the ruling, although the ACLU's Roger Baldwin was more subdued, opining that "the United States Supreme Court could not have come fairly to any other decision."[167] The *Times* praised the decision editorially, suggesting that "[i]t ought to abate the rancor of extreme radicals, while confirming the faith of the American people in the soundness of their institutions and especially in the integrity of their courts."[168] In ensuing days, the newspaper published a lengthy analysis by Felix Frankfurter, who praised the justices for writing "a notable chapter in the history of liberty,"[169] and a commentary observing that "[t]here is little public tendency [in Alabama] to protest the new trial ordered by the Supreme Court or to question the grounds on which it was ordered. Widespread [b]elief in this State that the Negroes are guilty does not prevent a great many Alabamians from suspecting that the trial itself was not fair to the spirit even if it was faithful to the letter of the law."[170]

The *Daily Worker* was not nearly so sanguine in its assessment of the Supreme Court's decision, which it branded as only a "partial victory." Emphasizing that the reversal of the convictions "does not mean that [the boys] go free," the Communist Party USA's newspaper warned that the decision simply "turns the Scottsboro boys back into the hands of the court which engineered the original frameups." The paper excoriated the NAACP as having "consistently played the role of assistant hangmen to the imperialists throughout the long history of the case."[171] It further charged that:

The Supreme Court verdict...is one of the most brazen and far-reaching maneuvers ever attempted by American capitalist government....Faced by growing mass distrust of the judicial machinery...; alarmed by the increasing sympathy and support for the Communist Party among the wide sections of the Negro masses, and hoping by this action to restore confidence in the judiciary in particular and capitalist democracy in general; aiming consciously at placating the mass anger aroused by the murderous frame-up, the Supreme Court verdict is supposed to confound all critics—especially the Communists.

The Supreme Court verdict...warns the Alabama lynchers that in using the legal machinery against Negroes, they must be more careful to avoid infractions of the code and—it tells them how to do it.

The Scottsboro boys still stand in the shadow of the electric chair. The demand, heard around the world and endorsed by millions of workers, is for their unconditional release.[172]

Attorney General Knight declined immediate comment on the Supreme Court's decision vacating the Boys' convictions and death sentences. Judge Hawkins, who had presided over the trials, predicted that retrials would be scheduled for the next regular term of the Jackson County Circuit Court, in March 1933. He additionally speculated that the defense would likely renew its efforts to secure a change of venue.[173] The *Birmingham News* reported that, "Informed of the verdict at Huntsville, Victoria Price, one of the alleged victims and principal state witness, said she was ready to appear against the Negroes in the new trial and that Ruby Bates, her companion in a 'hobo trip' from Chattanooga to her home, also would appear."[174] Meanwhile, still on death row in Kilby Prison, Haywood Patterson recalled, "On November 8, 1932, the boys shouted, they were so glad. Andy Wright, from his cell, read out loud that we fellows won a new trial."[175] The seven whose convictions had been overturned by the U.S. Supreme Court would soon be transferred to the Jefferson County Jail in Birmingham to await their retrial.[176]

In Judge Horton's Court

The Supreme Court's November 1932 decision in *Powell v. Alabama* invalidated the convictions of the seven boys under sentence of death. Using the obtuse language common to reversals, the justices "remanded [the cases] for further proceedings not inconsistent with this opinion."[1] Two of the boys were in legal limbo. Roy Wright's Scottsboro jury had been unable to return a sentencing verdict, resulting in a mistrial. A state court hearing on a habeas corpus petition filed on his behalf was postponed and then languished.[2] Eugene Williams's conviction had been invalidated by the Alabama Supreme Court; because he had not yet turned 16 at the time of the alleged crimes, his case should have originated in juvenile court. However, no action had been initiated to allow a juvenile court judge to consider the case. Both young men remained incarcerated although neither had lawfully been adjudged guilty. As a practical matter, they differed from the other boys only in that Roy was not confined in Kilby Prison and neither was scheduled for retrial. For the other seven, *Powell v. Alabama* represented a significant victory but a tenuous one. They would soon again face prosecution for rape.

This time, however, if the Supreme Court's decision was not to be an empty one, they would at least be represented by able counsel. The International Labor Defense was now squarely in command of the Boys' cases. Following its victory in Washington, DC, the ILD turned its thoughts to the new trials that would be conducted in Alabama. The organization had been criticized by the NAACP and others as exploiting the charges made against the boys to further the Communist Party's ambition of recruiting southern black workers to join its ranks. With the boys having been spared execution largely because of its efforts, the ILD was in a better position to refute this accusation. As Haywood Patterson's mother, Janie Patterson, said of the ILD at a rally in New Haven, "I don't care whether they are Reds, Greens or Blues. They are the only ones who put up a fight to save these boys and I am with them to the end."[3] The ILD still faced the difficult challenge of securing a lawyer for the Boys' retrial.

The fact that a new trial had been secured, and that a new lawyer would handle the defense, would not change the reality that the venue would remain an Alabama courtroom, presided over by an Alabama judge, and involving an Alabama jury. A lawyer unfamiliar with local customs, or even more risky, a lawyer perceived as an outsider, especially one affiliated with the Communist Party, could diminish or even doom chances for a not guilty verdict before the first witness was sworn. On the other hand, there was certainly no guarantee that a local attorney could overcome the community sentiments that already threatened to overwhelm the trial evidence. If the case was to be lost, it should not be lost without the most strenuous, and highly visible, fight possible. The ILD had to navigate these turbulent strategic waters.

The organization took action in January 1933 when William Patterson, a black attorney from Harlem and the national secretary of the ILD, wrote Samuel S. Leibowitz, another New York City lawyer, with an unusual request.

Dear Sir:

You no doubt have heard and are undoubtedly, if only from a legal point of view, interested in what has now become internationally known as the Scottsboro cases. Unquestionably it is the most important legal issue before the American courts. . . .

The new trials are tentatively set for March of this year. We are anxious to engage the most competent and able trial lawyer in this country for the purpose of insuring the best legal defense possible in order that the innocence of these boys may be established.

This is why we write this letter to you. After studying and combing the list of attorneys who we feel are competent to properly present this case, we have decided that you are eminently fit for this great task.

We have no money to offer you as a fee; if you undertake this task you will perhaps be compelled to spend considerable of your own funds. . . . We do have this to offer you: An opportunity to give your best in a cause which for its humanitarian appeal has never been equalled in the annals of American jurisprudence. You will not only be representing nine innocent boys, you will be representing a nation of twelve millions of oppressed people struggling against dehumanizing inequalities. . . .

We do not ask you as a condition of your acceptance as trial counsel to give up any of your social, economic or political views.

We are certain that you will give this matter your sincerest consideration and we hope you will favor us with a favorable reply at your earliest convenience.[4]

At the time he received Patterson's letter, Samuel Leibowitz was surpassed in reputation only by Clarence Darrow (who by then was 75 years old and nearing the end of his illustrious career) as the country's leading criminal trial lawyer. Born in Romania, Leibowitz (the family name originally was Lebeau) emigrated at age three with his parents, who were seeking relief from mounting anti-Semitism, and settled in New York City in 1897. He graduated from Cornell Law School in 1915 and relied on his superb intellect, unflagging self-confidence, and refined oratory—he had a magnificent baritone and was both a fine singer and actor—to gain a reputation as an outstanding criminal defense attorney. His clients included Al Capone, Harry Hoffman (for whom he secured an acquittal in 1929 on the retrial of a highly publicized Staten Island murder case), and singer Rudy Vallee (on a charge of speeding on the Brooklyn Bridge).[5] Before he left private practice to accept an appointment as a New York trial court judge in 1941, Leibowitz's record as a defense attorney in 78 murder cases reportedly was a remarkable 77 not guilty verdicts, one hung jury, and no convictions.[6]

Leibowitz was intrigued by the invitation to become involved in the Boys' defense, but also wary of the ILD and concerned about the potential politicization of the cases. His reply to Patterson included important stipulations as well as an expression of faith in the administration of justice in American courts.

Dear Sir:

While, as you are quite aware, your organization and I are not in agreement in our political and economic views, your letter arouses my sympathetic interest, because it touches no controversial theory of economy of government, but the basic rights of man.

Let me say at the outset that if I serve this cause, as you suggest I should, I will not serve it for money; nor will I permit you to repay the expense I may incur....

Some of my friends have advised me to take no part in this case. They fear that the defendants have been prejudged; that...they are doomed because their skins are black. I cannot partake of that opinion.

North and south, east and west, we Americans have a common tradition of justice. And if it is justice that these black men be adjudged innocent—if it is justice, I repeat—I cannot believe that the people of Alabama will be false to their great heritage of honor, and to those brave and chivalrous generations of the past, in whose blood the history of their State is written.

If the views I have expressed match yours, then I will accept the task of conducting the defense.[7]

Patterson's reply on behalf of the ILD signaled the beginning of an uneasy alliance. "The views you have expressed do not match ours, and yet despite the wide gulf that lies between us ideologically we stand ready to accept your services as trial attorney in the cases of the nine innocent Negro boys in Scottsboro.... The terms you have specified are acceptable to us."[8] Leibowitz thus assumed the role of lead defense counsel, conditioned on his being able to manage the case free of political influence.[9] He would be assisted by the ILD's Joseph Brodsky, who had entered the case immediately following the Boys' conviction and had earned respect for the quality of his advocacy before the Alabama Supreme

Court. George Chamlee, the veteran Chattanooga attorney whose heritage and familiarity with Southern ways would presumably help offset some of the difficulties that might confront the two transplanted New York City attorneys, and who like Brodsky had been working on the case for more than a year and a half, rounded out the defense team.

With the international attention that had centered on the case showing no signs of abating, the stakes were high for the prosecution and the State of Alabama as the retrials loomed. Alabama's Attorney General, Thomas G. Knight, Jr., who had represented the State before both the Alabama Supreme Court and the U.S. Supreme Court, announced that he would personally lead the prosecution in the renewed efforts to gain convictions. His resolve to do so solidified when it became clear that Leibowitz was planning to attack the grand jury that had indicted the boys and the petit juries before which they would be tried on the ground that blacks were systematically denied the chance to serve on those bodies. The Attorney General knew all too well that such a challenge, if successful, would have profound statewide ramifications. He vigorously disputed the allegation and "expressed indignant resentment at the 'interference' of outside elements in the administration of Alabama justice."[10]

Knight had indicated shortly after the Supreme Court's overturning of the convictions that he would not oppose a change of venue from Scottsboro for the retrials.[11] He maintained that "I want the people of all these United States to know that these defendants will get a fair trial. They had one when they were tried [originally] and convicted and they will get a fair trial regardless of what county of Alabama is chosen for their trial now."[12] Removal of the trial from Scottsboro would ensure that Jackson County jurors would not once again sit in judgment of the boys. The *New York Times* described the prospective jurors who were waiting in Judge Hawkins's courtroom in Scottsboro, while the change of venue motion was being resolved.

As the hearing proceeded, the jurors, twelve bewhiskered mountaineers in the overalls and boots uniform of the countryside, lounged in their chairs on a platform facing the bench and glared at the visitors from New York. Behind them sat twelve rows of lantern-jawed men of similar mien and costume. There wasn't a Negro in the court house or near it while the case was being considered.[13]

Although defense counsel had forcefully argued that Birmingham, Alabama's largest city, should be the new trial site, Judge Hawkins instead transferred venue to Decatur, in nearby Morgan County.[14] A town of 18,000 located some 65 miles west of Scottsboro, Decatur was just 25 miles from Huntsville, the home of Victoria Price and Ruby Bates. With a total population of approximately 46,000, Morgan County had about 10,000 more residents than Jackson County, although it was still decidedly rural.[15] The new venue meant that Attorney

General Knight would be assisted in prosecuting the case by Morgan County Solicitor Wade Wright. Jackson County Solicitor H.G. Bailey, who was responsible for the Scottsboro convictions, would join them at the prosecution table.

Judge James E. Horton, Jr. would preside over the trials. Horton lived in Athens, in neighboring Limestone County. Fifty-five years old, with a law degree from Cumberland University, Horton was born and raised in Limestone County and had served as a circuit judge in Alabama's Eighth Judicial District since 1922.[16] He stood 6' 2" and was lean and angular. The *New York Times* described Horton as "a Lincolnesque figure,"[17] a resemblance borne out by photos,[18] although he lacked a beard and occasionally wore glasses. He had an abiding respect for the law and was widely regarded as being principled and fair. The *Decatur Daily* left no room for mistake that Horton was a propitious choice. "The son of a judge, an able lawyer, chancellor, and then for over ten years circuit judge, honest and fearless, Judge Horton is well qualified to preside at the famous hearing."[19]

Trial proceedings were scheduled to begin Monday, March 27 in the Morgan County Courthouse. Its spacious second-floor courtroom, which included separate sections for white and "colored" spectators, seated 425 people. A statue in the courtyard featured a confederate soldier and the inscription, "Lest We Forget—This Monument is erected to the memory of those who offered their lives for a just cause, the defense of states rights."[20] National Guard troops had been summoned to Decatur as a precautionary measure,[21] and the armed soldiers maintained a visible presence. Conscious of the fact that he and the rest of the defense team were outsiders in this Southern community and courtroom, Leibowitz was intent on making a good first impression. The *Decatur Daily* reported that on his arrival:

Samuel S. Leibowitz, of New York, directing the defense of the negroes in the Scottsboro cases, said . . . that the people here had shown every courtesy and respect to himself and his associates. . . .

"The people here impress me as being honest, God fearing people who want to see justice done," Leibowitz said. "They have been cordial and friendly, and their cordiality and hospitality have been genuine."

"We of the defense are well pleased with our reception and feel that the people of Decatur want us to get a square deal."[22]

Adjoining this story, the *Daily* printed a front-page editorial musing about the momentous impending trials. The paper noted that "a court proceeding of widespread interest and considerable legal importance" had been transferred to the community, "without any suggestion whatever from our people. . . . Because Morgan county has been asked to shoulder a difficult civic burden, the eyes of the world have turned this way. Let the world see Decatur and Morgan as they really are, a fine little city, a splendid county and a citizenship without peer."[23]

The seven defendants, along with their two younger colleagues who were not scheduled for trial, would be transferred to the Decatur jail for the start of their trial, where they could be forgiven if they did not share the optimistic views that others were expressing. Not only would they again be on trial for their lives, but the jail, by all accounts, was abysmal. It had been condemned two years previously and since then considered "unfit for white prisoners," who were kept locked up in Huntsville.[24] Leibowitz objected to having to confer with the boys in the jail, describing it as "unfit for human habitation"[25] and "hardly 'fit for a pig.'"[26] Clarence Norris called it a "hellhole." The cells were "filthy,...the stink was sickening and rats the size of rabbits had the run of the place. But the bedbugs! There were millions of them, large as grains of rice. They crawled all over us at night and sleep was hard to come by."[27]

Meanwhile, the prosecution faced uncertainties about one of its prime witnesses and alleged victims, Ruby Bates. More than a year earlier, in January 1932, Bates had scrawled a handwritten letter to her boyfriend making a remarkable claim. The letter, bearing a January 5, 1932, date and a Huntsville address, read:

> dearest Earl
> I want too make a statement too you Mary Sanders is a goddamn lie about those negroes jassing me those policeman made me tell a lie...those negroes did not touch me or those white boys i hope you will Believe me the law don't...I know it was wrong to let those negroes die on account of me i hope you will Believe my statement Because it is the gods truth i hope you will Believe me i was jazzed But those white Boys jazzed me i wish those negroes are not Burnt on account of me it is those white Boys fault that is my statement, and that is all I know I hope you tell the law hope you will answer
> Ruby Bates
> P.S. this is one time that i might tell a lie But it is the truth so God help me.[28]

Huntsville, Alabama police coincidentally arrested a man, Miron Pearlman, for drunkenness on the same day the letter was dated and discovered the letter in his possession. Pearlman claimed that George Chamlee had paid him to get Bates drunk and then write a letter admitting that she had made up the rape accusation. On being questioned by the police, Bates confirmed that she had been drunk when she wrote the letter and in a sworn affidavit disclaimed the letter as wholly false. Chamlee vehemently denied that he was in any way involved with an attempt to bribe Bates to recant her story, although he acknowledged that Pearlman had contacted him about Bates. A subsequent investigation cleared Chamlee of any improprieties.[29]

With that unfortunate incident behind them, the prosecution encountered new difficulties with Bates as the retrial neared. She had disappeared.

On March 7, 1933, the *Huntsville Times* reported that Bates had been missing from her home for more than a week. Bates's mother speculated that she may have been kidnapped, and the police took a young man from New York City into custody pending further investigation.[30] On March 25, two days before Judge Horton was to open court in Decatur, Attorney General Knight conceded that Bates was still missing and her whereabouts were unknown.[31] He ordered the sheriffs of every county in Alabama to search for her.[32]

The accused were transferred under heavy security—their motorcade at front and rear featured machine gun-wielding law enforcement officers—from the Birmingham jail to the Decatur courthouse on Monday, March 27. A delay in transporting them caused the morning court session to be cancelled, so proceedings did not begin until 2:00 P.M. "The Negroes were chatting and joking among themselves as Judge Horton called the court to order."[33] The first business was a hearing on the defense's motion to quash the indictments. Before a packed courtroom, Leibowitz alleged: "For twenty-five years past the officials of Jackson County have systematically refused and neglected to place the names of Negroes on the jury rolls although some 600 of them residing in that county are qualified to serve and are barred solely because they are members of the African race."[34] *Time* magazine, which was covering what one newspaper had proclaimed to be "[t]he most highly publicized criminal case that modern courts have experienced,"[35] dolefully reported to the nation what the *Jackson County Sentinel* had editorialized about the defense motion: "A Negro on a jury in Jackson County would be a curiosity, and curiosities are sometimes embalmed."[36]

Attorney General Knight defended the selection of grand jurors as lawful and defied Leibowitz to prove his claim of race discrimination. The defense built its case over the afternoon and much of the next day by offering evidence that no blacks had been included on Jackson County grand juries in recent history, despite there being many qualified candidates. As the prosecution prepared to refute the contention that race explained the jury commissioners' failure to summon black grand jurors, Judge Horton decided that he had heard enough evidence. He abruptly denied the motion to quash the indictments. Leibowitz could not have been surprised by the ruling. He had raised the issue more with an eye toward preserving it for appeal in the event of a conviction than with the hope of aborting the trial. The *New York Times* observed that Leibowitz "smiled pleasantly and offered no argument against the exclusion of further testimony"[37] on the matter. The *Huntsville Times* reported that Judge Horton's unexpected action "apparently made no impression on the nine negro defendants, as they went ahead laughing among themselves."[38]

The State announced that it would proceed first against Haywood Patterson and thereafter join the remaining six defendants for trial. Leibowitz did not object to Patterson's case being severed from the others, although he reserved the right to insist on separate trials for the other accused boys.[39] The prosecution did not explain why Patterson would be isolated from the others and tried first. Perhaps the case against him was the strongest, in light of Victoria Price's anticipated testimony and with Ruby Bates still missing. Perhaps it was because Patterson, now 20, was one of the oldest and largest of the defendants. With a dark complexion and an ambiguous countenance that could be interpreted as surly, Patterson to some conjured the image of the quintessential black male predator, the perfect leading defendant from the prosecution's perspective to put before the all white jury that was certain to be impaneled.[40] Confronting the sea of white faces summoned for jury duty in the Morgan County Courthouse, Leibowitz presented another motion to be resolved before the trial could begin.

Just as he had challenged the makeup of the Jackson County grand jury responsible for the Boys' indictment, Leibowitz's new motion alleged that Morgan County's venire was unlawful because blacks were systematically denied the opportunity to serve on trial juries. Another round of legal wrangling ensued. Amidst charges of fraud in the jury lists and racial discrimination by the jury commissioners, the exchanges between Leibowitz and Knight became increasingly acrimonious. The hearing on the motion at one point was interrupted when Leibowitz introduced into evidence a copy of a booklet being sold outside of the courtroom entitled, "The Inside, Unpublished Story of the Infamous Scottsboro Trial." The tract presented a highly prejudicial account of the testimony offered in the first trials and included a denunciation of the Communist Party. Judge Horton dispatched deputy sheriffs with orders to bring the parties before him who were responsible for distributing the pamphlet. They returned moments later with three frightened teenagers in tow. The boys had been hired to hawk the pamphlets and apparently were oblivious to their contents or their potential ramifications for the trial. Judge Horton released them with a warning after Leibowitz volunteered that "he did not with to punish any one 'trying to earn a dollar in these times.'"[41] Judge Horton rebuffed Knight's attempt to introduce into evidence Communist Party literature that the prosecution complained was in wide circulation.

At the conclusion of the defense's showing on the motion challenging the venire, Judge Horton ruled that the State would be required to present evidence to negate the inference that unlawful discrimination accounted for the absence of blacks from Morgan County trial juries. Knight called a jury commissioner to the witness stand, who denied that race was considered in assessing potential jurors' qualifications. Almost immediately following this testimony, Judge Horton rejected the defense's attack on the venire. Leibowitz registered an exception to this ruling, again content that he had preserved the issue if an appeal proved necessary.[42]

By now, it was apparent that Leibowitz's aggressive examination of witnesses and his challenge to practices that had been unquestioned throughout Alabama's history had distressed many court observers. Somewhat defensively, Leibowitz insisted, "We are not launching a crusade. But we are doing everything we can to protect the rights of the boys who are defendants in this case."[43] He had to contend with derogatory snickering as he attempted to make his case challenging the jury pool and at one point turned to the courtroom audience and proclaimed, "I am tired of some people making a Roman holiday out of this case."[44] Emotions nearly boiled over during jury selection, when one member of the venire, a postmaster from Eva, crossed the bar, or court railing, separating the attorneys and court officials from the spectators and told Judge Horton, "Us jurors in Morgan County are not accustomed to taking the charge from the defendant's attorney, and we don't like it." The startled judge quickly admonished the man against making such interruptions. Leibowitz pressed prospective jurors on voir dire about whether they had heard threats made against himself or others associated with the defense because of his challenges to the jury system. "Invariably the answer was negative and frequently a prospective juryman grinned at the attorney as he replied."[45] Noting the antagonism aroused "among certain elements" in the community, the commander of the National Guard assigned five armed soldiers to stand watch outside of the apartment building where Leibowitz and his wife Belle were staying during the trial.[46]

Jury selection was complete by Friday evening of the first week of the proceedings. Eight of the twelve white men on the jury were from Decatur and the others were from the outlying towns of Falkville, Hartselle, Danville, and Joppa. Three were farmers. One was unemployed. Two were bookkeepers, one a banker, and one an accountant. One operated a filling station, one was a salesman, another a merchant, and one a barber. The foreman was a draftsman. Twenty-five prospective jurors had been excused because they already had made up their minds about the case, and four because they did not believe that circumstantial evidence was sufficient to support a conviction. Five were disqualified because of their opposition to capital punishment. Haywood Patterson, whose fate would be in their hands, "watched closely" as the defense lawyers and prosecutors exercised their peremptory challenges and the twelve jurors were seated.[47] Before ordering the jury sequestered in anticipation of the presentation of evidence when court resumed on Monday, April 3, Judge Horton made a most unusual appeal to them.

I have been judge of your court for a number of years and I feel I can say, with a degree of gratification...that so far as I have been able to see, all the jurors who ever sat before me have tried each case as far as they were able according to the law and the evidence, and to render a true verdict in every case.

...I have had occasion to preside at trials involving some who were rich and prominent and some who were not so rich or prominent; there were important cases and some that were not so important, but in all I have felt that true justice was meted out.

I have seen jurors with wet eyes and I have heard foremen read verdicts with a voice that quavered showing the agony experienced in reaching a verdict. Never have I known of a juror who flinched at performing his duty, wherever it might lie.

So far as the law is concerned, it knows neither native nor alien, Jew or Gentile, black or white. This case is no different from any other. We have only our duty to do without fear or favor.

...It would be a blot on the men and women of this country, a blot on all of you, if you were to let any act of yours mar the course of justice in this or any other case. I trust you will not show by discourtesy or violence anything but a proper regard for law and order. Your fellow citizens would bow their heads in shame if any act of yours were to interrupt the course of justice.

...I expect from you proper restraint and a fair decision according to the law and the evidence. We must be true to ourselves, and if we be true to ourselves we can't be false to any man.[48]

As they whiled away time over the weekend awaiting the start of the trial, the twelve jurors assembled jigsaw puzzles, played cards, enjoyed a Saturday fishing trip, and were escorted to a movie. On Sunday morning the group attended services at St. John's Episcopal Church, where they heard Reverend Peter Dennis deliver a sermon that made no direct reference to the legal proceedings that were so much on the minds of Decatur's citizens. Amidst the prayers and hymns included in the services, the jurors heard Rev. Dennis implore the congregation, "We, all of us, and I am speaking particularly to ourselves right here in Decatur, need to open our hearts to the heavenly spirit and to put away the things that led well-fed bodies and starved souls to nail the Lamb of God to the Cross on Calvary."[49] Easter Sunday was two weeks away.

National Guard troops opened the courthouse doors shortly after 8:00 on Monday morning. The courtroom immediately filled. "At least one-third of the seats...were given to Negroes."[50] Two black reporters were among the many newspaper correspondents in attendance. Only two women spectators were present.[51] One was Mary Heaton Vorse, who was described by local newspapers as a "writer for liberal publications."[52] Vorse later filed a story for *The New Republic* in which she offered her unflinching account of the woman who all parties assembled in court that morning would hear testify as the State's first witness.

Directly under Judge Horton in the witness stand sits Victoria Price. She claims to be twenty-one and looks older. It is impossible to exaggerate the girl's appalling hardness. She is more than tough. She is terrifying in her depravity. Her head comes in direct line with that of Judge Horton—a strange contrast. Between them, they compass the best and worst that this part of the country can produce.[53]

Victoria Price took the witness stand at 9:40. She wore a blue straw hat with a red feather, a black dress with white lace at the throat, and a necklace of glass beads. Three large rings adorned her left hand as she placed it on the Bible to be sworn.[54] On direct examination under Solicitor Bailey's gentle prompting, Price presented her account of what happened on March 25, 1931. Much as she had testified in Scottsboro, she described how she, Ruby Bates, and seven white boys were riding in a gondola shortly after the freight train pulled out of Stevenson, when a dozen black youths clambered over the top of a box car and intruded on them. The "negroes" knocked all of the white boys off the train except for Orville Gilley. The assailants removed her clothes and, while one held a knife to her throat and another held her legs, proceeded to rape her. She iden-tified Haywood Patterson as the third or fourth to assault her. Her "step-ins," which she said were torn off her, were admitted into evidence after Leibowitz withdrew an objection.[55] The direct examination lasted just 15 minutes, during which time she answered questions "in a clear low voice," with "[h]er eyes . . . lowered" and "her face stolid."[56]

Price transformed abruptly under Leibowitz's cross examination, which was variously described as merciless,[57] withering,[58] and "more like the dissection of a life than a cross-questioning."[59] The *Birmingham News* reported that, "The cross-examination was something that doubtless no other white woman has undergone in an Alabama court where a case of this nature was being tried."[60] As to Leibowitz, "Gone were his pleasant smile and injections of humor."[61] Also gone was Price's demure and composed demeanor. She shouted in anger at the defense lawyer and became argumentative, accusing Leibowitz of talking too fast and confusing her because of her lack of education. She claimed frequent memory lapses and several times denied Leibowitz's insin-uations, dismissing them as "some of Ruby's dope."[62] As Leibowitz "pressed searching questions regarding her past," the *New York Times* reported, Price's "lip curled and she snapped her answers in the colloquialisms of the 'poor white.'"[63]

It was clear at the outset that the cross-examination would be contentious. Price signaled her distrust of Leibowitz immediately when she balked about con-ceding that a model train that the defense lawyer had assembled resembled the Southern Railway train on which she allegedly had been assaulted. She protested that the train she was on was "lots bigger" and Leibowitz's was just "a toy."[64] She refused to reveal the year she was born, claiming that she had insufficient educa-tion to calculate it, as Leibowitz skeptically probed whether she was just 21 at the time of the reported rape.[65] The two dueled verbally the rest of the morning and into the afternoon, for more than three hours. Skilled interrogator that he was, Leibowitz would later characterize Price as one of the most difficult witnesses he had ever encountered.[66]

Leibowitz would eventually weave several strands of argument together in an attempt to demonstrate that the rape allegations were false. He would ask the jury to take stock of the physical evidence which, he contended, offered little support for the charge. Despite her claim that she had repeatedly been raped while lying on her back on jagged gravel, Price had only minor scrapes and insignificant bruises on her person. She was not overtly emotional when examined by physicians shortly after the alleged gang rape, nor did the physicians find quantities of semen or vaginal injuries indicative of a series of brutal sexual assaults. Moreover, despite the fact that the train had snaked for more than an hour and a half between Stevenson and Paint Rock, with the mostly full gondola being readily visible to observers, other witnesses offered little to corroborate her story.

Leibowitz additionally hoped to exploit Price's dubious past. Having spent time in jail for lewdness and prostitution, neither her character nor her credibility were beyond impeachment. The defense also would offer a theory to explain why Price would fabricate rape allegations. Leveling her accusation against the boys would deflect attention from her own actions and allow her to avoid being arrested for hoboing across state lines. And finally, Leibowitz would offer an explanation for the semen found in Price during her examination by physicians in Scottsboro that pointed to a source other than the six black youths who she claimed had raped her. He combined his grilling of the State's star witness with testimony elicited from other witnesses to advance the multiple defense themes.

Price had slipped to the ground in an apparent faint when she and Ruby Bates encountered the 50 or more armed men who had been summoned to the Paint Rock station following the report that a gang of blacks had thrown several white boys off the train. The initial report of rape was ambiguous. It was unclear whether the suspicion was verbalized as a question by one of the posse members or whether one of the women volunteered the accusation.[67] However the claim surfaced, Price and Bates were transported to the Scottsboro jail and from there to a doctor's office for examination. In anticipation of the physician's testimony, Leibowitz got Price to confirm that one of her attackers had hit her in the head with the butt of a gun, causing her to bleed above the eye.[68] Price also told Leibowitz that she was bleeding from "her privates."[69] Leibowitz asked her about the rapes and the resulting injuries to her back.

Q: [SAMUEL LEIBOWITZ]   They didn't spare you in any way, didn't try to make it comfortable for you in any way?
A: [VICTORIA PRICE]   No sir.
Q: Just like brutes?
A: Yes sir.
Q: You lay on your back there for close to an hour on that jagged rock screaming?
A: Yes sir.

Q: Was your back bleeding when you got to the doctor?

A: I couldn't say.

Q: When you got to the jail did you find any blood on your back?

A: A little bit.

Q: Are you sure about that?

A: I ain't sure, that has been two years ago.

Q: That is something you would remember?

A: I haven't tried to remember, I didn't think it would come up any more.

Q: To the best o[f] your recollection did you find a single drop of blood on your back when you were at the doctor's office?

A: I won't answer, I don't remember.[70]

Dr. R.R. Bridges, the second State witness, was one of two Scottsboro physicians who had examined Price and Bates on the afternoon of March 25, 1931. Although the other doctor, M.H. Lynch, had testified in Scottsboro, he would not be used in the Morgan County trials. The medical examination had taken place around 4:00 P.M., or roughly two hours after the alleged rapes. Solicitor Bailey established that Dr. Bridges had found scratches on the back of Price's wrist as well as three or four "pecan size" bruises on the small of her back and between her shoulders. He found no lacerations, about Price's vagina or elsewhere, although he offered that her vaginal tissue was redder than normal. He reported extracting semen—"lots of male germ"—from Price's vagina and inspecting it under a microscope. That examination revealed that all spermatozoa were "nonmotile" which, Dr. Bridges explained to the jury, "as a general rule" meant that they were no longer living.[71]

Leibowitz's cross examination probed the doctor for a great many details. "Before starting, Leibowitz suggested to Judge Horton that he give women an opportunity to leave the courtroom."[72] Referring obliquely to "the very clinical medical testimony" presented, the *New York Times* observed that "[a]t times [the two women in attendance] looked as though they wished they had not come."[73] Leibowitz initially got Dr. Bridges to explain that a drop of semen contains "millions of sperm" and that a "normal" seminal discharge is two to three drams, or one to two teaspoons of fluid. He elicited that although the spermatozoa swabbed from Price were nonmotile, sperm can live up to ten days in a woman's vagina. He even managed to establish that discharged semen might flow more quickly out of a prostitute, whose vagina was apt to be more "relaxed" than that of other women. Moving to observed physical injuries, Leibowitz prodded Dr. Bridges to explain that he had observed no wounds above Price's eye, no blood on her back, and no bleeding from her vagina. Her scratch was "little," and her bruises "minor"—just the type that might normally be caused by riding on top of gravel in a moving freight train.[74]

He asked the doctor whether either Price or Bates was "hysterical" or "nervous" when he examined them, to which Bridges replied, "Neither one." Driving home the point to the jury, Leibowitz incredulously asked:

Q: As a medical man can you conceive, can you imagine two young girls going through such a horrible experience as these girls claim they went through, with six negroes raping them and throwing them around in a box car, and then coming to a doctors [sic] office and not show any signs of hysteria, or any signs or [sic] nervousness?[75]

Leibowitz could not have been surprised when Attorney General Knight objected to the question. Solicitor Bailey tried to recover ground on redirect examination by getting the doctor to acknowledge that delayed hysterical reactions can occur and that when he saw Price and Bates again the next morning both women in fact were hysterical and crying. Judge Horton subsequently sustained an objection to Leibowitz's question about whether a person could simply "act" hysterical, although the defense lawyer succeeded in having Dr. Bridges explain that in addition to exhibiting no indication of hysteria, neither woman had an elevated heart or respiration rate when he first examined them.[76] Later in the trial, Leibowitz called Dr. Edward Reisman, a gynecologist from the University of Tennessee, as an expert witness in an attempt to bolster the points that he had already sought to establish through his examination of Dr. Bridges.[77]

In addition to trying to undermine the physical evidence that might have helped corroborate Price's accusation, Leibowitz tried to raise doubts about other aspects of the State's case. Price had testified that the gondola in which she and Bates had been repeatedly raped was filled to within 18 inches to two feet of its top. It would be expected, the defense lawyer intimated, that residents would have reported witnessing the assault as the train wended the hilly terrain between Stevenson and Paint Rock over the course of its hour and a half journey. The prosecution summoned just two witnesses who had observed unusual events consistent with Price's account. Lee Adams testified that he had observed several "negroes" in a gondola as the train was on its way out of Stevenson, one of whom gave "a lick" to somebody. Adams then saw two white boys walking back toward town, one of whom was bloodied. He made no mention of seeing any women and since Leibowitz did not contest that a fight between white and black boys had occurred on the train, he did not cross examine Adams at length.[78] Ory Dobbins, however, offered a far more vivid story.

On direct examination, Dobbins testified that as the train went by his home on March 25, just 40 yards away, he was standing on a hill and saw several blacks in a gondola with two white girls. One of the girls looked like she was trying to jump from the moving locomotive, said Dobbins, and as he watched "a negro" grabbed her and pulled her back into the car.[79] Dobbins had testified at Patterson's trial in Scottsboro and Leibowitz was ready for him on cross examination. Leibowitz once had deflected a compliment by explaining, "I'm not a great lawyer.... I'm only thorough."[80] He confronted Dobbins with a series of photographs showing the layout of his home and barn, the hill on which he said he was standing, and the railroad tracks. He then got Dobbins to concede that it essentially would have been impossible for him to have seen the train from his ostensible vantage point because the barn on his property would have blocked his view. Leibowitz also pointed out material inconsistencies between Dobbins's testimony in Scottsboro and his present story.

When Leibowitz asked Dobbins how he could tell that there was a woman in the gondola, Dobbins explained that she had on "women's clothes," a dress. This testimony was patently inconsistent with all other accounts, including Price's own, that both women had been wearing overalls over their dresses, thus shielding them from view. Leibowitz concluded his evisceration of the testimony by suggesting that since Dobbins had witnessed several black men scuffling with a white woman when the train passed by, he must certainly have proceeded immediately to report the attack. When Dobbins lamely conceded that he made no such report, Leibowitz wrapped up his cross examination.[81] The prosecution asked no further questions.

Leibowitz invoked the model train that he had assembled in an attempt to demonstrate that Price's testimony that a dozen black youths had jumped from an adjoining box car into the gondola in which she, Bates, and the white boys were riding did not jibe with how the train cars were aligned that day. His evidence strongly suggested that Price and Bates had been riding on a gondola that was positioned between other cars of that same type, well removed from the nearest box car.[82] One of the oddest moments of the trial involved an item of evidence that was used in support of the prosecution's case. Arthur Woodall, a deputy sheriff from Stevenson who helped transport the white boys who had reported being thrown off of the train to Scottsboro, testified on direct examination that he assisted in searching the nine arrested blacks at the Scottsboro jail. Woodall stated that he removed a knife from one of the boys, evidence that could have supported Price's claim that she had been raped at knifepoint. On cross-examination, Leibowitz attempted to raise doubts about the knife's ownership. A stupefying sequence of events is then reflected on the trial transcript.

Q: [SAMUEL LEIBOWITZ]   Did you ask the negro if it was his knife?
A: [ARTHUR WOODALL]   He said he took it off this white girl.
Q: Did you ask him if it was his knife?
A: He said that he took it off the white girl Victoria Price.
MR. LEIBOWITZ: If the Court please, the minute this witness said that, the Attorney General jumped up and dashed over to the door clapping his hands and I want that on the record and move for a mistrial. That is something I haven't seen in fifteen years experience at the bar. The Chief Prosecuting Officer for the State of Alabama conducting himself in

that fashion, and he has told me he wants to give these negroes a fair trial—jump up and clap his hands and dash out with a smile and laugh.

GENERAL KNIGHT: That remark is not true, but Your Honor I am sorry I went out.

MR. LEIBOWITZ: I never expected a display of that kind, I am mortified.

COURT: I accept the apology.

GENERAL KNIGHT: I should not have done it.

COURT: The attorney [*sic*] General regrets it.

GENERAL KNIGHT: I do and apologize to the court and to the jury and to the opposing counsel.

COURT: The Court did hear a sound, I wasn't looking at it—there doesn't seem to be any dispute in regard to the facts.

MR. LEIBOWITZ: I never saw anything like this in my life.

COURT: Gentlemen of the Jury don't consider that at all, that is not proper for you to consider, and do not let it influence you whatever.

GENERAL KNIGHT: I hope it won't influence them.

COURT: Overrule the motion.[83]

The *New York Times* described the incident as "the most dramatic moment of the day":

As the words fell from the lips of the witness, Mr. Knight . . . brought his hands down flat on the top of the counsel table, showed his elation and dashed into an anteroom, clapping his hands together once.

The Attorney General was out of the court room when Mr. Leibowitz made his protest, but his assistants sprinted after him and brought him back to apologize to the court and jury. He seemed nervous and chastened as he listened to the closing words of the defense lawyer's motion for a mistrial.[84]

Although the *Decatur Daily* opted to headline its afternoon edition, "Motion for Mistrial is Denied By Horton After Dramatic Moment," in reference to Knight's conduct,[85] the *Birmingham Age Herald* buried mention of the incident on an interior page, reporting blandly that "As [the witness] replied, Knight chuckled and with a clap of his hands turned to the witness room."[86]

Having attempted to highlight deficiencies in evidence that might tend to support Price's testimony, Leibowitz also did his best to discredit Price herself. His efforts were not always subtle. During one exchange, as Price evaded questions concerning her activities in Chattanooga on the evening preceding the alleged rapes, Leibowitz's frustration got the better of him.

Q: [SAMUEL LEIBOWITZ] You went to Chattanooga and got there about what time?

A: [VICTORIA PRICE] Oh, about seven or eight, six or seven, I don't know positive.

Q: That was Tuesday, March 24th?

A: I don't remember.
Q: The night before you claim you were raped?
A: I do know one thing those negroes and this Haywood Patterson raped me.
Q: That was the day before you claim you were raped—you are a little bit of an actress?[87]

Newspapers reported that Price had "screamed" at Leibowitz that Patterson had attacked her, and responded to his accusation that she was "a little bit of an actress" with, "You're a pretty good actor yourself,"[88] although the trial transcript captures neither her tone of voice nor her alleged retort.

Leibowitz's line of questioning was designed to raise doubts about Price's credibility. He hoped to undermine her innocuous account of traveling by train from Huntsville with Ruby Bates in search of employment in Chattanooga, their uneventful overnight stay, and their decision to board a train the next day intent on returning to Huntsville. He knew from studying the transcripts of the Scottsboro trials that Price had sworn that she and Bates had spent the night in Chattanooga with Mrs. Callie Brochie, who owned a home on Seventh Street, and whom Price described as a friend who took the two Huntsville women to the mills the following morning in their unsuccessful search for jobs. Price had not testified before the Decatur jury about these matters during her direct examination, and Leibowitz tried to get her to do so, prompting a heated objection from Knight.

GENERAL KNIGHT: I can't see the relevancy of the details of her going to Mrs. Brochie's and what she did in Chattanooga. I don't care what she did in Chattanooga, the only thing we are interested in is whether she was raped on that train.
MR. LEIBOWITZ: I am testing her credibility.
GENERAL KNIGHT: You know that is no proposition of law.
MR. LEIBOWITZ: Address your remarks to the Court.
GENERAL KNIGHT: You make it necessary to address them to you.
MR. LEIBOWITZ: I have been a gentleman, but I can be otherwise too.
COURT: Wait a minute, gentlemen, don't either one of you say anything. Gentlemen I am not going to have another word between you, ask the question and the Court will pass on it.[89]

After Price reaffirmed that she and Bates had spent the night of March 24 in Mrs. Callie Brochie's house on Chattanooga's Seventh Street, Leibowitz sprang his trap. Some members of the courtroom audience, those who read popular magazines and recognized the names leading up to the attorney's final question, saw it coming.

Q: Did you meet a man by the name of Florian Slappy [*sic*]?
A: No sir.
Q: Do you know a lawyer by the name of Evans Chew?
A: No sir.

Q: Do you know a man by the name of Epic Peters?

A: No sir.

GENERAL KNIGHT: I don't think that is relevant cross examination.

COURT: Is there anything further you want to ask in regard to these parties?

MR. LEIBOWITZ: Nothing further.

Q: By the way Mrs. Price, as a matter of fact the name of Mrs. Callie you apply to this boarding house lady, is the name of a boarding house lady used by Octavius Roy Cohn [*sic*] in the Saturday Evening Post stories—Sis Callie, isn't that where you got the name?[90]

GENERAL KNIGHT: We object.

COURT: Sustain the objection.[91]

Later in the trial, Leibowitz called his co-counsel George Chamlee to the witness stand. Chamlee explained to the jury that he had been an attorney in Chattanooga for over 40 years and that he had occupied an office on Seventh Street for 25 years. He described how Seventh Street was two miles from the train tracks, rather than the four blocks that Price had estimated she had walked to get there. Although intimately familiar with the eight blocks comprising Seventh Street and most of the people who resided there, Chamlee recounted how he had never heard of "Callie Brochie," that the City Directory included no listing for her, and that he had walked the length of Seventh Street vainly looking for a boarding house fitting the description offered in Price's testimony.[92] Another long time resident of Chattanooga, Roy and Andy Wright's sister, Beatrice Maddox, echoed Chamlee's conclusions.[93] Her testimony not only cast additional doubt on Price's veracity but doubtlessly was designed to remind the jurors that the young men who stood accused of committing such a heinous crime had families who cared about them, lives beyond their immediate predicament, and were more than simply the infamous "Scottsboro Boys."

Beyond efforts to undermine the specifics of Price's testimony, Leibowitz did his best to impeach her character. He asked Price whether she had been convicted of adultery, which she denied, and whether she had been convicted of lewdness with a man named Jack Tiller, which she denied, and finally whether she had been convicted of vagrancy, which she was not required to answer because Judge Horton sustained the prosecution's objection. Price in fact had been found guilty of those offenses and even served time in jail. However, she was convicted under the Huntsville City Code rather than of breaking the State's criminal law. Under Alabama law, city code violations were inadmissible to impeach a witness's credibility.[94] Although the jury was formally prohibited from taking note of Price's run-ins with the law, Leibowitz's pointed questions nevertheless succeeded in calling those indiscretions to the jurors' attention.

The narrow purpose behind attempting to cross examine Price about her prior convictions was to impeach her credibility by demonstrating past violations of the law. Strictly speaking, the precise nature of the offenses was not germane, beyond suggesting an untrustworthy character or a general lack of veracity. At the same time, the specific offenses in Price's background—most notably, lewdness and adultery—also could relate to the substance of the rape allegation. Leibowitz had not explicitly relied on such a theory, although he obviously would not be displeased if others were inclined to do so. As Attorney General Knight contested Leibowitz's efforts to raise Price's criminal past before the jury, he leaped to a conclusion that the defense attorney had not articulated, that Price's promiscuity could bear on issues of consent.

Q: [MR. LEIBOWITZ]   Jack Tiller was your boy friend?
A: [VICTORIA PRICE]   Before I left Huntsville, Alabama, he was.
Q: You and he were convicted together?
A: No sir.
Q: Convicted of lewdness?
A: No sir, not Jack Tiller, look and see if it is J. Tiller.
GENERAL KNIGHT: We object.
COURT: Sustain the objection.
GENERAL KNIGHT: We don't care whether this woman has been convicted for forty offenses, the charge is rape. She has never been convicted for living in adultery with a negro.
COURT: I would permit you to show any intercourse approximately within twenty four hours of this time.
MR. LEIBOWITZ: I desire to say this, and say it only because General Knight made that statement, I will prove she did consort with negroes time and time again, and I will prove it beyond a doubt.
GENERAL KNIGHT: We object.
COURT: When that comes up.
ATTORNEY KNIGHT: You prove it instead of saying it.
MR. LEIBOWITZ: I will prove it if you will let me.
COURT: Gentlemen I will let you show she had commerce with any man within a day before.
MR. LEIBOWITZ: Within a day or so before.
COURT: To account for any semen.[95]

Referring to this heated confrontation between Knight and Leibowitz, the *Daily Worker* disingenuously reported that, "Prosecutor Knight lost his temper and exclaimed, 'I don't care what her previous convictions or actions were— but she never lived with niggers.'"[96] Although ancillary to the Attorney General's objection that Price had not been "living in adultery with a negro," Judge Horton's ruling that the defense could "show any intercourse approximately within twenty four hours of" the charge marked a critical moment in the trial and represented a major tactical victory for Leibowitz. As would later become clear, a contrary decision would have been devastating to the defense's case.

In addition to hammering at the weaknesses in external evidence supporting the rape allegation and trying to undermine Price's credibility, Leibowitz attempted to supply the jury with an alternative picture of what had occurred. He first offered a theory about why Price would falsely claim that she had been raped. In one of the concluding questions of his cross examination, he suggested what her motivation may have been.

Q: Isn't the real reason why you are making these charges you were found hoboing on a freight train—
A: I was seeking work for my mother.
Q: And you saw the negroes had been captured by the people at Paint Rock and you thought you would be arrested for vagrancy for being a hobo on a train in company with negroes and at that time you determined to say they raped you to save yourself?
GENERAL KNIGHT: We object.
COURT: Sustain the objection.[97]

With that seed firmly planted, Leibowitz developed a counter narrative of the events leading up to the rape charge, relying both on his cross examination of Price and other witnesses and on evidence presented during the defense's case.

Leibowitz laid the foundation for what he would try to prove happened during his cross examination of Price. By all accounts of the trial, Price was so incensed by the relentless questioning that she was shouting at Leibowitz by the end of their exchange.[98]

Q: Did [Jack] Tiller, Ruby Bates and Lester Carter come to your home at one time about two or three nights, a short time, before you left Huntsville?
A: No one knew we were leaving but me and Ruby Bates, we were hunting work.
Q: Isn't it a fact that three days after you met Lester Carter you and he and Tiller and Ruby Bates went walking along the L & N Railroad tracks?
A No sir, we never have been on the railroad together.
Q Isn't it a fact that you had intercourse with Tiller on the ground while Ruby Bates had intercourse with Lester Carter right beside you?
A: No sir, I didn't.
Q A day or possibly thirty six hours before you were examined by the doctor?
A: I never was in Lester Carter's company before until I was in Scottsboro in jail.
Q: Did you have intercourse with Tiller a short time before you left Huntsville?
A: No sir.
Q: On the railroad yards?
A: I have told you three times, and I am not telling you any more—no sir I didn't.
Q: Did you that same night I refer to in the L & N yards, it started to rain that night, then did you go with Ruby Bates, Lester Carter and Tiller into a box car that night?
A: Explain that.
Q: A short time before you left Huntsville—
A: I told you I never was in Lester Carter's company until I was in Scottsboro.

Q: Did you go with Tiller into a box car?

A: No sir.

Q: And stay with Tiller all night in the box car?

GENERAL KNIGHT: We object.

A: No sir.

Q: Did you stay with Jack Tiller in the box car a short time before you left Huntsville, sleep with him all night, while Ruby Bates and a man by the name of Lester Carter stayed with you in that box car all night sleeping on newspapers?

A: I answered that four times and I am not answering it any more.

COURT: Did you?

A: Judge Your Honor, I said I didn't.

COURT: Very well, she said she didn't.

Q: Did you at any time that night have intercourse with a man by the name of Jack Tiller, the night I refer to?

COURT: The night before she went to Chattanooga?

MR. LEIBOWITZ: A night or two nights before that. I will be able to show by medical testimony the condition she was in, and I promise you I will connect it up, and you can hold me strictly to my promise—I will be able to show that the condition she was found in could have been caused two or three nights before that.

A: You can't prove that.[99]

Leibowitz's tough examination of Price, designed to lock her inescapably into her story more than with the expectation that she would change it, was risky. A contemporary observer, sensitive to the mood of the trial, reported that, "The audience in the courtroom could not forgive him for what he revealed about Victoria Price."[100] A later commentator explained why. "Leibowitz made the fatal mistake of regarding Victoria Price as a cut-rate prostitute. He was 'not accustomed to addressing Southern juries'...Too late the chief defense attorney realized that Mrs. Price had become a symbol of white Southern womanhood."[101] Reactions within and outside of the courtroom revealed mounting hostility toward Leibowitz and, by extension, his clients. During the trial's third day, Judge Horton received a report from the commander of the National Guard troops that "a mass meeting, to which 200 young men of the community were invited...was held in a hall near the court house...to 'protest against the manner in which Mr. Leibowitz has examined the State's witnesses.' There was talk...of riding the New York lawyer out of town and lynching the Negroes."[102] Judge Horton abruptly sent the jurors from the courtroom. Then, "in phrases that fell from his lips like the bullets he promised to lynchers,"[103] he issued a stern admonition to onlookers.

Whether or not there is the slightest danger the Court does not know; sometimes rumors come that may be absolutely untrue, but occasionally we reach that point where the Court feels that there should be something said along this line.... This Court intends to protect these prisoners, and any other persons engaged in this trial. Any man or any group of men that attempts to take charge outside of the law, are not only disobedient to the law, but are citizens unworthy of the protection of the State of Alabama.... [T]he soldiers here and the Sheriffs here are expected to defend with their lives these prisoners.... [T]he man who attempts it may expect that his own life be forfeited, or the guards that guard them must forfeit their lives....I am speaking with feeling, and I know it, because I am feeling it. I absolutely have no patience with mob spirit....Your very civilization depends upon the carrying out of your laws in an orderly manner....I will say this much; so far as I am concerned I believe I am as gentle as any man in the world; I don't believe I would harm any one wrongfully, but when it comes to a question of right and wrong, when it comes to the very civilization, men no matter how quiet they are, or how peaceful they are, there comes a time when they must take a stand either right or wrong. Now gentlemen I want that understood, and I will say this much; if there is any meeting in this town where such matters are discussed, where such thought[s] are brought forward, the men that attend such a meeting should be ashamed of themselves; they are unworthy citizens of your town, and the good people of this town look down on them. Now gentlemen I have spoken straight words; I have spoken harsh words, but every word I say is true, and I hope we will have no more of any such conduct. Let the jury return.[104]

The defense's first witness after the prosecution rested its case was Dallas Ramsey, a black man whose home abutted a hobo jungle near the railroad tracks in Chattanooga. Ramsey described having seen two white women in the hobo camp around 6:00 A.M. on March 25, 1931. He was able to pinpoint that date because he later read about the alleged gang rape in the Chattanooga newspaper. The paper had devoted prominent coverage to the story because four of the arrested boys were from that city. In a moment pregnant with drama,[105] Victoria Price was escorted into the courtroom and positioned before Ramsey. Despite venturing that Price had put on weight since he had seen her two years previously, Ramsey unhesitatingly identified her as one of the women he had seen. He went into detail about what he and Price had discussed, and testified that he had seen her scramble on board the train destined for Huntsville later that morning, accompanied by a man.[106] Ramsey's account was corroborated later during the defense's case by E. L. Lewis, a neighbor and also a black man, who reported talking with Price and a white man who he described as being one of Price's traveling companions. Lewis would identify that man as Lester Carter.[107]

After trying to discredit Price's story about where she had spent the night during her trip to Chattanooga, and her claim that her only traveling companion was Ruby Bates, Leibowitz continued to chip away at her testimony. He unsuccessfully attempted to introduce into evidence a copy of the Huntsville adultery ordinance that Price had been jailed for violating.[108] Next, he offered Beatrice Maddox and George Chamlee as witnesses, whose testimony suggested that Mrs. Callie Brochie and her Seventh Street boarding house were fictions.[109]

He then placed five of Haywood Patterson's original codefendants on the witness stand to refute the charges directly.

As he had two years earlier in his testimony at Scottsboro, Willie Roberson unequivocally denied fighting with white boys on the train or raping Price or Bates, and maintained that he had not even seen the women until after the train had stopped at Paint Rock. He explained that he had boarded the train with the hope of reaching Memphis and getting treatment for the syphilis and gonorrhea with which he was inflicted. His "private parts," he insisted, were "swollen a heap," and were laden with large sores. He was not wearing a "suspensory," which made it painful for him to walk, much less run or engage in fights, and he claimed that his condition rendered him incapable of having sexual intercourse.[110]

Olen Montgomery likewise offered a complete denial. He testified that he remained on an oil car at the rear of the train during the entire journey and knew nothing about a fight, the alleged rapes, or about any women being on the train. He additionally explained that he was blind in one eye and could not see well out of his other eye.[111] There was no doubt that Montgomery's vision was severely impaired. Describing a "dramatic interview...with the innocent Negro boys" in the Decatur jail, the *Daily Worker's* correspondent wrote floridly about becoming "aware of the eyes staring at me....The eyes were the eyes of the Scottsboro boys. Only seventeen eyes, for Olin [sic] Montgomery is blind in one and he peered between the heavy three-inch steel bars with his one good but near-sighted eye at the shadow on the wall."[112] On cross examination, Knight got Montgomery to concede that he did not know whether Haywood Patterson had raped Price.[113]

Ozie Powell testified that on March 25, 1931, he had traveled on a flat car from Chattanooga to Stevenson, where he got off the train to get cigarettes, and then took a position between a gondola and a box car. When he saw several "colored boys" crossing between the cars overhead, he climbed up to investigate. On doing so, he observed a number of black youths fighting with a group of white boys in a gondola a few cars away. He denied seeing any women and he denied committing rape.[114] Knight's aggressive cross examination included trying to get Powell to admit that he had told a different story at the Scottsboro trial. Powell's confusion during the cross examination was evident and it caused Leibowitz to elicit on redirect examination that Powell had completed only three months of schooling in his entire life.[115] Leibowitz's attempt to protect Powell from the Attorney General's questioning produced another testy exchange between the two lawyers.

MR. LEIBOWITZ: Would you mind stepping away from the witness and obstructing the jury's view General Knight.
GENERAL KNIGHT: Gentlemen, I am sorry if I have obstructed your view, I want the witness to hear.

MR. LEIBOWITZ: He can hear from where you are standing.
GENERAL KNIGHT: That is all right, I will stand where I want to.
MR. LEIBOWITZ: You are at liberty to climb up in his lap if you want to.[116]

Andy Wright and Eugene Williams offered considerably more detailed accounts of the fight that had broken out on the train between the black and white youths than had previously been supplied. Each denied having seen any women until after the train had stopped in Paint Rock, and each denied having anything to do with a rape. Cross examination focused on inconsistencies between their current stories and how they had testified in Scottsboro, but otherwise was not particularly damaging.[117] Wright's and Williams's testimony largely foreshadowed Haywood Patterson's own version of events, which Leibowitz held for last.

Leibowitz first led Patterson through the events that had precipitated the fight on the train. Patterson described how he was holding on to the side of a train car as the locomotive approached Stevenson, at which point: "Some white boy come walking along the side of the car, transferring from car to car, come along and stepped on my hand, and I asked the boy the next time he wanted to pass let me known [*sic*] and I would get out of his way; the boy spoke up and asked me what was my part about it if he knocked me off; I psoke [*sic*] up and told him if he did it again I would show him my part about it."[118] The train strained mightily up the substantial inclines along the route, moving so slowly that those clinging to it could easily jump off and swing back on again.[119] Several white boys did just that, collecting rocks in the process, which they threw at Patterson and other blacks riding on the train. Further words were exchanged, and then several black youths banded together to fight the white boys.

Patterson testified that he and others crawled into the fourth gondola from the nearest box car, where they began fighting five white boys. Two more white boys joined the fight, entering the gondola from the next car over, or five gondolas away from the closest box car. The blacks got the better of the whites, and all of the whites but two jumped off of the train; one ran away toward the engine, and Patterson and Andy Wright helped pull the other one back into the train so he would not be injured hitting the ground. Patterson identified the white boy they rescued as Orville Gilley who, he said, scrambled back into the adjoining gondola. Patterson noticed three or four other people in the neighboring car but paid little attention to them. He returned to his original position on the train, where he remained until the Paint Rock station. He denied having seen any white women on the train and emphatically denied raping anyone.[120]

On cross examination Knight peppered Patterson with questions about contradictory statements he had made at his original trial in Scottsboro. Patterson had sworn in Scottsboro that he had seen "all but three of these negroes ravish that girl" and he had specifically identified Charlie Weems as one of the rapists.

But his Scottsboro testimony was confused, at best. He subsequently retracted those allegations during his Scottsboro trial, insisting that he "did not see any negroes on top of either one of those girls," and that "I did not see any girls in there [on the train] until we got to Paint Rock."[121] Knight, of course, focused on the former, incriminating statements, but Patterson remained steadfast in his denials. He dismissed the Scottsboro proceedings in their entirety during the following exchange with the Attorney General.

Q: I will ask you if when you were in Scottsboro—you were tried at Scottsboro?
A: Yes, sir, I was framed at Scottsboro.
Q: Framed at Scottsboro?
A: Yes sir.
Q: Who told you to say you were framed?
A: I told myself to say it.[122]

Leibowitz and Knight clashed repeatedly as Knight continued his cross examination of Patterson. At one point, Leibowitz interjected:

MR. LEIBOWITZ: I have treated his witnesses with much more courtesy and with much more decency than he is showing this negro on the stand; he is running at him and shouting and pointing his finger at him, trying to embarrass him; he is only an illiterate negro, give him half a chance. I treated your witnesses with the utmost courtesy.
GENERAL KNIGHT: I am not ashamed with the way I am examining this witness.
MR. LEIBOWITZ: Don't rush up at him, nothing is going to be gained by that.[123]

At another point, another Leibowitz warning elicited a similar retort from the Attorney General:

MR. LEIBOWITZ: Don't point your finger at him trying to embarrass him.
GENERAL KNIGHT: I am not studying about embarrassing him, what I want to do—
MR. LEIBOWITZ: Don't point your finger in his face, or your pencil at him.
GENERAL KNIGHT: I will point anything I want to until the Court tells me not to.[124]

Reports of Patterson's trial testimony were far from uniform in the nation's press. Both the *New York Times* and the *Daily Worker* described how Patterson claimed during cross examination that he had been "framed" in Scottsboro.[125] That assertion, however, escaped mention in several prominent Southern newspapers, including both Birmingham publications. The *Birmingham News* instead reported that Patterson reacted with "outraged feeling"[126] in response to a portion of Knight's questioning, and the *Birmingham Age Herald* emphasized how Patterson "repeatedly denied"[127] making statements that were reflected in the Scottsboro trial record. The jurors nevertheless heard the complete testimony and Patterson, like the other accused boys, this time remained true to his story that he knew nothing about the women being raped.

The Boys' denials were to be expected. However, building toward the climax of his case, Leibowitz next produced a disinterested witness who offered dramatic support for their claims of innocence. Lester Carter was one of the white boys put off of the train during the fight about which much testimony already had been presented. But Carter, in his more than three hours on the witness stand,[128] had much more to offer, which he did with uncommon flair. "Carter gave the courtroom its greatest entertainment as he mixed flowery phrases with the jargon of tramps, gestured impressively, and delivered himself as if he might have been reciting some tale of adventure about the campfire of his beloved jungles. He kept his hands going, raised and lowered his voice, gave the impression that he was reliving the activities he was recalling, and at times reminded one of a high school orator."[129]

Carter testified that he met Victoria Price and a man named Jack Tiller in the Huntsville jail in 1931, where all were serving sentences for vagrancy. He was introduced to Ruby Bates at the jail, who was there visiting Price. After their release, Carter explained, the four of them visited together, once at the home of Price and her mother, and thereafter in a hobo jungle in Huntsville. In the hobo jungle, the two couples engaged in sexual intercourse. So close were they, said Carter, that at one point Tiller and Price slid down almost on top of Bates and himself. When it started to rain, the foursome retreated into a box car, where they again engaged in sexual relations. They also developed a plan to leave Huntsville and relocate in Chattanooga. Carter, Price, and Bates would hop a train, get established in Chattanooga, and then send for Tiller, who was married to another woman and could not come and go so freely.[130]

Attorney General Knight apparently was following Carter's testimony incredulously, as Leibowitz twice interrupted his questioning to protest. On the first occasion, the defense lawyer exclaimed:

MR. LEIBOWITZ: What is all this joke, what is this smiling about. I am going to quit unless it stops.
GENERAL KNIGHT: You can quit at any time you get ready.
MR. LEIBOWITZ: Such discourtesy to a witness—
GENERAL KNIGHT: It is very hard to control disgust, an expression of disgust.[131]

Moments later, Leibowitz again exploded:

MR. LEIBOWITZ: Your Honor when a man sits on the stands [*sic*] and sees all these faces in front of him, he has got enough hardship without a man standing there smirking at him and making facial expressions at him.
COURT: If that was done I am sure Counsel doesn't intend it.

GENERAL KNIGHT: I made no facial expressions at him; I think he should quit his argument, I am sitting here attending to my business.[132]

Continuing his testimony, Carter explained that pursuant to their plan, he, Price and Bates boarded the Chattanooga-bound train around 3:00 P.M. a day and a half after the described liaisons. They did not talk much during the trip because they feared being arrested for hoboing across state lines. They arrived in Chattanooga about 8:00 that same evening, and there met a young man who introduced himself as "Carolina Slim." The youth's real name was Orville Gilley. Gilley led them to a hobo jungle near the railroad tracks, where the four of them spent the night. The next morning, Carter described his interaction with "some negro men" who Bates and Price claimed had used bad language toward them while Carter and Gilley were gone looking for breakfast. Later that morning, Carter, Gilley, Price and Bates caught the train heading west toward Huntsville.[133]

They began their journey, said Carter, on the top of a box car but when the train stopped in Stevenson, the four of them relocated into the fourth or fifth car in a series of gondolas. They knew about the fight that had started between other white boys and black youths on the train and when it escalated after the train left Stevenson, Carter and Gilley joined in. Carter explained that he and most of the white boys jumped off the train during the fight, but Gilley and another stayed on board. Carter and other of the deposed whites walked to Stevenson, reported the fight with the black youths, and then were taken by car to Scottsboro. There they saw the arrested black youths as well as Price and Bates. All of them soon ended up in the Scottsboro jail.[134]

While they were being held in the jail, Carter heard Price tell Gilley that they would get paid for testifying against the "negroes," and that if Gilley didn't tell the same story she did, she would have him taken off the witness stand. Price again expressed concern that they would get arrested for hoboing. Gilley grew angry, asked Price why she wanted to make up a story, and told her she would go "to Torment" for telling her lies. Price, Carter said, retorted, "What the Hell do we care about negroes." Carter was released from jail after spending two and one half weeks there and explained that he had not been called to testify in Scottsboro. He eventually traveled to Albany, New York, intent on telling the state's highest official, Governor Franklin Roosevelt, what he knew about the case. Although he did not succeed in seeing Roosevelt, someone in the governor's office advised him to get in touch with Mr. Brodsky, in New York City. Carter followed that recommendation. He concluded his testimony on direct examination by stating that his first contact with Leibowitz was 2:00 that very morning.[135]

Solicitor Wade Wright conducted a lengthy cross examination that did not so much highlight vulnerabilities in Carter's testimony as allow him to provide additional details beneficial to the defense's case. The witness apparently relished the opportunity to rehash his testimony. "Carter grinned as Wright questioned him at length about the 'date' he and Tillery [*sic*] had at Huntsville."[136] He additionally volunteered that he and Bates not only had engaged in sexual intercourse prior to leaving for Chattanooga, but also while spending the night there in the hobo jungle, less than a day before the Scottsboro physicians would find semen in Bates's vagina. When Wright asked Carter whether Price and Gilley also had sexual relations in the Chattanooga hobo jungle, Carter responded, "Not that I know of."[137] Carter clarified during the cross examination that no part of the fight that had broken out on the train took place in the gondola in which Price and Bates were riding. He explained that he and Gilley climbed into the adjacent gondola to join in the fight. "The negroes didn't come into the car we were in, they were in the joining car."[138]

If Wright succeeded in damaging Carter's credibility, it may have been in his final questioning, when he bore in on Carter's relationship with Brodsky, a member of the defense team, with whom Carter had met during his trip to New York. Solicitor Wright, like some newspaper reporters, had not failed to notice that Carter was "well dressed [and] clean shaven."[139] Wright's pointed questioning began after he learned that Carter, a self-proclaimed hobo, had made his return trip from New York to Alabama by automobile.

Q: What kind of car did you come down in?
A: Chevrolet car.
Q: Who furnished the expenses for that trip?
A: I bought my meals.
Q: Where did you get the money?
A: Mr. Brodsky would give me three or four dollars along.
Q: Did he pay for your meals?
A: Yes sir.
Q: When you left from here up there you didn't have that kind of suit of clothes on you have got on now?
A: No sir, not this one.
Q: Where did you get that suit of clothes?
A: I bought it in New York.
Q: Who paid for it?
A: I paid for it out of the money I would get.
Q: That Mr. Brodsky let you have?
A: Yes sir.
Q: Do you know what that suit cost?
A: About eleven dollars.
Q: How long did you stay in New York in that room Mr. Brodsky rented for you?
A: Well I remained there, I said I was about two weeks going up, I remained around there a couple of weeks.[140]

At the conclusion of Carter's testimony, Leibowitz called E. L. Lewis, the black man who, along with Dallas Ramsey, had seen Carter and the two white women in the Chattanooga hobo jungle on the morning of March 25, 1931.[141] He then announced that the defense rested its case, "with a proviso,"[142] noting that additional witnesses might be called. Ever the master of timing, Leibowitz thus brought the proceedings to a temporary halt. The court went into "informal recess" as observers speculated about what the announcement heralded.[143]

Less than ten minutes later the gambit was revealed, as Ruby Bates made her entrance before a startled courtroom. Heads turned as Leibowitz called her name. The three State's attorneys shared a look of consternation.[144] Bates's whereabouts had been unknown since the end of February and her appearance as a defense witness on the heels of Lester Carter's testimony boded ominously for the prosecution. She was described as trim, with a "girlish figure,...dark complexion and downcast eyes;"[145] many thought her pretty.[146] Her attire, unusual by Decatur fashion standards, commanded immediate attention. The *Birmingham News* described Bates as "dressed in modish gray and well groomed," and printed a front-page photograph of her under the caption, "Girl Witness Dresses Well."[147] The *Huntsville Daily Times* commented on her "grey coat and close fitting hat to match."[148] The *New York Times* noted the sharp contrast between Bates's "stylish clothes" and the "calico skirt and black woolen sweater" that was Victoria Price's outfit.[149] Her new look did not escape Attorney General Knight's notice.

The courtroom was hushed as Leibowitz began his questioning. Judge Horton stood close, the better to scrutinize Bates's testimony. To allay suspicion that he had somehow engineered Bates's disappearance and dramatic emergence, Leibowitz first established that he and Bates had never met before that very moment.[150] Then, over the next ten minutes, Bates told her story; an account that repudiated what she had told the juries in Scottsboro and amounted to an admission that the rape charges had been fabricated. In every material respect, Bates corroborated Lester Carter's testimony and refuted Victoria Price's. Like all other witnesses, Price was not allowed in the courtroom while she was not testifying, but she was brought before Bates at one point so Ruby could identify her. During that confrontation, the two women "glared at one another. Mrs. Price was panting with anger and excitement. Attorney General Knight edged his way in between the two women and cautioned the State's main witness to 'keep your temper.' The Price woman was hurried out of court and the Bates girl continued her sensational evidence."[151]

Referring to March 23, 1931, the day before Bates and Price left Huntsville by train for Chattanooga, Leibowitz asked Bates:

Q: Did you have intercourse with Lester Carter that night?
A: I certainly did.
Q: Did Victoria Price have intercourse with Jack Tiller?
A: She certainly did.
Q: In your presence?
A: Yes sir.[152]

Bates confirmed that she, Carter, and Price left jointly for Chattanooga on March 24, while Tiller remained in Huntsville. She and Price did not spend the night in Chattanooga on Seventh Street in a boarding house owned by Mrs. Callie Brochie, but rather in a hobo jungle by the railroad tracks with Lester Carter and Orville Gilley, who they met shortly after arriving. She described their encounters with Dallas Ramsey much as Ramsey and Carter had described them. On March 25, she, Price, Carter and Gilley boarded the train back to Huntsville, occupying a gondola after the train pulled into Stevenson. The gondola was located next to the one where the fight between the black and white youths would soon come to a head.

Q: What happened?
A: And after a while there was a bunch of negroes come over and started fighting, they was all fighting and Lester Carter and this Gilley boy jumped over to help them out.
Q: You mean Lester Carter and Gilley left the gondola in which you were in and went into the next gondola where the fight was between the white boys and the negroes?
A: Yes sir.
Q: Then what happened?
A: The negroes put all the boys off but one, Orville Gilley and he came back in the car where we were.
Q: Then what happened, when you, Victoria and Gilley were there did the negroes come in that car where you were?
A: Not that I know of.
Q: Did any negro attack you that day?
A: Not that I know of.
Q: Did any negro attack Victoria Price that day?
A: I couldn't say.
Q: Did you see any negro attack Victoria Price that day?
A: No sir.[153]

When Leibowitz asked Bates why she had originally claimed that she and Price had each been raped by six Negroes, she replied, "I was excited." She explained that Price told the story "and I told it just like she told it."

Q: Did she [Price] tell you what would happen to you if you didn't follow her story?
A: She said we might have to lay out a sentence in jail.[154]

Leibowitz concluded the direct examination by getting Bates to explain that she had just arrived in Alabama from New York, where she had met a minister, Reverend Fosdick. Bates testified that after she told him the story about what had happened, Reverend Fosdick urged her to return to Alabama. She traveled by bus from New York City to Birmingham, and she had just arrived in Decatur from Birmingham.[155]

Bates's recantation did not settle well with many local residents. At one point during her testimony, Leibowitz called out a member of the courtroom audience for "snickering" and "referred to the spectators as 'rooters for this Negro's blood.'" Obviously concerned about further alienating the townspeople, "Defense Attorney George Chamlee, of Chattanooga, stated openly to the court that in the South courtroom audiences meant nothing by laughing, that they were all good folks of a kind he knew, and that he would vouch for them. Liebowitz [sic] accepted the explanation graciously."[156] Tension nevertheless mounted. Following the close of court that day National Guard troops with "riot guns" were assigned to guard Leibowitz, and Bates was removed by deputy sheriffs from her sleeping quarters around midnight and hidden.[157] In the meantime, however, Attorney General Knight began his cross examination.

Knight opened his examination by quizzing Bates about the gondola in which she and Price were riding. Not more than a minute or two into his questioning, and without warning, he pounced, abruptly switching topics.

Q: Where did you get that coat?
A: Well I bought it.
Q: Who gave you the money to buy it?
A: Well I don't know.
Q: You don't know, where did you get that hat?
A: I bought it.
Q: Who gave you the money to buy it?
COURT: Do you know.
A: Dr. Fostick [sic] of New York.
Q: He gave you that?
A: Yes sir.
Q: He gave you the money to buy the coat and hat?
A: He certainly did.
Q: What about the shoes?
A: I have had the shoes a long time.
Q: You say Dr. Fostick [sic] of New York gave you that hat and coat, didn't you know that when I asked you the first time?[158]

The devastating impact of this questioning would be clearer later if it was not immediately apparent. Having made his point about her New York wardrobe, Knight turned to a frontal assault on Bates's testimony. Bates of course could not dispute that she had perjured herself in Scottsboro, if she was not doing so in Decatur, and that she had written a letter more than a year ago retracting her accusation, only to repudiate the retraction as a drunken misstep. Knight hammered away at Bates for her inconsistencies and otherwise tried to undermine her testimony. She admitted to having syphilis before the trouble in Scottsboro, which Knight intimated undercut her story about engaging in sexual relations with Carter. Knight also pressed her about a meeting between the two of them two months previously, in which Knight had insisted that he "did not want to burn any person that wasn't guilty," that he wanted the truth, and that he "would punish anyone who would make you swear falsely." He ended the cross examination as he had begun, returning to the subject of Reverend Fosdick giving her money to purchase the clothes she was wearing.[159] During Knight's two hour cross examination, local papers reported that Bates appeared "obviously flustered"[160] and "confused," sometimes "biting her lips."[161] "On some of the sharp questions, Miss Bates held her head downward and would answer only at repeated insistence, and then slowly."[162] Bates never wavered, however, in her recantation of the rape charges.

Bates's testimony concluded the defense's case. Judge Horton declared a recess until 8:30 the next morning. Patterson's trial had just ended its fourth day, longer than the combined duration of the four trials conducted in Scottsboro two years previously.

The State offered rebuttal evidence when court reconvened on Friday, April 7. Dr. Carey Walker testified that he had treated Ruby Bates for syphilis and gonorrhea on May 20, 1931. He recounted how Bates confided that she had contracted the diseases "from these negroes" while being raped on the train. Leibowitz established on cross examination that Bates already had told her story in court in Scottsboro by the time Dr. Walker had examined her. He tried to minimize the significance of her disclosure, suggesting that it was only natural that she would have remained consistent with her well-known story while talking with the doctor.[163]

Attorney General Knight then examined Dr. J.H. Hall about medical aspects of sexual intercourse in an attempt to counter the earlier testimony of Dr. Reisman, the defense's expert. Dr. Hall cautioned that it was impossible to infer anything about how long ago intercourse had occurred based on finding nonmotile spermatozoa. He further stated that because semen seeps from the vagina following intercourse, it would not be possible to discern the number of men with whom a woman engaged in sexual relations based on the quantity of semen found in her vagina a few hours after intercourse. He finally opined that the emotional condition of a woman shortly after being raped was unpredictable and could be highly variable. He offered the example of soldiers sometimes maintaining great calm in the midst of and immediately following battle, only to collapse the following day.[164]

An obviously skeptical Leibowitz used the doctor's appearance as an opportunity to pose questions—some highly objectionable—that allowed him to recast the testimony in a light much more favorable to the defense.

Q: Let me ask you this question: A woman who has been hardened to rough life, a woman who has been a prostitute, a woman who has been in prison, served time in jail, a woman who has had the unfortunate experience of being subjected to the lowest and most vile elements of human life, that type of woman is less likely to faint isn't that a fact than the average woman we know and we all love, isn't that so?
A: Well you could hardly state that, I have seen some of the most ferocious looking men faint when you would stick them with a hypodermic needle....
Q: I will ask you this question; wouldn't you say that it is unusual and something strange that two women should both react in the same identical say [*sic*]; that an hour and a half afterwards they were both examined by a doctor scientifically as to their pulse and respiration and both act exactly in the same way, and that the next morning both again act the same identical way, both of them are crying or what might be called hysterical, wouldn't you say something looked a little suspicious?
GENERAL KNIGHT: We object....
Q: Suppose a woman says she was in a place for over an hour, the time it would take a train to go from Stevenson to Paint Rock, I am speaking of the average woman...[S]uppose she said she was in the middle of a fight with guns and knives there, and shooting, and she saw a man's head, the scalp being opened up and blood running out, she was grabbed and held over the side of a train and she was grabbed and pulled back and thrown down and her clothes torn down and some of them raped her; her legs were pulled apart and a knife was held on her throat and she was raped by one negro after another and she was a white woman; I am speaking of the average woman, don't you think she would have fainted long before she ever reached Paint Rock if that ever happened to her?
A: No sir, I wouldn't think so.
Q: You really mean that seriously?
A: Yes sir, I do.[165]

The prosecution next recalled W. H. Hill, the Paint Rock depot agent who had testified earlier in the trial. Hill specified that it was Ruby Bates who claimed that the two women "had been raped by the negroes" soon after she and Price got off the train. Leibowitz probed Hill's recollection only briefly, again employing his questioning more to communicate his theory of the case than to elicit information. He concluded his cross examination by asking Hill if he could say "whether the people in Paint Rock want to see these negroes sent to the electric chair."[166]

Knight had little success in strengthening the prosecution's case by examining Haywood Patterson and Ruby Bates, who he recalled to the witness stand. Nor was he able to extract helpful testimony from Vertus Frost, a prisoner who had been incarcerated in a death house cell next to Patterson and was prepared to describe damaging statements that Patterson purportedly made.[167] The case against Patterson thus was complete. The State rested and the attorneys prepared to deliver their closing arguments on the afternoon of Friday, April 7.

Alabama law allowed the prosecution to have the first and last word before the jury, with defense counsel's argument sandwiched in between. Jackson County Solicitor H.G. Bailey led off, introducing themes that would be repeated by the other State's attorneys when their turns came. Bailey had obtained death sentences against eight of the boys in Scottsboro, but he implored the Decatur jurors "to turn [Patterson] loose" if they were persuaded of his innocence. "[B]ut on the other hand," said Bailey, "if he is guilty, the state of Alabama wants you to send him to the electric chair." He then raised the specter of "sinister influences" at work regarding the defense's key witnesses, Lester Carter and Ruby Bates. Victoria Price, charged Bailey, "didn't come here in a hat bought in New York. She didn't come here in a New York coat.... We don't say that she is what she should have been. She has erred but our laws say no man shall lay a hand on a woman against her will."[168]

Wade Wright then took over. The Morgan County Solicitor had a booming voice, which he employed not only in his courtroom oratory but which also distinguished him as one of the region's finest all-day singers. Wright's fire and brimstone rhetoric inspired numerous courtroom spectators to nod their heads and emit occasional "No's" as he spoke. He told the jurors how the U.S. Supreme Court had ordered new trials in the case after Communist sympathizers took up the boys' cause. He deplored the assault on Victoria Price's character. He turned and pointed at the lawyers for the defense, including Leibowitz and the ILD's Joseph Brodsky, and roared, "Show them, show them that Alabama justice cannot be bought and sold with Jew money from New York."[169]

At that remark, Attorney General Knight fidgeted ruefully. The *New York Times* charged that Wright had "made a frank appeal to local pride, sectionalism, race hatred and bigotry."[170] The *Huntsville Daily Times'* Friday afternoon edition offered only a paraphrased description of the solicitor's argument, stating that he asked the jury, "Are you going to stand for justice being bought?"[171] The *Decatur Daily* further defused the statement with an apparent misprint, reporting that, "raising his voice until it carried to groups outside the courtroom," Wright asked, "'Are you going to stand for justice being sought?'"[172] But Leibowitz was clear about what he had heard. He jumped to his feet and immediately moved for a mistrial.

MR. LEIBOWITZ: We object, Mr. Wright just said to this jury, "are you going to stand here and see justice bought and sold with Jew money from New York" and I move for a mistrial.
COURT: Overrule the motion
MR. LEIBOWITZ: I except. I submit a conviction in this case won't be worth a pinch of snuff in view of what this man just said.

COURT: Gentlemen of the jury the statement made by Mr. Wright the Court rules is improper, and it is excluded from you. Gentlemen don't let that statement influence you in any way at all. The Court will ask you not to consider that statement.[173]

Not cowed in the least by Leibowitz's objection or Judge Horton's ruling, Solicitor Wright continued his onslaught. He argued that Ruby Bates had been unable to share information about her New York City trip with the jury "because part of it was in the Jew language." Of Lester Carter, he railed, "That man Carter is a new kind of man to me. Did you watch his hands? If he had been with Brodsky another two weeks he would have been down here with a pack on his back a-trying to sell you goods. Are you going to countenance that sort of thing?"[174] His ensuing comment brought another outraged motion for a mistrial from Leibowitz.

MR. LEIBOWITZ: I object, the learned Solicitor of Morgan County just stated Mr. Carter had been traveling all over the land of the United States of America; he just referred to Mr. Carter and said; "What does Mr. Carter tell you, may be it is Carterinsky now." We move for a mistrial.
COURT: Overrule that motion, but you are right I dont [*sic*] think that is proper argument. Gentlemen of the Jury I will exclude Mr. Wright's statement, so don't consider it.[175]

The following day, out of the jury's presence, Leibowitz and Brodsky would ask Judge Horton to remove the other Boys' trials to Birmingham, alleging that Wright's incendiary remarks "had incited the mob spirit so greatly that their lives would be endangered if they were forced to conduct the cases" in Decatur. Brodsky advised the court, "Since that speech was made in this court room attacking me, my race and the city from which I come, three men have threatened my life." For his part, Wright explained that "he had meant no harm and that he was only delivering his customary closing argument to a jury.... 'I've been prosecuting cases here a long time and the people hereabouts know how I speak.'"[176]

George Chamlee opened for the defense later that afternoon, when Wright finally finished his summation. Chamlee's position as the lone Southerner on the defense team could not have been more apparent, nor more urgent in attempting to quell animosities about outside influences that were rekindled by the prosecution's arguments. Chamlee embraced his role, introducing himself to the jury as the son of a Confederate soldier who had been born and raised in the South. He assured the jury that he shared their values, telling them that "I want to uphold the principals [*sic*] of womanhood in the South."[177] With these overtures Chamlee's job was largely complete. He briefly summarized the defense's position regarding the charges against Patterson and then yielded to Samuel Leibowitz.

Leibowitz's argument began on Friday afternoon, consuming over two hours, and despite Judge Horton's prodding, carried over into Saturday morning for another two hours. He addressed several preliminary matters before analyzing the strength of the evidence. He began by warning the jurors that their verdict would have wide ramifications: "Telegraph instruments throughout the world, this minute are clattering with the story of this trial.... [Y]ou are deciding more than the guilt or innocence of this Negro, you are deciding a world issue."[178] He lashed back at Solicitor Wright's argument, denouncing it as nothing more than "an appeal to prejudice, to sectionalism, to bigotry[.] What he is saying is, 'Come on, boys! We can lick this Jew from New York! Stick it to him! We're among our home folk.'" He disassociated himself from the Communist Party, stressing that he was not a crusader for social causes but only interested in seeing justice served. He confided to the jurors, "I'm not getting any fee in this case and I'm not getting a penny of expenses."[179]

Then, turning to the evidence, Leibowitz reminded the jury that the State's case rested on the slender reed of Victoria Price's testimony. "She is the only eyewitness."[180] Where, he asked, was Orville Gilley, the white boy who all parties agreed had been spared ejection from the fast-moving train during the fight with the black youths? Lester Carter and Ruby Bates swore that Gilley had spent the night of March 24 in the Chattanooga hobo jungle with themselves and Price, and had boarded the Huntsville-bound train with them on the morning of March 25. Price swore that she had never seen him before she and Bates encountered him in the gondola when the train left Stevenson. Gilley had been held in the Scottsboro jail as a material witness through the conclusion of the original trials. He testified only briefly in Scottsboro and he did not even appear before the Decatur jury. If he could corroborate Price's story, why was he not called to do so?[181]

He assailed Price's story, pointing out its inconsistency with the medical evidence; with how the train's box cars and gondolas were configured as the locomotive moved out of Stevenson toward Paint Rock; with the testimony of Dallas Ramsey and E. L. Lewis, who had seen Price in the Chattanooga hobo jungle; with the layout of Chattanooga's Seventh Street and with evidence about the existence of the elusive "Mrs. Callie Brochie"; with Lester Carter's evidence; and finally, with the testimony of Price's alleged co-victim Ruby Bates. Haywood Patterson was on trial for his life. Referring to his client, Leibowitz asked the jurors not to be swayed by passion or prejudice but to use "your reason as logical, intelligent human beings, determined to give even this poor scrap of colored humanity a fair, square deal."[182] Leibowitz challenged the jury: "Don't compromise on a jail term. This boy wants death in the electric chair rather than languish in prison for a crime he did not commit." He finished by reciting the Lord's Prayer. With a concluding, "Amen," he took his seat, visibly spent.[183]

Following a ten minute recess, Attorney General Knight addressed the jury with the last of the closing arguments. Disavowing that racial prejudice or religious animosity should figure into the jurors' deliberations, Knight joined Leibowitz in calling for "a verdict on the merits of the case."[184] He quickly launched into an attack on Ruby Bates who, he charged, had "sold out lock, stock and barrel." Contrasting the two women who were so central to the case, Knight shouted, "The state didn't dress Victoria Price up like the lilies of the field."[185] But Bates, on the other hand, "sold out for a gray coat and a gray hat."[186] Continuing with that same theme, Knight pointed at Haywood Patterson and challenged the jurors: "If you acquit this Negro, put a garland of roses around his neck, give him a supper and send him to New York City. There let Dr. Harry Fosdick dress him up in a high hat and morning coat, gray striped trousers and spats." He expressed outrage at the defense's treatment of Victoria Price, a woman that the State's evidence showed had been brutally assaulted. He ventured that he "did not believe a fly would light" on Price if it knew how the defense lawyers had characterized her, and argued that it was the defense's case, rather than the prosecution's that was "framed."[187] He protested, "We aren't lynching people in Alabama, legally or illegally, but the name of the State of Alabama has been lynched."[188] At one point referring to Patterson as "that thing," Knight concluded by asking the jury to return a guilty verdict and sentence of death.[189]

Judge Horton began his charge to the jury at five minutes past twelve. He cautioned the twelve men that the sole issue before them was whether Haywood Patterson had raped Victoria Price. "You are not trying whether or not the defendant is white or black.... You are not trying lawyers, you are not trying State lines."[190] He invited the jurors to scrutinize carefully the testimony of the two women who figured so centrally in the case and whose stories were in such opposition.

[Ruby Bates] admitted on the witness stand in this trial that she had perjured herself in the other case. In considering the evidence, you may consider not only her lack of virtue as admitted by her here, but also that she contradicted her previous testimony as perjured.

Regarding Victoria Price, there has been evidence here that she also was a woman of easy virtue. There has been evidence tending to show that she gave false testimony here about her movements and activities in Chattanooga. That evidence has not, except by her, been denied.

If in your minds the conviction of this defendant depends on the testimony of Victoria Price and you are convinced she has not sworn truly about any material point, you could not convict this defendant.[191]

He instructed the jury about the elements of rape, and about their duty to vote not guilty unless the prosecution's evidence proved each element beyond a reasonable doubt. He told the jurors that if they did convict, their further obligation would be to fix punishment; it was within their discretion to order imprisonment for a minimum of ten years or a maximum of any term of years, or else impose a sentence of death by electrocution. Then, a "prototype of Abraham Lincoln in every physical feature and mannerism," Judge Horton "digressed in his charge to make a speech of literary and simple beauty.... [H]e spoke not with silver oratory but in plain phraseology that further recalled the president who before him dealt with race problems."[192]

Of course, gentlemen, we all love our land; that is a natural sentiment of all people. Not that we are narrow in it. Why, the man who lives in the mountains of Switzerland or on the coast of the Adriatic loves his land—the savage loves his land. It is a natural feeling and it is a fine thing for a man to do to love his native country.

...[M]y people have always been a Southern people, and I have no desire to live anywhere else. I am getting old, and it is my home, my native land, and I want to see righteousness done and justice done, and we are going to uphold that name.

A great many of our parents no doubt were in the War between the States....My father and my 61-year-old grandfather, every relative over fifteen, were in the Southern army. I am not saying that to be boasting or anything that way, but to show that I as well as you have no desire to in any way do anything that would not reflect credit on the South, and whatever I say, and whatever I do, remember, it is for justice and right and that they may prevail.

We are a white race and a Negro race here together—we are here to live together—our interests are together. The world at this time and in many lands is showing intolerance and showing hate. It seems sometimes that love has almost deserted the human bosom. It seems that hate has taken its place. It is only for a time, gentlemen, because the great things in life, no matter what they are, it is God's great principles, matters of eternal right, that alone live. Wrong dies and truth forever lasts, and we should have faith in that.[193]

Thus, at the conclusion of more than a week's worth of testimony and argument, and with those words ringing in their ears, the jurors retired to deliberate on the fate of Haywood Patterson.

The jury remained behind closed doors that afternoon and into the night, until Judge Horton sent them to their hotel at 11:30. Many Decatur residents were in church the next morning, Palm Sunday, when the jury announced that it had reached a verdict. Judge Horton was notified in Athens and arrived in Decatur some 40 minutes later. The courtroom was less than half filled as the jurors filed in. Laughter had been heard from within the jury room a bit earlier and some of the jurors were smiling as they entered the courtroom. Leibowitz looked tired. Attorney General Knight twitched nervously. Haywood Patterson kept his eyes down. The jury foreman handed the verdict form to Judge Horton. It was 10:58 A.M., two years to the day that Patterson's death sentence had formally been pronounced in Scottsboro. Judge Horton reviewed the form and then announced the verdict to the courtroom: "We find the defendant guilty as charged and fix the punishment at death in the electric chair."[194]

No demonstrations followed the announcement. Haywood Patterson made no visible reaction. Judge Horton thanked the jurors for their service and discharged them. They had arrived at their verdict on the third ballot. The first produced unanimous agreement about Patterson's guilt. The second ballot, focusing on punishment, reflected 11 votes in favor of death, and one for life imprisonment. The third ballot garnered unanimity for the death sentence. Judge Horton's entry of judgment on the verdict and formal sentencing was delayed until April 17, upon Leibowitz's advising the court that he had to return to New York on other business and could not be available earlier. Leibowitz thanked Judge Horton, call-ing him "one of the finest jurists I have ever met." But he further stated, "I cannot say as much for a jury which has decided this case against the weight of evidence."[195] He later expressed his belief that the verdict was "a miscarriage of justice." Attorney General Knight replied, "I don't, not beyond a reasonable doubt." Leibowitz subsequently issued a statement, in which he branded the ver-dict "an act of bigots, spitting upon the tomb of the immortal Abraham Lincoln." He vowed, "We will fight until hell freezes over with every drop of blood in our veins to free these men, because they are innocent, as every reasonable human being that sat in the courtroom hearing the evidence must have felt."[196]

The verdict sparked intense reactions elsewhere. Telegrams protesting the con-viction and death sentence poured into Governor Miller's office from around the country. The ACLU denounced the outcome as "lynch justice," the Presbyterian Labor Temple declared the verdict to be "contrary to the evidence," the leader of the Socialist Party deemed it a "terrible miscarriage of justice,"[197] and the ILD decried the "monstrous lynch verdict."[198] The NAACP condemned the "racial prejudice" infecting the trial and swiped at the ILD by lamenting the fact that "communism was on trial as well." The National Urban League charged that the verdict demonstrated that "justice for the Negro in certain types of cases is absolutely impossible in some sections of the South." A rally in Harlem grew violent when a thousand or more people who had gathered to meet Leibowitz on his return to New York took to the streets and clashed with police.[199] The *Birmingham News* took evident satisfaction in observing that this "[h]and-to-hand fighting," which included a police officer "being beaten by a group of Negroes until white passersby drove them off...far transcends any disorders in Alabama in connection with the Scottsboro cases."[200] An ILD rally featuring Mrs. Janie Patterson, Haywood's mother, drew a crowd of 10,000 to New York City's Union Square, as plans were afoot to organize a protest march 50,000 strong on Washington DC.[201]

Editorial reactions to the verdict were widespread and mixed. The *Chicago Tribune* did not directly address the merits, but instead skewered "the radical agitators [who] descended upon the community in which the trial was to be held, insulting, blatant, insolently prejudicing the case and the character of the agencies of the law. They have shown no consideration for the defendants. Pretending to defend them from mob sentiment and race prejudice, they have done everything possible to inflame both. No Klux fanatic could do more to create conditions in which evenhanded justice is impossible than these pretended friends of the oppressed." The *Charleston* [South Carolina] *News and Courier* took a similar tack, declining to pass on the "[g]uilt or innocence of the 'Scottsboro boy'....If there has been no fair trial outside pressure on Alabama is chiefly respnsobile [*sic*] for it." The *Jackson* [Mississippi] *Daily News* both defended the verdict and denounced outsiders who had participated in and covered the trial.

The verdict rendered by the jury in the famous Scottsboro case, over in our sister state of Alabama, was in strict accordance with the law and the evidence.

High-priced lawyers hired by the National Association for the Protection of Colored People [*sic*], a moronic and utterly needless organization, have hurried home to collect their fees they didn't earn.

Big-time newspaper correspondents sent down from the North to write the story failed miserably. There was nothing to write about—just a common, ordinary trial in a country town that fell far short of the space it occupied. The big-time boys couldn't find even a remote resemblance to race prejudice in Decatur.[202]

With similar assurance, the *Huntsville Daily Times* declared:

The accused negro boy was given a fair trial, as free from excitement and prejudice and bias as was possible in the State of Alabama.

...Now that the case has been decided in the lower court, the International Labor Defense, the Communists and the other "red" elements of the country have launched their campaign to prejudice Alabama in the eyes of the nation and of the world. There is no limit, either of falsehood or dirty work, to which they will not stoop in their fanatical zeal.[203]

Somewhat ambiguously, the *Greensboro* [North Carolina] *Daily News* suggested that Alabama's "courts, its system and methods of justice, rather than the actual defendants, were on trial....[O]ne arrives at that question which remains unanswered: 'What constitutes a reasonable doubt in the eyes of an Alabama jury?'" Also not staking a clear position, the *Nashville Tennessean* declared that "The Scottsboro case should be a warning alike to both the North and the South. The trial has shown the South that until it has won a reputation for dealing justice to its citizens without regard to their race, its courts will not have the confidence of other sections of the nation. The North has had an opportunity to learn that meddling such as has been indulged in during the Scottsboro case hearings is likely to lead to injustice instead of the justice such meddling is proclaimed to foster." With less equivocation, yet making a similar point, the *Charlotte Observer* offered, "It is reasonably to be feared that prejudice and passion have come into unfortunate collision with evidence and facts.... If justice has been miscarried, it would be unfair and slanderous to the South to lay it to inherent racial bitterness and unfairness. If such prejudice swayed the mind of the jury at all, it was put in there by current circumstances rather than implanted by long-cherished and ingrained animosities against Negroes."[204]

The *New York Herald-Tribune* was not reluctant to condemn the proceedings. "It is useless for anyone, either in or out of Alabama, to pretend that the verdict of guilty rendered against the first of the nine Negroes to stand retrial in the Scottsboro cases will not be received with a profound sense of shock by justice-loving Americans." The *Hartford* [Connecticut] *Courant* characterized the verdict in Patterson's trial as "dismaying," and concluded that "the effort to escape popular hostility against the race of the defendants was apparently unavailing."[205] The *New York Times* opined that the "result comes as a surprise and a shock to those who had followed the evidence given in court.... [I]t was all too plain that the trial was conducted in an atmosphere intensely prejudiced against the accused Negro."[206] *Time* magazine ventured that "Southerners could not see how the jury could have decided otherwise. How could a man continue to live in a small southern town if everyone who passed him on the street knew that he was one of twelve who set at liberty a blackamoor who surely had fought whites, possibly had molested a white woman?"[207]

The unfavorable newspaper editorials were mild compared to Samuel Leibowitz's tirade delivered at a rally in New York City. In response to a question posed by a reporter about the verdict in Patterson's trial, Leibowitz was quoted as exclaiming: "If you ever saw those creatures—those bigots, whose mouths are slits in their faces, whose eyes pop out at you like frogs, whose chins drip tobacco juice, bewhiskered and filthy—you would not ask how they could do it." Not surprisingly, this candid assessment quickly found its way to Alabama, evoking an angry reply from Attorney General Knight:

If this statement was made by Leibowitz it can be taken only as a wail of a contemptible loser. Particularly in view of the fact that in his address to the jury, he lauded the people of Morgan county and the members of the jury to the skies. Referring to members of the jury, he characterized them as highly intelligent, painstaking and honorable men. This was before the jury returned a verdict sentencing Heywood [*sic*] Patterson to death for raping Mrs. Victoria Price.

I, like every other Southerner, resent his despicable slurs....

I was very glad, indeed, that Leibowitz's insincere flattery of the court, myself and the jury could not swerve the jury from a just verdict in this case when they believed, as I do, that Heywood Patterson was guilty beyond a reasonable doubt.

Leibowitz having borne his gift of compliments, now wants to take it back.[208]

The *Decatur Daily* reported Leibowitz's remarks and the Attorney General's rejoinder in its April 15 edition, just two days before Judge Horton had scheduled Patterson's formal sentencing and the consideration of motions in anticipation of Charlie Weems's trial, which was next on the docket. When Judge Horton opened court on April 17, Leibowitz remained in New York, leaving Joseph Brodsky to appear with Patterson. Knight represented the State. Horton turned first to Haywood Patterson, asking him if he had anything to say before sentence was imposed. "I ain't had a fair trial," Patterson responded. "Ain't seen no girls on that train. I ain't had a fair trial." Explaining that the jury had weighed the evidence and that it alone had responsibility for finding the facts, Horton proceeded to sentence Patterson to die in the electric chair. Execution was scheduled for June 16, but Horton suspended the sentence when Brodsky filed a motion for a new trial.[209]

Judge Horton then startled the courtroom with his announcement that the trials in all of the related cases were postponed indefinitely, owing to "a statement published which...makes it impossible to fulfill the high purposes of a court of justice."

I do not know whether the leading counsel for the defendant made the statement imputed to him. I am not stating that he did, but so far as it might influence this trial, it could make little difference whether he actually said it or not. The effect will be the same. The published statement was uncalled for. It was addressed to a panel of highly intelligent jurors, and men who wished to do what was right in the case. The statement of itself of necessity must make impossible any just and impartial verdict. The accused Negro must be a victim of this statement. His leading attorney would be a millstone about his neck.[210]

Judge Horton also expressed regret about Knight's responsive statement, which he said "contributed to the already heated atmosphere which surrounds this case." Knight rose quickly to his feet, proclaiming, "I have no apologies to offer for my reply to that statement."[211] The State of Alabama provided Patterson a fair trial, the Attorney General protested. "I cannot stand by and hear that jury maligned. No, we aren't bigots in the South." His "eyes flashing," Horton admonished Knight. "My statement clearly infers that the defendant's chief counsel was at fault. It is the duty of the court to see that the defendant has a fair trial." At that, Brodsky interjected that he did not believe that Leibowitz had made the comment attributed to him. "Leibowitz's view is that in Decatur and the South, the white workers are imbued with the idea of white supremacy, and that only in union of the white and negro workers, warring against the ruling class, can they gain their ends."[212] Brodsky's statement, the *Daily Worker* fairly cackled, caused Knight to "turn...purple with rage,"[213] and it also incensed Judge Horton. "'So long as I sit on this bench, every defendant, white or black, shall have a fair trial,' Judge Horton said, his voice rising and quivering with emotion."[214]

From New York, Leibowitz issued a statement speaking for himself on the matter. While reiterating his respect for "Judge Horton and the fair-minded people of the State," he made no attempt at brokering peace with the rest of its people.

That millstone around the necks of the Scottsboro boys is that Alabama attitude which made twelve Decatur jurors guffaw as they push Haywood Patterson toward the electric chair. It is a piece with the action of Attorney General Knight in gleefully clapping his hands during the trial and in calling a defendant made in the image and likeness of God "that thing."

...As for the rest [those people unlike Judge Horton and fair-minded Alabamians], the baying pack, the wolves of bigotry, who raised the Hitler cry of "Jew money from New York" because we dared to demand a square deal for a poor unfortunate whose skin was black, I stand pat. They are bigots. Their very faces do betoken it.[215]

With the remaining trials on hold and review of Patterson's conviction pending, the ILD continued to fan the fires of public opinion. Lester Carter and Ruby Bates appeared at rallies in New York City, where they proclaimed that the "Scottsboro boys are innocent," and where Bates attributed her contrary testimony at the original trial to being "excited by the ruling class of the South."[216] Protests continued throughout the United States, in Boston, Chicago, Hartford, Philadelphia, Baltimore, Omaha, Washington, DC, Birmingham, and elsewhere. Religious organizations expressed support for the boys, and interest remained high internationally. Meanwhile, the cases of Eugene Williams and Roy Wright were finally transferred to juvenile court for determination of whether they should be retained there or instead removed to criminal court for final disposition.[217] Judge Horton announced that he would rule on Haywood Patterson's motion for a new trial on June 22 in his hometown of Athens.

Court opened on June 22 with the expectation that Judge Horton would entertain argument on the defense's motion for a new trial, a necessary step en route to appeal of Patterson's conviction, and then deny relief. He had already ruled against the defense on several issues raised in the motion, including the exclusion of blacks from jury service, the prejudicial nature of Solicitor Wright's closing argument, and others. Leibowitz was not even in attendance, ceding Patterson's representation to George Chamlee and Osmond Fraenkel, a New York City attorney retained by the ILD. Attorney General Knight represented the State. The lawyers must have been taken aback when, without prefatory remarks or the traditional formalities, the judge began reading from a written opinion that he had prepared. Their surprise almost certainly turned to amazement—Knight "listened tensely with mounting color," as "smiles of satisfaction" dotted the faces of defense counsel—when it became apparent that Judge Horton was voiding Patterson's conviction.[218]

"Social justice is based on law, and its perpetuity on its fair and impartial administration."[219] With his fidelity to law reaffirmed, Horton detailed the reasoning in support of his decision. "The vital ground...is whether or not the verdict of the jury is contrary to the evidence. Is there sufficient credible evidence upon which to base a verdict?" The conviction depended on the veracity of Victoria Price's testimony, for which Horton vainly sought corroboration. "None of the seven white boys [present on the freight train] were put on the stand, except Lester Carter," who had contradicted Price. The medical examinations conducted within two hours of the alleged attacks revealed no major injuries and just a few small scratches and bruises. Despite the claim that Price had been raped multiple times, she appeared calm and her heart beat and respiration were normal. Only a modest quantity of semen was found in her vagina and the spermatozoa were nonmotile. "When we consider, as the facts hereafter detailed will show, that this woman had slept side by side with a man the night before in Chattanooga, and had intercourse at Huntsville with Tiller on the night before she went to Chattanooga...the conclusion becomes clearer and clearer that this woman was not forced into intercourse with all of these negroes upon that train, but that her condition was clearly due to the intercourse that she had had on the nights previous to this time."[220]

Horton wrote that it was implausible that there were no reliable witnesses to a rape perpetrated by twelve young men against two women as the train passed by several populated areas between Stevenson and Paint Rock. Equally incredible was the State's position that "in the end by a fortuitous circumstance just before the train pulls into Paint Rock, the rapists cease and just in the nick of time the overalls are drawn up and fastened and the women appear clothed as the posse sight them. The natural inclination of the mind is to doubt." Despite scouring the record, Horton found that "the State's evidence...fails to corroborate Victoria Price."[221]

Nor did Horton find Price herself believable. "Her manner of testifying and demeanor on the stand militate against her. Her testimony was contradictory, often evasive, and time and again she refused to answer pertinent questions." Horton similarly discarded Ruby Bates's testimony, implicitly excluding her account and that of other defense witnesses in all instances "unless the facts and circumstances so strongly corroborate that evidence that it appears true." His conclusion was unequivocal.

History, sacred and profane, and the common experience of mankind teach us that women of the character shown in this case are prone for selfish reasons to make false accusations both of rape and insult upon the slightest provocation, or even without provocation for ulterior purposes....

[T]he law declares that a defendant should not be convicted without corroboration where the testimony of the prosecutrix bears on its face indications of unreliability or improbability and particularly when it is contradicted by other evidence.

...It is therefore ordered and adjudged by the Court that the motion be granted; that the verdict of the jury in this case and the judgment of the Court sentencing this defendant to death be, and the same hereby is, set aside and that a new trial be and the same is hereby ordered.[222]

Judge Horton's ruling granting Patterson a new trial was front-page news in the *New York Times,* which also reprinted substantial excerpts from the opinion.[223] It naturally commanded headlines in the *Daily Worker,* which hailed the decision as "a great victory for the I.L.D. and the mass protest movement initiated by hundreds of thousands of persons throughout the world."[224] Two black newspapers, the Chicago *Defender* and the Baltimore *Afro-American,* welcomed the decision but tempered their reactions by questioning why Horton had not recognized the insufficiency of the evidence much sooner, at the trial's conclusion. The *Afro-American* additionally noted that while Patterson had won a reprieve, Alabama's discriminatory jury system also had been insulated from further review.[225] Alabama newspapers, including the *Decatur Daily,* the *Huntsville Times,* and the *Birmingham News* reported the decision in headlines. Their stories emphasized Horton's explanation in his ruling that he was bound under Alabama law to vacate the conviction absent persuasive corroboration of Price's testimony.[226] The *Birmingham News* included editorial praise for Horton's "irreproachable conduct of the trial of the so-called Scottsboro case in Decatur," and the "forthright manner in which he cuts through the maze of confusions...in trying these cases and doing simple justice by the defendants."[227]

Attorney General Knight promptly announced that the State would retry the case as soon as possible.[228] Behind the scenes, with the support of Alabama's former U.S. Senator Thomas Heflin, who wired the Attorney General about his "keen disappointment and resentment...over the strange and annoying action of Judge Horton in the Scottsboro rape cases," Knight began to take steps to ensure that Horton would not preside over any new trials.[229] For his part, Leibowitz praised Horton as a "courageous, brilliant lawyer" and, almost certainly posturing, opined that in light of "the judge's pronouncement I cannot see how the other cases can be prosecuted further."[230] Although Chamlee and Fraenkel, who were present in Athens to hear Horton's ruling, were similarly pleased, the ILD's Joseph Brodsky offered a different perspective. Before Horton's ruling on the motion for a new trial, Brodsky had observed that the judge had the opportunity to quash the indictment and the jury venire based on the defense's showing that blacks had systematically been excluded from the jury rolls, but that "[v]ery quietly, very politely, very 'decently' [Judge Horton ruled,] 'Motion denied.'"

This will give you some idea of the "fair-mindedness" of the judge....

He is a man who has been poisoned at the source. You cannot make a "fair" man out of him. He is honest according to his lights. But his lights are the lights of the Southern ruling class, oppressors of the Negro people....

He is "democratic" and "decent," but he has a water-tight compartment in his brain and can't see that this is merely language that covers the worst and most vicious type of unfairness.[231]

Decades later, Judge Horton's courage in resisting the tidal wave of prejudices that threatened Haywood Patterson's trial was memorialized in a made-for-television movie, "Judge Horton and the Scottsboro Boys."[232] Closer in time to the ruling, his decision to overturn Patterson's conviction ended his judicial career; he was defeated when he ran for reelection in 1934.[233] Horton was interviewed about the case on his Alabama farm in 1966, when he was 88 years old. During the course of the interview he made a startling revelation. On the third day of Patterson's trial, recalled the retired jurist, Dr. Marvin Lynch—the second of the Scottsboro physicians who had examined Victoria Price and Ruby Bates the afternoon of the alleged rape—urgently requested to speak with Horton. The two men conferred in the only private setting they could find, the courthouse restroom, while the court bailiff stood guard outside. There, Dr. Lynch confided that he had been dropped as a State's witness in the trial because he had told Attorney General Knight that he did not believe that the women had been raped.

"My God, Doctor," said Horton. "Is this whole thing a horrible mistake?"

"Judge, I looked at both the women and told them they were lying, that they knew they had not been raped," said Lynch. "And they just laughed at me."

Lynch had only recently opened his medical practice in Scottsboro. He reportedly told Judge Horton that he could not testify about what he had just revealed because it would ruin his professional career. Horton remained silent about the doctor's disclosure, believing that he could trust the jury to "reach the right decision. I felt it would be best if a jury returned a not guilty verdict."[234] When the jury did otherwise, and sentenced Patterson to death, Horton was impelled to act.

James E. Horton, Jr. died in 1973 at age 95.[235] He had been guided by a lesson captured in a Latin phrase that he had learned as a boy: *fiat justitia ruat coelum*—"let justice be done though the heavens may fall."[236] Shortly after his death, a plaque was installed in the Athens courtroom where he had announced his decision to vacate Haywood Patterson's conviction. The inscription on the plaque quoted from Judge Horton's admonition to the jury during Patterson's trial: "So far as the law is concerned it knows neither native nor alien, Jew nor

Gentile, black nor white. This case is no different from any other. We have only to do our duty without fear or favor."[237]

Following Judge Horton's June 1933 decision ordering a new trial, Haywood Patterson and his eight companions remained incarcerated, their futures uncertain. Ever conscious of the death chamber housing the electric chair in Kilby Prison, they had not tasted freedom in more than two years.

Judge James Horton peering over bench, listening to testimony of Dr. R.R. Bridges at Haywood Patterson's trial, April 1933. AP Photo.

Crowd gathers outside Decatur Courthouse, April 1933. AP Photo.

Ruby Bates testifies during Haywood Patterson's trial in Decatur, April 1933. AP Photo.

Prosecution witness Orville Gilley, at the second Decatur trial, November 1933. AP Photo.

The Scottsboro Boys and their attorney, Samuel Leibowitz, in Decatur, Alabama jail in 1933. Seated are Samuel Leibowitz and Haywood Patterson. Standing between the two guards are (left to right): Olen Montgomery, Clarence Norris, Willie Roberson (front), Andy Wright (behind Roberson), Ozie Powell, Eugene Williams, Charlie Weems, and Roy Wright. Courtesy of Brown Brothers.

Eight of the defendants in the Decatur jail in December 1933 during Clarence Norris's second trial. Standing are Charlie Weems (left) and Haywood Patterson. In front of Weems are Ozie Powell and Clarence Norris, behind Powell. To the right (front) are Willie Roberson and Andy Wright and (rear) Olen Montgomery and Roy Wright. Eugene Williams is not pictured. Courtesy of Brown Brothers.

Haywood Patterson, July 1937. AP Photo.

Clarence Norris on being released from Kilby Prison, September 1946. AP Photo.

Decatur Redux: Judge and Jury

Attorney General Thomas Knight, who was preparing to run for Alabama Lieutenant Governor in 1934, remained committed to renew the prosecution of the Scottsboro defendants following Judge Horton's June 1933 decision to grant Haywood Patterson a new trial. Although the *New York Times* reported in July that Horton would preside over Patterson's retrial and the trials of the other defendants,[1] the *Daily Worker* speculated that the cases would be reassigned to Judge William W. Callahan. The Communist newspaper disdainfully branded Judge Callahan as "one of the most notorious Negro-baiters and Ku Klux Klansmen in Alabama."[2] Haywood Patterson would later describe him as "the toughest, most freckle-faced bald-headed man I was ever up against."[3] Callahan officially assumed responsibility for the retrials in October, after Alabama Supreme Court Chief Justice John C. Anderson prevailed on Horton to step aside. The Chief Justice's request was widely believed to have been instigated by Knight, leading the *Birmingham Post* to warn that "critics of our courts will now charge, inevitably, that the State Supreme Court permitted Attorney General Knight to shop around until he found a judge who combined some of the qualities of a prosecutor with those of a jurist."[4]

The 70-year-old Callahan, a former prosecutor and state legislator, had been elected judge in Alabama's Eighth Circuit in 1928.[5] With a steely countenance, wire-rimmed glasses, and silver hair, Callahan looked, as one contemporary observer noted, "the way a Hollywood producer thinks a Southern judge should look."[6] He grew up on an Alabama farm and attended neither law school nor college. Like many of his era, he was admitted to the bar after privately reading the law.[7] In his view, the upcoming trials presented "the simple question of the guilt or innocence of the defendants." Believing that the proceedings had unnecessarily "become involved in a tangle of extraneous matters relative to Communist activities among the Negroes, interference of outsiders with Alabama justice and local pride," Callahan had confided to friends his intention to "debunk the Scottsboro cases."[8]

That mind-set, coupled with his concern that the trials were causing the involved counties to incur extravagant expenses, resulted in Judge Callahan's proceeding at a pace and with a purpose that differed dramatically from Judge Horton's court. As if to underscore the transfer of authority and difference in perspectives, Callahan at one point rebuked Samuel Leibowitz by reminding him during Patterson's trial, "Judge Horton can't help you [now]."[9] Callahan was unabashed about his intention to waste no time on collateral matters and "to put on speed" during the trials.[10] At one point he pressed so hard that Leibowitz virtually begged for relief.

MR. LEIBOWITZ: May we stop now, I can't continue, I am so tired.
COURT: I am very sorry, but we can't. I have been working all day, since 8:30 this morning
MR. LEIBOWITZ: I am just putting on the record that my nerves are just worn out, and that I can't proceed further now, in justice to my client, with the cross examination of this witness. It is now 6:10 P.M.
COURT: You can make up your mind that we are going to have to go on with the cases, or we would never get through.... I am going to stop at 6:30 until tomorrow morning....
MR. LEIBOWITZ: Judge, I am sorry but I can't go any further. I am sorry, and I don't mean to be discourteous. Mind and body can do only so much. My nervous system is all to pieces, and I have been on my feet here all day, Judge. I can't go on. I am tired.
COURT: I think tomorrow, I'll ask you to take a seat, and then you won't be so tired. You have been running up and down that train so much, you have about worn yourself out. Do you say that you are too sick to go on?
MR. LEIBOWITZ: I say that I am too tired to proceed.
THE COURT: Let's go on for fifteen minutes more.[11]

In addition to the punishing pace and duration of the proceedings, Judge Callahan imposed a number of rules evincing his no-nonsense attitude about the trials. The Decatur courtroom under Judge Horton's hand had bustled with the activity of newspaper reporters and their clacking typewriters, and of cameramen taking pictures of trial participants. Callahan insisted that reporters remain outside of the bar that separated trial participants from spectators and imposed a strict ban on photographs being taken on courthouse grounds. He admonished two photographers who had unwittingly violated his order, threatened them with sanctions in the event of repeat transgressions, and instructed them not to publish the pictures they had taken.[12]

Striving to maintain the relative normalcy of the trials, Judge Callahan also declined to request that National Guard troops be dispatched to help maintain order. The trials were scheduled to commence on November 27, with hearings on motions beginning a week earlier. Although the *Birmingham News* reported that the Decatur courthouse was "[b]ecalmed amidst defense contentions of imminent violence,"[13] the *New York Times* described "the scene and the very atmosphere of the court room [as] different and more tense than at any time in [Patterson's] previous trial."[14] Lynchings were very much in the news in the waning months of 1933, in Alabama and elsewhere. In Tuscaloosa, a mob had overpowered sheriff's deputies transporting three black men represented by the ILD who had been accused of rape and murder, and then opened fire on the captives, killing two of them.[15] Similar, widely publicized incidents of vigilantism had recently broken out in Maryland, Louisiana, and California. After Callahan denied the defense request that National Guard units be summoned to Decatur, Leibowitz appealed first to Governor Miller and then to President Roosevelt to intervene. Both chief executives demurred, entrusting local authorities to maintain order.[16]

Concerns about violence were not entirely speculative. The defense had filed a motion for a change of venue, alleging that a fair trial would be impossible in Decatur because it had been saturated with publicity from the original proceedings in Scottsboro and from Patterson's retrial before Judge Horton just months earlier. Leibowitz hoped to remove the trial to an urban center, preferably Birmingham or Mobile. Supporting the motion were affidavits filed by investigators who had recently scoured Morgan County, interviewing residents. Numerous affidavits reflected intense animosity against both the defendants and their lawyers.[17] The defense investigators reported hearing such opinions as "the niggers and their dirty Jew lawyers from New York should be lynched and burned; that too much time and money was already spent on the case and '30 cents of rope' would put an end to it soon enough; that the niggers were unquestionably guilty; [and] that even if they were not guilty they should burn anyway as a lesson to the rest of the niggers to keep them in their proper place and to stop raping our white women."[18]

Attached to the change of venue motion was a copy of a remarkable 60-page screed signed by a Grove Hill, Alabama, attorney, Woodford Mabry, that had been circulated throughout the area. Entitled, "A Reply to Southern Slanders," this document was laden with sentiments such as, "White supremacy should be established by law,"[19] and "History proves BEYOND THE PERADVENTURE OF DOUBT that the negro is an inferior race."[20] "It seems strange," said the circular, "that whenever a black fiend is lynched in the South for his hellish crime, the negro leaders and their Northern sympathizers never waste a tear upon the WHITE WOMAN who has been overtaken by a fate worse than death."[21] "The public. . .does not want SHYSTER LAWYERS to come into their state. . . to interfere with the administration of Justice in our Courts and it does NOT

WANT A RAPE-FIEND or assassin to live one minute longer than necessary to determine his guilt and put him in the electric chair."[22]

The prosecution team—led by Attorney General Knight and buttressed by Assistant Attorney General Thomas Lawson, Jackson County Solicitor H. G. Bailey, and Morgan County Solicitor Wade Wright—fiercely resisted the change of venue motion. An Alabama statute dictating that a trial's location could be changed just once supported the State's effort to keep the trial in Decatur, since venue previously had been transferred from Scottsboro, in Jackson County, to Morgan County. However, rather than relying exclusively on the statute, which the defense contended was unconstitutional, the prosecution insisted that a fair trial could be provided in Decatur. Several witnesses who were quoted in the affidavits prepared by the defense investigators appeared in court and not only denied having made the statements attributed to them, but swore that they had open minds about the rape allegations. The prosecution's counteroffensive established that some of the residents quoted in the affidavits had died long before the investigators reported speaking with them. With these revelations, Knight asked that bench warrants be issued to have the investigators arrested for perjury. Judge Callahan declined to issue the warrants, although he had no hesitation in denying the change of venue motion.[23] "I reckon that's about enough," he said from the bench. "I am told that I would make everybody happy if I granted this motion. If the facts warranted it, nothing would make me happier. However, they don't so warrant, and I'm going to deny the motion."[24]

With the denial of the change of venue motion, the defense team resigned itself to confronting jurors from the same community and of a similar ilk as those who had convicted Patterson just a few months earlier and sentenced him to the electric chair. Judge Callahan's ruling was not unexpected. But just as it dimmed Patterson's chances of securing a different trial verdict, it presented his lawyers with fertile issues to exploit on appeal in the event of another conviction. Leibowitz planned to renew his attack on Alabama's jury system; a challenge that he had initiated and lost in Judge Horton's court and which was rendered moot when Horton granted Patterson a new trial. Unlike the lost battle to remove the trial from Morgan County, and different even from the landmark right to counsel ruling in *Powell v. Alabama* stemming from the original Scottsboro trials, a decision invalidating the hallowed Alabama tradition of all-white juries would radically change the face of Southern justice. The stakes were high and Leibowitz relished the prospect of leaving such a legacy.

The first motion asked Judge Callahan to quash the venire from which the Morgan County trial jurors would be selected. The motion alleged that:

The venire of Petit Jurors from which is, or is to be drawn the Jurors who are to try your defendant on the indictment aforesaid, is void and was drawn and selected in a manner and by methods contrary to law, in that persons of the Negro race, duly qualified under the laws of the State of Alabama to serve as members of the Petit Jury...were excluded from the roll of Petit Jurors of Morgan County from which was drawn the venire of jurors...solely by reason of their race and color, as will appear more particularly hereinafter.[25]

Alabama law required county jury commissions to include on their jury rolls "the names of all male citizens of the county who are generally reputed to be honest and intelligent men, and are esteemed in the community for their integrity, good character and sound judgment." Jury service was further limited to men between the ages of 21 and 65, who were not considered unfit because of "permanent disease or physical weakness," who had never been convicted of a crime "involving moral turpitude," and who were able to read English. Exceptions to the last requirement were recognized for "a free holder or householder."[26] The motion to quash the venire contended that Morgan County included approximately 9,000 white and 2,000 black men qualified for jury service in 1932–1933, when the jury roll relevant to Patterson's trial was prepared, and that not a single a black citizen had served on a grand jury or trial jury in the county in the past 25 years.[27]

Judge Callahan agreed to consider the record challenging Morgan County's jury selection procedures that had been developed months earlier before Judge Horton, prior to Patterson's second trial. At that hearing, Leibowitz had first elicited from J. H. Green, the Morgan County clerk of court, that although he had seen more than 2500 citizens report for jury duty during his four years of service, he was quite certain that, "Not one of them was a colored man."[28] In rapid fashion Leibowitz followed with several black residents of the county—dentists, doctors, ministers, teachers, businessmen, undertakers—to establish their qualifications as jurors and to confirm that none had ever been summoned for jury duty or knew of other blacks who had. He had told Judge Horton that he was prepared to offer the testimony of more than 400 additional witnesses to substantiate that Morgan County included numerous blacks who were qualified for jury service, prompting a ruling that further testimony would be unnecessarily cumulative.[29]

Leibowitz then called J. A. Tidwell as a witness, one of the three members of the Morgan County Jury Commission responsible for placing names on the jury rolls. While acknowledging that the jury commissioners' job involved identifying male citizens reputed for their character, intelligence, and judgment, he conceded that he could not identify the names of any blacks on the jury roll. In response to the prosecution's questions, however, Tidwell insisted that he never considered race or color in making his decisions, and he denied that any prospective juror had ever been excluded because of race. When pressed by Leibowitz to explain the absence of blacks on the jury lists, Tidwell mentioned the numerous sources he consulted to identify qualified jurors, including the voter registration list, the city directory, the telephone directory, and word of mouth. He then asserted: "I do not know of any negro in Morgan County over 21 and under 65 who is generally reputed to be honest and intelligent and who is esteemed in the community for his integrity, good character and sound judgment, who is not an habitual drunkard, who isn't afflicted with a permanent disease or physical weakness which would render him unfit to discharge the duties of a juror, and who can read English, and who has never been convicted of a crime involving moral turpitude."[30]

The two other county jury commissioners submitted affidavits echoing Tidwell's sentiments. They had never rejected anyone from jury service based on race or color. Their only job was to measure citizens' qualifications against the statutory criteria and their decisions were based solely on those factors.[31] The jury commissioners' affirmations were enough for Judge Callahan. He ruled that the "mere absence of negroes" from the jury rolls was not conclusive. The law entrusted jury commissioners to exercise discretion; they were presumed to do so lawfully; they had testified under oath that they had not excluded anyone from jury service because of race; and thus the defense had failed to meet its burden of establishing unlawful racial discrimination. The motion to quash the Morgan County venire was denied.[32]

The *Daily Worker* complained bitterly that Callahan's ruling meant that "a jury commissioner's statement that he considered a Negro and discovered a reason why he was unfit, is sufficient evidence that the law is 'fairly' enforced."[33] The Communist Party newspaper asserted that the challenge to the venire had begged "the question of whether Negroes are to be granted their constitutional rights of participating in the legal machinery of the state which is now solely in the control of the white man." This action consequently had engendered far more "bitterness...than any charge that the Scottsboro boys allegedly attacked two white girls of very unsavory reputation."[34]

With the motion to quash the Morgan County venire rejected, but the record impressively developed for an appeal, the defense mounted a similar attack against Jackson County's grand juries, including the one that had indicted Patterson and his codefendants on March 31, 1931. The challenge to the indictment alleged that blacks had systematically been excluded from grand jury service in Jackson County because of their race and that although hundreds of qualified blacks resided in the county, "no negro has served on any grand jury or petit jury in Jackson County for more than twenty-five years."[35] As with the motion to quash the Morgan County venire, Judge Callahan agreed to consider evidence adduced at the hearing before Judge Horton when the indictment was first challenged. That hearing had revealed much about race relations in and around Scottsboro.

As a part of his showing before Judge Horton that no blacks had served on a Jackson County grand jury in recent memory, Leibowitz had subpoenaed

J.S. Benson, the editor of the Scottsboro newspaper, the *Progressive Age*. Benson, who had lived in Scottsboro for 14 years and had regularly followed court proceedings, admitted under Leibowitz's questioning that "I have never known of one single instance where any negroes were put on the jury roll, or on the roll from which the Grand Jury was drawn." Undaunted, Attorney General Knight inquired of Benson whether he knew "of any negroes in Jackson County *qualified* to sit on a jury."[36] The following exchange ensued, over Leibowitz's angry objections.

A: [MR. BENSON]   I know some good negroes as far as negroes go.

Q: [ATTORNEY GENERAL KNIGHT]   Do you know of any that possess the qualifications prescribed by the statute I just read you?

A: I think that sound judgment would get it, I think that sound judgment part, there are some good negroes with good reputation there, just as good as anywhere.

Q: The question of their judgment?

A: I don't think they are.

On redirect examination by Leibowitz, Benson elaborated:

A: I don't believe there are any negroes in our country [*sic*] that I would risk on a case where I was interested in it, where there is any law and justice and so forth. . . . Some of them has got education enough. But, as a matter of fact, I think they wouldn't have the character. I mean they wouldn't be honest. They will nearly all steal.[37]

Later during the hearing before Judge Horton, Leibowitz had questioned John Sandford, a black resident of Jackson County, in an attempt to demonstrate that Sandford met all of the statutory qualifications for jury duty and that he knew several more blacks who were similarly qualified. Leibowitz had prefaced his questions to Sandford by advising him that Alabama law required that jurors be "esteemed in the community for their integrity, good character and sound judgment." When given the chance to cross-examine Sandford, Attorney General Knight bore in on him, demanding to know the meaning of the word "esteem." Leibowitz thereupon lost patience with Knight, and with one of his Southern mannerisms—what the *New York Times* described as "addressing his questions to the Negroes. . . by their Christian names."[38]

MR. LEIBOWITZ: You are not going to bully this witness, or any other witness.

COURT: Make your objections to the Court.

MR. LEIBOWITZ: Ask the Attorney General to stand back a little bit, and just lower his voice, and stop sticking his fingers in the people's eyes.

COURT: Ask him the question.

Q: [BY MR. KNIGHT]   Will you please tell me what the word "esteem" means?

A: [BY MR. SANDFORD]   I might tell you if I had a dictionary, or something the other, I couldn't rememorize [*sic*] it.

Q: You swore these people possessed the qualifications of a juror he stated, didn't you?
A: According to my knowledge they did.
Q: And you think they are esteemed, do you?
A: The way he asked me, according to my knowledge.
Q: And you don't know what the word "esteemed" means, John?
MR. LEIBOWITZ: Call him Mr. Sandford, please.
MR. KNIGHT: I am not in the habit of doing that, Mr. Leibowitz.
COURT: That has nothing to do with this case.[39]

The sniping between Leibowitz and Knight extended to all matters of proof. Aware that his obligation was to prove a negative—that the jury roll from which Jackson County grand jurors were selected lacked the names of any black citizens—Leibowitz at one point had asked Judge Horton's "indulgence...to get the jury roll, and we will bring every living man on that jury roll if it takes twenty-five years to do it, and we will prove that they are white. If the Attorney General will not make a concession along that line I will be compelled to do it." Refusing to yield an inch, Knight retorted: "The Attorney General makes no concession whatsoever; prove your case."[40] The *Decatur Daily* reported that "spectators who had grown weary during questioning...regarding the qualifications of negroes for juries in Jackson county, leaned forward" with renewed interest during this exchange, as "[t]he nine negroes named in the indictment under question sat lined behind defense counsel table, flanked by two national guardsmen, laughing and joking among themselves, and looking at the comic sections of newspapers."[41]

Judge Horton had abruptly denied the motion to quash the rape indictment prior to Patterson's first trial in Decatur, before Leibowitz had the chance to substantiate his claim that no black citizen had ever served on a Jackson County grand jury. The defense lawyer consequently was left to make good on his vow to scour the Jackson County jury rolls in Judge Callahan's court, several months later. Presentation of evidence began on November 23, 1933, when Jackson County Jury Commissioner J.E. Moody appeared with the enormous volumes that included the county jury rolls prior to and including 1931. Moody and two fellow jury commissioners had not assumed office until March 1931, after the citizens eligible for service on the grand jury returning the indictments against the Scottsboro defendants already had been determined by the prior administration. When the new jury commissioners began their work, Moody had directed his clerk, J.D. Snodgrass, Jr., to draw two red lines at the end of the names appearing on each page of the jury rolls so the jury lists prepared by the new commissioners would be clearly separated from the lists previously compiled.[42] The books were arranged by precinct, with jurors' names organized alphabetically within each of Jackson County's 39 precincts. A new page was started within each precinct for each letter of the alphabet, resulting in hundreds of pages of jury lists being demarcated by the red lines.[43]

Spectators dozed and departed as Leibowitz methodically led C.A. Wann, the circuit clerk of Jackson County, and then Moody, page by page through the rolls in an attempt to demonstrate that no black citizens had ever been selected by the Jackson County jury commissioners.[44] The monotony ended late in the afternoon in a nearly empty courtroom, as Judge Callahan had drifted from the bench and was idly chatting with news reporters. "Moody read off the name of Hugh Sanford and said: 'He's a Negro.'"[45] This testimony crackled like electricity in the courtroom. As Moody continued through the pages, he recognized the names of five additional blacks, a discovery that the *Birmingham News* described as "perhaps the most significant development since the inception of the Scottsboro cases nearly three years ago."[46]

Leibowitz instantly suspected fraud. By a remarkable coincidence, "[e]very name of a Negro found on the old jury roll was written in the [same] position: on the line immediately above the red lines, and therefore in the space by custom left blank."[47] Moreover, when Leibowitz inspected the names of the blacks that had been written into the jury rolls, it was obvious to him that each name overlapped and had been written *on top of* the red lines. Hence, he concluded, the names had been added after the new jury commissioners had taken over, even though they purported to be on the lists compiled by the commissioners who held office when the grand jury that had indicted Patterson and the other Scottsboro defendants had been selected.

When Moody balked at confirming that the names were superimposed on the red lines,[48] Leibowitz summoned a handwriting analyst from New York, John V. Haring, to examine the lists. He also had Moody and Kelly Morgan, Moody's predecessor on the Jackson County jury commission between 1927 and 1931, produce handwriting samples. In the process, he elicited an admission from Morgan that the disputed names appeared to be in Morgan's writing. After Haring arrived in Decatur he inspected the jury rolls and completed a microscopic examination of the pages. The expert then offered a detailed if somewhat arcane opinion that the ink used to write the names of the black jurors appeared on top of the red lines drawn by the outgoing jury commissioner. He further opined that the names were written by Morgan's hand.[49] Leibowitz's case for establishing fraud in the jury lists seemed unimpeachable.

But Judge Callahan was not impressed. He intimated that Haring's expert testimony had been more of a liability than an asset to the defense's case, stating that, "until the expert took the stand, I was in grave doubt about the matter."[50] However, relying heavily on Haring's "unclear" and "different conclusions" with respect to the allegations, Callahan ruled that fraud had not been proven. "I must conclude that there were, at the time the grand jury was drawn that found this indictment, names of colored persons on the jury roll, and I overrule the motion to quash the indictment."[51] Leibowitz took immediate exception to the ruling.

The record that he had so carefully developed in an attempt to prove fraud and to document Jackson County's practices and policies concerning black citizens' participation on grand juries at least had ensured that the issues would be preserved for review on appeal in the event of Patterson's conviction.

Jury selection for Patterson's third trial began on Monday, November 27, 1933. That same day, the *Montgomery Advertiser* ran a front-page story depicting how a lynch mob of 6,000 in San Jose, California had overpowered jailers, seized two white men who had been arrested for kidnapping and murdering a local boy, and hanged them in a city park. California Governor James Rolph was quoted as saying, "This is the best lesson that California has ever given the country. We show the country that this State is not going to tolerate kidnaping."[52]

A packed courtroom watched as twelve of the first 36 veniremen examined for Patterson's trial were excused for holding "fixed opinions" about the case and another eight were discharged because they had scruples against capital punishment. Prodded by Judge Callahan's warnings that they were "taking too much time" and that many of the questions they posed to prospective jurors were "irrelevant," Leibowitz and co-counsel Joseph Brodsky of the ILD nevertheless continued to probe the panel of 100 white men for racial prejudices and any lingering effects of Solicitor Wade Wright's argument at the prior trial that the Decatur jurors should not bow to the influence of "Jew money from New York."[53] A jury of nine farmers, a truck driver, a painter, and a merchant was sworn in by mid-afternoon.[54]

Victoria Price was the state's first witness. This would be the seventh time Price would tell her story under oath, including her testimony before the Jackson County grand jury and five prior trial appearances. "She was 25 years old, she said, and with her nondescript blond hair tightly curled in ringlets, her face powdered and her lips just faintly rouged she seemed nearer that age than she did last Spring."[55] Jackson County Solicitor H.G. Bailey, the prosecutor in the original trials in Scottsboro, had Price retrace the events of March 25, 1931. The direct examination lasted only ten minutes.

Price recounted how she had seen Patterson, carrying a gun, among a band of a dozen black youths who jumped into the gondola in which she, Ruby Bates, and seven white boys were riding as the freight train navigated between Stevenson and Paint Rock. Patterson fired a shot from the gun and ordered, "All you white sons-of-bitches unload." Only Orville Gilley among the whites remained in the gondola as Price's clothes were torn off and she was repeatedly raped at knife point. Price testified that as she was being assaulted several other of the intruders were raping Ruby Bates. "After they had intercourse with me, that defendant there, Haywood Patterson, he said that they was going to carry us north and make us their women, or else they was going to throw us in the river." After the train came to a halt in Paint Rock, Price continued, she fell while stepping to the ground and did not "come to" until later, while seated in a store. She concluded by telling the jury that two doctors later examined her in Scottsboro.[56]

Leibowitz's cross-examination would keep Price on the witness stand until 6:30 that evening and well into the next day. Leibowitz exposed numerous contradictions between Price's testimony and the prior accounts she had given of her ordeal, including what had transpired during the fight between the black and white youths before the alleged sexual assaults occurred, the extent of her injuries, and her ability to identify the guns that she said had been wielded by her assailants. Price was often evasive and obviously agitated in response to the lawyer's questioning, making faces and occasionally "bordering upon panic." Judge Callahan once interceded with an admonition to Leibowitz to "treat the lady with more respect," and warned the combative defense attorney, "The more I shut you off the better shape you're in."[57] The judge continued to interrupt Leibowitz's examination of Price and tried to hurry him along, alternatively interjecting that Leibowitz's questions were "illegal,"[58] "a waste of time,"[59] "immaterial,"[60] were tantamount to "arguing with the witness,"[61] and were "useless."[62] The stymied Leibowitz grew visibly frustrated while noting repeated exceptions to the judge's rulings.

As distracting as Judge Callahan's demeanor and frequent interruptions were to the defense, his regrettable behavior paled in comparison to his devastating evidentiary rulings. Early in the course of Leibowitz's cross-examination Callahan made known that he considered Price's conduct prior to the time of the alleged rape to be irrelevant, a stance that completely scuttled the defense's efforts to suggest that semen detected during her medical exam in Scottsboro could be traced to recent consensual liaisons with Jack Tiller or Orville Gilley, that Price had fabricated material portions of the account of her trip to Chattanooga, including spending the night in a boarding house run by Mrs. Callie Brochie, and in other important respects. Leibowitz's first inkling of the judge's restrictions surfaced as he attempted to question Price about what had taken place on March 24, 1931, when she and Ruby Bates left Huntsville by train for Chattanooga.

Q: [BY MR. LEIBOWITZ] Wherever it was that you got on the train was anybody that accompanied you on the train?
COURT: I don't like to interfere, but I can't allow the time of the court wasted on matters so immaterial. You mustn't ask that question again.
MR. LEIBOWITZ: We reserve an exception.
Q: Had you had sexual intercourse with any man the night before you left Huntsville?
COURT: Wait a minute—
MR. KNIGHT: The state objects to that.
COURT: I sustain the objection.

MR. LEIBOWITZ: We except. May I state the reason?
COURT: No sir, at least I don't require it.
Q: Did you have intercourse with any man the day before that?
MR. KNIGHT: The state objects.
THE COURT: I sustain the objection.
MR. LEIBOWITZ: We except. I propose now to apprise the court, not in the presence of the jury, so that the jury may not be affected by the purpose of the question, to state the purpose of the question.
THE COURT: I decline to do that. I think I know...
Q: Did Ruby Bates have sexual intercourse, in your presence, with one Lester Carter the day before—
MR. KNIGHT: We object to that.
COURT: I sustain the objection.[63]

Rescued from having to retrace many of the troublesome details that had emerged during her testimony before Judge Horton, Price steadfastly insisted throughout Leibowitz's withering cross-examination that she had been raped by Patterson and several other blacks while Ruby Bates was assaulted by still others. Orville Gilley, according to her testimony, all the while remained crouched in a corner of the gondola. Gilley had not appeared at the earlier Decatur trial, but in light of his ostensible vantage point, he loomed as a powerful prosecution witness to corroborate Price's story.

Gilley would take the witness stand on the afternoon of November 28, following the appearance of State witnesses (W. H. Hill, Tom Taylor Rousseau, W. E. Brannum) who briefly described being among the men dispatched to Paint Rock to await the arrival of the freight train on March 25, 1931, and there seeing the defendants.[64] Others (Lee Adams, Tom Dobbins, Sam Mitchell) testified about seeing groups of white and black youths scuffling on the train as it traveled between Stevenson and Paint Rock.[65] Luther Morris offered the most dramatic testimony when he described being in the loft of his barn on the afternoon of March 25, 1931, about 50 feet from the railroad tracks, as the train rumbled by. Morris stated that he heard "screaming and hollering" and that he looked up and saw the "negroes putting the white boys off the train" and then "take ahold of" two white women as they "snaked them toward the bottom of the car."[66] Leibowitz did his best to cast doubt on Morris's ability either to hear (during one somewhat comical exchange, Leibowitz asked, "Your hearing was good on that day, was it?" and Morris replied, "How is that?"[67]) or see (photographs taken from the barn loft revealed that one standing there could not have observed what was happening in a gondola car, as Morris had testified[68]) the events that he had described. He further elicited Morris's concession that he had taken no action to report the shocking assault that he claimed to have witnessed, but instead routinely continued carrying out his chores.[69]

The prosecution saved its star supporting witness, Gilley, for last. Solicitor Bailey's direct examination of Gilley took only 15 minutes, although Leibowitz would keep him on the witness stand for an additional two hours and forty minutes of cross-examination.[70] Gilley proved to be at least as entertaining as he was enlightening. "[A] tall, dark, almost handsome youth with a toothy smile and long, slender, white fingers,"[71] Gilley resisted Leibowitz's characterization as a hobo, professing instead to be a street poet and entertainer who had traveled the country reciting verse. Although his testimony backing up Price's account of the alleged rapes would be damning, he even had Leibowitz chuckling at times as he recounted being known as "Carolina Slim" (not a name, he patiently explained, but rather his "moniker"[72]) and touting his minstrel skills. At one point, Judge Callahan cut him off, proclaiming, "That ought to be enough of that. I don't like poetry anyway."[73] Warming to the quirky youth, "and to catch every word of his story, the court-room crowd leaned forward with hands cupped behind their ears."[74]

Gilley described being in the gondola with Victoria Price, Ruby Bates, and six white boys when several black youths, led by Haywood Patterson with a pistol in hand, boarded the car. Echoing Price's testimony, Gilley told the jury that the intruders had demanded, "All you white sons of bitches unload."[75] He then delivered a vivid account of the ensuing assault.

Q: [BY SOLICITOR BAILEY]   What did you see this defendant do, over there, Haywood?
A: I saw the defendant over there go to both girls; had intercourse with both girls. . . .
Q: Tell us what was done, as you saw it?
A: Some were holding the girls, and some had a knife to their necks, some were holding their legs open; they were all around the girls at the time the raping was going on. . . . When I left the end of the car I was sitting in and got up to where the girls was—I didn't go to where the girls was until towards the last, and when I got up there I saw they were about to kill one of the girls; her eyes was bulging out and she was gasping, and I says to this boy that had the gun, "Why don't you make them quit, he is going to kill her" and he looked over and seen it, and told the boy that was on her then to get off'n her—he says "You are killing that girl, you have all done what you want."[76]

The attack lasted until roughly 15 minutes before the train stopped in Paint Rock, Gilley explained, at which time the black youths scrambled out of the gondola and scattered. With "the essential fact" of the assault thus confirmed—readers of the *New York Times* were greeted the next day with the story caption, "Price Girl's Story Upheld By 'Hobo'"[77]—Solicitor Bailey relinquished his witness for cross-examination.

Leibowitz fared marginally better before Judge Callahan in being allowed to examine Gilley than he had while questioning Victoria Price about events preceding the freight train's fateful journey through Alabama on March 25.

He remained largely stymied, however, by Gilley's answers. Gilley explained that he first met Lester Carter around dusk on March 24 next to a Chattanooga train track, when Carter approached him for a match. "Two girls come across 'long side of him; they were supposed to be with him."[78] Yet Gilley denied sleeping that night in the Chattanooga hobo jungle with Carter and the two women, Price and Bates, insisting that he had retired in a box car and did not see the threesome again until 8:30 the next morning. Gilley had managed to find sandwiches and coffee for breakfast, which he shared with Carter, Price, and Bates prior to their all boarding the westbound freight train; Gilley's destination was Memphis and the others were headed for Huntsville. They began their trip in an oil car and then switched to a gondola in Stevenson, where they were joined by several other white boys. Gilley denied knowledge of any fighting, rocks being thrown, or other trouble brewing on the train until the black youths stormed into the gondola.[79]

Although Gilley refused to back down from his claim that Patterson and his companions had raped Price and Bates, Leibowitz did his best to chip away at details of his testimony. Making use of the model train exhibit, Gilley had confidently affirmed that the assault had occurred in one of the two gondolas "next to the box car nearest the engine."[80] Leibowitz knew that he could exploit this answer because the train's configuration would have made it impossible for the black youths to have entered either of the identified gondolas from an adjoining rear box car, as both Price and Gilley had described. He was thwarted, however, when Attorney General Knight, who also recognized the vulnerability of this aspect of Gilley's story, adroitly led Gilley on redirect examination to confess that he had confused the front and rear ends of the model train, thus inverting the positions of the cars in question.[81] Gilley also remained largely "unruffled"[82] under Leibowitz's incredulous questioning about why he had failed to come to the women's aid or call for help during such a vicious assault, about his and Price's motivation to avoid being prosecuted for vagrancy or violating the Mann Act, and about his and his mother's accepting money from Attorney General Knight in anticipation of his court appearance. "He was," lamented the *Daily Worker*, "undoubtedly, the state's strongest witness."[83] With Gilley's testimony completed, the State rested its case.

Following descriptions of the freight train by two crew members who had been on duty on March 25, 1931, which cast doubt on Price's account of how the gondola in which she claimed to be riding when attacked lined up with other cars on the train, Haywood Patterson was placed under oath to testify in his own defense. "[D]ressed in neatly-pressed brown trousers, slip over sweater, blue shirt and tie with pin,"[84] the 20-year-old "coal black, six-foot" Patterson confronted the jury "of stern faced white farmers,...trying to make them believe that he and not his white accusers was telling the truth."[85] His words barely audible, Leibowitz had to ask him repeatedly to speak up as he told his story.

Patterson described how he and his three friends, Eugene Williams and Andy and Roy Wright, had hopped aboard a freight train in Chattanooga on the morning of March 25, 1931. He and Williams clung to an oil car and the Wrights perched next to them on a lumber car. The ride was uneventful until the train emerged from a tunnel at Lookout Mountain and began a slow ascent. Then they encountered several white boys, one of whom stepped on Patterson's hand as they made their way over the oil car. The white youths came by a second time, and one of them "come brushing by me and like to push me off the car.... I told him if he wanted by to let me know and I would let him by." This remark led to angry exchanges, "and we cussed each other for a while" until the white lads escalated the confrontation by throwing rocks at Patterson and his companions. Patterson later found out the names of the youths who had instigated most of the trouble: "Lester Carter and the Gilley boy."[86]

As the train resumed its journey following a brief stop in Stevenson, the white boys returned to throwing rocks. "Then more colored boys come over top of the train," complaining about the rock throwing, and "they all decided to go settle with the white boys." Patterson and his three friends accompanied this group, now comprising roughly a dozen black youths, to a gondola—"the fourth gondola from the box car, toward the caboose"—and there they encountered five white boys. As the scuffling began, two more whites joined the fray from the connected gondola. Patterson recognized the two latecomers as Carter and Gilley. All of the white boys jumped from the gondola during the fight except for Gilley who, at Patterson's insistence because of the now dangerous speed of the train, was pulled back into the car. Having taught the white boys a lesson, Patterson and his friends returned to their former positions on the train, where they remained until the locomotive stopped in Paint Rock. There, he, his friends, and the other boys, who Patterson did not previously know, were tied up and taken by truck to Scottsboro. Knowing nothing about women being on the train or an alleged rape, Patterson assumed that they had been arrested for fighting.[87]

Knight wasted little time on cross-examination in grilling Patterson about his testimony at his first trial, where he had denied raping Price and Bates but blamed some of his codefendants for doing so.

Q: [BY ATTORNEY GENERAL KNIGHT]   I will ask you, Haywood, if you, when you was tried at Scottsboro, didn't make the statement that you saw all of the negro boys who went into that gondola rape the women, but three?
A: I don't remember making a statement like that. I remember making a statement. I don't know anything of it; I was threatened with death or being killed if I didn't confess; they threatened me if I didn't tell.
Q: Where did they tell you that?

A: There at Scottsboro.

Q: Were you in court when they told you that?

A: In court and over at the jail.[88]

Patterson claimed that a National Guardsman had threatened him in Scottsboro, within earshot of the judge, telling him that he would be turned over to the mob "if we didn't say we done it." The same man, said Patterson, further declared that they ought to "give all niggers the electric chair; there's too many niggers in the world."[89] Throughout Knight's grueling cross-examination Patterson clung doggedly to his contradictory claims that he never made the statements attributed to him during his Scottsboro trial and that his accusations against his codefendants had been coerced. At one point, he discounted his Scottsboro testimony by telling Knight: "No sir, that is just a frame up."[90] Leibowitz, in the meantime, repeatedly objected to Knight's use of the Scottsboro trial transcript to impeach Patterson, arguing that the proceeding was a nullity in light of the Supreme Court's conclusion that Patterson and his codefendants had effectively been denied counsel. Unpersuaded, Judge Callahan overruled the objections. Then, making good on his pledge to keep the trials moving forward, Callahan interrupted Knight's cross-examination for a brief dinner recess, with testimony resuming at 7:15 P.M.

Knight wrapped up his questioning of Patterson when court reconvened that evening and then deferred to Leibowitz's brief redirect examination. After securing confirmation from Patterson that he, a black youth, knew the punishment that would follow on a conviction for rape, Leibowitz earned a sharp rebuke for the final question he posed; a question that invited the jurors to apply their own understanding of Alabama justice and simple common sense in resolving the conflicting stories told by Patterson and Orville Gilley.

Q: [BY MR. LEIBOWITZ] If you were on that railroad car raping two white girls, with eight or nine or ten other negro boys, would you have permitted for one minute, the presence of a white boy witness on that car all through the raping, or would you have thrown him off the car, kept him off the car the same as you did the other white boys?

MR. KNIGHT: We object to that.

COURT: I sustain the objection. It is palpably illegal and improper.[91]

The night grew late as more witnesses appeared. In a telling turnabout from the prior trials, Dr. Bridges, one of the two Scottsboro physicians who had examined Price and Bates the afternoon of the alleged gang rapes, appeared as a defense witness rather than a witness for the prosecution. As in Patterson's first Decatur trial, neither side called the other physician, Dr. Lynch. The *Birmingham News* reported that "[s]everal women, including Mrs. Leibowitz, were present when he gave his unprintable testimony of the girl's condition."[92]

In response first to Leibowitz's and then Knight's questioning, Dr. Bridges stated that when he first examined Victoria Price, at approximately 4:00 the day of the reported rapes, he observed no blood, cuts or swelling about her face, and saw only superficial scratches on her wrists and small blue marks on her back. Her pulse and respiration were normal. He removed seminal fluid from the walls of her vaginal canal, but his microscopic examination revealed only nonmotile spermatozoa, which he explained generally although not invariably signifies that the sperm are dead. The presence of the seminal fluid allowed him to conclude that Price had recently engaged in sexual intercourse, but he could not answer when. He estimated that ejaculate from six men would result in six to twelve teaspoons of fluid, but conceded that the entire quantity would not be retained vaginally.[93] As the attorneys appeared to have exhausted their lines of inquiry, "Judge Callahan told Bridges: 'You better hurry, doctor, before they think of some more questions.'"[94] He then was excused.

Dr. Bridges was followed to the witness stand in rapid succession by four of the young men who, like Patterson, stood accused of raping Victoria Price. Perhaps owing to the lateness of the hour, news coverage of the codefendants' appearance was minimal or nonexistent. The *New York Times* summarized their testimony in a single sentence: "All denied that they had 'touched a white girl.'"[95] A fuller account appeared in the *Birmingham News,* which reminded its readers that Patterson had fought with Willie Roberson, the first codefendant to offer supporting testimony, while they were confined in the Jefferson County jail. The report further pointed out that Patterson "held a grin on his face as the witness testified."[96] Leibowitz had Roberson describe his disabling symptoms to the jury—genital sores that caused such pain and swelling he could walk only with difficulty—to discredit that he either could have fought with the white boys on the train or taken part in a rape. Testifying that he knew nothing about any women on the train, a fight, or the alleged rapes, Roberson explained that when he was removed from a box car in Paint Rock, he assumed simply that "the white men just wanted all the niggers off the train."[97]

Ozie Powell offered a confused but exculpatory story in which he also denied knowing that women were on the train or having anything to do with a rape.[98] Powell was followed to the witness stand by Olen Montgomery, who told the jury that "one eye is out, and the other is weak." He claimed to have boarded an oil car toward the rear of the train in Chattanooga and to have remained there until he was arrested in Paint Rock. As such, he knew nothing about a fight, any women being on the train, or a rape.[99] Andy Wright who, unlike the others who had testified, knew Patterson and was with him throughout the train ride, offered the lengthiest testimony. He corroborated Patterson's account of how the fight between the white and black youths had started, and explained that he had helped Patterson pull Orville Gilley back into the gondola in order to spare

Gilley death or injury by jumping from the fast-moving train. When the fight was over, he said, he returned with Patterson to an oil tank car. Like the other defendants, he insisted that he saw no women on the train and knew nothing about a rape.[100] At the conclusion of Wright's testimony, at 9:30 P.M., Judge Callahan announced that court stood in recess until 8:30 the next morning.

As testimony unfolded in Patterson's trial, speculation swirled about a witness who was nowhere to be found in Decatur, who was rumored to be near death and undergoing a life-threatening operation, a vital witness whose transformation from Southern white woman-victim to Communist sympathizer-supporter of the Negro defendants could not have been more complete. "Ruby Bates Dying," announced the *New York Times,* quoting an urgent message wired by Leibowitz to a New York City colleague: "Have just learned Ruby Bates is dying. It is of the utmost importance that you get to her bedside immediately, preferably with a clergyman, and take her testimony at once. Preferably obtain it as an ante-mortem statement under the law."[101] The initial reports about Bates's condition soon grew less dire. The *Birmingham News* quoted an ILD spokesman that Bates had undergone "a major operation in a New York City hospital," and that she was "resting easily" even though "not entirely out of danger."[102] Bates's hometown newspaper, the *Huntsville Times,* sounded much less alarmed. "Ruby Bates, who made a sensational appearance in court...last April to repudiate her testimony in the original trials at Scottsboro...will not return for the new trials. First reports were that she was dying, but a check showed she had undergone an operation yesterday, but that her condition was not critical."[103]

When informed about Bates's precarious health, Leibowitz had requested a continuance to allow Bates's deposition to be taken in New York and then transmitted to Decatur so it could be read to the jury. Judge Callahan, however, remained committed to moving the trials forward and refused to countenance delay even if it meant that the jury would not hear Bates's repudiation of the rape charges. A dismayed Leibowitz entered yet another exception to the judge's ruling.[104] Callahan enforced his edict even when Leibowitz renewed his request, informing the judge that Bates's deposition had been completed and was en route to Decatur via air mail.[105] Because the deposition failed by hours to arrive before the close of the trial, Patterson's jury would decide his fate without hearing Bates's sworn evidence that the charged crimes had never been committed.

The trial resumed the morning of November 29, when Lester Carter strode to the witness stand. Carter was the defense's counterpart to Orville Gilley: a crowd-pleasing vagabond with his own colorful moniker ("the Knoxville Kid"[106]), described variously in news articles as being "inclined to verbosity,"[107] "garrulous,"[108] and "quaintly grandiloquent."[109] Through sometimes comical testimony, Carter would recount what had occurred on the train as it carried its freight and mélange of passengers from Chattanooga until he took leave of it outside of Stevenson. He also would describe his encounters with Price, Gilley, and other witnesses in the Scottsboro jail and thereafter. However, Leibowitz's immediate design was to have Carter reveal Price's and Bates's activities prior to March 25, as he had done at the trial before Judge Horton. His examination of Carter began on a rocky note before an irate Judge Callahan, who earlier had ruled that such matters were beyond the scope of the trial and therefore inadmissible.

Q: Did you know a girl named Ruby Bates?
A: I got acquainted with her through the Price girl during the time I was serving time in jail—
COURT: Never mind about the time you were in jail.
Q: Did you and Victoria Price, Ruby Bates and Jack Tiller go out together?
A: Yes sir—
MR. KNIGHT: We object to that.
COURT: Sustain the objection; that is not evidence. Mr. Witness you must not answer so quick. Whenever a question is asked and objected to, and the court holds that it is illegal, that puts it out of the case just as if it never happened.
MR. LEIBOWITZ: We except.
Q: I want to know,—now don't answer this until the court says you may,—if the night before you left Huntsville before this train ride, whether or not you, Victoria Price, Ruby Bates and Jack Tiller, that is you with Ruby Bates, and Jack Tiller with Victoria Price, in the presence of each other, did not have sexual intercourse—
COURT: That has been raised so often, Mr. Leibowitz; I have ruled on that very legal point a half dozen times, and there can't be anything in it except a vicious attempt to get something before the jury that I have ruled is improper.
MR. LEIBOWITZ: Your Honor, I won't press it further. I want to note an exception to the court's ruling, especially in view of the court's reference to counsel—
COURT: I am ruling according to the law as I understand it.
MR. LEIBOWITZ: I do this in justice to my client, in view of the court's characterization that defendant's counsel made a vicious attempt to force testimony into the record, I want to move for a mistrial.
COURT: I decline to do that. If that particular word is offensive to you, I will withdraw that. Gentlemen (to the jury) you will pay no attention to the expression "vicious attempt". Don't let that enter into your consideration or in your minds.[110]

Although repeatedly rebuffed in his efforts to have Carter make explicit what his questions implied about the recent sexual intimacy between Carter and Bates, and Tiller and Price, Leibowitz led his witness through an account of the fight that had broken out between the white and black boys on the train on March 25. Carter insisted that he, Orville Gilley, Price, and Bates were traveling alone in the gondola next to the car where the fight had taken place. When the other white youths called for help, he and Gilley climbed into the adjacent gondola but he did not join in the fight "because I seen we were out-numbered."[111]

The courtroom roared and drew a reproof from the bench when Carter explained to Atty. Gen. Knight, with appropriate gestures to demonstrate on the miniatoure [*sic*] train, why he entered the car where the fight was going on, but did not participate.

"You see," he said, leaving the witness stand, and pointing out on the train, "if I had gotten off here (indicating the rear of the car in which he had been riding) I might have gotten hurt. You always want to hop from the front end of a car and save your neck. Otherwise you might lose it."[112]

Carter further recounted how he had overheard a conversation in the Scottsboro jail between Victoria Price and Odel Gladwell, one of the white boys who, like Carter, had jumped from the train as the fight began to escalate, in which Price had implored Gladwell to pretend that he was her brother because she feared being prosecuted for hoboing.[113] However, Judge Callahan's evidentiary rulings had so severely diluted his testimony compared to the first Decatur trial that the *New York Times* reported, "Carter left the witness stand without having contributed much more than some expert testimony about the proper way to board and alight from a moving freight train. Not a word of the graphic description he gave last Spring of the romantic night he and Orville Gilley spent with the two girls in the hobo jungle near the freight yards in Chattanooga was permitted to creep into the record of this trial."[114]

The defense rested following the appearance of a few less central witnesses and after Leibowitz was allowed to read from transcripts of earlier trials in an effort to impeach Price's and other prosecution witnesses' testimony. The prosecution then rested following an unsuccessful attempt to introduce incriminating statements allegedly made by Patterson and Roy Wright in the Scottsboro jail on March 26, 1931, the day after their arrest.[115] The lawyers began their closing arguments at 3:30 on November 29, the day before Thanksgiving. Each side was limited to two hours.

Wade Wright addressed the jury first. Avoiding the vilification of "Jew money from New York" that had so unforgettably distinguished his argument in the first Decatur trial, Solicitor Wright this time "credited God with having placed witnesses along the railroad tracks" to corroborate the prosecution's case. He branded Patterson's testimony denying the attack against Price as so patently unbelievable that it supported the State's case. After 30 minutes of pulpit-pounding delivery he yielded to Solicitor H. G. Bailey, the original prosecutor of the Scottsboro defendants.[116] Bailey told the jurors they should repudiate the sinister proposition that "citizens of their neighboring county" had conspired to "frame the Negroes."[117] He dismissed Lester Carter as an outsider, claiming that he now "represent[ed] a certain stratum of the big city"[118] and was not to be believed. He finished by demanding the electric chair, the only acceptable punishment for the vicious assault against Price.[119]

Leibowitz then rose to face the jurors. He began by assailing Victoria Price, Orville Gilley, and even defense witness Lester Carter as "bums," "loafers," and "scum."[120] He asked the twelve men in the jury box to weigh their stories against the disinterested testimony of Dr. Bridges who, he pointed out, the prosecution had declined to summon as a witness, and who had examined Price a matter of hours after the alleged assault and found no bleeding, bruises, or other injuries consistent with a vicious gang rape on a bed of gravel. Extolling the ingenuity of his adversaries, he asked why they had not secured Price's clothing, which surely would have contained evidence of the sexual assault.[121] He branded Price "a white girl tramp" and lambasted her for her glaringly inconsistent testimony from trial to trial—testimony that was "so fantastic that if you came upon it in fiction you would toss the book away."[122] He concluded with an appeal to the jurors' sense of fairness. "Do justice. If this Negro is a rapist—hand it to him. If they've show [sic] this beyond a reasonable doubt. If you have a reasonable doubt, stand your ground like a man....Bring in a verdict of not guilty so that justice will be done between the State of Alabama on the one hand and the defendant, Heywood [sic] Patterson, on the other."[123] Judge Callahan then adjourned court at 6:00 until the next morning.

November 30 was Thanksgiving, but Judge Callahan pressed ahead with the trial. Leibowitz had used most of the time allotted for the defense's closing argument, leaving George Chamlee only a brief opportunity to address the jury when court reopened. Although the urbane Leibowitz appeared to be "a stranger in a strange land" in the Alabama courtroom, "handicapped by unfamiliarity with its customs,"[124] such was not the case with the Southern-born Chamlee. While acknowledging that Patterson had testified in Scottsboro that he had seen the white women attacked on the train by other black youths, Chamlee asked the jurors to dismiss that testimony. The jury could certainly appreciate, he suggested, that "a clever lawyer could make a Negro admit anything." They likewise could infer why a witness like Patterson "will say yes when he means no, and no when he means yes."[125] The reasonable doubts permeating the case, he argued, could only translate into a not guilty verdict.

Alabama law allowed the prosecution to have the first and the last word during closing arguments, providing Thomas Knight with a final opportunity to tout the strength of the State's case. He reminded the jurors that their verdict would be heard "in California and Canada and elsewhere,"[126] but in a reference that drew an angry objection and a motion for a mistrial from Leibowitz, implored that they not lose sight of the significance of their decision to Alabama. The Attorney General's precise words were not transcribed, but the Associated Press story reported in Alabama newspapers quoted Knight as arguing, "You cannot avenge what has been done to Victoria Price but you can stop it from being done to another woman."[127] The New York Times account paraphrased Knight differently, reporting that he asked the jury "to send Patterson to the electric chair, not to avenge Victoria Price but to stop attacks upon white women by Negro marauders."[128] When Leibowitz later recited his exception for the record, it appeared that the Associated Press quote may have been the more accurate, although the true implication of the Attorney General's remark may have been better captured by the *Times*. Leibowitz stated: "We object to the statement by the solicitor that if you cannot avenge the assault on Victoria Price, you cannot stop the attacks on our womanhood. We object to it because it is an appeal to the passion and prejudice of the jury. And I therefore now move for a mistrial."[129] Whatever Knight said originally, the jury also got the benefit of his retort to Leibowitz which, according to the *Times,* was as follows:

The Attorney General, his voice trembling with emotion, whirled on his feet...and said:
   "It certainly is. It is an appeal to passion."
   ...[T]he hostile hillsmen who crowded the second-floor room chuckled their delight and slapped each other on the back as Judge Callahan denied [Leibowitz's motion for a mistrial] and Mr. Knight continued.
   "We all have a passion, and that is a passion for protecting the womanhood of the State of Alabama and, when we do protect the womanhood of the State, it doesn't lie in the mouth of any man to tell you what's best for your Commonwealth," he said.
   "If you believe this defendant raped Victoria Price, be men enough to return such a verdict as you know and I know will be a deterrent to others."[130]

Knight finished his argument at 10:30. Then, in his one concession to the Thanksgiving holiday, Judge Callahan called a recess until 1:30, when he would begin his charge to the jury. "'I think, gentlemen,' said Judge Callahan, 'that we should all go to our firesides and give thanks to a divine providence for the blessings of the past year."[131] What Haywood Patterson may have been thinking about the past year can only be left to speculation. During the closing arguments he was described as having "a glimmer of everlasting hope in his almost expressionless face."[132]

If ever he entertained it, hope seeped quickly from Patterson's visage after court resumed and Callahan began his jury instructions. "As the judge began to speak, Patterson leaned forward in his chair intently. As one after another loophole was closed to him by the court's interpretation of the law, he sat back, slumping lower and lower in his seat, the picture of dejection."[133] While neither Patterson nor the twelve men sitting in judgment of him likely grasped all of the nuances of Callahan's hour and a half explanation of the law, the general tenor of the judge's words and his telling gestures and facial expressions could scarcely have been more damning. "The cold stenographic report of the charge," wrote F. Raymond Daniell for the *New York Times*, "does not convey the full force of its blow to the defense. Time after time the judge changed the intonation of his voice significantly and several times he glared in what seemed an unfriendly fashion at the defense counsel table while explaining to the jury that inference and innuendo were not evidence."[134]

Patterson's defense was predicated on his having had no contact whatsoever with Victoria Price. It had nothing to do with the issue of consent. Judge Callahan nevertheless took pains to instruct the jury about the presumptions it could and should indulge under Alabama law regarding sexual relations between black men and white women.

Where a woman charged to have been raped, as in this case, is a white woman, there is a very strong presumption, under the law that she will not and did not yield voluntarily to intercourse with the defendant, a negro, and this is true, whatever station in life the prosecutrix may occupy, whether she be the most despised, abandoned or ignorant woman of the community, or a spotless virgin, or a daughter of a home of luxury and learning. The law forbids rape, and that law is made for all and reaches out its protecting arm for all, regardless of color, creed, or station in life. It is the glory of the law of this state, and of all the states of this Union, that its protecting arms encompass all womankind. If she has been violated unlawfully, she may appeal to the courts with an abiding faith that no accusing finger can point to her erring past or hopeless future, as an excuse for denying to her full protection of the law.[135]

Departing sharply from Judge Horton's application of the law, Callahan told the jury that, "The law would authorize a conviction on the testimony of Victoria Price alone....The law does not require corroboration."[136] Yet that instruction proved to be gratuitous, as Callahan quickly followed it by noting that Price's testimony "has been corroborated by the testimony of the witness Gilley" and "is further corroborated in that there was semen in [her] vagina and on other parts of the private parts."[137] Then, somewhat perversely in light of his repeated rulings that thwarted Leibowitz's efforts to establish that the semen detected in Price was likely to have originated from her consensual relations with Jack Tiller or Orville Gilley before the claimed rape, Callahan mused:

The finding of semen certainly establishes one point, or one fact, and that is that Victoria Price had sexual intercourse with a man. Then, the question on that point arises, how come it there [sic]? This must be met from the evidence or from reasonable conclusions drawn therefrom....It is subject to explanation, but gentlemen of the jury it must be explained by the evidence, or natural, logical conclusions to be drawn from the evidence, and evidence means evidence in the case. No mere suspicion, without evidence, that it could have been some other time or by some one else is a sufficient answer or explanation.[138]

Continuing, Callahan informed the jurors that because Patterson had been accused of rape and would suffer punishment if convicted, the law presumed that he was "an interested witness" and his testimony could be evaluated accordingly. But he warned the jury—a jury, like all others preceding it in the Decatur court-house, comprised exclusively of white men—that:

Something has been said through this case in argument about the defendant's being a Negro.

I would be ashamed of you if that is to enter into your consideration for search for truth in this case. No man is worthy to be in the jury box that would reach the guilt or innocence of a man on any such contemptible grounds.[139]

Callahan wound to a conclusion by instructing the jurors that if they were convinced that the State had proven its case against Patterson beyond a reasonable doubt, their verdict should be guilty and they should assign one of two punishments: death or imprisonment for a term not less than ten years or "any amount above that, that you see fit, according to the evidence.... Take this case, gentlemen, and give it your consideration."[140] As the jurors prepared to take leave, "Mr. Leibowitz rushed up to the bench followed by Attorney General Knight and a whispered conference ensued."[141] Incredibly, Callahan had neglected to inform the jury that it had another verdict option: that Patterson was not guilty. He corrected himself before the bemused jurors departed. "I believe I forgot one thing about the forms of the verdict. I gave you the forms of the verdict on conviction. If after considering all of the evidence in this case, you are not satisfied beyond a reasonable doubt that the defendant is guilty as charged, then he ought to be acquitted, and must be, under the law, and the form of your verdict in that event would be, 'We, the jury find the defendant not guilty.'"[142] The jury retired to determine Patterson's fate at 3:05 P.M.[143]

As determined as ever to bring "the Scottsboro cases" to a resolution, Judge Callahan began questioning the new venire called for Clarence Norris's trial that Thanksgiving afternoon, immediately upon Patterson's jury beginning its deliberations. The judge's standard questions included: "Have you such an opinion or prejudice against this defendant or his race that would prevent you from trying his case according to the law and the evidence, and finding a verdict accordingly?" "Are you opposed to capital or penitentiary punishment?"[144] The venire was so badly depleted by responses to these questions that more men had to be summoned to court for jury duty. To Leibowitz, the numerous prospective jurors who admitted having formed an opinion about Norris's guilt based on what they had heard or read about earlier trials strongly supported his argument for a change of venue. To Callahan, however, the venire members' candor in admitting their lack of impartiality lent confidence that the remaining jurors were in fact unbiased and able to provide Norris a fair trial.[145]

Meanwhile, Patterson's jury had not reached a verdict by dinnertime. Sensing the jurors' fatigue, Judge Callahan called a halt to their deliberations and dispatched them to a hotel for the night. He issued strict orders that they carry on no discussions about the trial. A rumor circulated that the jury had agreed that Patterson was guilty but remained divided about his punishment.[146] The next day, Friday, December 1, brought more of the same. Jury selection inched forward for Norris's trial while Patterson's jury returned to their deliberations at 8:30 and continued through lunch and into the late afternoon. Finally, at 5:00, just as Callahan was about to swear in Norris's jury, a knock on the door heralded that the jurors in Patterson's case had arrived at a verdict.

The courtroom waited tensely as Patterson, surrounded by six deputies, was ushered in wearing manacles. Then, "the jury, grave of face, and slow of step, filed in." "The silence," wrote T.M. Davenport for the Associated Press, "was electric."[147] The *New York Times* account continued:

> "Gentlemen," asked Judge Callahan, "have you agreed upon a verdict?"
>
> "We have," said Mr. Russell [the foreman of the jury].
>
> The words came in a whisper. The muscles in Patterson's neck grew taught.
>
> Mr. Russell stepped forward and handed the slip of note paper which he had been clutching in his right hand to John Green, the court clerk.
>
> It took Mr. Green almost a minute to flatten out the paper, which was moist and crumpled. He then read the fateful words:
>
> "We find the defendant guilty as charged and fix his punishment at death."
>
> The wisp of a smile that had lingered on Patterson's lips almost like a smile in death changed to a malevolent leer as his angry eyes swept from the jury to the judge and back again. Once his big body twitched and his right arm came up. He was like a caged animal about to lunge at a keeper who had mistreated him.[148]

The *Times'* dramatic report was contradicted by other news dailies only in its description of Patterson's reaction. The *Birmingham News* reported that "[t]he defendant, who has twice before heard juries pronounce the sentence of death for him, showed not the slightest concern as the fatal words of the decree were read."[149] The Associated Press agreed with this more stoic characterization of Patterson: "The negro who twice before has heard identical words read into his case, appeared unmoved."[150] The *Daily Worker* concurred: "When the verdict...was brought in, Patterson's face was immobile."[151] Leibowitz, for his part, appeared braced for the trial's outcome. When asked to comment on the verdict, the veteran lawyer tersely replied, "We'll do our talking before the Supreme Court of the United States."[152]

Others were not so restrained. William Patterson, the national secretary of the ILD, branded the result "outrageous" and a "legal lynch verdict."[153] The *Daily Worker* announced major demonstrations to "climax a week of open air protest meetings in Harlem, whose working-class population is seething with indigna-tion over the lynch preparations by the Decatur court."[154] Four Communist demonstrators snarled sidewalk traffic by chaining themselves to a Broadway light pole and haranguing theatergoers with chants of "Free the Scottsboro boys," and more than 3,000 sympathizers joined a march through Harlem protesting Haywood Patterson's conviction.[155] Within days of the verdict, religious leaders—"Protestants, Catholics and Jews, clergy and laymen alike"—led a crowd of more than 1,500 in New York City in denouncing lynching. They adopted a unanimous resolution "calling upon President Roosevelt and the Governor of Alabama to see to it that the defendants in the Scottsboro case receive a fair trial."[156] Among the "flood of communications" in the wake of the verdict "was a letter to Judge Callahan from San Jose, California, protesting against what was called 'the mob spirit' here."[157] As news of Patterson's conviction and death sentence rippled beyond the Decatur courtroom, a different jury began to hear evidence there against Clarence Norris.

Norris, for one, did not believe that his jury was materially different from the one that had condemned Patterson. "The jury looked like a lynch mob," he later recalled, "a bunch of tobacco-chewing, snuff-dipping, overalled crackers in muddy shoes."[158] Nine were farmers. One was a carpenter, another an oil salesman, and the last a railroad employee. All twelve men, of course, were white.[159]

Norris's trial resembled Patterson's in other respects, as well. The combative Leibowitz continued to clash with his familiar nemeses—Victoria Price, Attorney General Knight, and Judge Callahan. A furious Callahan erupted when Leibowitz revisited the issue of Price's alleged sexual indiscretions prior to her rape claim, which the jurist had repeatedly ruled were irrelevant. His rebuke prompted the defense lawyer to lodge yet another motion for a mistrial.

Q: [BY MR. LEIBOWITZ]   I am going to ask you, Mrs. Price, if you spent the night in Chattanooga in a wooded section near the railroad yards?
COURT: I see that you have gone far enough with it, myself, to make that question illegal and I sustain the objection to it.
MR. LEIBOWITZ: We except.
Q: I must ask just one more question,—don't answer it until objection is made and ruled on by the court. Did you, there that night, in and about the railroad yards in Chattanooga, have sexual intercourse with one Lester Carter, or one Gilley, in company with Ruby Bates?
MR. KNIGHT: We object to that.
COURT: I sustain the objection. Mr. Leibowitz, that question was so palpably illegal that you ought not to have asked a question like that.
MR. LEIBOWITZ: I except to the admonition of the court and move for a mistrial.
COURT: The motion is overruled.[160]

Price clung to her story on direct examination and throughout Leibowitz's grueling cross-examination. Under Solicitor Bailey's questioning she repeated her account of the black youths' threat as they stormed the gondola in which she was riding—"All you white sons of bitches unload"—and she embellished her previous testimony by adding that "they said they were going to take us north and make us their women, or else throw us in the river one."[161] She unhesitatingly identified Clarence Norris as among the six who had raped her. She chillingly told of being pinned down and held at knifepoint during the assault, while beside her others were raping Ruby Bates.

Price denied on cross-examination that she and Bates had traveled from Huntsville to Chattanooga with Lester Carter the evening before the alleged rapes, or that she had even set eyes on Carter before encountering him in Chattanooga. She likewise denied having met Orville Gilley that evening, insisting that she first saw him on March 25 during the train ride back to Alabama. She admitted knowing Jack Tiller, describing him as "my guard" rather than as a boyfriend, but was spared answering whether she had been convicted of committing adultery with him when Callahan broke in and warned Leibowitz, "You've gone far enough."[162] She maintained that her lips "was kin'ly busted" following the assault, and that her whole face was swollen and bruised.[163] When she professed an inability to describe the size of the individual pieces of chert, or gravel, in the gondola in which she said she was attacked, Leibowitz pressed her to answer: "You can't or won't [describe the size]—which is it?" This inquiry prompted another explosion from Callahan, who lectured the lawyer, "That question is improper and you have no right to ask it. It is my business to see that the witness is fairly treated."[164]

Price was flustered by Leibowitz's unrelenting cross-examination. She claimed numerous times no longer to remember details of the two and one-half year old incident. "Frequently she turned her eyes toward Mr. Knight before answering the defense lawyer's questions. Mr. Leibowitz at last protested, asking the witness if she were 'looking for signals.' Judge Callahan flared up, declaring that he would not allow 'such tactics' in his court room."[165] Price's testimony finally came to an end. As in prior trials, a verdict would hinge on the jury's willingness to credit her testimony. Ensuing witnesses would do little more than shore up or help erode her essential narrative. None, quite clearly, could rival Victoria Price's importance to the Scottsboro prosecutions.

Leibowitz's best chance to refute Price's accusation, if he had any at all, was to offer persuasive physical evidence that an attack could not have occurred as she had described it, through the testimony of a disinterested witness with a stellar reputation in the community. Those qualities were best embodied in Dr. Bridges, the Scottsboro physician who had examined Price and Bates just hours after the alleged rapes on the afternoon of March 25, 1931. Leibowitz's theory of the case—the theory that he was asking the jury to accept in lieu of Price's account—was developed in the lengthy question he put to Dr. Bridges during Norris's trial.

Q: Tell us, doctor, supposing a woman had been hit in the head with the butt end of a gun —let me put it this way, suppose that a woman came into court and testified, that is assuming a state of facts for the purpose of hypothetical question—assuming that a woman came into court and testified that she had been hit on the head with the butt end of a gun, the wound from which bled—

MR. KNIGHT: I object to the question.

COURT: I will wait until he gets through.

Q: (Continued)—and supposing further that she states that she was seized very violently, and states further that she was struck several blows in and about different parts of the body, including the face, and supposing that she was picked up and held over the sides of a gondola car by her legs, and then pulled back around, and thrown down on some rough material know as chert, and suppose then and there one of the assailants pushed her head, that is the head, in a violent fashion, put his hand on her face roughly, and supposing further that this man that threw her down had intercourse with her, and supposing that while the intercourse was going on, he tore at her breasts, taking hold of her in and about the breasts, and suppose that six men in succession had intercourse with this woman, against her will, while she was struggling and squirming, and resisting, on this rock, or chert, and suppose, doctor, that she lay on this rock or chert on her back and on her side for over an hour, screaming and struggling with these heavy men on top of her, and suppose after that, she was taken off, and suppose that she claimed that she was in a faint, for a few moments, and was taken to a nearby point to a doctor's office—what would you expect to find on her body—can you state with a reasonable certainty what would be found on her body; would you find more evidence of violence and assault than a mere couple of scratches on the wrist and forearm, or the throat?

MR. KNIGHT: We object to that.

COURT: The objection is well taken. The question is not based on the evidence.[166]

Leibowitz, of course, believed that his question indeed was based on and accurately reflected the evidence regarding Price's allegations. He excepted to Callahan's ruling, although he doubtlessly was content to have been allowed to propound his elongated hypothetical question for the jury's consideration. He employed a similar tack—offering key elements of the defense's theory of the case through a question that was predestined to call for an inadmissible answer—during his examination of Lester Carter.

Q: [BY MR. LEIBOWITZ] Who introduced you to Ruby Bates?

A: [BY LESTER CARTER] Victoria Price and Jack Tiller.

Q: Was that while you were still in [the Huntsville] jail?

A: Yes sir.

Q: After you got out of jail, did you see Ruby Bates in Huntsville?

A: Yes sir.

Q: Did you not, on the night before you left Huntsville, together with Ruby Bates and Victoria Price and Jack Tiller, go to a lumber yard in train yards there, and did you not have intercourse with Ruby Bates there that night, and did not Victoria Price have intercourse, in your presence, with Jack Tiller?

MR. KNIGHT: We object to that.

COURT: I sustain the objection. That question is not legal and highly improper and you will pay no attention to it.

MR. LEIBOWITZ: Exception.[167]

From an evidentiary standpoint, Norris's trial differed from Patterson's in two significant respects. First, whereas Patterson's jury had heard Patterson and four of the other Scottsboro defendants testify in denial of the charges, neither Norris nor any of the others who stood accused took the witness stand at Norris's trial. Leibowitz may have concluded, in light of the outcome in Patterson's case, that having Norris or his companions testify was simply too risky or would be counterproductive. Allowing Norris to take the witness stand to deny the rape charge would have opened the door for damaging cross-examination regarding his testimony at his prior trial in Scottsboro, where he had protested his own innocence but claimed to have witnessed Price and Bates being attacked by all of his codefendants, including Haywood Patterson. Although Patterson had similarly testified about having seen the two women assaulted on the train during his Scottsboro trial, the fact that Norris had named Patterson as one of Price's assailants would have put Leibowitz in an awkward position smacking of a potential conflict of interest between his clients.

The second major evidentiary difference in the two trials lay in the fact that Norris's jury heard Ruby Bates's testimony, albeit via written interrogatories secured at her New York City hospital bed. Patterson's jury had reached its verdict without considering Bates's testimony after Judge Callahan refused to delay the trial for even a day to permit delivery of the interrogatories. At Norris's trial, Leibowitz read from the transcript of Bates's sworn examination and cross-examination, which had been conducted just days earlier as Bates recuperated from abdominal surgery. Significant portions of Bates's testimony were excluded by Judge Callahan in response to objections. The jury consequently did not hear the following answers that Bates supplied to the interrogatories.

On March 23rd, in the afternoon about 5:30, it was nearer 6 o'clock Victoria Price, Lester Carter and Jack Tiller and myself walked up the Pulaski Pike.... We went off into a side road. We walked along this road until we came to a big ditch and then we saw these vines on each side of the ditch where we couldn't be seen. We got over in the vines. There were sexual intercourse between both couples, Lester Carter with myself and Jack Tiller with Victoria Price. Later in the night it began raining, so we moved from there and walked to the N.C. & St. L. Railroad...and we found a box car there on the side track. We got into the box car and later in the night there was sexual intercourse again....

[On March 24, Lester Carter, Victoria Price, and I] got on this freight train going to Chattanooga, we got in a box car.... The train pulled into Chattanooga that night about 8:30.... While we was looking for [a box car to spend the night in], Orville Gilley was coming meeting us.... When we couldn't find a box car, Orville Gilley said that he knows a place, he knew was the hobo jungle, a place where we could rest.... Lester Carter and myself spread out on Lester's overcoat on the ground and laid down and we dozed off to sleep. That's all that happened that night that I remember.

...On the morning of March 25th, Lester Carter and Orville Gilley went again for something to eat....Victoria Price looked over into another place where there was a bunch of hobos and she said, "If I knew that Lester and the other bo[y]—who introduced himself to us as 'Carolina Slim' and later told us his name was Orville Gilley—would not come back soon, we would go over there and make some money from these boys."... [After Carter and, later, Gilley returned] we went down to the freight yards. We sat at the freight yards until the freight train pulled in going west.[168]

On the other hand, Norris's jury did hear Bates's responses to interrogatories that focused on what happened after she, Price, Carter, and Gilley boarded the freight train on the morning of March 25.

When the train started to pull out [of Stevenson, Alabama], we got into a gondola and besides this gondola there was several other gondolas....Shortly after the train pulled out...there was some white boys come to the next car from where we was, a gondola, and they said something and Lester Carter was talking to them....I noticed that there was some negroes come into this car from the top of the box car from the direction of the caboose. Then when these negro boys got to where these white boys was, there was a fight. I don't know what the fight was about, but most of these white boys got off the train. Lester Carter also got off the train. Orville Gilley started to get off...but was pulled back in the car by one of the negro boys. After then the negro boys disappeared. I did not see them any more until there was some boys taken off the train at Paint Rock.

...[After the train arrived in Paint Rock] there was some negroes taken off the train and placed under arrest and Victoria Price and myself was also placed under arrest and Orville Gilley was also put under guard by the Sheriff. Victoria Price made out like she fainted. She was taken into a store where I was also taken a few minutes later....When she began to talk, she was asked about what happened. So she told them that we were attacked by some negro boys.

...[After they were taken to the Scottsboro jail, Price] had told the Sheriff that we had been raped and she made up the story of how we had been raped and she was telling me the story. I told her that I do not know whether I will or not, because it is not true. She was telling me that I must tell these things, as she was pointing them out to me....I also heard her tell Lester Carter that he must tell that we had been raped by these negro boys....Victoria Price reminded me during all this time that I must tell what she did. She said that unless I did tell what she did, I would get her in trouble. She would have to serve a jail sentence....Lester Carter asked Victoria Price why she wanted to tell what she did on these boys for. Victoria Price said that she didn't give a darn for all of these niggers, let them hang them all and Lester Carter told her that she should be ashamed of herself....

[Q]: Did you testify...that six negroes raped you and six negroes raped Victoria Price and one of the negroes held a knife at your throat?
A: Yes, sir.
[Q]: Was that testimony true?
A: No, sir....

[Q]: Did Haywood Patterson, Ozie Powell, Willie Roberson, Andy Wright, Olen Montgomery, Eugene Williams, Roy Wright, Charley Weems and Clarence Norris, or any of them, assault either you or Victoria Price on March 25, 1931?
A: No.[169]

The presentation of evidence concluded on Monday, December 4. The lawyers' arguments were shorter and less barbed than in Patterson's trial. During Leibowitz's hour long oration, sandwiched between the arguments of Solicitor Wright and Attorney General Knight, he asked why a national spectacle should be made of "a contemptible frame-up by two bums." In an attempt to neutralize his status as an outsider from New York, working hand in hand with the International Labor Defense and representing a black defendant, he reminded the jurors that "we [are] all American citizens." He then deliberately played on the jurors' regional pride.

If you have a reasonable doubt, hold out. Stand your ground, show you are a man, a red-blooded he-man—a Southern gentlemen, ready to do justice even to this lowly, insignificant worm of a Negro boy. If the State had showed his guilt, I'd be the first to hang him. But this State has failed to do this. Its case smells to heaven. We've had enough of this expense, enough opprobrium upon this State of Alabama. Let's end it now.[170]

Judge Callahan's charge to the jury followed the lawyers' summations. The *New York Times* had become openly disenchanted with Callahan over the course of Patterson's and Norris's trials, and offered increasingly unflattering depictions of the judge and his conduct. During its coverage of Norris's case, the *Times* had gone out of its way to point out that "[t]he judge...was criticized today by *The Birmingham Post* in an editorial headed 'A Questionable Trial.'"[171] And while reporting on the charge to Norris's jury, the newspaper noted that "Judge Callahan peered over his spectacles at the representatives of Northern newspapers" as he explained that the law "protects all womankind regardless of...their race or color." The judge remarked that Alabama's law resembled that of many states, including New York. "As he pronounced the name of the Empire State,... Judge Callahan allowed his voice to rise and he cast a challenging look at Mr. Leibowitz."[172]

Meanwhile, the *Birmingham News* also was transparent in its allegiance. As Norris's trial neared conclusion, the Alabama newspaper featured in its headline that "Leibowitz Handed Stern Rebuke in Trial in Decatur." Its page one story elaborated:

Looking straight at the attorney, who has displayed an unpleasant mood from the time he entered court, Judge Callahan told him he had noticed the throwing of pencils on the table and other evidence of resentment to the court's rulings....

Newspaper men had commented on the defense attorney's attitude several minutes before the judge took open cognizance of it. The attorney had shot his questions like barbed darts during his cross quiz, and prior to that had objected to nearly every direct question from the prosecution, had been overruled almost as often, and had entered exceptions with a grating emphasis.[173]

Leibowitz noted several specific exceptions to Callahan's jury instructions, "pressing the judge almost as though he were a hostile witness."[174] The lawyer remained furious about what—in his mind—amounted to being duped during Patterson's trial into the erroneous belief that he could take a general exception to the jury instructions and thereby preserve issues relating to the charge for appeal.[175] He thus painstakingly detailed his requests for modifications to Judge Callahan's charge, eliciting a few begrudging concessions but for the most part simply protecting the record for appeal. Norris's jury finally retired at 6:17 P.M. At the jurors' request, they would not begin their deliberations until the next morning.[176]

When Norris's trial began, Leibowitz reportedly had expressed guarded optimism about his client's chances. "For the first time since the International Labor Defense brought him into the Scottsboro case, he said, he was hopeful of obtaining a jury verdict of 'not guilty.'"[177] Norris's outlook was much bleaker. "Mr. Leibowitz...didn't understand that no matter what evidence he produced to the contrary, a Southern jury would never acquit a Negro of the charge of rape brought against him by a white woman. It didn't matter whether the woman had been raped or not, the code of the South at that time was that the word of the lowest white person was proof enough against the most influential black citizen."[178] The jury deliberated throughout the day on December 5. Still unable to reach a verdict by 9:30 that night, the jurors were consigned to hotel rooms with orders to resume their deliberations the next morning. "The jurors were a haggard-looking group when the judge ordered them brought into court tonight. Some had their collars open at the throat, some were perspiring, and some looked as angry as though a careless individual had just stepped upon their corns."[179] Rumors surfaced that the jurors were deadlocked and that a mistrial might result.

In the meantime, Judge Callahan granted Leibowitz's motion for an indefinite postponement of the remaining trials pending the outcome of Patterson's and, if necessary, Norris's appeals. The other trials "would be but a futile gesture," Leibowitz contended, if the constitutional questions raised during the earlier trials, centering on the jury selection procedures employed in Jackson and Morgan Counties, were resolved in the defense's favor. Tension built while Norris's jury continued to deliberate. Callahan appointed two additional sheriff's deputies to watch over Leibowitz, who already was being protected by two beefy New York City police officers.[180]

Finally, at 11:20 on the morning of December 6, a knock on the door of the deliberations room signaled that the jurors had something to report. Norris was brought into court, surrounded by deputies, with Haywood Patterson also in tow. The jurors were escorted into the courtroom, solemn faced, as rain beat down outside. They had arrived at a verdict. They had received their instructions 41 hours earlier, devoting 14 hours to deliberations. A piece of paper bearing their verdict was transmitted to Judge Callahan, who studied it, paused, then read aloud, "We the jury find the defendant guilty as charged in the indictment and fix his punishment at death." Norris appeared unmoved. A woman who worked in the courthouse gasped. Reporters slid from their seats to wire news of the verdict to their papers. Otherwise, silence filled the Decatur courtroom. Judge Callahan thanked the jurors for their service and then discharged them.[181]

First Patterson, and then Norris were formally sentenced to death by Judge Callahan. When asked if he had anything to say before sentence was pronounced, Patterson replied, "Yes sir, I am not guilty. I have been sentenced to the electric chair three times for something I am not guilty of."[182] Leibowitz's biographer provided an unflattering account of the ensuing imposition of sentence—an account not substantiated by other reports and conflicting with stories reporting that Leibowitz was the only defense lawyer present during the sentencing proceeding.[183]

"Heywood" [sic], Callahan said, smacking his lips, "the jury has found you guilty of rape." He lingered over the word "rape," mouthing it as though reluctant to let it go, and it came out "raaaaaaaape." He continued, "It now is my duty to pronounce sentence upon you. You shall be taken to Kilby Prison and there the warden is to do execution upon you by applying a current of electricity to your body of sufficient voltage to cause your death, and he is to keep it applied until you are dead." He turned away, and then remembering that he had left something out, he again addressed Patterson, adding perfunctorily, "May God have mercy on your soul."

Brodsky finally exploded at what he (and reporters who were present) felt to be the sadistic attitude of Callahan, and before Leibowitz could stop him he half arose, looked straight at Callahan and said firmly and very audibly, "And may God have mercy on yours." There was a shocked silence for a moment. Leibowitz pulled the white-faced, shaking Brodsky down.[184]

Clarence Norris's sentencing followed. Clasping his hat in hand as Callahan inquired whether he had anything to say, Norris, like his codefendant, protested his innocence. "Yes sir, I am not guilty of this charge. It was framed up against me." The judge replied that he had "nothing to do with the verdict"; he was only entering judgment on the jury's decision, as was his duty.[185] This time, Callahan neglected to invoke God's mercy.[186] He fixed February 2, 1934, as the date of both executions, although the appeal notices Leibowitz filed automatically resulted in a stay pending further judicial review. Before being taken from the courtroom, Patterson asked Judge Callahan to allow him to remain locked up in Birmingham's Jefferson County Jail instead of being returned to death row in Kilby Prison, explaining that an inmate at Kilby had made death threats against him. Callahan declined the request, disavowing authority to act on it and assuring Patterson that the warden of the prison would look out for him.[187] Patterson and Norris thus were transferred to death row while the remaining Scottsboro defendants were returned to the Jefferson County Jail as their cases remained stalled pending Patterson's and Norris's appeals. Leibowitz made his way to a train station under heavy security, and headed home to New York City.[188]

The *Daily Worker* reported that mass demonstrations had cropped up "all over [the] country"—in Buffalo, Cleveland, New York City, Philadelphia, Minneapolis, Toledo, Chicago, and Pittsburgh, in Scotts Run, West Virginia, Rock Island, Illinois, Youngstown, Ohio, and elsewhere—in protest of the "lynch verdicts" in the Scottsboro cases.[189] Although Leibowitz's return to New York City following the trials generated an enthusiastic reception and inspired a few large rallies,[190] reaction to the verdicts generally was considerably less widespread and more restrained than the Communist Party newspaper suggested. More than two and one-half years after the first round of death sentences, and six months after Judge Horton had nullified Haywood Patterson's second date with the electric chair, mention of the cases had grown increasingly unlikely to trigger the impassioned outrage once aroused. The country had not forgotten about Scottsboro, but with repetition and the passage of time, reactions had dulled to accounts of the trial injustices.

Of course, there was far from universal agreement that injustices had occurred. Newspapers and other outlets offered diverse opinions about the cases and what the verdicts signified. The *Montgomery Advertiser* scored the *New York Herald Tribune* when the latter paper referenced "the old prejudices and passions" that enveloped Haywood Patterson's trial, when it suggested that Judge Callahan's jury charge "fell short of complete impartiality," and when it concluded that the verdict "must be viewed by every disinterested observer as a shocking miscarriage of justice." The Alabama paper replied:

It is duly noted that *The Herald Tribune* racks its brain in an attempt to find some reason for which Heywood [*sic*] Patterson should be tried again, some manner in which Patterson may "prove his innocence."

Has it not occurred to The Herald Tribune that after three trials in which the Negro has been found guilty three times that the Negro IS guilty?[191]

The *Memphis Commercial Appeal* similarly concluded that justice had been provided in the three jury trials—with identical outcomes—in Patterson's case.

About all that the Scottsboro case has demonstrated is that it is often a long time between a verdict of guilty and fulfillment of the court's sentence.

By this time it would seem that those who have gone to such pains to defeat justice in Alabama would be convinced that the first verdict in the Scottsboro case was correct.

But for the meddlesome interference of agencies outside the state the case of the seven Scottsboro defendants would have been disposed of in the usual manner long ago. It now appears that it will be one of those interminable things which ultimately results in the original point of dispute being entirely lost sight of.

The most extraordinary phase of the Scottsboro affair is the patience of Alabama courts and of Alabama citizens. None will ever be able to charge that there was hasty action.[192]

The newspaper representing the transplanted trials' hometown, the *Decatur Daily*, reminded its readers that the citizens of Morgan County "did not welcome the 'Scottsboro case,'" which had been thrust upon them only when "Judge Hawkins quite properly" ordered a change of venue from Jackson County. It marveled with evident sarcasm that "[t]he defendants, the attorneys, the reporters, the sob-sisters and 'observers' who gathered here...have departed—intact, whole of person and enjoying good health."

Thus have the critics been dumbfounded, thus has the lie been given to the cry of "lynch plot" which was raised by the International Labor Defense and echoed, in milder form, by those who should have possessed better sense.

Thus has the judgment of Judge W. W. Callahan, presiding, been vindicated and thus has the honor of the people of Morgan county been upheld!

...[I]n view of the entire absence of any untoward incident whatever here, isn't it reasonable to ask those newspapers which have been so busily engaged in "panning" us (including some of our own state newspapers) to have the decency to accord us at least a public acknowledgement that Judge Callahan's judgment was sound and his faith in the people of this county and neighboring counties was not misplaced?[193]

Not content to let the matter rest there, the *Decatur Daily* launched follow-up editorials on succeeding days. The first announced that "we await with pleasure the words of commendation to flow" from the many newspapers "in our own state and others" that had warned of the "mob spirit" threatening the Scottsboro trials and were so busily "telling us how to conduct ourselves." The editorial continued:

Now that the shoe is on the other foot, we wonder just when these monthly journals with their far-fetched news stories, their "brilliant" editorial writers and their cartoonists, all having no conception whatsoever of the people of Decatur, Alabama, will have to say. All their predictions seem to have come to dismal failure.

There was no mob at Decatur, Alabama, and we wonder somewhat if some of these loud talkers, at least, are not disappointed?[194]

Then, to leave no doubt about the identity of the offending Alabama journalist, the *Decatur Daily* singled out columnist John Temple Graves, whose opinions appeared regularly in the *Birmingham Age-Herald* as well as the *New York Times.*

Mr. Graves, for no apparent reason, has taken occasion several times to tell the people of Decatur and Morgan county how they should conduct themselves. Mr. Graves has attempted to tell the people of Decatur and Morgan county many things of this section [of the State].

May we humbly suggest to the columnist that he desist from further column chatter until he learns more of his subject. If he cares to learn the people of this section, we are very happy to extend an invitation. Meanwhile may we suggest that he keep quiet until he knows the facts.[195]

Another Alabama newspaper, the *Birmingham Post,* had been skeptical about Judge Callahan and his conduct of the Decatur trials. It predicted that the judge's several evidentiary rulings and his general demeanor would yield a "record of this trial, when it comes to review by the U.S. Supreme Court, [that] will not be a favorable commentary on Alabama judicial procedure."[196] *Time* magazine's impression of Patterson's trial also was unmistakably negative. Its account described Victoria Price as a snuff-chewing, "twice-married mill-hand, onetime vagrant" whose story of the alleged rape was "in language so foul that newshawks could not print it....At a dozen points Victoria Price contradicted the story she had told at the two earlier trials." The magazine reported how Judge Callahan "bickered and interrupted" continuously as Leibowitz cross-examined Price.

Glaring frequently at Lawyer Leibowitz and intoning his words, Judge Callahan spent nearly two hours explaining to the jury how they could find Patterson guilty. When he had finished Lawyer Leibowitz and Attorney General Thomas Knight, the prosecutor, went up to the bench, [and] whispered hastily in his ear. "Oh yes," said the judge, facing the jury. "I overlooked one thing. If you are not satisfied beyond all reasonable doubt that the defendant is guilty as charged, then he ought to be acquitted."[197]

Scarcely three months later, *Time* reported positively on playwright John Wexley's *They Shall Not Die,* which it described as "an angry review of the Scottsboro Case."

On the premise that the rape charge against the nine young blackamoors was a frame-up, the play doggedly follows the pattern of the news from the alleged attack aboard a freight train through the first trial to the Supreme Court and on to the second trial. In fact a Manhattan lawyer named Samuel Leibowitz desperately defended the Negroes against a death penalty. In the play a Manhattan lawyer named Nathan G. Rubin...does the same job, emerging in a final courtroom scene as the hero of the piece. As in real life one of the two girl accusers, Lucy Wells..., repudiates her testimony in the first trial, makes a star witness for the defense in the second. Villains of the piece are the police who maltreat

Playwright Wexley's Cookesville boys in a brutally realistic first act; the race-prejudiced crowd in the courtroom; two foul-tongued prosecuting attorneys who denounce "Jew money from New York." After listening to Lawyer Rubin's solemn summation, the jury goes off-stage to bring Playwright Wexley's last curtain down with a burst of obscenely scornful laughter. A better playwright than most polemists, Playwright Wexley lost his temper in They Shall Not Die. Yet somehow his journalistic vehemence does not ruin his play.... [I]t succeeds in its purpose to arouse opinions and emotions on a controversial subject.[198]

While these dramatically different portraits of the Scottsboro cases were represented in the media, in an attempt to inform and influence public opinion, the litigants refocused their efforts on the courts. And the courts—from Judge Callahan to the state's and nation's highest tribunals—although insular by design, could not be immune to the sentiment generated about the most recent convictions and capital sentences.

Alabama rules of procedure and extraneous calamities soon combined to produce a potentially disastrous setback in Patterson's appeal. Patterson's jury had returned its guilt and sentencing verdicts on December 1, 1933. Judge Callahan formally entered judgment on the verdicts on December 6, at the same time he entered judgment against Norris. Leibowitz understood that he had 30 days following the convictions in which to file motions for a new trial, a necessary step in advance of an appeal. Because the trial transcripts were not yet available to prepare the motions, Leibowitz had asked Judge Callahan on December 1 for an extension of the 30 day filing deadline in Patterson's case. Callahan eventually granted two filing extensions, the first on December 29, and another on January 25, 1934. The latter order set February 24 for a hearing on the motions for a new trial for both Patterson and Norris. When the parties appeared for the hearing, Attorney General Knight was poised for action. He moved to dismiss the new trial motions, citing a statutory requirement that such motions must be filed before the expiration of the term of court in which the trials were completed, or December 23 in these cases. Over the defense's heated protests, and the ILD's charge that he had "deliberately misled" the attorneys into missing the filing deadline, Judge Callahan granted the State's request, ruling that he had no jurisdiction to consider the untimely motions for a new trial in either Patterson's or Norris's case.[199]

Diving into the particulars of Alabama law, the defense lawyers thought they had found a solution to this new obstacle. They uncovered a rule of procedure that allowed a criminal appeal to be perfected by filing a bill of exceptions within 90 days of the entry of final judgment. Believing that judgment had been entered in both cases on December 6, 1933, but wary of the fact that Patterson had been convicted on December 1, defense lawyers placed the necessary paperwork on an airplane on February 28, 1934, with the intent of filing the bills of exceptions in court the next day. Fate intervened. The airplane carrying the papers crashed en route to Alabama. Duplicate copies of the documents were not received and filed until March 5. As a result, Patterson's appeal was vulnerable to dismissal if the courts used December 1 as the beginning of the 90 day window.[200]

Assistant Attorney General Thomas Lawson urged the Alabama Supreme Court to reject Patterson's appeal in reliance on that theory when the cases were presented for argument on May 25. For his part, Knight defended the jury selection procedures and addressed other defense claims, including limitations placed by Judge Callahan on the examination of Victoria Price. Leibowitz shared time with constitutional expert Osmond Fraenkel, who argued the jury issues, and George Chamlee, in urging reversal of Patterson's and Norris's convictions. In addition to pressing that blacks had systematically been excluded from jury service in Jackson and Morgan Counties, Fraenkel accused the Jackson County jury commissioners of making a "desperate effort" to sustain the indictments through the "most brazen, rank and amateurish kind of forgery." Knight soft-pedaled the forgery contention. "I'm not here to say whether names of negroes were forged on the jury rolls," he told the justices. But he insisted that "[t]he selection of jurors rests within the discretion of the jury commissioners," and warned that "[i]f this court, with no evidence showing negroes were excluded, holds that a systematic exclusion of negroes took place, then the court is constituting itself the jury commission of every county in Alabama."[201] Chief Justice Anderson, the lone dissenter when the Alabama Supreme Court first considered appeals in the Scottsboro cases in 1932, once again presided over the arguments. Associate Justice Thomas Knight, Sr., the Attorney General's father, also listened intently as the lawyers presented their cases.

Life continued behind bars for the nine defendants while the appeals were pending. As Patterson had feared, he and Norris were transferred to Kilby Prison, in Montgomery, where they remained under sentence of death. They watched as guards led other prisoners to keep their dates with the electric chair.[202] The other Scottsboro defendants remained in the Birmingham (Jefferson County) Jail, where the two youngest, Eugene Williams and Roy Wright, continued under the uncertain jurisdiction of the juvenile court, and the rest awaited retrial on the criminal charges. In late March, three years to the day that they were arrested for rape, the warden of the jail placed Williams, Roy and Andy Wright, Willie Roberson, and Ozie Powell in solitary confinement for diverse infractions and "a long series of disturbances" that had accumulated over their extended stay in the facility. "They . . . have been nothing but a source of trouble ever since they have been here," said the warden.[203] As their restrictions continued into April amidst allegations that they were being starved, beaten, and tortured, Leibowitz promised to seek Governor Benjamin Meeks Miller's intervention to impel an immediate impartial investigation.[204] Still, they were required to endure the

Spartan conditions of solitary confinement well into the summer, far longer than the normal limit of two to three weeks.[205]

Meanwhile, the ILD arranged for Ruby Bates to join several of the Boys' mothers, Janie Patterson, Ida Norris, Mamie Williams, Josephine Powell, and Viola Montgomery, to pay a visit to the White House. The women sought an audience with President Franklin Roosevelt to implore him to "pardon...their 'innocent' sons." White House police informed the delegation that the President was unavailable, but promised to notify him about their attempt to see him. Their visit fell on Mother's Day.[206]

The Alabama Supreme Court unanimously affirmed Patterson's and Norris's convictions on June 28, 1934. No one had expected a different outcome. Defense attorneys from the outset had considered the state appeal to be little more than a formality before they sought review in the U.S. Supreme Court. Yet the state court's disposition of Patterson's appeal now loomed as a significant obstacle to that quest. Speaking for the court, Justice Bouldin accepted the State's argument that the bill of exceptions was submitted too late to allow Patterson's appeal to be considered. "The time for presenting bills of exceptions runs from the date of the judgment of guilty [December 1, 1933], not from the date of sentence [December 6]. The bill of exceptions was presented March 5, 1934, the ninety-fourth day. This was too late."[207] The state court's refusal to entertain the appeal meant that the Patterson's claimed constitutional violations could be insulated from review by the U.S. Supreme Court. In principle, the four-day tardiness in filing the bill of exceptions (as calculated by the state supreme court) meant that no court beyond Judge Callahan, either state or federal, would consider the essential fairness of Patterson's trial. Justice Bouldin's opinion set "Friday, the 31st day of August, 1934...for the execution of the death sentence according to law....All the Justices concur."[208]

The state high court did address the several issues raised in Norris's appeal, although it found no reason to upset his conviction or sentence. Justice Gardner's opinion dwelled at greatest length on the claim "that persons of the negro race, duly qualified under the laws of Alabama to serve as members of the grand jury that found the indictment...were excluded from the list from which said grand jury was drawn...solely by reason of their race or color."[209] Framing the issue just as Judge Callahan had, Justice Gardner explained that the jury commissioners' job "was not so much a matter of exclusion as of selection so as to obtain for that important function of judicial government those best suited for such important service."[210] Many citizens, of both races, simply failed to meet the high standards for inclusion for jury duty. Courts should be loath to impugn impermissible motivation to jury commissioners who, by necessity, are entrusted with discretion in selecting capable grand jurors. In an apparent effort to bolster the conclusion that Jackson County's jury commissioners had exercised their discretion well, the opinion pointed out that J. S. Benson, the "editor of the local newspaper and evidently widely informed as to the county and its citizenship, and who knew 'nearly all' of the negroes there, testified that while he knew some good negroes, with good reputations, yet he would not be willing to say there were any that possessed the necessary qualifications for jury service, and he based his opinion upon the requirement of good judgment. It was his view those he knew lacked that sound judgment that should characterize a juror."[211]

Failing to discern the relevancy of the alleged fraud in the appearance of names of black citizens on the Jackson County jury rolls to the claim of unconstitutional discrimination, the state supreme court opinion "pass[ed] it by without any expression of opinion thereon."[212] The court's rejection of the challenge to the Morgan County jury venire mirrored its reasoning on the grand jury claim. "We have previously observed the high standard of qualification for jury service. . . . We are of the opinion the proof clearly shows. . . that these [jury] commissioners did fairly and honestly endeavor to discharge their duty, and did not in fact discriminate against the negro race in the selection of the jury list."[213] Other claims raised on Norris's appeal—the denial of a change of venue, Judge Callahan's allegedly prejudicial conduct toward the defense lawyers, limitations placed on the cross-examination of Victoria Price about prior convictions and her alleged "adulterous relations. . . the night before the commission of the alleged crime, or even the night before leaving Huntsville," and relating to the jury instructions—also were rejected.[214] "Let the judgment, therefore, stand affirmed. . . . All the Justices concur."[215] Norris's execution, like Patterson's, was scheduled for August 31.[216]

Two weeks later, the defense filed motions for rehearing with the Alabama Supreme Court, prompting a stay of execution for both Patterson and Norris. The state supreme court denied Attorney General Knight's request for a special session to consider the motions. Defense lawyers thus were assured that they would have time to ask the U.S. Supreme Court to intervene when the justices opened their new Term of Court in October.[217]

The court challenges focused public attention on the fairness of Alabama's justice system. Some issues were systemic, most notably the practices and procedures that consistently produced all-white juries. Others were case-specific, including Judge Callahan's evidentiary rulings that had inhibited the defense from developing an alternative explanation for the semen found during Victoria Price's medical examination and his repeated clashes and displays of impatience with Leibowitz. If Alabama needed a diversion to allow public discussion of these issues to recede while attention shifted to different topics, it soon received one. The new developments placed the defense lawyers in the Scottsboro cases in a glaring and unflattering spotlight, and in the process fractured the tenuous alliance between Leibowitz and the ILD.

On October 1, 1934, police arrested two ILD lawyers in Nashville, Tennessee and charged them with attempting to bribe Victoria Price to change her testimony. When authorities took the two New York City lawyers, Daniel Swift and Sol Kone, into custody they also seized $1,500, in one dollar bills, from the men's car. A third man, J. W. Peerson, of Huntsville, Alabama, had been arrested two days earlier with Price in his car as the two were en route to Nashville. Peerson was held as the alleged go-between who had made arrangements for Price to meet the two lawyers in Nashville. Price reputedly had been offered $500 earlier in the summer if she would sign an affidavit swearing that her rape claims were false, an amount that later was increased to $1,000. She told Huntsville police about the plan, who encouraged her to play along with it. After arresting Peerson, the Huntsville police arranged for law enforcement authorities in Nashville to apprehend the men who allegedly had promised to pay Price for her recantation. Swift and Kone were promptly extradited to Alabama, as Attorney General Knight insisted that "no means will be spared" in bringing the men "to the bar of justice. Certainly, where persons have attempted to thwart the ends of justice in one State, no matter where they may be temporarily domiciled, they should be extradited."[218] New York Governor Herbert Lehman and Alabama Governor Benjamin Miller exchanged wired communications over the incident, and the arrests and extradition made headlines in Alabama newspapers and were reported nationally.[219]

Leibowitz was furious on learning about the arrests. He issued a statement disavowing any knowledge of the plan and threatening to withdraw from the case unless the ILD agreed to bow out.

I cannot continue as counsel in the Scottsboro case until the Communists are removed from all connection with the defense. In taking this position, I believe I am acting in the best interests of my clients of whose innocence I am as certain today as when I first took up their cause.

The events of the past week in Alabama have convinced me there is no other course left open.... I knew nothing of the activities of the two men from the International Labor Defense who were arrested in Nashville, charged with attempting to bribe Victoria Price. The defense needed no such help....

The Communists have raised huge sums of money by the exploitation of this case through paid-admission mass meetings throughout the country and kindred forms of lucrative ballyhoo. I gave my services free.

...Until all secret maneuverings, ballyhoo, mass pressure and Communist methods are removed from the case, I can no longer continue. I am not deserting the Scottsboro boys. I have given of my best and am prepared to continue to do so to the end that the Scottsboro boys shall not die.[220]

Leibowitz's accusations and ultimatum brought a swift and vitriolic response from the ILD. The *Daily Worker* accused him of making "vicious, slanderous attacks upon the International Labor Defense,"[221] of "treachery,"[222] and announced to its readers that Leibowitz had "withdrawn completely from the case."[223] The Communist newspaper claimed that Leibowitz had resigned after Wallace Pollak, the skilled constitutional lawyer who had successfully argued *Powell v. Alabama* in 1932, had agreed to represent Patterson and Norris in the Supreme Court. It printed a statement issued by the ILD asserting that Leibowitz had "put his personal and political ambition above the interests of the Scottsboro boys."[224] The *New York Times* quoted the ILD's Joseph Brodsky, Leibowitz's co-counsel throughout the Decatur trials, "as declaring that he 'never was so disappointed in anyone as I am in Mr. Leibowitz,' saying he feared the attorney was 'more interested in personal aggrandizement than in the welfare of the defendants.'"[225]

On October 4, amidst the bribery allegations and the attorneys' verbal warfare, the Alabama Supreme Court declined to rehear Patterson's and Norris's appeals. It fixed December 7 as their new execution date.[226]

Haywood Patterson and Clarence Norris found themselves at the vortex of this maelstrom. In urgent need of legal counsel to take their cases to the U.S. Supreme Court, the two young men again became caught up in a confusing tug of war regarding their representation. Leibowitz first laid claim to their allegiance. With Leibowitz's support, several black clergymen from Harlem visited Patterson and Norris at Kilby Prison. They secured signed statements from the youths and their parents requesting that Leibowitz represent them and that the ILD withdraw from their cases.[227] Almost as quickly, the ILD succeeded in getting Patterson and Norris to do an about-face. The young men withdrew their requests to have their cases handled by Leibowitz and signed letters asking the ILD to proceed on their behalf.[228] Mrs. Janie Patterson wrote Leibowitz that she wanted "Mr. Brodsky, Mr. Frankel [*sic*], and Mr. Pollak...to handle my boy's appeal and I don't want you or anybody connected with you. You just stay away from Haywood. I want you to leave him alone."[229] A lengthy sequel of commitments, severances, and recommitments involving the youths and the competing legal factions followed.

Leibowitz tried to bring stability and gain control over future litigation by helping to organize the American Scottsboro Committee "to carry forward the legal defense" of the Scottsboro cases. Composed of black New York City ministers, businessmen, and newspaper publishers, and including entertainer Bill "Bojangles" Robinson, the Committee approved Leibowitz as counsel for Patterson and Norris and announced plans to expand into a national organization.[230] Although it clearly lacked the authority to decide who would serve as the defendants' lawyer and it dissolved the following year,[231] the Committee's brief life span did not signify its irrelevance. In the short term, the American Scottsboro Committee was instrumental in helping to sway public opinion in Leibowitz's favor. Its more enduring contribution consisted of serving as the progenitor of later initiatives designed to solve the perpetually thorny problem of how to unify the interest groups competing for control of the Scottsboro cases.

The paperwork that had to be filed in the U.S. Supreme Court to keep Patterson, Norris, and the legal issues in their cases alive could not await resolution of the lawyers' in-fighting. Leibowitz and the ILD reached an uneasy agreement. If the justices deigned to grant review, Leibowitz would represent Clarence Norris and, at the behest of the ILD, Osmond Fraenkel and Walter Pollak would argue Haywood Patterson's case. Fraenkel and Pollak prepared the petitions asking the Supreme Court to address the important constitutional issues presented and filed the supporting briefs in both cases. The Alabama Supreme Court agreed to postpone Patterson's and Norris's executions until February 8, 1935, to allow the nation's highest court time to decide whether it would act.[232] On January 7, 1935, the Supreme Court announced that both cases had been added to its docket.[233] Arguments were scheduled for February 15. The impending executions once again were put on hold.

Leibowitz was a trial attorney. He was accustomed to grappling with ambiguous and disputed facts, engaging in fast-paced examination of witnesses, and making emotionally charged appeals to juries. He had never before argued in the U.S. Supreme Court, where a lawyer's trade is carried out much differently. In an appellate tribunal, and certainly one as august as the Supreme Court, a premium is placed on deliberate, logical argumentation. Lawyers are expected to carefully analyze and apply prior court decisions dispassionately to facts already established in the lower courts and now frozen in a cold record. He was nervous as he faced the eight robed justices—Justice James McReynolds, the notoriously conservative Southerner who had issued a one sentence concurrence in *Powell v. Alabama* when the Court voided the original Scottsboro trials, had recused himself without explanation—to ask that Clarence Norris's conviction be overturned.[234]

His argument began in appropriate moderation. It warmed as he assailed the rape indictment and the lengthy absence of blacks from Jackson County grand juries. As his oration perceptibly shifted to trial attorney mode, Leibowitz decried the fraudulent addition and forgery of names of black citizens in the jury rolls. He was interrupted with a question from Chief Justice Charles Evans Hughes: Could Leibowitz prove his claim of fraud? Having had the foresight to have the jury rolls brought to the Supreme Court (then still housed in the Capitol Building although it would move later that year to its own, new building across the street[235]) Leibowitz had the huge volume carried to the bench for the Chief Justice's inspection. Hughes studied the pages, focusing on the names that appeared to be superimposed on the red lines. When he finished, each of the justices in turn examined the book, some with the aid of a magnifying glass. As this extraordinary scene unfolded, and the justices reacted visibly to what their eyes revealed, Leibowitz could not have helped but feel optimistic about his argument.[236]

Leibowitz's argument began late in the day on a Friday. When his time expired, the Court adjourned until the following Monday. Thomas Knight, Jr., recently sworn in as Alabama's Lieutenant Governor, and an experienced Supreme Court advocate, then responded for the State. Addressing the Jackson County jury rolls, Knight frankly confided, as he had done before the Alabama Supreme Court, that "I cannot tell you whether or not those names were forged. I simply take the position that I do not know."[237] That matter was irrelevant, he maintained, to the larger constitutional issue. On that score, Knight unapologetically defended the jury commissioners of Jackson and Morgan Counties, insisting that they had performed their duties carefully and faithfully by including only qualified and capable citizens for jury duty, and excluding none by reason of racial discrimination. Knight subsequently addressed the issues raised in Patterson's case, which Walter Pollak argued for the defense.[238]

Six weeks later, on April 1, 1935, the justices announced their decisions. Chief Justice Hughes spoke for a unanimous (8-0) Court in *Norris v. Alabama,* the lead case, and in *Patterson v. Alabama,* which commanded separate attention because of its peculiar procedural posture. The headlines in the afternoon *Decatur Daily, Huntsville Times,* and *Birmingham News* were identical on the day of the Court's decision: "New Scottsboro Trials Ordered."[239] And although new trials for Norris and Patterson would be the immediate result of the Court's rulings, the broader implications were profound. A body blow had been delivered to a cultural mind-set. The second Supreme Court decision in the Scottsboro cases would irrevocably alter the face of Southern justice. Owing to the inevitable lags between pronouncing a rule, enforcing it, and acceptance and assimilation of its principles, the change would not be immediate. But it would be inexorable. There would be no going back to a legal system that carried out its business in reliance on all-white juries.

Norris v. Alabama did not announce a new principle of law. Chief Justice Hughes noted at the outset that "[t]here is no controversy as to the constitutional principle involved." Previous decisions had unambiguously established that the Fourteenth Amendment's Equal Protection Clause forbids states (and county jury commissioners) from relying on racial discrimination to deny otherwise qualified black citizens the opportunity to serve on grand and petit juries. "The question," said the Chief Justice, "is of the application of this established principle to the facts disclosed by the record."[240] The Court's ruling was important because of its skeptical appraisal of the factual basis on which Alabama had claimed fidelity to its obligation to administer the laws equally; a skepticism signifying that the constitutional prohibition against racial discrimination would be more than an empty promise.

With regard to the controversy concerning whether the names of black residents of Jackson County had fraudulently been added to the grand jury roll, Hughes observed that the books in question "were produced on the argument at this bar and were examined" by the justices. Rebuking both Judge Callahan and the Alabama Supreme Court, he reported, "We think that the evidence did not justify" rejection of the claimed fraud.[241] But this point of contention paled in comparison to the justices' repudiation of the Alabama courts' willingness to accept the "mere general asseverations" offered by the jury commissioners in explanation of the decades-long absence of blacks from grand jury lists. "Something more" was required.

Why were these names excluded from the jury roll? Was it because of the lack of statutory qualifications? Were the qualifications of negroes actually and properly considered?... The commisioner's answer to specific inquiry upon this point was that negroes were "never discussed."...

We think that the evidence that for a generation or longer no negro had been called for service on any jury in Jackson county, that there were negroes qualified for jury service, that according to the practice of the jury commission their names would normally appear on the preliminary list of male citizens of the requisite age but that no names of negroes were placed on the jury roll, and the testimony with respect to the lack of appropriate consideration of the qualifications of negroes, established the discrimination which the Constitution forbids. The motion to quash the indictment upon that ground should have been granted.[242]

The Chief Justice used the same reasoning to condemn the Morgan County jury venire from which the twelve white men comprising Norris's jury were drawn.

[The] showing as to the long-continued exclusion of negroes from jury service, and as to the many negroes qualified for that service, could not be met by mere generalities. If, in the presence of such testimony as defendant adduced, the mere general assertions by officials of their performance of duty were to be accepted as in adequate justification for the complete exclusion of negroes from jury service, the constitutional provision—adopted with special reference to their protection—would be but a vain and illusory requirement. ...[W]e find it impossible to accept [the]...sweeping characterization of the lack of qualifications of negroes in Morgan county [offered by a testifying jury commissioner]. It is so sweeping, and so contrary to the evidence as to the many qualified negroes, that it destroys the intended effect of the commissioner's testimony.[243]

Haywood Patterson, of course, had been indicted by the same Jackson County grand jury as Norris, and tried by a Morgan County jury selected through identical procedures. None could dispute the accuracy of Chief Justice Hughes's conclusion that "[t]he federal question now sought to be presented on behalf of

Patterson is precisely the same as that which we have considered and decided in Norris's Case."[244] The problem, of course, lay in Alabama's reliance on a state procedural rule—requiring the timely filing of a bill of exceptions to preserve issues for an appeal—as a bar to review of the federal questions. Employing a velvet hammer befitting his stature, the Chief Justice deftly expressed assurance that the Alabama courts would not want a procedural lapse, under these unique circumstances, to send Patterson to the electric chair as his codefendant received a new trial.

The state court decided the constitutional question against Norris, and it was manifestly with that conclusion in mind that the court approached the decision in the case of Patterson and struck his bill of exceptions. We are not satisfied that the court would have dealt with the case in the same way if it had determined the constitutional question as we have determined it. We are not convinced that the court, in the presence of such a determination of constitutional right, confronting the anomalous and grave situation which would be created by a reversal of the judgment against Norris, and an affirmance of the judgment of death in the companion case of Patterson, who had asserted the same right, and having regard to the relation of the two cases and the other circumstances disclosed by the record, would have considered itself powerless to entertain the bill of exceptions or otherwise to provide appropriate relief....At least the state court should have an opportunity to examine its powers in the light of the situation which has now developed. We should not foreclose that opportunity....

[W]e vacate the judgment and remand the case to the state court for further proceedings.[245]

The defendants' supporters had held out hope that another Supreme Court reversal, in combination with the passage of time—more than four years now separated the first and most recent chapters of the Scottsboro case—and the presumed waning of emotions, would bring the prosecution to an end. Now, perhaps, reason would prevail. Alabama could cut its losses. The young men, who by then had spent roughly a quarter of their lives behind bars, and Victoria Price, who had so frequently been subjected to intrusive, public, and even openly hostile courtroom examination, could begin to put this unpleasant part of their pasts behind them. But it was not to be. "New indictments to prosecute the Scottsboro attack cases 'to their conclusion,' will be sought promptly, Lieut. Gov. Thomas E. Knight Jr. of Alabama announced" immediately on receiving news of the Court's rulings.[246] Albert Carmichael, who had been elected to replace Knight as Alabama's Attorney General, echoed that the cases "will be prosecuted vigorously."[247]

Leibowitz hailed the Supreme Court decisions as "a triumph for American justice," for his clients and many others. "The victory just won for the 'Scottsboro boys' in the Supreme Court of the United States is the culmination of the hopes and ambitions of 15,000,000 Negro souls in America."[248] The *New York*

Times agreed. In an editorial entitled "Justice for Negroes," the *Times* opined, "This judgment shows that the highest court of the land is anxious to secure and protect the rights of the humblest citizen."[249] The *Times* additionally reported that news of the decision "received prominent display...in British newspapers. It was featured as the biggest news of the day in The Liberal News Chronicle, which also carried an editorial asserting, 'the Supreme Court struck a tremendous blow for the rights of the American Negro generally.'"[250]

Other editorial reaction was significantly more restrained, including among Alabama's newspapers. In that state, the more positive end of the spectrum was represented by the opinion of the *Birmingham Age-Herald*.

It appears quite clear from the court's decision, considered as to its general effect as distinguished from its particular application in the cases it decided, that Alabama and all Southern states should realistically confront the supreme dictate laid down for them in regard to the service of Negroes on juries....

While not underestimating the delicacies involved, *The Age-Herald* nevertheless sees no reason for great alarm as a result of that necessity. There remain legal safeguards against the inclusion of unqualified persons on juries, whether those persons be white or colored....

Our racial relations have progressed to the point where the human problems of such an obedience ought not to be insuperable or greatly frightening to either race....

Let the Scottsboro cases now be promptly and fairly prosecuted and concluded in the light of this clear-cut Supreme Court ruling. Let us confront and assume the responsibilities which that decision generally emphasizes.[251]

Other papers opted essentially to damn the Supreme Court's judgment by conferring no praise, and simply laying out the implicitly bleak options confronting Alabamians for future trials. The *Huntsville Times,* for example, told its readers:

[A] definite choice must be made.

One of these is to abandon prosecution of the Scottsboro negroes and turn them loose in order to continue an old custom with respect to jury service that has prevailed since, or even before, the Civil War.

Even that, however, will not cure the situation entirely. In event another case should arise, in which a negro is the defendant, it could, if he were able to bear the expense, be appealed to the U.S. Supreme Court, where, under Justice Hughes' opinion, it would be reversed.

The other alternative of the dilemma raised by this decision of the Supreme Court is for us to change our custom, and to place the names of negroes on the jury rolls of counties.

The number of them, quite probably, would be limited, but occasionally a member of the negro race would be drawn for jury duty.

Sooner or later, the decision must be made between these two courses of action.[252]

The *Birmingham News* took a similar tack.

The conclusion is inescapable, it seems to *The News,* that Alabama will have to take steps to correct the situation criticized by the Supreme Court wherever it holds true. If this should not be done, every case, either of a major or a minor nature, involving a Negro defendant, hereafter tried in Alabama, could conceivably be appealed to the United States Supreme Court, and each conviction set aside, where Negroes are excluded from the jury rolls.[253]

The *Montgomery Advertiser,* conversely, made no bones about its distaste for the Supreme Court's ruling. Grover Cleveland Hall lambasted the decision on the newspaper's editorial pages.

Alabama jury commissioners must immediately put the names of reputable Negro citizens in their jury boxes. Otherwise we cannot hope again to have the Supreme Court of the United States affirm the findings of a State court wherever a Negro's liberty or life is at stake....

Otherwise, we wish to say that Mr. Hughes's pontifical deliverance is a lot of baloney.

Here is the Supreme Court of a great republic...reversing the verdict of an oathbound jury upon the ground that it does not like the color scheme of that jury....

The Advertiser may be dumb, as well as "lost and ruint," but to save itself it cannot see what the political rights and privileges of Negroes in Alabama have to do with the guilt or innocence of the gorillas who are charged with criminal assault upon two women, it being agreed that rape is a felony under the law in this backward State....

It seems to The Advertiser that if the Supreme Court of the United States...had a more sensitive regard for the victims (actual and potential) of felonious assault and less regard for the politically dispossessed in the home State of these victims, it would not devote an entire opinion to an academic political question, but would offer some comment on the evidence by which the gorillas aforesaid had been convicted.

...Rape happens to be a capital crime in Alabama.

We are sorry that the Supreme Court of the United States seems to have no immediate interest in this phase of the subject.[254]

Whatever the true gauge of public opinion in Alabama regarding the latest reversals in the Scottsboro prosecutions, including the more general issues spawned by them, it would fall to State and local officials to implement the Supreme Court mandate. Like the newspaper editorial writers, jury commissioners and other court officials could embrace the Court's opinion and their obligations under it with varying degrees of enthusiasm. In practice, their responses could either effectively nullify or else give real meaning to the constitutional principles reaffirmed in the Court's ruling. Thus it was not a trivial matter when Governor Bibb Graves, who had just assumed office in January (Graves earlier served as Alabama's governor from 1927 to 1931, before beginning another four-year term in 1935), issued instructions to solicitors and judges throughout the State that he expected their compliance with the Supreme Court's decision.

The governor's directive came four days following the Court's ruling, after it was set back a day because of apparent "strong opposition among high State officials."[255] The delayed response had not gone unnoticed, as newspapers reported on the conspicuous "[s]ilence [that had] clothed official circles in Montgomery...on the effect of the U.S. Supreme Court's decision."[256] Although his statement was somewhat begrudging, and stopped short of endorsing the justices' ruling, Governor Graves made clear that he expected Alabama officials to observe it. He attached a copy of *Norris v. Alabama* to the letter that he transmitted to each of the State's solicitors and judges.

Holdings of the United States Supreme Court are the supreme laws of the land. Whether we like the decisions or not, it is the patriotic duty of every citizen and the sworn duty of every public officer to accept and uphold them in letter and spirit.

I have received the Supreme Court's decision in the Scottsboro case, holding in effect that when there is systematic exclusion of Negroes from juries, it is discrimination against the race in violation of the United States constitution.

This decision means that we must put the names of Negroes in jury boxes in every county in the state.

Alabama is going to observe the supreme law of America....

It is unusual for the governor to undertake to suggest to the judicial department things which under our state policy are peculiarly within its jurisdiction. However, I have a duty to perform and an oath to abide by.

In the exercise of this power, I am writing our trial judges enclosing a copy of that opinion and saying that I do not assume or intimate that the contents of their jury boxes in any way fails to conform to all legal requirement, but suggesting that in the event there be any non-conformity, they speedily take proper steps to remedy any defects.[257]

Alabama newspapers responded in resoundingly favorable terms to the governor's action. The *Birmingham News* captioned its next-day editorial, "Gov. Graves Performs His Duty Admirably."[258] The *Huntsville Times* commended the governor for his "courageous action...in advising trial judges and solicitors that the names of properly qualified negroes should be placed in the jury boxes of every county in the state."[259] The *Birmingham Age-Herald* lauded Graves for acting "promptly, decisively and courageously," and the *Selma Times Journal* and Montgomery's *Alabama Journal* were similarly complimentary.[260] The *Montgomery Advertiser* was comparatively dour, supporting the governor's policy statement, expressing reservations regarding its implementation, and continuing to rail against the Scottsboro defendants.

We think it is the function of the Governor to point the way, and so we are glad, but not surprised, that Governor Graves should have acted in the forthright manner that he did. He could not have done less.

...Everybody knows that there are hundreds of Negroes in Alabama who are qualified by native intelligence and personal character to serve on a jury drawn to hear any cause....

Nevertheless the great majority of Negroes are not yet prepared for the responsibilities of jury service, and for the information of Mr. Charles Evans Hughes The Advertiser will here say upon its own responsibility that the great majority of Negroes in Alabama are not likely to be summoned for jury duty in the future. If they are the respectable practitioners at the bar on both sides of a cause will strike their names.

Finally and in conclusion: The Advertiser does not believe that if the 12 Apostles, returned to life, should declare the Scottsboro infants guilty, the Supreme Court of the United States would affirm the verdict....

The Advertiser believes that the State of Alabama should resolutely prosecute these sucklings to the bitter end!

...Let Alabama continue to drop these sucklings into the laps of the ponderous, querulous old men who quaver aimlessly in the chambers of the Supreme Court of the United States.

The dignity of a self-respecting State can demand no less.[261]

Outside of Alabama, the Atlanta-based Commission on Interracial Cooperation commented that, "The sooner we begin to work out this and other problems involving the normal civil rights of the minority groups, the better it will be for all concerned. Gov. Graves is to be commended for his leadership in this direction."[262] The *New York Times* editorialized, "Governor Graves of Alabama deserves the approbation of the country at large for his prompt action in directing the circuit judges and solicitors throughout the State to accept and uphold the decision of the United States Supreme Court 'in letter and in spirit.'"[263] John Temple Graves applauded the governor's action as an example of "a political realism and an executive courage," and was cautiously optimistic about prospects for more fundamental reforms. "Not only are the ideas of Southern white people changing but the Negro himself is continually improving and many who would have held him unfit for the duties and rights of citizenship a decade or so ago consider him qualified today. It is safe to suggest that the South is not half as shocked at the prospect of Negro jurors as it is at the threat of another Scottsboro trial."[264]

Since Alabama's Lieutenant Governor and Attorney General were already on record as vowing to renew the prosecution of Patterson, Norris, and the other defendants, "the threat of another Scottsboro trial" plainly loomed. Nevertheless, the two young men most directly affected by the Supreme Court's decisions could not help but be relieved when informed about the rulings in their death row cells. "'That "shore" is good news,' [Norris] said grinning, 'I'm mighty happy.'" Patterson "broke into boisterous laughter, halting intermittently to shout 'A new trial—a new trial.'" The other young men, still confined in the Birmingham Jail, let loose with "shouts of joy" on receiving the news.[265] With the future so utterly beyond their control—to be determined by the actions, whims, and deliberations of an uncertain mix of prosecutors, defense lawyers, witnesses, jurors, and judges—the nine accused youths could not be faulted for fully savoring their present reprieve.

Denouement

It is rare for a criminal prosecution to result in a landmark U.S. Supreme Court ruling. It is extraordinary for a case to recapture the justices' attention and inspire a second groundbreaking decision. Yet this unlikely progression involving the epochal right to counsel and jury selection issues resolved in *Powell v. Alabama* and *Norris v. Alabama* distinguished the Scottsboro trials. The federal constitutional claims were all that blocked Alabama's efforts to convict and execute the young men involved in these cases—at least all of them except Eugene Williams and Roy Wright, whose age deprived the state criminal courts of jurisdiction—following their convictions for raping Victoria Price. The defense could not assume that the Supreme Court would again provide a safety net as new prosecutions loomed. Leibowitz's first maneuver was to try to thwart new trials by publicly calling on Alabama Governor Bibb Graves to bring an end to the Scottsboro cases in late April 1935, just a month after the Supreme Court's ruling in *Norris*.

He asked the governor to pardon the defendants or, in the alternative, to appoint a special fact-finding committee composed "of such men as Bishop W. G. McDowell of the Alabama Diocese, Episcopal Church, and some of the heads of the colleges of the State"[1] to investigate the charges. Leibowitz stipulated that he would willingly accept such a committee's findings in order "to bring a stop to this carousel of hate." Seeking to distance himself and his clients from the International Labor Defense and the Communist Party, he charged that "[s]ubversive elements...have...exploited the unfortunate plight of these helpless youths for the purpose of raising huge sums of money with which to carry on political propaganda avowedly seeking to tear down our form of government." He called the prosecution an exorbitantly expensive and "dastardly frame up," and branded the convictions "a mockery of justice." "I plead with you," he wrote the governor, "to put an end to this mad pursuit of these boys."[2]

Governor Graves greeted the overture with icy silence. The following day, Victoria Price swore out nine new warrants accusing each of the defendants of rape, a step calculated to ensure their continuing confinement pending their re-indictment.[3] In a taunting editorial, the *Decatur Daily* praised the governor for not listening to Leibowitz's "tom-foolery" and reminded its readers that Leibowitz "once had the effrontery to tell New York newspapers that Morgan county citizens were tobacco chewing ignoramouses or worse." "Since when," asked the *Daily*, "did Alabamians need the advice of a New York lawyer on how to operate their law courts? Since when did it become necessary for a New York attorney to tell us when to substitute fact-finding commissions for the jury system in this state?" It tartly concluded: "If the governor designs [*sic*] to reply at all, The Daily trusts that his reply will be confined to a terse invitation to accept residence in a region said to possess the warmest climate in the universe."[4]

Events over the ensuing months ground inexorably toward another round of trials. In mid-May, in response to the U.S. Supreme Court's mandate, the Alabama Supreme Court formally ordered that the original indictments against Clarence Norris and Haywood Patterson be dismissed.[5] Legislation was enacted in August authorizing Alabama jury commissioners to purge their old jury rolls, now suspect in light of the Supreme Court ruling, and create new ones.[6] The following month, Lt. Governor Thomas Knight, Jr., whose successor as state Attorney General, Albert Carmichael, had appointed him as special prosecutor in the Scottsboro cases, announced that he would pursue new indictments in Jackson County and retry the defendants in Morgan County.[7]

The task of presenting evidence to the new grand jury fell to Jackson County Solicitor H.G. Bailey, who had obtained the original indictments and convictions in the Scottsboro cases. On November 13, 1935, Victoria Price appeared to testify before the Jackson County grand jurors. One black man served on the 18-member grand jury. Creed Conyers, a farmer and the chairman of the board of trustees of the Negro schools in Paint Rock, was the first black to have served on a Jackson County grand jury since slavery had been abolished. The grand jury returned a true bill of indictment charging each of the nine original Scottsboro defendants with two counts of rape, one naming Victoria Price as the victim and the other naming Ruby Bates. Two-thirds of the grand jurors were required to concur for a true bill of indictment; the specific votes to indict the Scottsboro defendants were not reported.[8] In Morgan County, Judge William W. Callahan indicated that he did not know when the new trials would take place. "'All I know is what I saw in the morning papers,' said Judge Callahan, adding that he had given the matter no thought."[9]

Patterson, Norris, and their seven companions remained incarcerated follow-ing their victory in the Supreme Court. They were entering their fifth year behind bars, having been shuttled between Kilby Prison while under sentence of death and the Birmingham jail after their capital sentences were set aside, and locked up in the deplorable Decatur jail during their trials in Morgan County.[10] Meanwhile, controversy erupted anew over who would represent them in court. As the *Decatur Daily's* salvo against Leibowitz, his intemperate remarks, and his status as a "New York lawyer" suggested, his continuing partici-pation in the cases risked representing more of a liability than an asset. The involvement of ILD lawyers and their affiliation with the Communist Party was another alienating factor to most Alabamians. The alleged attempt by ILD attorneys to bribe Victoria Price to change her testimony in October 1934 (their indictments were *nolle prosequied* in May 1935 after the two New York lawyers failed to appear to answer the charges[11]) had further riven the uneasy partnership among the defense attorneys. The American Scottsboro Committee, formed shortly after the bribery allegations were made in response to the dissolving rela-tionship between Leibowitz and the ILD attorneys, had accomplished little to resolve the disputes regarding trial counsel.[12]

With eight of the young men solidly committed to Leibowitz's continuing representation, and Haywood Patterson equivocating, the ILD blinked. Repre-sentatives of the ILD invited a meeting in October 1935 with a number of organizations that the ILD had previously denounced as infidels and puppets of capitalism, including the NAACP, the ACLU, the American Scottsboro Committee, and others. Following two months of sometimes heated discussion, a compromise agreeable to the involved organizations and Leibowitz was ham-mered out. Leibowitz would remain on the case but local counsel—a Southern lawyer familiar with the ways and the people of Morgan County—would be enlisted to take a leading role in the retrials. A new coalition was formed in December, the Scottsboro Defense Committee.[13]

Allan Knight Chalmers, the engaging, Yale-educated pastor of the Broadway Tabernacle who had a long-standing interest in the Scottsboro cases, chaired the new committee.[14] Chalmers immediately set to work to enlist the backing of prominent Alabamians. He sought the support of the religious community and newspaper representatives, including Grover Cleveland Hall of the *Mont-gomery Advertiser*, and steered the delicate negotiations regarding defense coun-sel.[15] Leibowitz had solicited the advice of James Horton, the courageous judge who had presided over Haywood Patterson's first trial in Morgan County in 1933 and later vacated his conviction, about a good local lawyer to assist with the defense. Horton, who had resumed a law practice following his unsuccessful bid for reelection, had recommended Clarence L. Watts, a native of Huntsville.[16] Chalmers succeeded in retaining Watts for the princely sum of $5,000.[17]

The defendants' arraignments were scheduled for January 6, 1936, in Judge Callahan's court.

When the nine young men appeared before Judge Callahan for arraignment, residents of Decatur "showed scant interest in the proceedings."[18] John Temple Graves reported that "Alabamians still are divided on the merits of the case," but in light of "all the noise, bitterness, notoriety and expense that attended the earlier trials...[are] of one mind in the wish to be rid of the thing for better or for worse."[19] The clerk of court read the first indictment: "The Grand Jury of [Jackson] County charge that before the finding of this indictment Haywood Patterson, whose name to the Grand Jury is otherwise unknown than as stated, forcibly ravished Victoria Price, a woman, against the peace and dignity of the State of Alabama."[20] Clarence Watts entered a not guilty plea on Patterson's behalf. This ritual was repeated for all of the other defendants except the two youngest, Eugene Williams and Roy Wright, whose cases still awaited processing in juvenile court.

Callahan quickly dismissed the defense's motion to have the trials removed to federal court. The motion had alleged that Alabama law allowed only a single change of venue, and that it was impossible to secure a fair trial in the state courts and the poisoned atmosphere of Morgan County.[21] He thereafter denied a motion to transfer the trials to Jefferson County (Birmingham), or "such other county as may be just and proper,"[22] ruling that the defense had failed to establish that a Morgan County jury could not be impartial.[23] He similarly rebuffed the defense's effort to have Lt. Governor Knight removed as special prosecutor in reliance on a state constitutional prohibition against officials' simultaneously holding two paid offices.[24] He set Patterson's trial for two weeks hence, January 20.[25] The *New York Times* ruefully observed that the onset of the trial closely coincided with "the birthday anniversary of General Robert E. Lee," as it commented: "Three times before, once as a friendless Negro hobo and twice as a potential martyr for the Communist party, Patterson has been tried, convicted and condemned to death for the alleged attack on Victoria Price.... Inquiry among the townsfolk...indicated today that while Northern interference with the 'course of Alabama justice,' is still strongly resented, there is a disposition to regard the case with profound apathy."[26]

John Evans was among the one hundred citizens summoned for jury duty for Patterson's trial. A janitor who worked in the Decatur courthouse,[27] Evans was one of twelve blacks in the venire. None would serve on Patterson's jury. The black venire members appeared ill at ease in the courtroom and Judge Callahan's demeanor did little to reassure them. When one of them made his way toward the jury box, which for generations had been inhabited by whites only, Callahan cut him off by interjecting, "Here, boy, sit over there!"[28] Seven of the blacks who reported for jury duty were disqualified for cause: two claimed statutory exemptions based on their employment (one was a doctor, another a teacher); two were older than 65; and three expressed opposition to capital punishment. The other five black venire members were struck peremptorily.[29] Which side struck the prospective jurors was not disclosed, although the prosecutors— Knight, Solicitor H.G. Bailey from Jackson County, and Solicitor Melvin Hutson from Morgan County—were unlikely to be eager to see blacks on Patterson's jury.

The courtroom was only half full when the State opened its case on the morning of January 21. The seats filled rapidly as Solicitor Bailey examined the first witness, Victoria Price. Testifying before a jury for the eighth time, Price's story by now was familiar. She described how Patterson, brandishing a pistol, was one of several blacks who clambered into the gondola in which she, Ruby Bates, and several white boys were riding, how the "colored boys...[ordered], 'All you white sons-of-bitches unload,'" and how Patterson struck her in the head with his gun before he and five of the other black youths raped her.[30] In keeping with the defense team's strategy of featuring local counsel in the trial, Leibowitz sat by while Clarence Watts cross-examined.

Price appeared "truculent"[31] and was often forgetful while responding to Watts's hour-long questioning. Callahan for the most part refused to allow Watts to probe about Price's activities prior to March 25, 1931, the day of the alleged rape, volunteering at one point before any of the prosecutors had occasion to object that he failed to see the materiality of whether she had seen Jack Tiller on the night of March 23 or March 24.[32] Before the day ended, Watts made multiple motions for a mistrial, basing one on Callahan's "attitude [and] lack of patience" and his "irritability in the presence of the jury."[33] A writer reporting on the trial for *The New Republic* described Callahan as "an impetuous, biased old man," elaborating: "To the outsider, Callahan's behavior in court seemed unbelievable. He did not hesitate to belittle the evidence of the defense, making slighting remarks about witnesses, excluding testimony as to the character of the complainant, Victoria Price, and continually badgering the lawyers. His attitude was in every way that of the community."[34]

Price's testimony was damning, but the prosecution this time would not have the benefit of Orville Gilley's corroboration. Gilley, the lone white boy who had remained on board the train following the scuffle that had broken out between Stevenson and Paint Rock involving the white and black youths, had testified during Patterson's 1933 trial before Judge Callahan that he had witnessed Price being raped. He was presently in custody in Tennessee, however, following assault and robbery convictions.[35] A new state's witness had nevertheless materialized, Obie Golden, a guard who was employed at Kilby Prison when Patterson was on death row there. Over Watts's strenuous objection, Golden testified that while he was on duty on the evening of November 22, 1934, Patterson had asked to see the warden and then confided to Golden that he had "messed with them girls."[36] Leibowitz ripped into Golden on cross-examination, demanding to know why the guard had not asked Patterson to sign a confession or otherwise made a written record of it, and getting him to admit that Patterson did not repeat the alleged confession when the warden saw him the next morning. Golden nevertheless stood by his story.[37]

The prosecution next called several witnesses who had appeared in earlier trials to testify about aspects of the train's passage between Stevenson and Paint Rock on the day in question. The closest any of them came to offering direct support for Price's account was Luther Morris's insistence that he "absolutely saw" several "darkies" put their hands on the white girls after throwing the white boys off the train as it headed west past his house.[38] The State rested late in the afternoon and Watts began presenting the case for the defense. Court adjourned shortly before 5:30.

When the trial resumed the next morning, the jury was read portions of Dr. R. R. Bridges's previously transcribed testimony that focused on his examination of Victoria Price following the alleged rape. The physician was ill and unable to make a personal appearance in court. Lester Carter testified next. Watts's attempts to have Carter explain how Price had engaged in consensual sexual relations with Jack Tiller shortly before making the rape charges were repeatedly squelched by Judge Callahan. When Watts tried to state the purpose of the testimony for the record, Callahan cut him off, insisting, "It is just of such character and so patently illegal I don't think it is proper for you to state your purpose." Watts persisted. "If the court please, we are not offering this testimony now on the issue of the woman's credibility, but undertaking to offer it for the purpose of accounting for a physical state of affairs." Callahan remained unmoved. "I am through, and I sustain the objection."[39]

Under Knight's cross-examination, Carter conceded that he "clumb" off the train following the fight with the black youths, leaving Price and Ruby Bates behind in the gondola.[40] Seeking to exploit a tactic that had worked so effectively when he had examined Ruby Bates during Patterson's trial before Judge Horton, Knight bore in on Carter about where the witness had acquired the clothes he was wearing. Carter, however, proved to be a more formidable challenge for the Lieutenant Governor than was Bates.

Q: [MR. KNIGHT]   I believe you testified Mr. Brodsky had given you the clothes you had on?...
A: [LESTER CARTER]   No sir, he didn't give me any clothes.
Q: I don't mean the same clothes—
A: These are the trousers I have had on at every trial.
Q: All right.
A: I can't wear a bathing suit down here.[41]

Carter, who contributed little of substance in light of Callahan's restrictive rulings, was followed to the witness stand by Haywood Patterson. Leibowitz conducted the direct examination, during which Patterson steadfastly maintained his innocence and flatly denied Golden's claim that he had made an admission of guilt. As was his wont, Leibowitz did his best to underscore the fantastic nature of the rape charge through his questioning. "I am going to ask you if you would have dared under any circumstances to ride along with two white women on an open car, along that railroad, by all these stations and all these houses, by these roads,—would have dared to rape a white woman on that car in view of people along that railroad?"[42] Although an objection to the question was sustained, Patterson's answer did not really matter. On cross-examination, solicitor Hutson, who "blustered and stormed about" while displaying "obvious scorn and disbelief,"[43] attempted to impeach Patterson by recalling his Scottsboro trial testimony, where he stated that he had seen all of the defendants except his three friends from Chattanooga rape Price and Bates. Leibowitz protested that the Scottsboro trial was a nullity in light of the Supreme Court's conclusion that Patterson and his codefendants lacked effective counsel, but Callahan allowed Hutson's questions.[44]

Later that day and into the next, Olen Montgomery, Willie Roberson, Ozie Powell, and Andy Wright testified in Patterson's defense and professed their own innocence. The defense rested toward the middle of the afternoon. The lawyers then readied their closing arguments.

Solicitor Hutson not only argued, he "roared" at the jurors. "Don't go out and quibble over the evidence," he exhorted. "Get it done quick. His voice rose to a crescendo as he choked back a sob evoked by his own eloquence."[45] In making his impassioned call for Patterson's conviction he reminded the jurors that they would have to go home and confront their neighbors after announcing their verdict. "He pleaded for a sentence of death lest 'the white women of this glorious state have to arm themselves with six-shooters around their middles in order to protect the sacred parts of their bodies.'"[46] He demanded justice on behalf of Victoria Price. "'She fights for the womanhood of Alabama,' he shouted."[47]

Clarence Watts adopted a contrasting style. Calm and deliberate, the Huntsville attorney reminded the jurors that "I am your friend and neighbor." He assured the panel that "I have never stood before a jury and defended a man I believed guilty of an attack."[48] Whereas Hutson had asked for a verdict to protect the women of Alabama, Watts stressed the need to protect the innocent. "It takes courage to do the right thing in the face of public clamor for the wrong thing, but when justice is not administered fairly, governments disintegrate and there is no protection for any one, man or woman, black or white."[49]

Thomas Knight argued last. Like Watts, Knight adopted a conversational tone before the jurors. He was brief and to the point. His argument summarized the evidence supporting Patterson's guilt. He asked the jury to act on the evidence, to return a guilty verdict, and impose punishment of death.[50] Evening had arrived. Judge Callahan asked the jurors whether they would rather retire until morning or return after dinner to receive their instructions. Eerily reminiscent of Solicitor Hutson's admonition to "[g]et it done quick," one panel member responded, "Let's come back tonight and get it over with."[51] Others concurred. Callahan declared a recess until 7:30 P.M.

Judge Callahan began his charge after dinner. Although recognizing that "there is no claim by the defendant...that the prosecuting witness, Victoria Price, gave her consent, but on the contrary...the defense is made that the defendant did not have sexual intercourse with the prosecutrix,"[52] Callahan nevertheless told the jury, as he had in prior cases: "Where a woman charged to have been raped, as in this case, is a white woman, there is a very strong presumption under the law that she will not and did not yield voluntarily to intercourse with the defendant, a negro, and this is true whatever station in life the prosecutrix may occupy, whether she is the most despised, abandoned or ignorant woman of the community, or a spotless virgin from a home of luxury and learning."[53] Contrary to Judge Horton's interpretation, he instructed the jurors that "[t]he law does not require that [Victoria Price] be corroborated by some other witness" to sustain a conviction for rape.[54] Before allowing the jurors to retire for the night, he told them that they had two punishment options if they found Patterson guilty: death or a term of imprisonment of at least ten years or "any number of years above ten that you feel that the evidence justifies you in fixing."[55]

The jury began deliberating at 8:30 on the morning of January 23. As the jurors discussed Patterson's fate, jury selection began for Clarence Norris's trial. Although a panel of twelve white men was chosen to hear the evidence against Norris by day's end, they would not sit in judgment of him. Attorneys for both sides and Judge Callahan later agreed to postpone Norris's and the other defendants' trials because Dr. Bridges's continuing illness rendered him unavailable as a witness.[56] Late that afternoon Patterson's jury delivered word that it was ready to report. The jurors were escorted into the courtroom at almost precisely 5:00. They had arrived at a verdict.[57]

Patterson was guilty as charged. Then came the stunning sentencing decision. His punishment was not fixed at death, but rather 75 years imprisonment. The mixed verdict brought different reactions. The *Montgomery Advertiser* focused on the sentencing verdict. "Negro Is Saved From Chair By Jury At Decatur," read its page 1 headline.[58] Other Alabama newspapers likewise featured the prison sentence in headlines.[59] The *Birmingham Age Herald* reported, perhaps hyperbolically, that Patterson's case "represents probably the first time in the history of the South that a Negro has been convicted of a charge of rape upon a white woman and has been given less than a death sentence."[60] Seated at counsel table, prosecutors Knight, Hutson, and Bailey were "visibly stunned" when the foreman announced the sentencing decision.[61] Chalmers, the chair of the Scottsboro Defense Committee (SDC), concurred that the prosecution was "[s]hocked by Patterson's seventy-five year sentence."[62] Victoria Price said, "I don't think it was enough punishment."[63] The *New York Times* editorialized:

Once more a white Alabama jury has brought in a verdict of guilty in the case of the Negro youth Haywood Patterson, charged with attacking a white woman. But this time something—a lingering doubt regarding the evidence, a twinge of conscience, fear of an irrevocable act—impelled the jury to fix a sentence, not of death, but of imprisonment for seventy-five years. As three previous juries had voted for a death sentence, this is a sign that the temper of Alabama juries has at least slightly changed. Whether because of the manner in which the defense was this time conducted, or because the years of outside criticism and the attitude of the Supreme Court have at last begun to take effect, the Scottsboro boys can now regard their case as not altogether hopeless.[64]

In contrast, others decried the injustice of the guilty verdict. "The conviction is an outrage," proclaimed the Scottsboro Defense Committee, and a "challenge to the conscience of the nation."[65] Norman Thomas, former candidate for president of the Socialist Party, charged that Patterson's conviction stemmed from "popular hysteria. It is not supported by the evidence."[66] Leibowitz acknowledged that the verdict "is the first break we have gotten." But he also vowed to fight it "until hell freezes over."[67] Patterson told Judge Callahan as he stood for the formal pronouncement of sentence, "I am not guilty and I do not think justice has been done."[68] He later told Leibowitz, "I had rather die than spend another day in jail for something I didn't do."[69]

The sentence apparently stemmed from the convictions of the jury foreman, John Burleson, a tea-totaling farmer and devout Methodist who had serious reservations about Patterson's guilt. He thought Price's testimony was incredible. Unable to dissuade his fellow jurors from voting to convict, Burleson reportedly prevailed on them to "compromise" by sentencing Patterson to prison instead of death.[70] "It is difficult for Northerners to believe that the verdict of seventy-five years represented any kind of victory for the defense," observed a contributor to *The New Republic*. "But when one realizes that the state in its plea never suggested an alternative for the death penalty...and that the Judge broadly hinted as to the necessity of the extreme penalty, the compromise becomes all the more remarkable." Yet the remarkable nature of the verdict was not cause to celebrate. "[T]he fact that hits you between the eyes is that these Scottsboro boys have had the benefit of expert legal defense, pitiless publicity and the confidence of a large part of the civilized world, and...they have been unable to obtain the most elementary justice."[71]

On January 24, with the other trials postponed and their business in Decatur concluded for the time being, Haywood Patterson and his eight companions were readied for transportation back to the Birmingham jail. They were placed in the back seat of police cars, handcuffed to one another in groups of three, and began the 90 mile trip to the south at 1:00 P.M. Morgan County Sheriff J. Street Sandlin drove the middle car. He was accompanied in the front seat by Deputy Ed Blalock. In the back seat of the car, directly behind Sandlin, Roy Wright was handcuffed to Clarence Norris, seated in the middle, who in turn was handcuffed to Ozie Powell. As the caravan proceeded down the Bee Line Highway and began descending Lacon Mountain, just a mile and a half from the Cullman County line, the car that Sheriff Sandlin was driving careened wildly, its siren wailing, and then screeched to a halt on the roadside. A shot rang out. Deputy Blalock stumbled out of the car, bleeding profusely from a knife wound to his throat. Ozie Powell slumped in the back seat, a bullet fired from Sheriff Sandlin's gun lodged in his head. State Highway Patrolman J. T. Bryant, in the car to the rear, rushed to give aid. Lieutenant Governor Knight, whose car was at the end of the caravan, directed his driver to take Blalock immediately to the nearby Cullman hospital. The cars containing the prisoners continued to Birmingham, where Powell was given over to a hospital and the other defendants delivered to jail.

Beyond the obvious wounds suffered by Blalock and Powell, what had happened remained unclear. As the facts began to emerge, outside observers and newspaper writers rushed to give definition to the dramatic turn of events. Telegrams and letters "from the East, West, North and as far South as Kentucky" flooded the Governor's office expressing outrage at Powell's shooting.[72] From New York City, Socialist Party leader Norman Thomas accused Alabama law enforcement officers of displaying "[p]assion, prejudice and incompetence" in their handling of the prisoners.[73] Congressman Arthur Miller of Chicago asked that "a thorough investigation" be made of the shooting, while International Labor Defense representatives decried the "dastardly attack" made on Powell and the "lynch spirit" responsible for it. A New York City organization, the Federal Negro Theater Local City Projects Council, telegrammed, "We condemn murderous assault on Ozie Powell innocent victim of Scottsboro frameup...and demand immediate indictment of attackers." The Louisville Pen and Hammer Club argued for the "immediate, unconditional release [of the] Scottsboro boys to save their lives...[and] prosecution of sheriff for murderous assault and impeachment [of] Judge Callahan."[74]

Alabama officials fired back. Governor Graves, who ordered 50 National Guardsmen to stand ready for action in the wake of the incident, expressed resentment at accusations that inadequate precautions had been taken to safeguard Powell and the other prisoners.[75] He issued a statement declaring,

"The officers did their full duty and are to be commended for handling a most delicate and deplorable situation in an efficient manner."[76] Lieutenant Governor Knight similarly commended the officers. Responding to Norman Thomas's accusation, Knight said, "Every officer present took every possible step to assure the safe delivery of the prisoners to Birmingham. There not only was no 'passion and prejudice' displayed, but every officer tried efficiently to do his duty—and did it."[77]

Newspaper editors quickly joined the fray. The *Birmingham News* immediately opined that the law enforcement officers handled:

a desperate situation...most commendably....That the officers' defense of themselves did not go so far as it might have is a fact which is bound to reflect credit everywhere on the character of Alabama officers and law and order in this state in general, and in the highly publicized Scottsboro case in particular. At the same time, this latest act of violence on the part of some of the Scottsboro defendants should convince all their sympathizers everywhere that, whether these Negroes are guilty or innocent of the charge on which they are being tried, they are—or at least some of them are—vicious men, and not the lamb-like victims of circumstance which the more irresponsible and prejudiced champions of their cause have pretended to believe them to be.[78]

The *Birmingham Age Herald* editorialized that, "It Could Have Been Worse."

Although there are many doubtful elements in this attempted escape of some of the Scottsboro defendants, Alabama has reason to be glad that the result was no worse than the slight wounding of one officer and one defendant. In view of the tense emotions wrapped up in the case, it is fortunate that the attempt to escape was thwarted and that no one was seriously hurt.

As it happens, however, justice in Alabama should rate a bit higher than before.... [The officers'] conduct should be an answer to unjust charges that Southern officers are always quick on the trigger when Negroes accused of rape attempt to escape....

The incident also serves to show the character of the defendants....While one can urge justice for them, no one in the light of their continued conduct can believe that the Negroes are peaceful, pure-minded boys. This attack, with their previous conduct while in jail, stamps them as reckless and vicious and without regard for law.[79]

The *Montgomery Advertiser* predicted that Powell's shooting would mean that "Alabama will be stigmatized anew as a lynch State: it will be falsely charged that the prisoners were the victims of official brutality." However, the paper lamented, "This is 'just one of those things.'...Race prejudice had nothing to do with it."[80] Two days later, the Montgomery newspaper quoted appreciatively from a *Baltimore Evening Sun* editorial that concluded that Alabama could not possibly avoid criticism over the incident, no matter where the truth lay. "'Too much passion and prejudice have been aroused by the Scottsboro case to permit, henceforth, any cool, objective examination of anything connected with it. If an archangel came down from Heaven and swore to the truth of [Sheriff] Sandlin's story, there are people who would still believe that the affair was an attempt to murder Powell; and to date there are no archangels in sight.'" The *Advertiser* reiterated: "The latest episode was merely another in which this State had no other choice than to make the best of circumstances that were not of its asking. Such observers as *The Evening Sun* who try to maintain the impartial view may be assured of that."[81]

For its part, the *New York Times* refrained from blaming Alabama officials for this latest development in the Scottsboro case and appeared willing to assume that Ozie Powell bore responsibility for it. It nevertheless expressed concern about the incident's aftermath and seized the opportunity to renew its criticism of Judge Callahan for his conduct of the trials.

The rash act of Ozie Powell in stabbing a deputy sheriff who was taking him to jail has heaped new coals upon the fires of bitterness surrounding the famous Scottsboro case. It makes death sentences for all the Negroes accused with him of attacking two white women almost certain and it raises a question of the wisdom of appealing from the verdict of the jury which condemned Haywood Patterson to a life in prison.

It is probable, however, that the Negroes whose trials were indefinitely postponed after Patterson's fourth conviction could be brought back here tomorrow without danger of a lynching.

There were few indications at the court proceedings this week of the hysteria which marked the earlier trials. This is undoubtedly because the citizens of Morgan County feel reasonably sure that, with Judge W. W. Callahan presiding, there will be no miscarriage of justice as they see it.[82]

Although opinions took form and were verbalized rapidly, the facts surrounding Deputy Blalock's stabbing and Ozie Powell's shooting proved more stubborn. The accounts emerging from witnesses' statements were anything but harmonious. From the lunchroom and filling station that he operated roughly 100 yards away, G. F. Anderson noticed the car operated by Sheriff Sandlin swerve off the road and stop. When he heard a shot he sprinted toward the car and watched as the sheriff got out holding his smoking pistol. Anderson saw Blalock step out of the car from the passenger's side, holding a bloody handkerchief to his throat as a pool of blood began to form in the road. "I looked into the rear of the car and the two Negroes on the left were holding their hands above their heads. They kept repeating, 'Boss, we haven't got anything on us. You can search us, we haven't got nothing on us at all.'" Powell, seated on the right in the back of the car, was bleeding from his head. "It looked to me like a part of his forehead had been torn away."[83]

Sheriff Sandlin reported that Powell, whose left hand was handcuffed to Clarence Norris but whose right hand was free, without warning or provocation had taken a knife to Deputy Blalock's throat in a desperate escape attempt. At the same time, the sheriff said, Roy Wright, whose left hand was free, launched a knife attack against him while he struggled to maintain control over the car. As he activated the siren and brought the car to a halt, "I saw Powell get hold of Blalock's gun. I let go of Wright, pulled out my gun and fired. That ended it all."[84] Sandlin later insisted that "the whole thing was planned by some outsiders and I believe they are white. I don't believe the negroes could have plotted the attack themselves."[85]

Roy Wright denied the sheriff's accusations. "I didn't have a knife and I didn't try to cut the sheriff. I know he would have killed me instead of shooting Ocie [sic] if I had had a knife and tried to cut him." Wright also disavowed any plan to escape. "We wouldn't try to escape now that things look better for all of us," he said, in an apparent reference to Patterson's avoiding a death sentence at his trial.[86] Clarence Norris, who had been handcuffed to Roy Wright on his left and to Ozie Powell on his right in the back seat, corroborated Wright's denials and disagreed with material aspects of the sheriff's account.

Ocie [sic] and Officer Blalock had been talking about the case and about the attorneys in the case shortly before Ocie cut the officer. Ocie had sassed the officer, and the officer had slapped him.

A few minutes later Ocie reached his free hand into his pocket and got his knife. He opened it then he reached over and cut Officer Blalock's throat. That was when the trouble started.[87]

Roy Wright later elaborated on Norris's explanation, recounting that the deputies transporting the defendants to their arraignment before Judge Callahan in early January had advised them to tell the judge that they no longer wanted Leibowitz and Watts to represent them and to request court-appointed counsel. The lawyers only wanted to make "a million dollars on you and then drop you," the deputies argued. They maintained that such a move also would cause Thomas Knight to leave the case. Ultimately, the defendants were told, "it will not go so hard against you." As he, Norris, and Powell were being driven back to the Birmingham jail following Patterson's conviction, Wright continued, Sheriff Sandlin and Deputy Blalock pressed them about why they had not taken the advice they had received and fired Leibowitz and Watts.

Ozie said, "Oh, I'd rather have those lawyers than any I've ever seen," and turned to me. He then said: "Damn, what they're talking about."

The fellow that got cut was sort of turned around in his seat with his back to the windows and his left hand nearest to Powell. He slapped Ozie as soon as he had made that remark and Ozie got his knife out of his pocket and slashed at him....

With that Ozie dropped the knife to the floor of the car. The High Sheriff started blowing his siren and put his foot on the brake and stopped the car. We all threw our

hands up as the car stopped. The High Sheriff. . .pulled out his gun and pulled open the
door a little bit and pointed the gun inside the car and said:

"I'm going to get rid of all of you."

He fired one shot at Powell. Soon afterward Mr. Knight and Mr. Lawson rolled up on
the other side.[88]

Deputy Blalock's account, on the other hand, closely resembled Sheriff Sandlin's story.

Three of the Scottsboro boys were in the rear seat of our patrol car. We were coming up
Lacon Mountain about 15 miles north of Cullman. . . .

The Negroes were handcuffed together. Ocie [sic] Powell's left hand was chained to the
Negro next to him. His right hand was free.

Without saying anything Powell all of a sudden reached over and attacked me.
He stabbed me in the right side of my neck. And then again. . . .

We began shooting and some of the shots seemed to hit Powell in the head.[89]

Despite the knife attack and loss of blood, Deputy Blalock miraculously was
not critically injured. His neck wounds were sutured at the hospital and he was
allowed to go home that same day. Ozie Powell's injuries were more serious,
although he too would survive. He was operated on and bullet fragments were
removed from his brain. Newspaper reporters were at Powell's hospital bed when
he was questioned on the day of the shooting.

Ocie [sic] Powell, gaunt and muscular, suffering from shock and apparent fright, with a
bullet lodged in his skull, Friday night lay on an examination table at Hillman Hospital
and told his version of the knife attack on Deputy Blalock.

"I stabbed the white man because he was talking about killing me," the Negro said in
the presence of deputies and doctors as they worked over him.

Powell, a hollow-eyed Negro though a large-framed man, shivered as he told the story
of the knife attack and the shooting. . . .

The Negro talked incoherently about the actual attack. . . .

"The white man was talking about killing me, and I was scared," Powell said.

"I got the knife three days ago from a Negro grocery boy who delivers things to the
county jail in Decatur. . . .I don't know all his name," Powell said, "but we call him
Earnest. . . ."

"I didn't have my mind on causing any trouble," the Negro said, "but I got scared
when the white man got to talking about killing me."[90]

Samuel Leibowitz was on his way back to New York City when he learned about
the deputy's being stabbed and Powell's being shot. He quickly reversed course and
returned to Alabama to check on his clients and investigate what had happened.
Following interviews with Powell, Roy Wright, and Norris, he branded allegations
that the knifing had been part of an escape attempt as "so much poppycock."

Does the Sheriff of Morgan County claim that three Negroes shackled together in the rear seat of a rapidly moving automobile, with only two doors leading to the front compartment, with two men in that automobile armed to the teeth, this car preceded in front by an automobile carrying two other armed officers of the law and followed by still another car with armed guards and with State highway patrolmen as an escort, did attempt to escape by using a penknife?

If that is the contention of the Morgan County Sheriff, we dare say that the public will demand further enlightenment.

If it was not an attempt to escape, perhaps the Sheriff will be kind enough to give the public all of the facts that provoked this unfortunate occurrence.[91]

In the ensuing days, the delivery boy who Powell had named as providing him with the knife was identified, taken into custody for questioning, and subsequently released.[92] At Governor Graves's behest, the Alabama State Highway Patrol investigated the shooting and issued a report that accepted Sheriff Sandlin's and Deputy Blalock's claims that Powell had attacked the deputy without provocation and was shot as he struggled for control of Blalock's gun.[93] Roy Wright's role in the incident remained disputed. Morgan County Solicitor Melvin Hutson originally promised that the grand jury would hear evidence in mid-February at its next regularly scheduled session to determine whether Powell and Wright should be indicted.[94] However, the grand jury apparently was not asked to consider the case when it next met and no charges were immediately forthcoming.[95] In the meantime, Powell was released from the hospital to the medical ward at the Birmingham jail.[96] His mother traveled from Atlanta to visit him. Afterwards, she was quoted as saying that they had decided to replace Leibowitz with other counsel,[97] a report that Leibowitz dismissed as an attempt by Alabama officials to drive a wedge between him and his clients.[98] The Scottsboro defendants, now young men ranging in age from 18 to 24, were returned to solitary confinement in the Birmingham jail.[99] Their future appeared as bleak and uncertain as ever.

Public sentiment about the Scottsboro cases had waxed and waned since March 1931, when reports about Victoria Price's and Ruby Bates's allegations, the Boys' arrests, and the gathering of angry crowds in Alabama first burst into the national limelight. The ambiguous verdict in Haywood Patterson's most recent trial hinted at a softening of the antipathy directed against the defendants in the racially and politically charged incident. Conversely, Ozie Powell's attack on Deputy Blalock and the response that it evoked, in the form of a bullet to Powell's head, threatened to rekindle passions to their former heights. Another critical juncture had emerged in the ongoing controversy. The future course of public opinion now, more than ever, was vital to the cases' resolution.

From the time "the Scottsboro boys" originally achieved notoriety, through the stabbing and shooting incident in January 1936, interest groups and the media had engaged in fierce competition to shape public attitudes about the cases and stamp them with symbolism and meaning. Public discourse was carried out in other representations as well, including literature and the arts. Renowned African American author Langston Hughes, who visited the Tuskegee Institute in Alabama shortly after the original trials had concluded in Scottsboro, was distressed about the lack of interest and concern surrounding the verdicts that he perceived at this black institution. Hughes later accepted an invitation to speak at the University of North Carolina and his remarks as well as a poem inspired by the Scottsboro cases were published in late 1931 in the radical magazine, *Contempo*.[100] Hughes excoriated the South, American justice, and the silence engulfing the black community about the Boys' plight. "If these 12 million Negro Americans don't raise such a howl that the doors of Kilbee [*sic*] Prison shake until the 9 youngsters come out...then let Dixie justice (blind and syphilitic as it may be) take its course, and let Alabama's Southern gentlemen amuse themselves burning 9 young black boys till they're dead in the State's electric chair."[101] His Scottsboro-inspired poem, *Christ in Alabama,* lashed out in stark verse against Southern hypocrisy and racism.[102] In 1932 Hughes collaborated with artist Prentiss Taylor to publish *Scottsboro Limited,* comprising poems, a play, and several lithographs vividly depicting images of injustice and oppression. Hughes authored another Scottsboro-related poem in 1936, *Ballad of Ozie Powell.*[103]

Another book motivated by the cases, *Scottsboro, Alabama,* was published in Seattle in 1935. This work included 118 linoleum prints portraying racial injustices confronting African Americans throughout history, culminating with the events associated with Scottsboro.[104] Playwright John Wexley penned *They Shall Not Die,* a loosely disguised account of the Scottsboro cases, which opened on Broadway in February 1934.[105] F. Raymond Daniell, the *New York Times* correspondent who had covered the Decatur trials, believed that the play so eloquently captured scenes from the Alabama courtroom that it resembled a "dream walking," lacking only "the rich bouquet of perspiration and the acrid affluvia of stale tobacco juice." A reviewer for the NAACP was less complimentary, dismissing Wexley's play as "propaganda for the Communist party."[106]

The Scottsboro boys were also heralded in music, song, and dance. Songs from the early and mid-1930s included "The Scottsboro Boys Shall Not Die," "Song for the Scottsboro Boys," and "The Death House Blues." A blues ballad entitled "Scottsboro Boys" by folk legend Leadbelly (Huddie Ledbetter) warned, "[G]o to Alabama, and you'd better watch out."[107] Literary and visual artists as well as musicians overwhelmingly decried injustices that they identified with the Scottsboro charges and trials, and with Southern traditions more generally. The publicity that focused on and regenerated from the cases originally had been instrumental in sparing the young men's lives.[108] Following the episode in which Ozie Powell slashed Deputy Blalock's throat, however, the intense public interest

in the legal proceedings was a mixed blessing for those working on the defendants' behalf. Alabama officials were acutely aware of the relentless public scrutiny
and they could ill afford to offer concessions that could be interpreted as legiti-
mizing the criticisms arising from these outside sources.

Chalmers, the chair of the New York based SDC, understood that a favorable
resolution for the young defendants hinged on allowing Alabamians a dignified,
face-saving means of disposing of the cases. He knew that the same factors that
earlier had been responsible for sparing the boys—the intervention of the ILD,
Leibowitz's participation, and the interest shown in the cases by the Northern
press and internationally—now threatened to be impediments. "It is axiomatic,"
Chalmers maintained, "that if one intends to change society, he will not be
successful if he works from the outside."[109] He thus sought to mobilize local
support for the defendants in an effort to counterbalance the perception that
Alabama and the South could only preserve their honor against outside attack
by fighting to the bitter end. Following months of tense and often discouraging
negotiations, Chalmers's labors bore fruit. The Alabama Scottsboro Fair Trial
Committee came together in late April 1936 under the leadership of Dr. Henry
Edmonds, pastor of the Birmingham Independent Presbyterian Church and the
chair of the Alabama Commission on Interracial Cooperation.[110]

The Alabama committee included church leaders, newspaper editors, lawyers,
and other prominent state citizens. Its name had been carefully chosen; all on the
committee agreed that the young men deserved a fair trial, but many were
unwilling to embrace the proposition that they were innocent. The SDC's orien-
tation was quite different. The New Yorkers dominating that committee were
firmly convinced that the Scottsboro defendants had been falsely accused. The
contrasting views about the Boys' innocence made for an uneasy alliance between
the two groups from the outset and had important implications for how the cases
should be resolved. Whereas the Alabama committee considered strategies
centering on guilty pleas and reduced sentences, the SDC flatly rejected
compromises that would require an admission of guilt.[111]

The Alabama committee also was concerned about Leibowitz's continuing
involvement in the cases, believing that he embodied so many of the reasons
why state officials felt compelled to persist in their prosecution that he had
become an albatross around the Boys' necks. Although it ultimately relented
from demanding Leibowitz's ouster, correspondence critical of the New York
lawyer and otherwise detailing the committee's plans for working to resolve the
cases was leaked to Lieutenant Governor Knight in June. Knight wasted no time
in sharing the correspondence with the press. This untimely and awkward disclosure not only pierced the veil of secrecy under which the committee had been
operating but, predictably, infuriated Leibowitz.[112] A few days later, Chalmers
issued a press release scolding Knight for his interference with the defense efforts

and affirming that "Samuel S. Leibowitz is chief counsel for the Scottsboro boys and there is no basis for any impression to the contrary."[113]

As summer yielded to autumn and winter approached, the cases stagnated. The boys remained in solitary confinement in the Birmingham jail for such an alarmingly long time that their supporters were concerned about their psychological and physical health. The Alabama Scottsboro Fair Trial Committee worked at such a glacial pace, and with so few results and so much bickering, that it was almost a relief to Chalmers and the SDC when it disbanded in January 1937. After Clarence Watts and Alabama Attorney General Albert Carmichael engaged in an unproductive dialogue about the cases in October 1936, Chalmers believed that he could no longer sit quietly.[114] He thus opened a very public discussion about the Boys' condition and the prospects for settling the cases.

Chalmers's chosen forum was a December 9, 1936, dinner address in Asbury Park, New Jersey before the Department of Race Relations of the Federal Council of the Churches of Christ in America, an event which a *New York Times* reporter had been assigned to cover. Chalmers described how the Boys' lengthy isolation in the Birmingham jail had plunged them into "utter despair," causing him to warn that, "Justice must come soon or for some of them it may be too late." Then came his revelation. The SDC had received "'very good assurances from sources close to the prosecution' of the readiness of Alabama to drop the cases against four of the defendants." When contacted in Montgomery, Thomas Knight denied that any such agreement had been made. He said he did not know the basis of Chalmers's assertion, and reaffirmed his intention "to continue with the prosecution of the Scottsboro defendants." Chalmers maintained that Knight's denial was *pro forma* and expressed confidence in his information. He further volunteered that although he could not reveal names, the affected defendants included two who "were under age" and one who "is partly blind."[115]

Whether prompted by Chalmers's gambit or acting independently of it, Knight traveled to New York City from Alabama with Attorney General Carmichael just after Christmas for a clandestine visit with Leibowitz. Their agenda was to reach an agreeable settlement of the Scottsboro cases. According to Leibowitz's biographer, Knight broached the subject by confiding, "This damn case is costing the taxpayers of Alabama a lot of money. It is proving itself a nuisance politically and every other way. We're sick and tired of the Scottsboro boys, let's sit down and find some solution to the case that will satisfy you and allow us to save face."[116] Although he was convinced of the young men's innocence, Leibowitz also was a realist. He knew that the defendants still awaiting trial faced steep odds in Alabama and that it would be a long shot to rely once again on the U.S. Supreme Court to correct the injustices associated with their cases.

He was willing to hear Knight out, although he insisted that none of his clients would plead guilty to rape and that any settlement would have to be in all of their best interests.

Negotiations continued over the next several weeks, into February 1937. Carmichael and Leibowitz reportedly arrived at an agreement whereby Ozie Powell would be prosecuted only for the assault on Deputy Blalock; the rape charges against Clarence Norris, Charlie Weems, and Andy Wright would be dropped but each would plead guilty to assaulting the white boys on the train and essentially be sentenced to the time they already had served behind bars; all charges would be dismissed against Olen Montgomery, Willie Roberson, Eugene Williams, and Roy Wright; and Haywood Patterson would withdraw his appeal with the promise that his 75 year prison sentence would later be reduced. The SDC reluctantly acquiesced to the plan. Carmichael still had to obtain Judge Callahan's endorsement and promised to present the proposed settlement to him. Then came a disquieting breakdown of communications. Without explanation, prosecution representatives became unresponsive to defense inquiries about the agreement. Concerns that the negotiations had unraveled later proved well founded. It appeared that Judge Callahan, ever the defendants' nemesis, had scuttled the proposed settlement, insisting that he would never accept a "fifty dollar fine for rape."[117]

Lieutenant Governor Thomas E. Knight, Jr. died on May 17, 1937. He was a month shy of his 39th birthday. His death followed an extended illness that culminated in liver and kidney failure.[118] The state capitol, where his body lay in state in a casket adorned by an Alabama flag fashioned of sweet peas and carnations, was closed pending his funeral. Governor Graves lamented that "Alabama has lost her most prominent young man....He was brilliant and true....I could not have loved him more had he been my own."[119] Even in death, Knight was associated with the Scottsboro cases, as they were mentioned early and often in his obituaries. Describing him as "the special prosecutor in the Scottsboro case," the New York Times wrote that Knight's "court conduct [was] characterized by intensity, self-confidence and sincerity. Even adverse critics of the prosecutor admitted that they thought he really believed in the guilt of the Negroes."[120] Calling his death a "tragedy," the Birmingham News similarly noted that "Mr. Knight became most famous as prosecutor in the Scottsboro case." It editorialized: "There are many, including this newspaper, who did not share his position in this case; but no one, we believe, questioned his sincerity or failed to recognize the ability with which he performed his duty as prosecutor."[121]

Within a week of Knight's death, Judge Callahan announced that the trials of the remaining Scottsboro defendants would begin on July 6, 1937, in the Decatur courthouse.[122] Before Callahan acted, the New York Times had forecast that

Knight's death would facilitate the cases' resolution. "Scottsboro Case Held Near an End...Politics Now No Factor," read the caption introducing John Temple Graves's article.

Now that death has withdrawn Mr. Knight and that Mr. Leibowitz is entrusting much of the defense to an Alabama attorney, Clarence L. Watts of Huntsville, there is promise of an end to the six-year-old case.

...More and more now there is talk here of such a compromise. The sentiment of the Alabama Bar Association, although not officially expressed, is believed to be in this direction, as is that of the Alabama Scottsboro Committee, an organization of fifty or more prominent citizens, devoted originally to obtaining what was termed "an unencumbered trial."

...The people of Alabama are weary of the Scottsboro case to the point of a very genuine apathy now toward the disposition of it. More than anything else, they want an end to it. It is of no political value to anybody any more and in that fact there is much promise.[123]

Alabama newspapers not only printed rumors of an impending compromise,[124] some actively promoted one. Chalmers had succeeded in winning over Grover Cleveland Hall, the editor of the *Montgomery Advertiser,* who for years had supported the Boys' prosecution. Hall now lobbied for a settlement of the cases in an editorial that was reproduced in several other Alabama papers. In his editorial, entitled "Lay Down This Body of Death," Hall advocated bringing an end to the cases. "Nothing can be gained," he argued, "by demanding the final pound of flesh."[125] Two days later, on June 14, the Alabama Supreme Court announced its decision affirming Haywood Patterson's conviction and 75-year prison sentence. Although he did not author the opinion, Associate Justice Thomas Knight, father of the late former prosecutor and Lieutenant Governor, joined the court's decision.[126]

Leibowitz was not surprised to learn that the Alabama Supreme Court had found no error in Patterson's trial. His only comment regarding the decision was, "[W]e're going to the United States Supreme Court." When asked about the July 6 trials scheduled in the other cases, he said simply, "[W]e'll be there."[127] All the while, reports circulated that the trials would never take place because a settlement was imminent.

As the heat built to suffocating intensity in the first week of July in northern Alabama, hopes for a compromise began to fade. On July 5, Judge Callahan insisted that he "knew nothing" about a pending settlement and ordered the eight defendants to be transported from Birmingham to Decatur for the opening of court the next morning.[128] The following day, in a nearly deserted courtroom, Clarence Norris and Charlie Weems were arraigned on the indictments returned in November 1935 by the Jackson County grand jury—a body selected in conformance with *Norris v. Alabama*—and Clarence Watts entered a plea of not guilty to them. Norris's trial was scheduled to begin on July 12, and Weems's on July 15. Callahan announced a plan to conduct two trials a week until all of the defendants' cases were resolved. Morgan County Solicitor Melvin Hutson dismissed rumors of a compromise. "I know nothing about a proposition to settle these cases on a basis of assault as carried by some of the newspapers," he said. "These defendants are guilty of rape or nothing. If they are guilty of rape, they should be punished as the law directs; and if they are not guilty, they should be acquitted by a jury."[129]

And so jury selection began on schedule in Clarence Norris's trial. One black man was among the 35 prospective jurors in the regular venire, and two more were in the supplemental venire required under Alabama law for capital cases. None survived to pass judgment in the case. One was disqualified because he opposed the death penalty and the prosecution struck the other two as the venire was whittled to the final panel.[130] For the third time, Norris's fate would be decided by an all white jury, amidst "the cries of babies and the whir of electric fans in the sweltering court room with its Jim Crow spectators' section, and its separate drinking fountains for white and black."[131]

To no one's surprise, the first witness for the prosecution was Victoria Price. Making her ninth appearance before a jury, Price was "modishly" dressed, wearing a checked frock with red flowers and a wide-brimmed straw hat.[132] Her story was familiar. She identified Norris as one of the black youths who had stormed into the gondola in which she and Ruby Bates were riding. Ordering the whites to "unload," Norris and several others proceeded to rape her while she was held at knifepoint. Price was considerably less decisive on cross-examination. She cited the lapse of more than six years since the incident for her imperfect memory and the confusion of having testified in numerous trials to explain inconsistencies between her present narrative and earlier versions of the event. After much wrangling, Leibowitz was allowed an answer to his question of whether she had made up the rape story "to cover your own violation of the law in going to Chattanooga with a man for immoral purposes."[133] Her response was a defiant "No!"[134] Then, employing a new tactic that may have been designed to shame the otherwise shameless Price, Leibowitz summoned Mrs. Emma Bates, Ruby Bates's mother, to stand before the witness to be identified. Furious about this staged confrontation, Price stood by her story that she had gone to Chattanooga in search of work and snapped, "Ruby Bates asked me to go with her."[135]

Judge Callahan continued his jousting with Leibowitz during Price's cross-examination. At one point, he warned the lawyer against overreaching but then with mock charity excused him, to the titters of the courtroom audience, "because I realize that you are young and inexperienced."[136] The defense later took a new tack and asked witnesses to describe Price's reputation in the community. Their opinion, in a word, was that her reputation was "bad." A former

Huntsville deputy sheriff testified that he would not believe Price even if she were under oath and had sworn on a stack of Bibles. Clarence Watts subsequently told the jury during his summation that "there's not a white man in Alabama that would convict another white man on [Price's] testimony."[137]

The prosecution produced several additional witnesses, as it had in prior trials, who testified about seeing the fight between the black youths and the white youths as the train steamed between Stevenson and Paint Rock. Some of the witnesses claimed to have seen the blacks in the company of the two white women who later accused them of rape. A deputy sheriff testified that Norris had discussed the rape charges with him and "pointed out the rest of the eight boys and accused them of it but denied it himself."[138] Orville Gilley, who had corroborated Price's account of the rapes in trials conducted in late 1933, did not testify. The State rested its case late in the afternoon of July 13.

The life span of the Scottsboro cases had exceeded that of some of the material witnesses, including Dr. R. R. Bridges. Dr. Bridges had examined Price in Scottsboro shortly after the reported rapes and had reported several facts about Price's physical condition—including normal respiration and heart rates, insignificant scratches or bruising, and finding a modest amount of immotile spermatozoa in her vagina—that, according to the defense, belied her story. The doctor's testimony from a prior trial was read to Norris's jury, as were portions of the previously recorded testimony of Lester Carter. As in prior trials conducted before Judge Callahan, the jury would not hear Carter's account of his and Jack Tilley's recent liaisons with Ruby Bates and Victoria Price. Norris's jury did hear Carter's recollection that Price had exclaimed while in the Scottsboro jail following the alleged attack that she and Bates had tried to escape from the train when it pulled into the Paint Rock station, "but there was so damn many men there we couldn't get away."[139] The defense wrapped up its case with little additional fanfare. "It was an old, old story for...Leibowitz,"[140] who knew that his client's fate again hinged almost exclusively on the weight of Price's testimony.

The rhetoric of the lawyers' closing arguments stirred the sultry courtroom following the largely dispassionate reading from trial transcripts and the witnesses' testimony. Calling Price's assailants "fiends from hell,"[141] Assistant Attorney General Thomas Lawson reviewed the evidence and asked the jurors to dispatch Norris to the electric chair as "a warning to other rapists and a protection for the womanhood of this state."[142] In response, Clarence Watts, after proudly noting his own Southern heritage, called on his fellow Alabamians to demonstrate their evenhandedness and acknowledge the flimsiness of Price's tale by turning Norris loose. Leibowitz also hammered at Price's credibility, labeling her story a frame-up and a series of "damnable lies," but alternatively suggesting that she was "more to be pitied than blamed."[143] The veteran lawyer compared Price's testimony to "an eggshell—hollow in the inside, and easily broken."[144]

Without wavering about Norris's claimed innocence, Leibowitz subtly attempted to suggest that, at a minimum, the case did not warrant capital punishment. Alabama law entrusted juries with broad sentencing discretion in rape cases, he argued, specifically to allow distinctions to be made between assaults involving a "train-riding bum and a decent woman."[145]

Morgan County Solicitor Melvin Hutson had the last word. Not to be outdone, he assured the jury that "I know [Norris] is guilty, and I think Mr. Leibowitz knows he is guilty"—a representation that infuriated Leibowitz and occasioned his immediate motion for a mistrial, which Judge Callahan just as promptly denied.[146] Hutson urged the jurors to return a death sentence against Norris, saying that he wished the penalty "could be 'written in golden letters across the Alabama sky,' so that outsiders never again would meddle with her affairs."[147] The courtroom had grown so stifling in the midsummer heat that Judge Callahan had stepped down from his elevated bench to be closer to the floor. After Hutson finished his argument the judge ordered a recess until the next morning, when he would deliver his two and one-half hour charge to the jury.

The jury began deliberating at 10:50 on the morning of July 15. It reached a verdict less than four hours later, completing its work more rapidly than any jury since the original trials in Scottsboro. Clarence Norris sat impassively as he was found guilty of rape and sentenced to death.[148] Leibowitz vowed to appeal. "I'm in this thing until hell freezes over," he said. "I'll take the case on twenty trips to the Supreme Court if necessary."[149] On receiving news of Norris's death sentence in London, where he was attending to other business, Chalmers, the head of the SDC, broke down and cried.[150] From New York, the SDC issued a statement attributing Norris's conviction to "race prejudice," rather than credible evidence. "[M]illions of people all over the world are shocked and horrified at the verdict," said Roger Baldwin in the statement, as he called on "all persons to rally to the defense and intensify the fight for the liberty of these youths."[151]

An exhausted Clarence Watts, who had wilted under the oppressive heat and the strain of Norris's trial, informed Judge Callahan that he was too ill to continue. He returned to Huntsville to convalesce. Watts's unavailability caused a postponement of Charlie Weems's trial, which was to have ensued on the heels of Norris's. It was not immediately clear whether Andy Wright's case would begin on time the following Monday. With the defense's knowledge that few legal issues remained in play that were likely to evoke the U.S. Supreme Court's intervention, and with State representatives weary from the financial and political toll that the trials continued to exact, rumors persisted that the remaining cases would be settled.[152]

When Andy Wright's trial date arrived on July 19, Clarence Watts remained ill and was unable to participate. Leibowitz and his associate from New York City,

William Richter, appeared at Wright's side and announced that they were ready to go forward. Reflecting on Clarence Norris's recently completed trial, F. Raymond Daniell of the *New York Times* had written, "Like actors in a revival of an old play, the characters in Alabama's famous Scottsboro case came into court this week, repeated their familiar lines with the same old gestures, and the curtain dropped on the expected denouement, a verdict of guilty and a sentence of death. What changes there were in characters, scenery and atmosphere were superficial ones."[153] Few observers expected a different sequence of events or outcome in Wright's trial. Thus, many were surprised when prosecutors announced that the State was withdrawing its quest for the death penalty in exchange for the defense's willingness to forgo the larger special venire required for capital cases, a deal Leibowitz later described as "like being asked to swap a turkey for a horse."[154] Assistant Attorney General Thomas Lawson explained that Wright was "one of the younger Negroes" involved in the case and was "not regarded by the state as a leader of the attacks." Lawson remained mum about whether the State would refrain from seeking death sentences in the other scheduled trials.[155]

Speculation continued that at least some of the cases would be settled short of a trial. The *New York Times* reported that prosecutors had advised Victoria Price that she could recant her accusations without fear of being charged with perjury, an overture that did not diminish her resolve to keep telling her story. The *Times* further indicated that a knowledgeable source had "hinted...that an important announcement would be made before the end of the week regarding the disposition of" several of the outstanding cases.[156] In the meantime, after the lone black member of the venire was excused, an all-white jury was impaneled for the trial of Andy Wright.[157]

Other than the State's decision not to seek the death penalty, little distinguished Wright's trial from previous ones. Victoria Price stuck fast to her claim that she had been raped despite being confronted by Leibowitz with numerous inconsistencies between her present testimony and prior sworn versions of her account. Judge Callahan and Leibowitz continued to clash as Callahan enforced his ruling that Price's conduct and whereabouts before the March 25 train ride during which she allegedly was raped were irrelevant. Leibowitz had Dr. Bridges's testimony read to the jury, imploring the jury to pit the objective facts revealed by the physician's examination against Price's story that she had just been gang-raped by a half dozen assailants. Late in the afternoon of July 20, Solicitor Bailey demanded Wright's conviction, telling the jury that the rape laws were "designed to protect the virtue of our women, regardless of their reputation or station." He was followed by Solicitor Hutson, who asked the jury to impose a prison sentence "equal to life imprisonment," which he suggested would be in the range of 50 to 75 years. The jury returned its verdict the following day. It answered the prosecution's call and then some, finding Wright guilty as charged and sentencing him to 99 years in prison.[158]

With Norris sentenced to death and Andy Wright handed a prison term even longer than the State had requested, Leibowitz's frustrations boiled over as Charlie Weems's trial began. Prosecutors had dropped their quest for a death sentence for Weems, just as they had done for Andy Wright. Nevertheless, Leibowitz's anger was evident during his cross-examination of Price, who immediately became entangled in a maze of contradictions and began shouting defiantly at the defense lawyer. Judge Callahan intervened, warning Leibowitz that, "It is not too late for the court to enforce its orders. Your manner is going to lead to trouble, Mr. Leibowitz, and you might as well get ready for it."[159] Out of the jury's presence, Leibowitz moved to have Price's "perjured" testimony struck from the record, which Callahan impatiently dismissed as "a grandstand play."[160] Lester Carter testified for the defense that Price had told him while they were both locked up in the Scottsboro jail that "There was no rape," yet had asked him to back up her story so she would not get into "trouble over riding a train."[161] The trial moved along rapidly and the presentation of evidence gave way to the attorneys' closing arguments.

As Leibowitz faced the twelve white jurors he startled the courtroom by predicting, and all but demanding Weems's conviction. "I don't expect an acquittal," he declared. "If Melvin Hutson will ask for 50 years, the verdict will be 99 or something like that."[162] Leibowitz's remarks followed Solicitor H.G. Bailey's argument, which had dwelled at length on the outside influences associated with the case. "I'm sick and tired of this sanctimonious hypocrisy," Leibowitz shouted. "It isn't Charlie Weems on trial in this case. It's a Jew lawyer and New York State put on trial here by the inflammatory remarks of Mr. Bailey."[163] Characterizing Bailey's summation as a "song of hate, coated with prejudice and hypocrisy,"[164] Leibowitz branded as "poppycock" the suggestion that blacks received the same measure of justice as whites in Alabama. He recounted how he had examined more than a thousand prospective jurors from Morgan County, not one of whom admitted to harboring racial prejudices, only to be told repeatedly by whites, outside of court, that "a Negro did not have a chance" of beating a charge of raping a white woman. A vexed Judge Callahan paced the floor as Leibowitz addressed the jury, while Assistant Attorney General Thomas Lawson stalked out of the courtroom.[165]

Solicitor Hutson rose to respond. "How would you like to have your daughter on that train with nine Negroes in a car?" he thundered.[166] He accused Leibowitz of shamelessly posturing for the press, to the prejudice of his client. "If he hasn't premeditatedly tried to convict that negro for publicity purposes, then I don't know what I'm talking about."[167] The defense lawyer, Hutson continued, had "insulted not only the members of the jury but the citizenry of this county."

The evidence required a guilty verdict, he insisted, and he invited the jurors to sentence Weems to as many as a thousand years in prison.[168] The jurors heard Judge Callahan's instructions and began deliberating shortly before 2:30 on July 23. They announced their verdict the following morning. Weems was guilty of raping Victoria Price. His punishment was 75-year imprisonment.

Weems's jury finished its work, and Judge Callahan accepted its verdict and discharged its members, on Saturday, July 24. Few spectators were in the courtroom when the rest of the Scottsboro cases suddenly cascaded to a resolution, bearing out the weeks of murmured predictions that a settlement would preempt at least some of the scheduled trials.

Ozie Powell was brought out first. He conferred briefly with Leibowitz and then stood before Judge Callahan, who read the indictment charging Powell with assault with intent to commit murder for the January 1936 slashing of Deputy Blalock. Callahan asked Powell for his plea and Leibowitz instructed his client, "Don't plead guilty unless you are guilty." Powell indicated that he was. "I'm guilty of cutting the deputy," he said. At that, Solicitor Hutson announced that the State would *nolle prosequi,* or dismiss, the outstanding rape indictment. Hutson urged Judge Callahan to impose the maximum sentence on Powell for the assault charge, 20 years, and the judge obliged.[169] Powell later was transported from Decatur to Montgomery's Kilby Prison to begin service of his sentence, along with Andy Wright, Charlie Weems, and Clarence Norris (the lone defendant under sentence of death). Haywood Patterson already was incarcerated at Kilby, pursuant to his earlier conviction and 75-year sentence.[170]

Then, in what Leibowitz later described as "nothing short of a miracle,"[171] and "probably the greatest victory in the life of the Negro people of America since the War Between the States,"[172] Thomas Lawson approached the bench and quietly told Judge Callahan that the rape indictments against the remaining four defendants—Olen Montgomery, Willie Roberson, Eugene Williams, and Roy Wright—were being *nolle prosequied.* Leibowitz already was making his way out of court as the announcement was made. He presented the release order to a jailer and hurried the four bewildered young men, who had no inkling that their freedom was imminent, into waiting cars that sped north under police escort to the state line and beyond. "Thus," said the *New York Times,* "in a tangle of inconsistencies, ended the famous Scottsboro case."[173] The *Birmingham News* headline read, "Four of Negroes in Attack Cases Given Freedom."[174] The *Age-Herald,* Birmingham's other paper, adopted a different perspective, one shared by the many Alabamians who had grown weary and disenchanted with the cancerous proceedings. Its headline all but sighed with relief: "Alabama Courts Free of 'Scottsboro' Cases."[175]

In a lengthy statement, the "Scottsboro case prosecution staff" explained the decision to grant four of the defendants their outright release.

The prosecution is convinced beyond any question of a doubt, after going through eleven trials of the Scottsboro cases, that the defendants who have been tried are guilty of raping Mrs. Victoria Price in the gondola car, as she has recited upon the witness stand. Her testimony is corroborated by reputable witnesses so as, in our opinion, to convince any fair-minded man that these defendants did participate in throwing these white boys off the gondola car and raping Mrs. Victoria Price.

But, after careful consideration of all the testimony, every lawyer connected with the prosecution is convinced that the defendants, Willie Roberson and Olen Montgomery, are not guilty.

The doctor who examined Willie Roberson the day after the commission of the crime states that he was sick, suffering with a severe venereal disease; and that in his condition it would have been very painful for him to have committed that crime; and that he would not have had any inclination to commit it. He has told a very plausible story from the beginning: That he was in a box car and knew nothing about the crime.

Olen Montgomery was practically blind and has told a plausible story, which has been unshaken all through the litigation, which put him some distance from the commission of the crime. The state is without proof other than the prosecutrix as to his being in the gondola car, and we feel that it is a case of mistaken identity. Mr. Bailey, Mr. Lawson and Mr. Hutson all entertain the same view as to these two Negroes, and in view of the doubt generated by the fact that their physical condition was as stated above, the fact that two men were seen in a box car by a disinterested witness, which tends to corroborate Willie Roberson, we feel that the policy of the law and the ends of justice would not justify us in asking a conviction in these two cases.

Two of the defendants were juveniles at the time this crime was committed. According to a careful investigation by the attorney-general's office, we are convinced that at the time of the actual commission of this crime one of these juveniles was 12 years old and the other one was 13; and while they were in the gondola car when the rape was committed, counsel for the state think that in view of the fact they have been in jail for six and a half years the ends of justice would be met at this time by releasing these two juveniles, on condition that they leave the state, never to return.[176]

The State's exit from the cases was anything but clean. One of the defendants (Clarence Norris) remained under sentence of death, although it was commonly believed that the governor in due course would commute the sentence to a term of imprisonment; three of the defendants (Haywood Patterson, Charlie Weems, and Andy Wright) were serving prison sentences that ranged between 75 and 99 years; the rape case against Ozie Powell had been dropped following his conviction and 20-year prison sentence for assaulting Deputy Blalock; and charges had been dropped altogether against four of the defendants (Olen Montgomery, Willie Roberson, Eugene Williams, and Roy Wright), although each already had spent six and a half years behind bars. Reaction to these incongruous outcomes was mixed.

Victoria Price's hometown newspaper, the *Huntsville Times,* bid an editorial "Good Riddance" to "these destructive, hate-breeding gutter cases." Its sympathies clearly lay with the State, which had "suffered bitterly" because of a "dirty campaign by the International Labor Defense and other defense organizations to vilify and abuse the judicial system and processes of justice of Alabama." It openly expressed "contempt and dislike" for Leibowitz. As to the four "negroes [who] got their freedom,...New York is welcome to them."[177] The *Tuscaloosa News* sounded a similar note. "The people of Alabama are exceedingly tired of seeing this case used as a sounding board for political bombast in the East and as a money-raising tear-jerker for radical elements throughout the world."[178]

The *Birmingham News* editorialized, "At Last We Are Rid of the Scottsboro Case," concluding that "a great and troublesome burden has been lifted from Alabama." It hailed the resolution of the cases as "a triumph of common sense and moderation." It nevertheless was troubled by the four cases ending in convictions for rape and called for the governor to make an "adjustment" in them: "Either all nine Negroes were guilty or none was."[179] The *Birmingham Age-Herald* similarly lauded the dismissals granted to four of the defendants, but expressed "renewed doubt of the guilt of those now under conviction....It is not too much for those who believe in the innocence of all the defendants to hope that at length, under the effect of this settlement and the quieting of feeling which it should be permitted naturally to produce, a satisfactory disposition of the remaining cases may be achieved." It warned, however, that "provocative agitation to that end likely would have the reverse effect."[180]

The *Chattanooga Times,* which at the outset of the cases had shown little sympathy for the defendants, including the four who called Chattanooga home, now voiced a different opinion. "There is not a sadder story in the annals of American jurisprudence than that of the Negroes who for the past six years have lived in the shadow of the electric chair," intoned the newspaper. It had little enthusiasm for the "compromise [which] involves a demand for the slow death of the defendants through long prison sentences instead of quick death by electrocution." There is "every reason to believe," the editorial concluded, "either that the Negroes are not guilty...or that the doubt is too great to warrant conviction."[181]

Stephen Roddy, the first Chattanooga lawyer involved in defending the boys in the original Scottsboro trials—whose dubious assistance resulted in the Supreme Court's insistence in *Powell v. Alabama* that due process of law requires minimally adequate representation in capital cases—had died by the time the cases resulted in this uneasy resolution. However, George Chamlee, the Chattanooga attorney enlisted by the ILD and who ably assisted Leibowitz during the early Decatur trials, remained active. Chamlee ventured that "[t]he Scottsboro cases were the greatest miscarriage of justice that ever disgrace[d] a great state in 100 years." He concluded that "Attorney General Lawson has rendered the state of Alabama a real service in his action by dismissing four of these nine colored boys, and now Gov. Graves ought to pardon all the other five and release them from prison."[182]

For the *New York Times,* John Temple Graves observed that "Southern reaction to the Scottsboro case compromise is as varied as the fates meted out to the defendants." Many Alabamians "describe the case as a horrible example of the evils of outside interference and of Communist efforts to capitalize upon racial and sectional feeling." And many citizens remained "strongly convinced that the four Negroes who were released should have been prosecuted." However, outside of Alabama, "Southern comment seems generally to praise the compromise and to expect Gubernatorial clemency for the Negroes left with life or death sentences....Nowhere in the South, apparently, is there praise for the Northern groups and organizations which have interfered in the case, even though there are many here who admit that, without this interference, the defendants would have been dead and buried long ago."[183]

Writing in *The Nation,* Morris Shapiro called the settlement a "farcical finale which left the state in the anomalous position of providing only 50 per cent protection for the 'flower of Southern womanhood.'" He maintained that "Alabama justice has yielded to expediency in the Scottsboro case. No other explanation is possible." He then proceeded to offer his own, cynical explanation for the conflicted posture of the "case which has become a stench in the nostrils of the more literate minority of" state residents. "After six and a half years the high-pitched, screechy voice of Victoria Price has begun to sound a little hollow and tinny to 'Buster' Lawson, whose eyes are on the attorney-generalship of Alabama. If it weren't for that latter fact nine Negroes instead of four might be free today."[184]

Chalmers, of the SDC, considered the resolution an unacceptable "double cross"[185] and vowed to keep fighting to obtain the freedom of the incarcerated youths. The SDC compiled editorial reactions from newspapers throughout the country that criticized or were skeptical about the fractured compromise, publishing them in a pamphlet entitled, *4 Free, 5 in Prison—on the same evidence.*[186] For example, the *Akron Journal* asked, "Why Only Four?" It speculated that, "Perhaps Alabama has good reasons for not making the dismissal unanimous. The nation would be interested to know what they are." The *Camden Courier* proclaimed, "The State of Alabama comes off without honor or even dignity in the 'settlement' of the Scottsboro case....If [Victoria Price] is wrong about [the identity of] two, why is it assumed she is right about the seven others?" The *Buffalo Times* charged that "the evidence against the five [*sic*] now freed was exactly the same as they used to put Norris in the shadow of the electric chair. If Olen Montgomery deserves to go free, so do Patterson and Weems. And if Patterson, Norris and Weems are guilty, so is Montgomery."[187]

The reactions of the young men most directly affected by the prosecutors' action predictably were mixed, as well. On first being released, the four gaining freedom "came running out of the jail, laughing and smiling."[188] One of them exclaimed, "Gee, I haven't been so happy since I was 2 years old."[189] In contrast, as Charlie Weems stood before Judge Callahan for sentencing, just before the prosecution *nolle prosequied* the rape charges leveled against several of his companions, he told the jurist, "I didn't get a fair trial. I didn't get justice."[190] Clarence Norris, whose execution was scheduled for September 24 by Judge Callahan—a date automatically stayed by the filing of his appeal—also proclaimed his innocence when he was formally sentenced. "The jury didn't find me guilty—they just thought they did," he said. "I was convicted of a crime I never thought of committing."[191] After the other cases were settled, Norris reported from the Birmingham jail that he was "lonesome," that he had not heard from Leibowitz, and that he knew nothing about rumors that his death sentence would be commuted.[192] Andy Wright, facing a 99-year prison sentence, wrote a doleful letter on the evening that his brother and three of the other original defendants were released. The letter was published in *The Nation*, where it was captioned, "Plea from a Scottsboro Boy."

Dear Sirs: I am quite sure you all have read the outcome of my trial, and seen that I was given a miscarriage of justice. I feel it is my duty to write you all the facts of my case, which you perhaps overlooked, or perhaps it was not published in the papers. I was framed, cheated, and robbed of my freedom....

The 19th day of July, 1937, I was retried and sentenced to 99 years' imprisonment.

Now I wish to call your attention to how the judge charged the jury. He charged them in a perjury way....

How can I receive justice in the state of Alabama, especially of Morgan County, when perjury is used against me and my attorneys too? And I beg you, dear friends, readers, all stick together and work and struggle together and see that justice be brought to light. Let us all pull and struggle together and see that justice be done. It is not that I hate to go to prison, but I am innocent, and the slander is being thrown on our race of people and my family, is my reason of wanting to fight harder than ever.

ANDY WRIGHT
Montgomery, Ala., July 24[193]

While five of the young men festered in Alabama prisons, the other four were greeted by thousands of cheering supporters when they arrived by train at New York City's Pennsylvania Station. Separated by just two days from more than six years of confinement, and having never traveled outside of the South, let alone to the hub of the nation's largest city, the youths understandably were "goggle-eyed" and not a little bewildered by the raucous reception.[194] A giddy Leibowitz punched through the crown of the straw hat he was wearing, an act he explained that was designed to help purge some of the "grime of Alabama." He warned that there would be "no exploitation, no barnstorming, no theatricals of any kind" for his charges.[195] Any embarrassments or transgressions involving the liberated defendants would not only reflect adversely on them, but could damage the chances of their less fortunate colleagues to gain freedom.

Notwithstanding these ambitions, little more than three weeks passed before the four who had won their release had fallen under the wing of the entrepreneurial Reverend Thomas Harten and announced that they were no longer under Leibowitz's supervision. They appeared on stage at Harlem's Apollo Theatre as "the Scottsboro Boys."[196] They were hardly recognizable. The *Decatur Daily* described them as "[c]ompletely citified....All dress in natty new clothes and wear their hair slicked to a bright polish. Two even sport canes."[197] Earlier, they had appeared alongside Ruby Bates, Norman Thomas, Roger Baldwin, and Mrs. Ada Wright before an estimated crowd of 4,500 at New York City's Hippodrome. At that rally, Leibowitz had disclosed details of an agreement that he had reached with Alabama Attorney General Albert Carmichael and the late Lieutenant Governor Thomas Knight, Jr. that would have allowed the defendants to plead guilty to assault charges and be freed within five years. The deal fell through, Leibowitz speculated, because Judge Callahan blocked it, but he now implored Carmichael to carry it out. "Come forward like a man and a true American citizen who loves liberty and justice and fair dealing," Leibowitz cajoled, "and say to the Governor of Alabama: 'I have given my word that these boys should be given their freedom within two years, and I ask you to honor my promise.'"[198]

The SDC, in the meantime, redoubled its efforts on behalf of the five young men who remained incarcerated. Chalmers worked closely with several Alabamians, including Grover Hall, Henry Edmonds, and attorney Forney Johnston, who were committed to that same cause.[199] When the U.S. Supreme Court announced in late October, shortly after opening its 1937 Term, that it would not review Haywood Patterson's conviction,[200] it became apparent that whatever relief might be granted would have to come from the Alabama governor, and not the courts. John Temple Graves wrote that it would not be unrealistic to expect such action.

The [previous] release of the four Negroes has...set people of the State to stand the "shock" of freedom for all the rest with the exception of Ozie Powell, who is under an additional charge of a knife attack upon a deputy sheriff in January, 1936.

Another factor tending to make the thought of Executive action in behalf of the remaining defendants more popular here is that the case seems to be now closed to what was called "outside interference" and that if anything is done for the Negroes it will be the work of Alabama itself, not that of "New York Attorneys" or radicals.

Still another favorable factor, and one which involves national opinion rather than local, is the political future which Governor Bibb Graves is believed to have in mind for himself.

Forbidden under Alabama law to succeed himself as Governor, he is thought to desire some Federal post....

But the most favorable factor of all is Alabama's great weariness with the Scottsboro case and all its works.[201]

The campaign to free the imprisoned Scottsboro defendants thus focused on Governor Graves. The Alabama Committee arranged a meeting with the governor just before Christmas. Chalmers, who also was invited to attend, was ecstatic about the outcome. His contemporaneous memorandum regarding the discussion reflected that Governor Graves believed that "the position of the state is untenable with half [of the defendants] out and half in on the same charges and evidence." Although he declined to "make any promise that would look like a deal," and stated that he would not take action "as long as there was any pending appeal before the courts," he concluded: "My mind is clear on the action required to remedy this impossible position. When the cases come before me I intend to act promptly. I cannot be any clearer than that, can I?"[202] Chalmers was convinced that this "was the big break for which we had all been waiting. It had come at last."[203]

Time moved slowly as Clarence Norris's, Andy Wright's, and Charlie Weems's appeals awaited disposition in the Alabama Supreme Court. Nearly six months later, on June 9, 1938, the court affirmed Wright's and Weems's convictions.[204] The following week, in an opinion written by Justice Knight, father of the late Lieutenant Governor and long-time special prosecutor in the Scottsboro cases, the state supreme court upheld Clarence Norris's conviction and death sentence. The decision further "ordered that Friday, the 19th day of August, 1938, be and the same is hereby fixed and set for the execution of the defendant."[205] On July 5, Governor Graves commuted Norris's death sentence to life imprisonment.[206]

The next step for the incarcerated defendants lay with the Alabama Board of Pardons, a body that conducted hearings and made nonbinding recommendations to the Governor regarding executive clemency. The three-member Board was chaired by Attorney General Albert Carmichael and included State Auditor Charles McCall and Secretary of State D. H. Turner. Chalmers appeared before the Board on August 16, intent on asking its members to recommend that all five of the young men be released to the custody of the SDC. He was surprised to learn that the Board would consider only the requests made on behalf of Haywood Patterson and Ozie Powell because Norris, Weems, and Andy Wright still had time to seek further judicial review of their convictions. Chalmers did not expect a favorable recommendation from the Board. He regarded the Board's consideration as little more than an obligatory ticket to be punched on the way to the governor's office. His suspicions were reinforced early in the hearing. While pleading his case on behalf of "these boys," McCall interrupted him, icily pointing out that those remaining in custody were "men, not boys."[207]

The next day, the Board unanimously voted against recommending relief for Patterson and Powell, and formally ruled that the requests made for the three other defendants had been filed prematurely.[208] Yet Chalmers was not discouraged. To the contrary, he was more certain than ever that he would soon be escorting all of the young men from prison. At the conclusion of the Board's hearing, Governor Graves had invited Chalmers and several members of the Alabama Scottsboro Committee into his office. Then, according to Chalmers, the governor stated unambiguously, "It is my intention to parole the boys in Dr. Chalmers's custody and in the custody of his Committee. I intend to do this as soon as I have put my proposal before the Pardon Board and as soon as it has agreed to my plans."[209] When the Board of Pardons ruled against the release applications filed on behalf of Norris, Weems, and Andy Wright on October 11,[210] the time was ripe for the governor's intervention.

Governor Graves originally planned to take action on October 24 but then pushed back the anticipated favorable announcement one week. Chalmers expected that all of the young men except Ozie Powell, whose stabbing of Deputy Blalock distinguished his case from the others, would be released on October 31. He had made preparations to retrieve them and his airplane ticket from New York to Alabama was in his pocket when he received a devastating telegram on October 29. The governor had changed his mind.[211] The immediate cause of this reversal of fortune apparently was a disastrous series of meetings that the governor had with the five defendants when they were brought from prison to his office on October 28 so he could interview them. Haywood Patterson had come armed with a five-inch blade fashioned from a file, which was detected during a search just prior to his meeting with the governor. Graves found Ozie Powell belligerent, Charlie Weems and Andy Wright evasive, and Clarence Norris angry and threatening to kill Patterson over a disagreement they had had in prison. "I'll kill him," Norris reportedly pledged to the governor about Patterson. "I never furgits."[212]

Graves was repulsed and mortified by what he saw and heard. He subsequently told Grover Hall, who had been lobbying with Chalmers for the defendants' release, "They will humiliate you, Grover, they will humiliate Dr. Chalmers...and all other decent sponsors. They are anti-social, they are bestial, and they are unbelievably stupid and I do not believe they can be rehabilitated in freedom."[213] Chalmers nevertheless pressed for a meeting to ask the governor to reconsider. He and Hall were granted an audience with Graves in early November but the governor was not moved. Not easily dissuaded, Chalmers turned his sights on Washington, DC, where he first secured a letter of support from Hugo Black, the former U.S. Senator from Alabama and now an Associate Justice on the U.S. Supreme Court. He then invoked the assistance of President and Mrs. Roosevelt. Although Graves's political career in Alabama was in little apparent jeopardy, since his tenure as governor was ending in just two months, and though he had long admired the president, he evaded Roosevelt's entreaties and remained firm in his decision. He would not grant the incarcerated five their freedom.[214] He publicly announced his decision on November 15.[215]

Chalmers pleaded with Graves to reconsider. He met with the governor once more on December 12. After repeating his previously made arguments, Chalmers told Graves that if he would not make good on his earlier pledge to release the young men, Chalmers would feel obliged to make public the correspondence that documented the governor's breached promises. He recalled that Graves, who "seemed frightened," told him, "I can't go through with it. I am finished politically if I do. . . . What you can do, I do not know. You will do what it seems necessary for you to do. I, however, know very well what they can do."[216] Two weeks later, the SDC published a pamphlet, *Scottsboro: A Record of a Broken Promise,* that followed through on Chalmers's warning. The pamphlet compiled documents laying bare "a record of the negotiations with Governor Graves from the first conference throughout 1938," which corroborated Chalmers's claim that the governor had reneged on assurances that the young men would be granted their freedom. In light of Graves's failure to take action, the SDC announced that it "is now centering its efforts on a pardon campaign directed to the new Governor of Alabama, Frank Dixon, and will continue its work until complete and unconditional freedom is won for all of the defendants."[217] Several newspapers issued harsh critiques of Alabama's continuing intransigence toward the Scottsboro defendants upon the revelation of Graves's inaction,[218] although Graves still refused to budge.

The disclosure of the behind-the-scenes discussions with Governor Graves rankled and alienated several members of the Alabama Scottsboro Committee who had been working with Chalmers and the SDC on the defendants' behalf. Grover Hall, who respected Graves even though he disagreed with him, believed the action was impolitic. Hall declined to help Chalmers arrange a meeting to discuss the Scottsboro cases with Graves's successor, Frank Dixon, who took office in January 1939. Still, Chalmers believed that he "had no choice." If there was any hope of winning executive clemency, he thought it lay with Graves as he neared the end of his term rather than Dixon, who was about to begin his. "We had to take the steps that we did," said Chalmers, "and we had to suffer the consequences."[219]

Haywood Patterson, Clarence Norris, Ozie Powell, Charlie Weems, and Andy Wright bore the full brunt of the failed efforts. Although Chalmers and a few other dedicated individuals and organizations continued to work for their release, by 1939 memories of Scottsboro and the involved protagonists were fading rapidly from public consciousness. As early as Haywood Patterson's fourth trial in January 1936, which had ended in a conviction and 75-year prison sentence, the *New York Times'* F. Raymond Daniell warned about the case's impending obscurity and the predictable consequences.

Patterson's life has been saved. He has been condemned to a penitentiary sentence longer than even the most optimistic actuary would reckon his life probabilities. For Mr. Leibowitz, who boasts that few of his clients ever have gone to the electric chair, it is a victory, but for Patterson it is what? A Negro in jeopardy of his life is a potential martyr, but a Negro in jail for the rest of his life for a sordid crime is a forgotten man.[220]

In 1939, the Alabama legislature transferred authority from the governor to the Parole Board to make pardon and parole decisions. Chalmers and Grover Hall, who found it impossible to harbor ill will against his "Yankee" friend,[221] renewed their efforts to gain the defendants' release. They worked diligently but suffered one disappointment after another until Hall's untimely death in January 1941.[222] In the meantime, Andy Wright succumbed to a "prison psychosis" and grew increasingly despondent. Clarence Norris lost a finger to a prison mill machine and began to lose hope that he would ever again taste freedom. Charlie Weems, who had been critically injured by a prison guard early in the service of his 75-year sentence, did his best to avoid trouble and blend inconspicuously into prison life. Haywood Patterson was transferred to Atmore Prison in southernmost Alabama, where he cultivated poisonous snakes and earned a reputation as an incorrigible prisoner and homosexual predator.[223]

Charlie Weems was the first of the Scottsboro defendants to be paroled. He was released from prison in November 1943, some twelve and a half years following his March 25, 1931, arrest in Paint Rock. He settled into a job in an Atlanta laundry. His reentry into society was perhaps the least eventful of all of the young men who had been ensnared in Alabama's justice system. He suffered no reported future problems with the law or other unusual adjustment problems.[224]

Andy Wright gained release in January 1944. He was assigned a job in a Montgomery lumberyard, which he found intolerable because of an overbearing supervisor, strict regulations, and dangerous working conditions. He married within months of leaving prison. In September, nine months after leaving prison, he fled his job and left Montgomery, thus violating parole. Wright went to Mobile, where his wife's mother lived. He was prevailed upon to return to Montgomery with an understanding that his parole would not be revoked. He secured a job at a grocery store and remained out of trouble for nearly two years. Then, however, his marriage failed, he bolted to Chicago, and he was returned to prison in Alabama. He was in and out of prison between late 1946 and the summer of 1947, and then served another three years behind bars after being involved in a traffic accident in which he was charged with reckless driving and driving without a license. He was paroled again in June 1950. Then 38 years old, and having spent nearly half of his life incarcerated since his arrest for rape, he spoke about Victoria Price when he was let out of prison. "I'm not mad because the girl lied about me," Wright said. "If she's still living, I feel sorry for her because I don't guess she sleeps much at night."[225]

Andy Wright was authorized to leave Alabama and with Roy Wilkins's assistance found work in Albany, New York. The next year, Wright's world threatened to fall apart once again. He was arrested on July 11, 1951, for the first-degree rape of a 13-year-old Albany girl. He denied the allegation, insisting that the girl's foster mother had manufactured the charge, taking advantage of his status as one of the Scottsboro boys, and that he had done nothing more than buy the girl a dress. Thurgood Marshall, then championing various civil rights causes as lead counsel with the NAACP, including the campaign to desegregate schools, helped locate a lawyer to defend Wright. After spending eight months in jail awaiting trial, Wright faced another all-white jury on yet another rape charge. This time, he was in a New York courtroom and his alleged victim was black. The jury deliberated for little more than an hour before delivering its verdict. Wright, announced the foreman, was not guilty. Shortly thereafter, Wright was convicted of assaulting his wife. He received a suspended sentence on the condition that he leave Albany. He drifted to Cleveland and then to New York City, where he settled in 1955.[226]

Clarence Norris was paroled on January 6, 1944, the same day that Andy Wright first won release. He was 32 years old. The last of the defendants to have a death sentence lifted, Norris's first taste of freedom since 1931 paralleled Wright's experiences in several respects. Like Wright, his first work was in a Montgomery lumberyard, which he found oppressive and unbearable. Like Wright, he married within months of being paroled. And like Wright, he absconded in September 1944. After the Parole Board rejected his request to have his parole transferred to Ohio, Norris concluded that "I just couldn't take any more from those rotten crackers."[227] He boarded a train for New York City. Shortly after his arrival, he met with Chalmers, Morris Shapiro, and Roy Wilkins, who persuaded him to return to Alabama after receiving assurances that the Parole Board would not return him to prison. He was instead returned to the same job and supervisor that he despised at the Montgomery lumberyard. That arrangement lasted only briefly. On October 18, after Norris complained to the parole authorities about his employment situation, he was promptly returned to prison. He had been free just over nine months.[228]

Norris remained in prison for two more years, until gaining release on September 27, 1946. He reunited with his wife just long enough to learn that she no longer wanted the marriage. Norris reached his breaking point with this latest blow. Once again violating his parole, he left Alabama, traveling first by train to Atlanta, where he had a brief, chance encounter with Charlie Weems, and then to Cleveland, where his mother, two of his sisters, and other relatives lived. He surprised his mother, who tearfully greeted him and took him into her home. Norris found a job, assumed his brother's name, and lived uneventfully with his mother until police officers showed up at her house looking for him. He then moved into a boardinghouse and eventually remarried, although the marriage soon disintegrated. Norris stayed in Cleveland until 1953. Then, still wanted by the Alabama authorities, he relocated in New York City.[229]

Ozie Powell remained in prison until gaining release in June 1946, about three months prior to Norris's second release date. He was paroled after serving nine years of his 20-year sentence for stabbing Deputy Blalock. Never the same since the bullet from Sheriff Sandlin's gun embedded in his brain, Powell was allowed to leave Alabama and return to his native Georgia. There is no record of his returning to Alabama or of his involvement in further legal difficulties.[230]

Haywood Patterson would not be paroled. He found another way to gain his freedom. On July 17, 1948, after spending 17 years behind bars, Patterson escaped from Kilby Prison. He had contrived to work on Kilby's expansive prison farm. As the sun began to set on that summer evening, he made a break with several other prisoners through the tall cornstalks and into the countryside. Eluding dogs, airplanes, and search parties, and traveling mainly at night, Patterson distanced himself from the prison grounds. Ironically, he took passage on a train, hiding in a tool compartment until the locomotive reached Opelika, Alabama, approximately 60 miles east of Kilby. He narrowly evaded a search party there and set off again on foot. Six days after leaving the prison grounds he reached the Georgia state line. He hopped another train, reached Atlanta, and then found a train to his hometown of Chattanooga. He stayed there just long enough to locate some relatives and beg a few dollars from them. Then he was off again, traveling by train and bus to Detroit, where his sisters lived. "The day after I got there my sisters cooked a great home-coming meal," Patterson later recalled. "I tasted beer for the first time. I was thirty-six years old when I had my first glass."[231]

The FBI caught up with Patterson two years later. He was placed under arrest in Detroit on June 27, 1950.[232] Alabama immediately sought his extradition. "Sitting in jail with his suspenders loose and his eyes glinting with bitterness, Patterson said hopefully that he couldn't believe Michigan would send him back to Alabama. 'Alabama is the rottenest place in the world,' he said. 'They make criminals there....Hell, they [want] to kill me.'"[233] Patterson got his wish. Michigan Governor G. Mennen Williams declined to honor Alabama's extradition request and a federal judge ordered Patterson's release.[234]

He did not stay out of trouble long. He was arrested in December 1950 and charged with murder for stabbing another man to death in a Detroit barroom brawl.[235] Patterson claimed that he had acted in self defense. A jury convicted him of manslaughter in September 1951 and he was sentenced to a six- to 15-year term of imprisonment. Shortly thereafter, he was diagnosed with cancer. He died in prison on August 24, 1952, at age 39.[236] The *New York Times'* account of his demise was starkly captioned, "'Scottsboro Boy' Dead."[237]

Meanwhile, the young men who had gained their freedom as a part of the compromise of July 1937 also struggled with the outside world. Olen Montgomery was arrested and jailed in Detroit in 1940 "when the complainant, a Negro woman, ran into a police station and declared he had threatened her with a knife." He was released from custody after the woman refused to sign a warrant charging him with rape.[238] He had been unable to make a go of his aspiration of becoming a professional musician, was unwilling to engage in menial labor, remained handicapped by poor vision, and had taken to heavy drinking. He bounced between New York City, Detroit, and Atlanta, where his mother lived, and called frequently on the NAACP for money, transportation, and other assistance. Plagued by alcohol-related problems and often destitute, Montgomery returned to his hometown of Monroe, Georgia in the mid-1940s and settled there temporarily. In 1952 he was back in New York City, where he was charged with disorderly conduct after being detained for sleeping on a subway. The charge was dismissed after the NAACP intervened on his behalf.[239]

Willie Roberson drew the attention of both *Time* magazine and the *New York Times* following his July 1942 conviction for disorderly conduct. The *Times* described how Roberson, "one of the defendants in the Scottsboro case," had been found guilty of "annoying a young white woman" on a Brooklyn subway. He must have experienced a flashback to his Scottsboro trial when the judge lectured him before imposing a 90-day jail sentence that, "The women of this city must be able to feel safe on the streets and subways at all times. We of the courts must help the city to protect all women."[240] Roberson also was jailed in 1942 following a fight that broke out in a Harlem social club, although he protested that he was not involved and was simply a victim of circumstances.[241]

Eugene Williams may have made the smoothest adjustment. Like Olen Montgomery, Williams had dreams of becoming a professional musician but soon discovered the same shoals on which the hopes of countless aspiring New York City musicians before him had been dashed. He moved west to join relatives in St. Louis. In 1938, Chalmers held Williams out as an example of what the defendants who still remained incarcerated might achieve if granted their release. He bragged about Williams in a letter that he sent Bibb Graves when the Alabama governor was still considering paroling the young men who remained in prison. Chalmers quoted a newspaper article in his letter, which revealed that, "Eugene Williams, age twenty, one of the Scottsboro boys, was enrolled at [Kansas City's] Western Baptist Seminary recently. The Home Mission Board of the National Baptist Convention is financing his education."[242] Chalmers did not report whether Williams succeeded in his studies, but nor were there reports of future difficulties in Williams's adaptation to life after the Scottsboro trials were behind him.

The same could not be said about Roy Wright, the youngest of the Scottsboro defendants. Originally taken under wing by Bill "Bojangles" Robinson, the famous song and dance man who entertained in Harlem, on Broadway, and before audiences nationwide, Wright enrolled in vocational school, served in the army, married, and found a job. He and his brother Andy frequently visited after Andy finally secured his release from prison. Roy joined the merchant marine and, away from home for long stretches of time, harbored suspicions that his wife was unfaithful to him. In 1959, more than two decades after being turned loose by the Alabama justice system, the younger Wright shot and killed his wife. He then took his own life.[243]

Clarence Norris had officially been a fugitive from justice since he had absconded from Alabama in 1946 in violation of his parole. Yet in his mind, he was a fugitive from injustice. He had spent 15 years in Alabama prisons, including more than four years under sentence of death, for a crime that he had always maintained he had not committed. His life had been eventful since moving to New York City in 1953. He had been involved in numerous scrapes with the law, during which he could only hope that the authorities would not discover that he was a wanted man in Alabama. They never did. In 1956, Norris paid a visit to Samuel Leibowitz, who had been a trial judge in Brooklyn since 1941. Despite his years as a criminal defense attorney, Leibowitz had earned a reputation as a hard-nosed, law and order judge. Leibowitz's support of capital punishment and his general willingness to impose harsh penalties had earned him the nickname, "Sentencing Sam."[244] Norris told Judge Leibowitz that he, too, believed in the death penalty, "if the person is guilty of a crime that merits" it. Norris imposed a further caveat: "when whites deserve it, they should be executed just as the blacks are."[245]

Norris eventually remarried and he and his wife had two daughters. In 1970, with his fugitive status and conviction for raping Victoria Price continuing to gnaw at him, Norris decided that he owed it to himself and his family to try to clear his name. "My kids were growing up and they didn't even know who I was. I didn't want them to find out someday I was a convicted rapist without knowing my side of the story."[246] He enlisted the help of the NAACP, which began exploring Alabama's receptivity to nullifying Norris's parole violation a quarter century after he had fled the State. When Norris became impatient with how slowly this process was unfolding, he placed a telephone call directly to the Alabama Department of Corrections and explained his situation. He was told by the person on the other end of the call, "Yes, we want you back and I will do everything in my power to get you back."[247] Norris thereafter allowed the NAACP to press the matter on his behalf.

The plan was not only to erase Norris's parole violation, but to secure a full pardon. Alabama law stipulated that "Any person whose sentence to death has been commuted by the Governor"— as had occurred in Norris's case—"shall not be eligible for a pardon unless sufficient evidence is presented to the Board of Pardons and Paroles to satisfy it that the person was innocent of the crime for which he or she was convicted, the board votes unanimously to grant the person a pardon, and the Governor concurs in and approves the granting of the pardon."[248] Norris and his supporters thus had their work cut out for them.

Progress was slow but it was steady. The NAACP located a law firm in Montgomery, Alabama that was willing to help. The lawyers arranged a meeting in April 1976 with the Alabama Attorney General's office to explain Norris's present circumstances and his quest. From New York, the NAACP asked for and received the help of several prominent people, including New York City Mayor Abraham Beame and U.S. Senator Jacob Javits, who wrote letters on Norris's behalf.[249]

The Scottsboro case was revived and thrust once again before the American public in April 1976 with the release of a made-for-television movie that aired on NBC, "Judge Horton and Scottsboro Boys." A reviewer described the essential story line.

John McGreevey's script focuses on the second trial of the Scottsboro boys. In 1931, all nine [sic] had been found guilty and sentenced to death. The 1933 retrial, set in a Decatur, Ala., courtroom was presided over by Judge James E. Horton, a respected jurist and member of the local Establishment. Thrown into a confrontation with blatant racism, Judge Horton sticks to the letter and spirit of the law. His reward is a ruined career.[250]

Judge Horton's opinion voiding Haywood Patterson's 1933 conviction because it was contrary to the weight of the evidence loomed as large in 1976 as it had when it originally issued, only this time it garnered the support of an Alabama official. On August 5, 1976, Alabama Attorney General William Baxley wrote the Alabama Board of Pardons and Paroles with a recommendation that Norris be pardoned. He stated his belief that Norris was innocent. Baxley relied extensively on and referred directly to Judge Horton's opinion in reaching his conclusion. Despite this endorsement, Norman Ussery, the Chairman of the Board of Pardons and Paroles, was not moved. Ussery replied, "It is my feeling that as long as Mr. Norris is a fugitive from justice and there is an outstanding warrant against him, it would not be proper even to consider him for a pardon at this time."[251]

Negotiations ensued. Letters of support poured in for Norris. Newspaper editorials urged Alabama to act. Ussery relented and a compromise was reached.

The Board of Pardons and Paroles advised Norris in a letter dated October 22, 1976, that a majority of the Board had "voted to void the delinquency taken in your case. . .and reinstate you on parole but without supervision. We have further ordered that you be granted a Conditional Release from supervision."[252] The Board members then unanimously affirmed their belief in Norris's innocence and, pursuant to Alabama law, recommended to Governor George C. Wallace that Norris be pardoned. Governor Wallace acted on October 25, 1976.

Clarence Norris, the sole surviving "Scottsboro Boy," was pardoned yesterday by Gov. George C. Wallace of Alabama and asserted happily in New York City that "a man should never give up hope."

Mr. Norris, now 64 years old and a warehouseman for the City of New York, spoke at a news conference. . . .

Freed from all charges, Mr. Norris said that he had "no bitterness against the people who did me wrong."[253]

A month later, Norris returned to Alabama for the first time since 1946 to accept his pardon personally. "It's a far different time from when I left," he said. "I only wish the other eight boys could be here today—their lives were ruined by this thing too."[254] With his innocence officially acknowledged, Norris left Alabama and returned to New York City. "[T]he last survivor of the 'Scottsboro Boys' rape case, which became a symbol of racial injustice in the Deep South in the 1930s," Clarence Norris died on January 23, 1989, at age 76.[255]

The Lessons of Scottsboro

The Scottsboro boys were unwitting participants in a sociolegal drama that ranked among the most highly publicized and spectacular trials of the twentieth century. They had aged from adolescence at the time of their arrest in 1931 to manhood when the last of them left Alabama's prison system in 1950. Many of them struggled to adapt to life outside of prison and some did not live to see the 1960s. With Clarence Norris's death in 1989, all of the principals in their trials had passed away: Thomas Knight, Jr., their chief prosecutor, died more than a half century earlier; the irascible Judge William Callahan—74 years old when he sentenced Norris to death in 1937—had succumbed decades ago; Judge James Horton passed away in 1973; their chief defense lawyer, Samuel Leibowitz, died in 1978; and their accusers, Ruby Bates, who recanted her accusation, passed away in 1976, and Victoria Price, who did not, died in 1982.[1] With the passage of the years, their stories receded from public awareness, even where they had begun. In 1969, the *New York Times* announced, "In Scottsboro, Few Remember the Criminal Trial That Brought Prominence to the Town 38 Years Ago."[2]

Much as the media had given visibility and meaning to the Scottsboro cases in the 1930s, it would fall largely to the media to revive the cases and redefine their significance for ensuing generations. Most people got their information about the cases in the 1930s from printed sources, where newspapers and interest group publications dominated, although poets, songwriters, playwrights, and novelists offered perspectives, as well.[3] Television did not become a household fixture for another two decades. Many Americans who were not old enough to follow the cases when they originally were newsworthy received their first history lesson about the charges, trials, and their aftermath through the somewhat unlikely format of a made-for-television movie. NBC broadcast "Judge Horton and the Scottsboro Boys" in April 1976. The script, based on Dan Carter's prize-winning book,[4] was prepared by Hollywood writer John McGreevey.[5] More than 40 million viewers watched the two-hour docudrama.[6]

The television dramatization emphasized themes of racial injustice and the courageous, principled, and career-ending stand of Judge Horton as he vacated the conviction and death sentence returned by a Decatur jury in Haywood Patterson's second trial. Critics lauded the portrayal and the movie received an Emmy nomination, although some scholars were not impressed. One lamented the script's neglect of the Communist Party and the International Labor Defense's role in saving the Boys' lives, its inattention to the division of opinion about the case between North and South, and characterized the broadcast as a "perversion of the Scottsboro symbol to millions of Americans."[7] Nor were Victoria Price and Ruby Bates favorably impressed.

The producers of "Judge Horton and the Scottsboro Boys" erroneously believed that Price and Bates had died prior the show's being aired. In fact, both women were very much alive. Although McGreevey attempted to hew to the transcript of Patterson's trial in his television script, his depictions were not always precise. One deviation involved Leibowitz's attempt to undermine Price's credibility during his cross-examination of her in Judge Horton's courtroom. Leibowitz had asked Price during the trial "if she had 'ever heard of any single white women being locked up in jail when she is the complaining witness against negroes in the history of the State of Alabama?'" The television script embellished this question by inserting "for perjury" after "locked up in jail." Price actually had been held in jail as a material witness and not because she had been suspected of lying under oath. At another juncture, the television show portrayed ILD attorney Joseph Brodsky as asserting that the defense had succeeded in establishing "that Victoria Price was a whore." Although the defense had presented evidence to this effect, the statement attributed to Brodsky was nowhere to be found in the trial record. These and other alleged misrepresentations caused first Bates and then Price to sue NBC for invasion of privacy, defamation, and libel.[8]

Ruby Bates died shortly after her lawsuit was filed. Price, who had remarried and adopted her husband's surname of Street, forged ahead with her claims. She sought $6 million in damages. The case came to trial in July 1977 in the U.S. District Court in Winchester, Tennessee, roughly 65 miles west of Chattanooga and 45 miles north of Scottsboro. Few prospective jurors had ever heard of the Scottsboro boys or their rape trials. For the first time in 40 years Victoria Price Street swore before a jury that she had been raped. On cross-examination, the attorneys representing NBC brought out numerous inconsistencies between Mrs. Street's current testimony and the evidence presented during the Alabama criminal trials. Several other witnesses testified, including McGreevey and Carter for the defense.[9]

The trial concluded with NBC's lawyers reading aloud from Judge Horton's opinion in which he explained why he had overturned Haywood Patterson's conviction in 1933. The jurors listened to the recitation with interest. However, they were not allowed to return a verdict in the civil suit. At the conclusion of the evidence and the attorneys' arguments, the judge dismissed the lawsuit, relying in part on the First Amendment and in part on insufficiency of evidence to support Victoria Price Street's claims.[10] The Sixth Circuit Court of Appeals affirmed the dismissal, but after the U.S. Supreme Court agreed to review this decision, Street and NBC settled the case. Terms of the settlement were not disclosed. The agreement ensured that the Supreme Court would not make yet another ruling involving the Scottsboro cases.[11]

Viewers who missed "Judge Horton and the Scottsboro Boys" had other opportunities to watch television shows and movies that included both loosely based dramatic versions and serious educational accounts of the cases. At the former end of the spectrum was a television movie, broadcast on Court TV in 1998, "Crime Stories: The Scottsboro Boys." Another dramatic representation followed in 2006, the film "Heavens Fall." This Hollywood production, directed by Terry Green and starring Timothy Hutton as Samuel Leibowitz, generated little public interest. The Public Broadcasting System (PBS) aired "Scottsboro: An American Tragedy" in 2001. Nominated for an Academy Award, this critically acclaimed and illuminating documentary included original film footage and soundtracks as well as insightful commentary about the social significance of the cases.

Several books designed to introduce younger readers to the trials and describe their place in American history also were published on the cusp of the 21st century.[12] Earlier fictional works had developed themes and used imagery that may have evoked suggestions of Scottsboro to those knowledgeable about the cases. Millions of Americans who absorbed Harper Lee's gripping 1960 novel, *To Kill a Mockingbird,* which depicted a black man convicted of raping a white woman in Alabama in the 1930s, or saw Gregory Peck star as Atticus Finch in the 1962 movie based on the book, might have been impressed by the resemblance to the Scottsboro cases.[13] Richard Wright's *Native Son* featured Bigger Thomas as a young black man accused of raping and murdering a white woman. The book, first published in 1940, emphasizes social and legal injustices confronting blacks and has elements of similarity to Scottsboro. The parallels are not entirely coincidental since Wright reported on the Scottsboro trials in the 1930s for the Communist Party newspaper, the *Daily Worker.*[14]

All attempts to revive Scottsboro in the national psyche, whether by television, movie, or in print, required explaining the cases anew, and ascribing meaning to them, for generations that considered the 1930s a part of the distant past.

In contrast, the legal precedent established by the Supreme Court's rulings in *Powell v. Alabama,* involving the right to counsel, and *Norris v. Alabama,* prohibiting racial discrimination in jury selection, had solidified the cases' place in American constitutional law. However, even in this respect, time was dulling their luster. With the due process revolution in criminal procedure worked by the Warren Court in the 1960s, and the inevitable accretion of the law through subsequent rulings, these landmark Scottsboro-era decisions were more widely recognized for their historical value than their contemporary significance.

Other legal developments brought rule changes that would have markedly altered the Scottsboro prosecutions if they had been initiated today. In the first place, none of the young men now would be on trial for their lives. Four decades after Judge Callahan sentenced Clarence Norris to death for the last time, the Supreme Court ruled that capital punishment is unconstitutionally excessive for the crime of rape.[15] Most of the Scottsboro boys would have enjoyed double immunity from the death penalty because of their age. The justices ruled in 1988 that the Eighth Amendment's prohibition against cruel and unusual punishments protects 15-year-olds against execution, and in 2005 the Court limited the death penalty to offenders at least 18 years old at the time of their crimes.[16] The Scottsboro jury's willingness to sentence 13-year-old Eugene Williams to death would be considered especially shocking today, although the practice was not unconstitutional in 1931; children as young as 14 were executed in this country as late as the 1940s.[17]

The high-stakes drama of capital trials command public attention like few other criminal cases. Nor is the legal system immune to the uncommon significance of capital cases. When the death penalty is sought, the accompanying glut of publicity and intensified community interest in a case's outcome have a heightened potential to jeopardize the accused's rights to a fair trial and an impartial jury. U.S. Supreme Court Justice Felix Frankfurter once observed, "When life is at hazard in a trial, it sensationalizes the whole thing almost unwittingly."[18] The change of venue from Jackson County to nearby Morgan County certainly did not insulate the Scottsboro defendants from the prejudicial publicity and the inflamed community sentiment surrounding the charges. Media-fueled interest in the cases explained the urgency of the defense's efforts to remove the trials to Montgomery if not to federal court.

Elected trial judges owe their careers to voters from the same communities where crimes are charged and justice is dispensed. Some judges may be influenced, consciously or not, by the intense pressures associated with capital cases.[19] The accused almost inevitably suffers in such circumstances. Judge Horton's invalidation of Haywood Patterson's conviction in June 1933 is a dramatic example of judicial independence in the face of such threats. Horton demonstrated extraordinary fortitude in withstanding community sentiment when he granted

Patterson a new trial, yet he also suffered the consequences. His tenure as an Alabama trial judge came to an abrupt end in the following election. Judge Callahan, in contrast, frequently played to the Morgan County courtroom audiences. His courtroom demeanor and rulings mirrored many of the attitudes and prejudices of the surrounding community.

Appellate judges likewise can be affected by the magnitude of capital cases. State supreme court reversals of capital convictions and sentences sometimes become campaign issues in contemporary elections, and can cause voter disaffection and result in judges' non-retention. Rose Bird's ouster as chief justice of the California Supreme Court in 1986 is one of several instances of the political vulnerability of appellate judges who vote to overturn verdicts in capital trials.[20] Yet by the same token, defendants under sentence of death sometimes benefit by their condemned status. The Supreme Court has recognized that death is different from other punishments because of its unique severity and finality, and those same qualities have been known to inspire especially rigorous judicial review of capital convictions and sentences.

U.S. Supreme Court Justice Robert Jackson once confessed that, "When the penalty is death, we, like state court judges, are tempted to strain the evidence... in order to give a doubtfully condemned man another chance."[21] Several landmark Supreme Court rulings, including *Powell v. Alabama* and *Norris v. Alabama,* have been issued in cases involving state criminal defendants under sentence of death.[22] One such case was decided in 1936, on the heels of the High Court's Scottsboro rulings. *Brown v. Mississippi* saw the Supreme Court overturn murder convictions and death sentences imposed on three black defendants after state law enforcement officers had unabashedly coerced confessions from them. While testifying at the trial, a deputy sheriff was asked how severely one of the defendants had been whipped before confessing. "Not too much for a negro," the deputy responded, "not as much as I would have done it if it were left to me."[23] The Court's decision and related events have been described as "a 'Scottsboro' case in Mississippi."[24]

Ironically, the threat of capital punishment can be both a curse and a blessing for accused and convicted offenders. The nation's attention was focused on Scottsboro and Decatur for the early trials when the risk was high that the rape charges would result in the Boys' execution. Public attention waned during the later trials but never so dramatically as when imprisonment instead of death was the prescribed punishment. Outside of Allan Knight Chalmers and a few other dedicated individuals, concern largely gave way to indifference among both the public and the judiciary when the defendants' death sentences were nullified and replaced by lengthy terms of imprisonment.

The defendants' fates were decided by all-male, all-white juries in the Scottsboro and Decatur trials, including the four concluded after the Supreme Court's 1935 ruling in *Norris v. Alabama.* Alabama law at the time limited jury service to men, while custom and tradition limited jury service to whites. Although women participated on juries in some American jurisdictions as early as the nineteenth century, by World War II 20 states in addition to Alabama still barred women from jury service. The Supreme Court did not prohibit this practice until 1975.[25] Opinions are mixed about what role, if any, gender plays in a juror's assessment of a rape accusation. Some attorneys subscribe to the view that women jurors tend to be more skeptical than men of rape charges,[26] and there is some evidence that women who grew up before the 1960s, when more permissive attitudes about sex began to emerge, are especially likely to discount rape claims made by women whose behavior they interpret as having contributed to their alleged victimization.[27]

Even if women had been included on juries in the Scottsboro cases, and even if they had adopted a more critical attitude in evaluating Victoria Price's testimony, the defense would have faced an uphill battle in trying to negate the many other factors working against the defendants. Altering the racial composition of the jury might have had a bigger impact on the deliberations, although a different outcome still may have been unlikely in the social and cultural context within which Alabama courtrooms operated in the 1930s. Enough blacks would have had to have been represented on the jury to insulate the minority group jurors from external community pressures, as well as to counterbalance the internal decision-making dynamics of a predominantly white jury. Evidence does suggest that the racial makeup of juries can affect case outcomes in modern capital trials. In general, black defendants are treated less punitively, particularly in capital trials involving white victims, as the number of black jurors increases.[28] Death sentences are imposed less frequently when one or more blacks, especially black men, serve as jurors in cases involving black defendants and white victims.[29]

Even after *Norris v. Alabama* was decided in 1935 and Governor Bibb Graves directed county jury commissioners and trial judges to comply with the ruling, blacks were not well represented on Alabama jury venires. Moreover, the few black citizens who were included on the jury rolls and called to court almost never had the chance to serve in criminal trials. In capital cases, prospective jurors who voiced opposition to the death penalty were routinely disqualified for cause, that is, by operation of law. Venire members not excused for cause still had to survive peremptory challenges, which attorneys used to strike prospective jurors who they suspected would not favor their cause. Lawyers were not required to explain their decisions to strike potential jurors. Both the death qualification process and peremptory challenges took their toll on the black citizens represented on trial venires.

Owing in part to perceptions of unequal treatment by the justice system, blacks historically have expressed significantly greater opposition to capital punishment than whites.[30] Simple opposition to the death penalty was sufficient reason to excuse potential jurors for cause in capital prosecutions when the Scottsboro cases were tried. Contemporary legal standards for dismissal are more demanding. Citizens no longer are automatically disqualified from serving on capital juries because they have principled reservations against the death penalty. Prospective jurors can only be disqualified for cause in capital trials if their beliefs are so strong that they would be unwilling even to consider imposing a death sentence or their attitudes about capital punishment would substantially impair their ability to follow the law.[31] Although the standards for dismissal are more demanding, the death qualification process continues to result in disproportionate underrepresentation of blacks who are otherwise eligible to serve on criminal trial juries.[32]

Prospective jurors who survive death qualification remain vulnerable to removal through the lawyers' exercising peremptory challenges, as illustrated in another case from Alabama that reached the Supreme Court in 1965. Like the Scottsboro cases, *Swain v. Alabama*[33] involved a young black man who was sentenced to death by an all-white jury for raping a 17-year-old white woman. The trial in *Swain* occurred in 1962, but there was no record of a black ever having served on a criminal or civil jury in Talladega County, where the crime allegedly occurred. Although the names of qualified black citizens appeared on the county jury rolls, as required by *Norris v. Alabama,* the absence of black trial jurors owed to the struck-jury system employed in Alabama for exercising peremptory challenges. The 19-year-old defendant in *Swain* invoked the Supreme Court's ruling in *Norris* to challenge the long-standing practice in Talladega County of using peremptory challenges to exclude blacks from jury service.

The Supreme Court rejected his claim, owing in part to the justices' professed inability to attribute the absence of black jurors exclusively to the actions of Talladega County prosecutors. Almost perversely, the record suggested that defense lawyers often took the initiative in striking black potential jurors and/or concurred in prosecutors' decisions to do so, thus leaving responsibility for the challenges unclear.[34] The majority opinion in *Swain* additionally refused to infer that the prosecutor in the rape case under review had been motivated by racial discrimination simply because he struck all six of the black prospective jurors on the venire. "The presumption in any particular case must be that the prosecutor is using the State's challenges to obtain a fair and impartial jury to try the case before the court. The presumption is not overcome and the prosecutor therefore subjected to examination by allegations that in the case at hand all Negroes were removed from the jury or that they were removed because they were Negroes. Any other result, we think, would establish a rule wholly at odds with the peremptory challenge system as we know it."[35]

The *Swain* rule essentially immunized prosecutors against claims that they were using peremptory challenges in a racially discriminatory fashion. The presumption that impermissible racial bias motivated the removal of one or more black prospective jurors would never be indulged in an individual case, and few defendants had the wherewithal to demonstrate the consistent pattern of prosecutorial strikes over time that the Court required to support such an inference. What the justices had given with one hand in *Norris* they had effectively taken away with the other in *Swain*: an all-white jury was an all-white jury whether produced by excluding blacks from the venire or through the exercise of peremptory challenges.

More than 20 years passed before the Court righted course and overruled *Swain,* thereby deposing a rule that had crumbled under the weight of its own "crippling burden of proof."[36] In criminal trials today, prosecutors (as well as defense lawyers) may be required to come forward with legitimate, race-neutral reasons for exercising peremptory challenges, or else be found in violation of the Constitution.[37] Although the internment of *Swain* was progressive in principle, in practice fleshing out racial motivation has proven to be so daunting that some Supreme Court justices have figuratively thrown in the towel and advocated the elimination of peremptory challenges.[38]

If racial biases are difficult to detect and substantiate in lawyers' decisions to strike potential trial jurors, they are even more elusive in the context of capital sentencing, where prosecutors initially must determine whether to seek a death sentence, and where punishment responsibility ultimately is left to the judgment of twelve jurors. Each juror in each of the trials in the Scottsboro cases swore that racial prejudice would not affect his consideration of the evidence or his performance as a juror. With the surprising exception of Haywood Patterson's fourth trial, where a single forceful juror persuaded his colleagues to impose a prison sentence instead of death, and Roy Wright's 1931 trial in Scottsboro, where seven jurors voted for death even though prosecutors had requested only a prison sentence because of Roy's tender years, each and every juror asked to return a death sentence in the Scottsboro and Decatur prosecutions did so. The young men's guilt was a foregone conclusion. Yet, were these outcomes attributable to the fact that the accused offenders were black and Victoria Price was white, that a heinous crime had been committed, or to some combination thereof? And how could an outside observer hope to penetrate either the closed doors of the jury room or the jurors' minds and make such a determination?

Modern death penalty law is little closer to responding to the threat of race discrimination in capital cases than was true in the 1930s. The Supreme Court's most direct consideration of whether racial prejudices fatally contaminate death-penalty decisions occurred in *McCleskey v. Kemp,*[39] a 1987 ruling involving a Georgia defendant who was convicted of murder and given a capital sentence.

The challenge was based on a comprehensive statewide empirical study that concluded that the odds of a death sentence being imposed in murder cases with white victims were 4.3 times higher than in otherwise similar cases with black victims. The discrepancies in capital charging and sentencing decisions were especially pronounced in black defendant-white victim killings, such as was involved in *McCleskey*.

The justices split 5-4 in rejecting the argument that the evidenced racial disparities compelled the conclusion that unlawful racial bias had infected the decisions made in McCleskey's case. They similarly refused to hold that the evidence demonstrated an unacceptable risk of system-wide racial discrimination in Georgia's capital cases. Justice Lewis F. Powell, Jr. authored the majority opinion. Following his retirement from the Supreme Court, Powell indicated that he would have decided *McCleskey* differently if given another opportunity. The retired justice further volunteered to his biographer that he "would vote the other way in any capital case."[40] But the Court's original ruling remains the law and it has essentially preempted challenges to the administration of the death penalty based on statewide evidence of racial disparities in capital charging and sentencing decisions. Studies in many states, like the Georgia study examined in *McCleskey*, have produced evidence that white victim cases are significantly more likely than similar black victim cases to cause prosecutors to seek and juries to impose death sentences.[41] In this respect, the Scottsboro boys were ahead of their time.

Defense attorneys repeatedly insinuated during the Scottsboro defendants' trials that Victoria Price was a prostitute and sexually promiscuous in an effort to undermine her claim that she had been raped. Judge Horton was generally receptive to the offers of evidence. He admitted testimony that Price and Ruby Bates had engaged in sexual intercourse in the days immediately preceding the alleged rapes with, respectively, Jack Tiller and Lester Carter, and that the women had spent the night before the fateful March 25 train ride in a Chattanooga hobo jungle with Orville Gilley and Carter. His conclusion that Price's rape claim lacked corroboration helped him overturn Haywood Patterson's conviction as being inconsistent with the greater weight of the evidence. In contrast, Judge Callahan consistently and adamantly refused to allow the defense to delve into the women's conduct before March 25, the day of the alleged rapes, including their prior sexual activity and history. He charged the jury that the law indulged a heavy presumption that a white woman would not consent to sexual relations with a black man. He also ruled that corroboration of a complainant's testimony was unnecessary to support a rape conviction.

The trials thus presaged several controversial issues regarding the law of rape that emerged during the 1970s and 1980s, when an outcry arose that rape victims were made to endure indignities, humiliation, and renewed trauma as a result of their treatment within the criminal justice system. Reforms ensued in state and federal law that were designed to protect victims against having their reports of rape greeted with skepticism and distrust, against having their private sexual lives unnecessarily exposed during cross-examination, and attempting to buffer them from the secondary victimization that many experienced through their interactions with law enforcement and court personnel.[42] The enacted protections would vindicate Judge Horton in some respects and Judge Callahan in others. Neither judge's rulings were perfectly consistent with contemporary laws governing the proof of rape.

Modern laws firmly reflect that evidence concerning an alleged rape victim's prior consensual sexual relations is both logically irrelevant and prejudicial, and that reputation evidence regarding promiscuity is presumptively inadmissible at a rape trial. As a general rule, complaining witnesses are protected by rape shield laws from being examined about their prior consensual sexual relations with others. Contrary to prevailing attitudes of an earlier era, contemporary law rejects the inference that because a woman is unchaste—that is, because she has consented to have sexual intercourse with other men in the past—she is more likely to have consented to the sexual conduct at issue in a rape trial. Similarly, reputation evidence regarding promiscuity is considered irrelevant both with respect to the complaining witness's propensity to consent to sexual relations and to her general credibility. The requirement that a rape complaint must be corroborated by independent evidence also largely has been eliminated. In these respects, Judge Callahan's insistence that Victoria Price's reputation as a prostitute was irrelevant and that evidence regarding her prior sexual conduct was inadmissible, and his refusal to require independent corroboration of her rape allegations, are superficially consistent with current laws of rape.

Yet Callahan's rulings would be considered erroneous in most respects under modern law and would likely invalidate the rape convictions returned in the Scottsboro prosecutions. Consent was never at issue in the trials. For that reason, if for no other, Callahan's repeated instructions to Decatur juries that the law strongly presumed that a white woman would not consent to sexual relations with a black man were utterly and bizarrely irrelevant. Moreover, his refusal to allow the jury to hear evidence about Price's and Bates's consensual sexual liaisons with Tiller, Carter, and/or Gilley in the days prior to the alleged rapes almost certainly would be prejudicial error even under today's restrictive evidentiary standards.

The defense had not sought to inform the jury about Price's prior sexual encounters to suggest that she was thereby more likely to have consented to sexual intercourse with the defendants on the train. Having denied ever seeing Price on the train, and certainly disputing that they had engaged in sexual intercourse with her, consent formed no part of the young men's defense. Instead, evidence of her prior sexual conduct was offered as an explanation for the semen that

Dr. Bridges detected in her vagina shortly following the alleged rape. The modest amount of immotile spermatozoa and semen the physician discovered would have been perfectly consistent with Price's having engaged in sexual intercourse with Tiller or Gilley during the 24 to 48 hours prior to the alleged rape. It could have suggested that one or both of those men—and not the defendants—were the source of the semen. Contemporary rape shield laws include an exception to the general rule against evidence of past sexual behavior that applies when the evidence "is offered to prove that a person other than the accused was the source of semen, injury or other physical evidence."[43] Paying homage to Judge Horton's ruling in the trials, and rejecting Judge Callahan's, this exception is sometimes referred to as the "Scottsboro rebuttal provision."[44]

Not only legal developments, but scientific ones, would be crucial in arriving at contemporary verdicts in the Scottsboro cases. Few, if any, scientific innovations rival the dramatic impact that DNA evidence has had on the criminal justice system. Although largely a tool for linking offenders to their crimes through the biological evidence they leave behind, its analogous powers of exclusion make DNA analysis a potent mechanism for establishing innocence. The Scottsboro defendants' guilt or innocence, and whether Victoria Price's testimony was true or false, could have been conclusively determined if the semen removed from Price and Bates following their rape claims had been preserved and if the technology for DNA analysis had been available when the young men were accused of their crimes.

If DNA testing had been developed shortly after their convictions became final, for example in the late 1930s or early 1940s, the Scottsboro defendants would have been in a position similar to thousands of prisoners in the late 20th century. They would have been tried and found guilty before this science existed, yet still incarcerated when it became available to confirm or refute their guilt. The vast majority of crimes do not involve biological evidence such as semen, blood, or saliva, on which DNA analysis depends, so the new technology is far from a magic bullet for determining the truth in criminal prosecutions.[45] Nevertheless, by 2007, at least two hundred people convicted of crimes in the United States had been exonerated by post-conviction DNA test results. Those individuals had served an average of twelve years in prison before it was discovered that they had been wrongfully convicted and they were released. Fourteen of them had been convicted of capital crimes and sentenced to death.[46] Rape cases are not immune from mistaken identifications. DNA tests performed by the FBI in approximately 10,000 rape cases excluded roughly 20 percent of the reported suspects; matches were found in about 60 percent of the cases, and the rest of the analyses were inconclusive.[47]

DNA exonerations represent just the tip of the iceberg of cases involving miscarriages of justice. Because evidence suitable for DNA testing does not exist in the great majority of criminal cases, it is impossible to know how many innocent people have been convicted of crimes nationwide. One study produced evidence of 340 wrongful felony convictions in the United States over the 15-year period 1989–2003. Wrongful convictions were conservatively defined as involving people officially recognized as not guilty of the crimes for which they were convicted. The actual number of innocent people wrongly convicted of crimes almost certainly is many times greater.[48] After soliciting the views of experienced actors within the criminal justice system, some scholars have conjectured that erroneous convictions occur in less than one percent of felony cases. Translating that estimate into a 99.5% accuracy rate, the sobering total of innocent people convicted of felonies would exceed 6,000 annually, with a much higher number in misdemeanor cases.[49]

Clarence Norris's pardon by the State of Alabama amounted to an official recognition of his innocence and, by necessary implication, the innocence of the eight young men accused with him. Had the ILD not come to their aid following the convictions and death sentences returned in Scottsboro in 1931, and had not the U.S. Supreme Court twice ordered new trials, at least seven of them—Eugene Williams and Roy Wright being the exceptions—almost certainly would have been executed. Debates about their innocence largely would have been buried along with them. Under any circumstances, after-the-fact recognition of innocence can offer only small consolation to the unfortunate individuals who wrongfully suffer conviction and incarceration. As a case in point, the nine young men swept up in the Scottsboro prosecutions spent a total of more than 90 years behind bars for a crime that the State responsible for their convictions acknowledged decades later did not occur.

It is unlikely that any defense attorney, no matter how skilled and resourceful, could have overcome the many factors that combined to produce the youths' convictions in the Scottsboro and Decatur trials. As a practical matter, the confluence of race, region, politics, and inflamed community sentiment that distinguished the cases created an overwhelming and essentially irrefutable presumption of guilt. The trials nevertheless have long been associated with assistance of counsel issues. The defendants' legal representation ran the gamut from worst to best, with both extremes sometimes personified in the same lawyer who so valiantly championed their cases, Samuel Leibowitz.

Judge Alfred Hawkins's assignment of "all the members of the [Scottsboro] bar" to represent the nine defendants at their initial arraignment, followed by his confusing colloquy at the outset of the trials with attorneys Stephen Roddy and Milo Moody, resulted in the lawyers going forward without preparation or a coherent strategy to defend the boys against capital charges. Those circumstances gave rise to the Supreme Court's landmark right to counsel ruling in *Powell v. Alabama.* So "casual" and untimely was this appointment process that the lawyers' performance denied the boys—"young, ignorant, illiterate, surrounded by hostile sentiment, haled back and forth under guard of soldiers, charged with an atrocious crime regarded with especial horror in the community where they were to be tried"—the essentials of due process of law.[50] The justices' decision in *Powell* provided the cornerstone three decades later for *Gideon v. Wainwright*,[51] which guaranteed all poor people charged with felonies the right to court-appointed trial counsel.

Powell v. Alabama is an especially significant ruling because the Supreme Court's invalidation of the Boys' convictions and death sentences affirmed that a criminal defendant is owed more than the simple presence of counsel. The justices' ruling meant that minimal performance standards must be met if the attorney's constitutional role is to be discharged. The courts have struggled with how to define the threshold requirements for effective assistance of counsel, adopting only general guidelines for identifying substandard performance and the resultant harm to the defendant's case that must be established before a criminal conviction is overturned.[52] Some observers continue to maintain that quality defense representation too frequently is lacking, including in capital cases, and that court-appointed counsel too often are underpaid, overworked, and lack the experience, training, and/or resources to be truly effective advocates.[53] Those deficiencies were certainly evident at the Scottsboro Boys' first series of trials. Yet after the young men shed Roddy and Moody as their lawyers they would have little reason to complain about their attorneys' capabilities.

When Samuel Leibowitz entered the Scottsboro cases, the boys' trial representation was in the hands of one of the country's best criminal defense lawyers. Leibowitz was a brilliant, experienced, and skilled tactician. He also was hard working and always exquisitely well prepared. Not even Leibowitz, however, was ready for what greeted him in Decatur, Alabama, upon his arrival from New York City. For all of his talent, Leibowitz suffered from his status as a New Yorker in a Southern courtroom. He not only was a New Yorker, but a Jew, as local solicitors were eager to remind the Decatur juries, and one who had been brought into the case by the International Labor Defense, an affiliate of the American Communist Party. The invectives directed against the lawyer intensified when he exploded before the Northern press about the "bigots" who served as jurors in Decatur, who "drip[ped] tobacco juice, bewhiskered and filthy," as they sentenced Haywood Patterson to death in Judge Horton's courtroom. When those remarks found their way back to Alabama it became unclear whether the New York lawyer's presence on the defense team was a bigger asset or liability to the boys. Recognizing his tenuous posture, Leibowitz eventually yielded principal trial responsibilities to Clarence Watts, an Alabama native with a law practice in neighboring Huntsville.

Another confounding aspect of Leibowitz's advocacy involved his simultaneous representation of all nine of the accused. Although the defendants' cases were connected, they also differed in significant respects. Some of them had given statements denying their own involvement but claiming they had witnessed the other young men raping Price and Bates. Olen Montgomery and Willie Roberson suffered physical disabilities that made it questionable from the outset whether they were capable of jumping from car to car and fighting with the white boys on the train or raping the two women. Although a unified defense could well have been in all of the young men's best interests, no judicial inquiry was made concerning the Boys' awareness of the potential divided loyalties confronting Leibowitz or their willingness to proceed with him as their lawyer notwithstanding the conflict of interests he may have faced in representing them.[54] In the end, some of the young men who did not benefit by the compromise worked out in the summer of 1937, who remained incarcerated as four of their companions walked out of jail, expressed confusion, if not resentment and a sense of betrayal, at the differential treatment.

Although the legal issues in the Scottsboro cases are both important and enduring, they pale in comparison to the lasting social significance of the trials. The Scottsboro cases speak volumes about America, about the country's hopes and fears regarding race relations, class distinctions, regional mores and cultural traditions, political divides, and about the media and its representation of social and legal injustices. Even though the trials were concluded in the 1930s, the prison sentences served by 1950, and the principals all deceased by the 1980s, Scottsboro lives in history as a courtroom drama nonpareil. The cases portray a complicated vortex of issues that have undergone definition and redefinition, and that in many respects continue to defy final resolution.

In January 2004, amidst television cameras and radio and newspaper reporters, a crowd gathered near the Jackson County Courthouse in Scottsboro to dedicate a historical marker commemorating the Scottsboro Boys' trials and their struggles for justice. "Why has it taken so long for this day to arrive?" asked one woman who attended.[55] Another in attendance volunteered, "It's the right thing to do and the right time to do it. All the principles [sic] are dead—the secrets of the war can now be told." A few of the locals ruminated that if the train had only gone a bit faster or just four miles farther on March 25, 1931, it would have crossed the county line. Scottsboro would have been "spar[ed]...its infamy," and the defendants forever known as the "Huntsville Boys." The mayor ventured that any city's name in the land could be substituted for Scottsboro. "Would a mob have shown up in another town? Are our people any more prone to emotion than another group of people? Scottsboro is part of the American story."[56]

An 87-year-old black man who attended the ceremony, one of the few who could remember the cases firsthand, recalled that the mob scene following the

Boys' arrest "was frightening" and that death threats were leveled against the jailed suspects.[57] He applauded the town's move to install the plaque on the courthouse lawn. "I think it will bring the races closer together," he said, "to understand each other better." Another person at the gathering ventured, "We can not change the course of human events that began on March 25, 1931, but we can unite to heal the longstanding wounds."[58] One Scottsboro resident perhaps best captured the significance of the marker that was installed more than seven decades after the conclusion of the trials in the Jackson County Courthouse. "'The "Boys" are dead,' said Sheila Washington,...who grew up in a black household where her father hid a book about the case inside a trunk. 'But the story still lives.'"[59]

It would be a tragedy if the story of the Scottsboro boys were forgotten. If their story does not endure, the tragedy of the broken lives of Olen Montgomery, Clarence Norris, Haywood Patterson, Ozie Powell, Willie Roberson, Charlie Weems, Eugene Williams, Andy Wright, and Roy Wright will only be compounded. If their cases are not remembered it will be a tragedy for the system of laws and the men and women charged with administering them. And if they and their cases are forgotten it will be a tragedy for a nation concerned with securing social and legal justice for all of its people.

Notes

INTRODUCTION

1. Norval Morris, *Madness and the Criminal Law* (Chicago: The University of Chicago Press 1982), p. 73.

2. Ray Surette, *Media, Crime, and Criminal Justice: Images and Realities* (Pacific Grove, California: Brooks/Cole Publishing Co. 1992), pp. 82–83.

3. Richard V. Ericson, Patricia M. Baranek, and Janet B.L. Chan, "Media and Markets," in *Crime and the Media,* edited by Richard V. Ericson (Brookfield, Vermont: Dartmouth Publishing Co. 1995), pp. 3–31, at pp. 15–18.

4. At the time of their arrest, the accused in the case ranged in age from 13 to 20. All were African American. The term "boys" may have been age-appropriate for at least some of youths, but of course it also can be considered racially pejorative. When the young men are described as "the Scottsboro Boys," the intent here is to be faithful to common contemporary references and not to be racially offensive.

5. The Supreme Court ruled in *Coker v. Georgia,* 433 U.S. 584 (1977) that capital punishment is constitutionally excessive for the crime of raping an adult, and hence violates the Eighth Amendment's prohibition against cruel and unusual punishments. There is some uncertainty about whether *Coker's* prohibition against capital punishment applies when the rape victim is a child.

6. The Supreme Court ruled in *Roper v. Simmons,* 543 U.S. 551 (2005) that the Eighth Amendment forbids the execution of offenders who were younger than 18 at the time they committed their crimes.

CHAPTER 1

1. Gordon V. Axon, *The Stock Market Crash of 1929* (New York: Mason & Lipscomb 1974), p. 72.

2. Thomas Holt, "The Lonely Warrior: Ida B. Wells-Barnett," in *Black Leaders of the Twentieth Century,* eds. John Hope Franklin and August Meier (Urbana, Illinois: University of Illinois Press 1982), 39–61, p. 42.

3. Dan T. Carter, *Scottsboro: A Tragedy of the American South* (Baton Rouge: Louisiana State University Press, rev. ed. 1979), pp. 5–6; American Experience, "Scottsboro: An American Tragedy," http://www.pbs.org/wgbh/amex/scottsboro/peopleevents. The youths' ages are reported elsewhere slightly differently. For example, in Robert Leibowitz, *The Defender: The Life and Career of Samuel S. Leibowitz 1893–1933* (Englewood Cliffs, New Jersey: Prentice-Hall), p. 187, Weems is described as being 21, Patterson, Andy Wright, and Roberson as 17, Powell as 16, and Williams as 14. Newspaper stories and other writings occasionally used other spellings for the young men's first names, including "Heywood" (for Haywood Patterson), "Ozzie" or "Osie" (for Ozie Powell), and "Charley" (for Charlie Weems). The standard spellings are used throughout this book.

4. See the autobiographical account provided in Haywood Patterson and Earl Conrad, *Scottsboro Boy* (New York: Bantam Books 1950), pp. 1–2, an account that is largely confirmed through other sources.

5. James Goodman, *Stories of Scottsboro* (New York: Vintage Books 1994), pp. 3–4.

6. Carter, note 3, at p. 25; Goodman, note 5, at p. 4.

7. Carter, note 3, at p. 4, citing Scottsboro *Jackson County Sentinel,* March 26, 1931, and Huntsville (Alabama) *Daily Times,* March 26, 1931.

8. Carter, note 3, at p. 5, citing Scottsboro *Jackson County Sentinel,* March 26, 1931, and Huntsville (Alabama) *Daily Times,* March 26, 1931.

9. Goodman, note 5, at pp. 4, 8.

10. Patterson and Conrad, note 4, at p. 3; Goodman, note 5, at p. 5.

11. Carter, note 3, at pp. 6–7; Goodman, note 5, at p. 21.

12. Goodman, note 5, at p. 5.

13. Goodman, note 5, at pp. 12–13, *quoting* the *Jackson County Sentinel,* March 25, 1931 (but reporting "friends" instead of "fiends"; Douglas O. Linder, "The Trials of 'The Scottsboro Boys,'" found online at http://www.law.umkc.edu/faculty/projects/FTrials/Scottsboro/SB_acct.html.

14. *Huntsville Daily Times,* March 25, 1931, p. 1.

15. Ibid.

16. Margaret Vandiver, *Lethal Punishment: Lynchings and Legal Executions in the South* (New Brunswick, New Jersey: Rutgers University Press 2006), pp. 9–10; Stewart A. Tolnay and E.M. Beck, *A Festival of Violence: An Analysis of Southern Lynchings, 1882–1930* (Urbana, Illinois: University of Illinois Press 1995).

17. Carter, note 3, at pp. 8–10.

18. Michael J. Klarman, "*Powell v. Alabama*: The Supreme Court Confronts 'Legal Lynchings'," in *Criminal Procedure Stories,* edited by Carol S. Steiker (New York: Foundation Press 2006), 1–44, at p. 2; Leibowitz, note 3, at p. 186.

19. *New York Times,* March 26, 1931, p. 21.

20. *Birmingham News,* March 26, 1931, pp. 1–2.

21. Michael J. Klarman, "The Racial Origins of Modern Criminal Procedure," 99 *Michigan Law Review* 48 (2000): 52–57.

22. *Montgomery Advertiser,* March 27, 1931, p. 4.

23. *Birmingham News,* March 26, 1931, p. 2.

24. *Birmingham News,* March 27, 1931, p. 1.

25. *Birmingham News,* March 30, 1931, p. 2.

26. "Nine negroes were indicted separately and jointly on two counts of criminal assault against two Huntsville girls..." *Birmingham News,* March 31, 1931, p. 1.

27. *Powell v. State,* 224 Ala. 540, 141 So. 201, 204 (1932).

28. *Powell v. Alabama,* 287 U.S. 45, 50 (1932).

29. *Birmingham News,* March 31, 1931, p. 1.

30. *Powell v. Alabama,* 287 U.S. 45, 59–60 (1932), citing Ala. Code § 5567 (1923).

31. Carter, note 3, at pp. 19–20.

32. *Powell v. Alabama,* 287 U.S. 45, 56 (1932).

33. Carter, note 3, at pp. 17–18.

34. Goodman, note 5, at pp. 24–25.

35. Charles H. Martin, "The International Labor Defense and Black America," 26 *Labor History* 165 (1985).

36. *Daily Worker,* April 2, 1931, pp. 1, 3.

37. *Montgomery Advertiser,* March 26, 1931, p. 1.

38. *Jackson County Sentinel,* March 26, 1931, p. 1, quoted in Carter, note 3, at p. 13.

39. *Progressive Age,* March 26, 1931, p. 1, quoted in Carter, note 3, at p. 13.

40. *Huntsville Daily Times,* March 26, 1931, p. 1.

41. *Huntsville Daily Times,* March 26, 1931, p. 8.

42. *Huntsville Daily Times,* March 25, 1931, p. 1.

43. *Huntsville Daily Times,* March 26, 1931, pp. 1, 8.

44. *Huntsville Daily Times,* March 30, 1931, p. 8.

45. *Daily Worker,* April 7, 1931, p. 1.

46. Diane Miller Sommerville, "The Rape Myth in the Old South Reconsidered," 61 *Journal of Southern History* 481 (1995): 483–486.

47. Sommerville, note 46, at 488. Sommerville argues that whites' perception about hypersexuality among black males may not have become widespread until the 20th century. Diane Miller Sommerville, *Rape and Race in the Nineteenth-Century South* (Chapel Hill: University of North Carolina Press 2004), pp. 10–11.

48. W.F. Cash, *The Mind of the South* (New York: Alfred A. Knopf 1970), pp. 115–116.

49. Peter W. Bardaglio, "Rape and the Law in the Old South: 'Calculated to excite indignation in every heart,'" 60 *Journal of Southern History* 749 (1994): 754.

50. Dennis D. Dorin, "Two Different Worlds: Criminologists, Justices and Racial Discrimination in the Imposition of Capital Punishment in Rape Cases," 72 *Journal of Criminal Law & Criminology* 1667 (1981); Marvin E. Wolfgang and Marc Riedel, "Race, Judicial Discretion, and the Death Penalty," 407 *Annals of the American Academy of Political and Social Science* 119 (1973).

51. Hollace Ransdall, *Report on the Scottsboro, Ala. Case* (May 27, 1931) (unpublished), reprinted in full at Professor Doug Linder's "Famous American Trials" Web site, http://www.law.umkc.edu/faculty/projects/FTrials/scottsboro/SB_HRrep.html.

52. Ibid.

53. *New York Times,* March 26, 1931, p. 21.

54. *Birmingham News,* March 26, 1931, p. 2.

55. *Huntsville Daily Times,* March 2, 1931, pp. 1, 8.

56. Patterson and Conrad, note 4, at p. 4.

57. Ibid. at p. 11.

58. Ibid. at p. 23.

59. Ibid. at p. 25.

60. See http://www.law.umkc.edu/faculty/projects/FTrials/scottsboro/SB_bSBs.html; http://www.pbs.org/wgbh/amex/scottsboro/peopleevents/p_williams.html; http://www. pbs.org/wgbh/amex/scottsboro/peopleevents/p_lwright.html; http://www.pbs.org/wgbh/ amex/scottsboro/peopleevents/p_awright.html.

61. See http://www.pbs.org/wgbh/amex/scottsboro/peopleevents/p_weems.html; http:// www.law.umkc.edu/faculty/projects/FTrials/scottsboro/SB_bSBs.html.

62. Clarence Norris and Sybil D. Washington, *The Last of the Scottsboro Boys* (New York: G.P. Putnam's Sons 1979) pp. 18, 27–38.

63. See http://www.pbs.org/wgbh/amex/scottsboro/peopleevents/p_montgomery.html; http://www.law.umkc.edu/faculty/projects/FTrials/scottsboro/SB_bSBs.html.

64. See http://www.pbs.org/wgbh/amex/scottsboro/peopleevents/p_roberson.html; http://www.law.umkc.edu/faculty/projects/FTrials/scottsboro/SB_bSBs.html.

65. See http://www.pbs.org/wgbh/amex/scottsboro/peopleevents/p_powell.html; http:// www.law.umkc.edu/faculty/projects/FTrials/scottsboro/SB_bSBs.html.

CHAPTER 2

1. Dan T. Carter, *Scottsboro: A Tragedy of the American South* (Baton Rouge, Louisiana: Louisiana State University Press, rev. ed. 1979), p. 21.

2. *Montgomery Advertiser,* April 7, 1931, p. 1, quoting J.S. Benson, editor of the (Scottsboro) *Progressive Age.*

3. *Huntsville Daily Times,* April 6, 1931, p. 1; see also *Montgomery Advertiser,* April 7, 1931, p. 1

4. *Daily Worker,* April 7, 1931, pp. 1, 3.

5. *Huntsville Daily Times,* April 6, 1931, p. 1.

6. *Norris v. Alabama,* 294 U.S. 587, 590 (1935), quoting Alabama Code § 8603 (1923).

7. Haywood Patterson and Earl Conrad, *Scottsboro Boy* (New York: Bantam Books 1950), p. 10.

8. Faust Rossi, "The First Scottsboro Trials: A Legal Lynching," 29 *Cornell Law Forum* 1, 4 (Winter 2002), available on-line at http://www.lawschool.cornell.edu/pdfs/Winter2002 Forum.pdf.

9. Carter, note 1, at p. 22.

10. Clarence Norris and Sybil D. Washington, *The Last of the Scottsboro Boys* (New York: G.P. Putnam's Sons 1979), p. 22.

11. Carter, note 1, at p. 18, quoting Memorandum of Walter White on Conversation with Hollace Ransdell, May 2, 1931, Legal Series, Scottsboro Case, File Box 1, National Association for the Advancement of Colored People Collection, Library of Congress, Washington, DC.

12. James Goodman, *Stories of Scottsboro* (New York: Vintage Books 1994), p. 41.

13. Patterson and Conrad, note 7, at p. 8.

14. *Weems and Norris v. Alabama,* Transcript of Record, Supreme Court of the United States, 22 United States Supreme Court Records and Briefs, No. 100, p. 85, October Term 1932.

15. *Powell v. Alabama,* 287 U.S. 45, 53–56 (1932).

16. *Powell et al. v. Alabama,* Brief for Petitioners 52, United States Supreme Court, in *Weems and Norris v. Alabama,* Transcript of Record, note 14.

17. Rossi, note 8, at p. 4; Carter, note 1, at p. 23.

18. *Weems and Norris v. Alabama,* Transcript of Record, note 14, at pp. 18–21.

19. *Huntsville Daily Times,* April 6, 1931, p. 1; Carter, note 1, at pp. 23–24.

20. The indictments on which the prosecution proceeded in the three sets of trials later reviewed by the U.S. Supreme Court are provided at *Weems and Norris v. Alabama,* Transcript of Record, note 14, at p. 1; *Patterson v. Alabama,* Transcript of Record, Supreme Court of the United States, 22 United States Supreme Court Records and Briefs, No. 99, p. 1, October Term 1932; and *Ozie Powell, Willie Roberson, Andy Wright, and Olen Montgomery v. Alabama,* Transcript of Record, Supreme Court of the United States, 22 United States Supreme Court Records and Briefs, No. 99, p. 1, October Term 1932.

21. *Weems and Norris v. Alabama,* Transcript of Record, note 14, at pp. 96–97.

22. *Huntsville Daily Times,* April 6, 1931, p. 1.

23. *Montgomery Advertiser,* April 7, 1931, p. 1; *Huntsville Daily Times,* April 6, 1931, p. 1.

24. *Weems and Norris v. Alabama,* Transcript of Record, note 14, at pp. 22–24. The trial record prepared for purposes of appeal consists primarily of a summary of witnesses' testimony, presented in the form of a narrative, and not verbatim accounts of attorneys' questions and witnesses' answers. However, verbatim transcriptions of testimony and exchanges between counsel and the trial judge occasionally are provided, including when important to an issue raised on appeal. For the most part, quoted material from the trials corresponds to the narrative summaries, rather than the precise language that the witnesses may have used. Much of the original flavor of the narratives is attempted to be preserved, including word choices, the lack of capitalization of "negroes," and in related respects.

25. *Weems and Norris v. Alabama,* Transcript of Record, note 14, at pp. 24–32.

26. *Weems and Norris v. Alabama,* Transcript of Record, note 14, at pp. 33–34.

27. Ibid., at pp. 34–36.

28. Ibid., at pp. 37–38.

29. *Huntsville Daily Times,* April 7, 1931, p. 1.

30. *Weems and Norris v. Alabama,* Transcript of Record, note 14, at pp. 38–41.

31. Ibid., at pp. 42–48.

32. Ibid., at pp. 48–51.

33. Ibid., at pp. 51–54.

34. Ibid., at pp. 55–56.

35. Ibid., at pp. 56–58.

36. *Huntsville Daily Times,* April 7, 1931, p. 1.

37. Ibid. For another report of the defense lawyers' attempt to negotiate life sentences for the defendants in exchange for guilty pleas, see *Birmingham News,* April 7, 1931, p. 1.

38. *Weems and Norris v. Alabama,* Transcript of Record, note 14, at p. 58.

39. Ibid., at p. 59.

40. *Huntsville Daily Times,* April 7, 1931, p. 1.

41. *Weems and Norris v. Alabama,* Transcript of Record, note 14, at pp. 59–62.

42. *Patterson v. Alabama,* Transcript of Record, note 20, at p. 21.

43. Ibid., at 22–26.

44. *Montgomery Advertiser,* April 8, 1931, p. 1.

45. *Patterson v. Alabama,* Transcript of Record, note 20, Petition for New Trial, at p. 54.

46. *Birmingham Age Herald,* April 8, 1931, p. 1.

47. *Patterson v. Alabama,* Transcript of Record, note 20, at pp. 27–30.

48. Ibid., at pp. 30–32.

49. The Transcript of Record incorrectly identifies the witness as Ory "Robbins" instead of "Dobbins." Ibid., at p. 34.

50. Ibid., at pp. 32–35.

51. Ibid., at pp. 35–38.

52. Ibid., at pp. 39–41.

53. *Birmingham News,* April 8, 1931, pp. 1–2.

54. *Montgomery Advertiser,* April 8, 1931, p. 1; *Birmingham Age Herald,* April 8, 1931, p. 1 ("Threatens Judge").

55. *New York Times,* April 9, 1931, p. 31.

56. Ibid. The article attributed a statement to Judge Hawkins that, "More than 1,000 members of the Alabama National Guard have been stationed here to protect" the defendants. Other newspapers reported that the judge had said "More than 100" National Guardsmen had been assigned, which accords with the actual number. See *Birmingham News,* April 8, 1931, p. 2, which also provides a fuller account of the quoted officials' statements.

57. *Patterson v. Alabama,* Transcript of Record, note 20, at pp. 42–43.

58. Ibid., at pp. 44–45.

59. Ibid., at pp. 45–46.

60. Ibid., at pp. 46–48.

61. Ibid., at pp. 48–49.

62. Ibid., at p. 50.

63. *Birmingham News,* April 8, 1931, p. 1.

64. *Ozie Powell, Willie Roberson, Andy Wright, and Olen Montgomery v. Alabama,* Transcript of Record, note 20, at pp. 22–24.

65. Ibid., at pp. 24–26.

66. *Huntsville Daily Times,* April 8, 1931, p. 1.

67. *Montgomery Advertiser,* April 9, 1931, p. 1.

68. *Ozie Powell, Willie Roberson, Andy Wright, and Olen Montgomery v. Alabama,* Transcript of Record, note 20, at pp. 26–28.

69. Ibid., at pp. 28–30.

70. Ibid., at pp. 30–33.

71. Ibid., at pp. 33–35.

72. Ibid., at pp. 36–37.

73. Ibid., at pp. 38–39.

74. Ibid., at pp. 39–40.

75. Ibid., at pp. 41–42.

76. Ibid., at pp. 42–48.

77. Ibid., at pp. 48–52.

78. *Huntsville Daily Times,* April 9, 1931, pp. 1, 10.

79. *Birmingham Age Herald,* April 9, 1931, p. 1; *Montgomery Advertiser,* April 9, 1931, p. 1; *Huntsville Daily Times,* April 9, 1931, pp. 1, 10.

80. *Montgomery Advertiser,* April 10, 1931, p. 1.

81. *Birmingham Age Herald,* April 10, 1931, p. 3.

82. *Montgomery Advertiser,* April 10, 1931, p. 1; see also *Birmingham Age Herald,* April 10, 1931, p. 3.

83. *New York Times,* April 10, 1931, p. 52.

84. *Daily Worker,* April 9, 1931, p. 1.

85. *Daily Worker,* April 11, 1931, p. 1.

86. *Daily Worker,* April 9, 1931, p. 1.

87. *Daily Worker,* April 11, 1931, p. 1.

88. *Montgomery Advertiser,* April 10, 1931, p. 1.

89. *Huntsville Daily Times,* April 10, 1931, p. 1.

90. *New York Times,* April 11, 1931, p. 40; *Montgomery Advertiser,* April 11, 1931, p. 1; *Huntsville Daily Times,* April 10, 1931, p. 1; *Birmingham Age Herald,* April 11, 1931, p. 1.

91. *Daily Worker,* April 11, 1931, p. 1.

92. *Huntsville Daily Times,* April 10, 1931, p. 1; *Birmingham Age Herald,* April 11, 1931, pp. 1–2.

93. Norris and Washington, note 10, at p. 25.

94. Patterson and Conrad, note 7, at p. 12.

95. *Birmingham Age Herald,* April 11, 1931, p. 1.

96. *Daily Worker,* April 11, 1931, p. 1.

97. *Daily Worker,* April 13, 1931, p. 1.

98. *New York Times,* April 26, 1931, p. 2.

99. *Daily Worker,* April 16, 1931, p. 1.

100. Quoted in *Montgomery Advertiser,* April 14, 1931, p. 4.

101. *Montgomery Advertiser,* April 14, 1931, p. 4.

102. *New York Times,* June 21, 1931, p. 53.

103. Carter, note 1, at p. 146; *New York Times,* July 12, 1931, p. 9.

104. Quoted in Edmund Wilson, "The Freight-Car Case," 68 *The New Republic* 38 (August 26, 1931): 40.

105. 261 U.S. 86 (1923). See Hugh T. Murray, Jr., "The NAACP versus the Communist Party: The Scottsboro Rape Cases, 1931–1932," 28 *Phylon* 276 (1967): 279; Raymond Pace Alexander, "The Upgrading of the Negro's Status by Supreme Court Decisions," 30 *Journal of Negro History* 117 (1945): 127–29.

106. Carter, note 1, at pp. 52–53.

107. Wilson, note 104, at 40–41; Murray, note 105, at 277–78.

108. Carter, note 1, at p. 72.

109. *Daily Worker,* April 24, 1931, p. 1.

110. *New York Times,* July 6, 1931, p. 17; Murray, note 105, at 276.

111. Carter, note 1, at pp. 67–72.

112. Wilson, note 104, at 42.

113. Murray, note 105, at 283.

114. Goodman, note 12, at p. 71; Carter, note 1, at pp. 69–70, pp. 88–89; Daniel Pfaff, "The Press and the Scottsboro Rape Cases," 1 *Journalism History* 72 (1974): 75.

115. Beth Tompkins Bates, "A New Crowd Challenges the Agenda of the Old Guard in the NAACP, 1933–1941," 102 *American Historical Review* 340 (1997): 344, quoting Mark Naison, *Communists in Harlem During the Depression* (Urbana, Illinois: University of Illinois Press 1983), p. 62.

116. Frederick G. Detweiler, "The Negro Press Today," 44 *American Journal of Sociology* 391 (1938).

117. Pfaff, note 114; Carter, note 1, at pp. 68–69, 88–90; Goodman, note 12, at pp. 68–71.

118. Pfaff, note 117, at 74, 76.

119. Felecia G. Jones Ross, "Mobilizing the Masses: The *Cleveland Call and Post* and the Scottsboro Incident," 84 *Journal of Negro History* 48 (1999).

120. Goodman, note 12, at p. 64.

121. Patterson and Conrad, note 7, at p. 20.

122. Goodman, note 12, at pp. 111–12; Robert Leibowitz, *The Defender: The Life and Career of Samuel S. Leibowitz 1893–1933* (Englewood Cliffs, New Jersey: Prentice-Hall 1981), p. 192.

123. *New York Times,* June 28, 1931, p. 18.

124. *New York Times,* June 29, 1931, p. 18; *New York Times,* June 30, 1931, p. 3.

125. *New York Times,* June 30, 1931, p. 9; *New York Times,* July 8, 1931, p. 9; *New York Times,* July 11, 1931, p. 9.

126. *Time,* June 22, 1931, available at http://www.time.com/time/archive/printout/ 0,23657,741838,00.html.

127. *New York Times,* July 14, 1931, p. 21.

128. *New York Times,* September 6, 1931, p. 25.

129. *Birmingham News,* January 21, 1932, p. 1; *New York Times,* January 22, 1932, p. 17.

130. *Birmingham News,* January 22, 1932, pp. 1, 2.

131. *Daily Worker,* January 22, 1932, pp. 1, 3.

132. *Birmingham News,* January 22, 1932, pp. 1, 2.

133. *Powell v. State,* 141 So. 201 (Ala. 1932).

134. *Weems v. State,* 141 So. 215 (Ala. 1932).

135. *Patterson v. State,* 141 So. 195 (Ala. 1932).

136. *Powell v. State,* 141 So. 201, 203-04 (Ala. 1932).

137. Ibid., at pp. 207–08.

138. Ibid., at p. 210.

139. Ibid., at p. 211.

140. Ibid., at p. 213.

141. Ibid., at pp. 214–15.

142. *Daily Worker,* March 25, 1932, p. 1.

143. *New York Times,* March 25, 1932, p. 6.

144. *Birmingham News,* March 25, 1932, p. 6.

145. *New York Times,* March 27, 1932, p. 25; *New York Times,* March 31, 1932, p. 44.

146. *New York Times,* May 1, 1932, p. E6.

147. See, for example, *Gitlow v. United States,* 268 U.S. 652 (1925); *Whitney v. California,* 269 U.S. 530 (1925).

148. *New York Times,* May 17, 1932, p. 2; *New York Times,* May 24, 1932, p. 20.

149. *Powell v. Alabama,* 286 U.S. 540 (1932).

150. *New York Times,* June 1, 1932, p. 8.

151. *Daily Worker,* May 6, 1932, p. 1; *Daily Worker,* May 7, 1932, p. 1.

152. James A. Miller, Susan D. Pennybacker, and Eve Rosenhaft, "Mother Ada Wright and the International Campaign to Free the Scottsboro Boys, 1931–1934," 106 *American Historical Review* 387 (2001): 404.

153. *New York Times,* October 9, 1932, p. 22.

154. *New York Times,* October 11, 1932, p. 19; *New York Times,* October 12, 1932, p. 14.

155. 261 U.S. 86 (1923).

156. See Richard C. Cortner, *A Mob Intent on Death: The NAACP and the Arkansas Riot Cases* (Middletown, Connecticut: Wesleyan University Press 1988).

157. *Moore v. Dempsey,* 261 U.S. 86, 89–90 (1923).

158. 237 U.S. 309 (1915).

159. *Moore v. Dempsey,* 261 U.S. 86, 91 (1923).

160. Brief for Petitioners, *Powell et al. v. Alabama,* 22 United States Supreme Court Records and Briefs, Nos. 98, 99, 100, October Term 1932.

161. Brief for Respondent, *Powell et al. v. Alabama,* 22 United States Supreme Court Records and Briefs, Nos. 98, 99, 100, October Term 1932; *New York Times,* October 11, 1932, p. 19.

162. *Powell v. Alabama,* 287 U.S. 45, 52 (1932).

163. Ibid., 287 U.S., at 56–57.

164. Ibid., 287 U.S., at 68–71.

165. *New York Times,* November 8, 1932, pp. 12–13.

166. *New York Times,* November 8, 1932, p. 1.

167. *New York Times,* November 8, 1932, p. 11.

168. *New York Times,* November 8, 1932, p. 20.

169. *New York Times,* November 13, 1932, p. E1.

170. *New York Times,* November 13, 1932, p. E5.

171. *Daily Worker,* November 8, 1932, p. 1.

172. *Daily Worker,* November 8, 1932, p. 4.

173. *New York Times,* November 8, 1932, p. 13.

174. *Birmingham News,* November 8, 1932, p. 2.

175. Patterson and Conrad, note 7, at pp. 27.

176. Norris and Washington, note 10, at pp. 61.

CHAPTER 3

1. *Powell v. Alabama,* 287 U.S. 45, 73 (1932).

2. *New York Times,* January 17, 1933, p. 4.

3. Dan T. Carter, *Scottsboro: A Tragedy of the American South* (Baton Rouge: Louisiana State University Press, rev. ed. 1979), p. 144.

4. Quoted in Quentin Reynolds, *Courtroom: The Story of Samuel S. Leibowitz* (New York: Farrar, Straus and Company 1950), pp. 249–50.

5. Robert Leibowitz, *The Defender: The Life and Career of Samuel S. Leibowitz 1893–1933* (Englewood Cliffs, New Jersey: Prentice-Hall, Inc. 1981), pp. 2–8, 50–78, 144–47.

6. Samuel Liebowitz [*sic*], http://www.law.umkc.edu/faculty/projects/FTrials/Scottsboro/SB_bLieb.html.

7. Quoted in Reynolds, note 4, at pp. 251–52.

8. Ibid., at p. 252.

9. Leibowitz, note 5, at pp. 189–90.

10. *New York Times,* March 11, 1933, p. 28.

11. *New York Times,* December 23, 1932, p. 12; *New York Times,* December 24, 1932, p. 5.

12. *New York Times,* March 8, 1933, p. 14.

13. *New York Times,* March 8, 1933, p. 14.

14. *Decatur Daily,* March 8, 1933, p. 1.

15. Transcript of Record, *Norris v. Alabama,* Supreme Court of the United States, No. 534, October Term, 1934, p. 478.

16. Douglas O. Linder, "Without Fear or Favor: Judge James Edwin Horton and the Trial of the 'Scottsboro Boys,'" 68 *University of Missouri at Kansas City Law Review* 549 (2000): 553, 563.

17. *New York Times,* March 28, 1933, p. 6.

18. *New York Times,* March 29, 1933, p. 7.

19. *Decatur Daily,* March 27, 1933, p. 1.

20. Linder, note 16, at 555.

21. *Decatur Daily,* March 24, 1933, p. 1.

22. *Decatur Daily,* March 27, 1933, p. 1.

23. *Decatur Daily,* March 27, 1933, p. 1.

24. *New York Times,* March 18, 1933, p. 30.

25. *New York Times,* March 30, 1933, p. 4.

26. *Decatur Daily,* April 5, 1933, p. 1.

27. Clarence Norris and Sybil D. Washington, *The Last of the Scottsboro Boys* (New York: G.P. Putnam's Sons 1979), p. 64.

28. A copy of the letter is printed in Bates's handwriting in the *Daily Worker,* February 13, 1933, p. 1. The *Daily Worker* had reported the existence of the letter, and the Alabama authorities' alleged suppression of it, in January 1932. *Daily Worker,* January 15, 1932, p. 1. Copies of the letter are reprinted in Haywood Patterson and Earl Conrad, *Scottsboro Boy* (New York: Bantam Books 1950), pp. 215–16 (bearing the incorrect date of January 5, 1933), and in Norris and Washington, note 26, at p. 266 (also bearing the incorrect date of January 5, 1933). See also Carter, note 3, at pp. 186–87.

29. Carter, note 3, at pp. 186–88.

30. *Huntsville Times,* March 7, 1933, pp. 1–2.

31. *Decatur Daily,* March 25, 1933, p. 1.

32. *New York Times,* March 26, 1933, p. 17.

33. *New York Times,* March 28, 1933, p. 6.

34. *New York Times,* March 28, 1933, p. 6.

35. *Huntsville Times,* March 26, 1933, p. 1.

36. *Time,* March 20, 1933, available at http://www.time.com/time/archive/printout/ 0,23657,745379,00.html.

37. *New York Times,* March 29, 1933, p. 7.

38. *New York Times,* March 29, 1933, p. 7

39. *Birmingham Age Herald,* March 29, 1933, pp. 1–2.

40. See *Scottsboro: An American Tragedy,* PBS Home Video (2001). See generally Jennifer L. Eberhardt, Paul G. Davies, Valerie J. Purdie-Vaughns and Sheri Lynn Johnson, "Looking Deathworthy: Perceived Stereotypicality of Black Defendants Predicts Capital-Sentencing Outcomes," 17 *Psychological Science* 383 (2006).

41. *New York Times,* March 29, 1933, p. 7; *Birmingham Age Herald,* March 29, 1933, pp. 1–2.

42. *New York Times,* April 1, 1933, p. 34.

43. *Huntsville Times,* March 29, 1933, p. 1.

44. *Huntsville Times,* March 30, 1933, p. 2.

45. *Birmingham News,* April 1, 1933, p. 2.

46. *New York Times,* April 1, 1933, p. 34.

47. *Birmingham Age Herald,* April 1, 1933, pp. 1–2.

48. *New York Times,* April 1, 1933, p. 34.

49. *New York Times,* April 3, 1933, p. 34; *New York Times,* April 2, 1933, p. 5; *Decatur Daily,* April 1, 1933, p. 1.

50. *Huntsville Times,* April 3, 1933, pp. 1–2.

51. *New York Times,* April 4, 1933, p. 10.

52. *Huntsville Times,* April 3, 1933, p. 2; *Decatur Daily,* April 3, 1933, p. 1.

53. Mary Heaton Vorse, "The Scottsboro Trial," 74 *The New Republic* 276 (April 19, 1933): 277.

54. *New York Times,* April 4, 1933, p. 10.

55. Trial Transcript, *State of Alabama v. Haywood Patterson,* pp. 9–15 Decatur, Alabama, March-April, 1933, microfilm collection, Cornell Law School.

56. *Birmingham News,* April 3, 1933, p. 2.

57. *Birmingham Age Herald,* April 4, 1933, p. 1.

58. *Huntsville Times,* April 3, 1933, p. 1.

59. Vorse, note 53, at p. 277.

60. *Birmingham News,* April 4, 1933, p. 14.

61. *Birmingham News,* April 3, 1933, p. 1.

62. Trial Transcript, *State v. Patterson,* note 55, at p. 87.

63. *New York Times,* April 4, 1933, p. 10.

64. Trial Transcript, *State v. Patterson,* note 55, at p. 17.

65. Trial Transcript, *State v. Patterson,* note 55, at p. 26.

66. Carter, note 3, at p. 206.

67. Trial Transcript, *State v. Patterson,* note 55, at pp. 202, 795–96 (testimony of W.H. Hill); ibid., at 732 (testimony of Ruby Bates).

68. Trial Transcript, *State v. Patterson,* note 55, at p. 34 (testimony of Victoria Price).

69. Trial Transcript, *State v. Patterson,* note 55, at p. 66 (testimony of Victoria Price).

70. Trial Transcript, *State v. Patterson,* note 55, at p. 64 (testimony of Victoria Price).

71. Trial Transcript, *State v. Patterson,* note 55, at pp. 161–67 (testimony of R.R. Bridges).

72. *Birmingham News,* April 4, 1933, p. 14.

73. *New York Times,* April 4, 1933, p. 10.

74. Trial Transcript, *State v. Patterson,* note 55, at pp. 172–73, 175–81 (testimony of R.R. Bridges).

75. Trial Transcript, *State v. Patterson,* note 55, at p. 174 (testimony of R.R. Bridges).

76. Trial Transcript, *State v. Patterson,* note 55, at pp. 188–94 (testimony of R.R. Bridges).

77. Trial Transcript, *State v. Patterson,* note 55, at pp. 506–28 (testimony of Dr. Edward Reisman).

78. Trial Transcript, *State v. Patterson,* note 55, at pp. 244–54 (testimony of Lee Adams).

79. Trial Transcript, *State v. Patterson,* note 55, at pp. 255–58 (testimony of Ory Dobbins).

80. Vorse, note 53, at p. 277.

81. Trial Transcript, *State v. Patterson,* note 55, at pp. 259–86 (testimony of Ory Dobbins).

82. Trial Transcript, *State v. Patterson,* note 55, at pp. 132–40 (testimony of R.S. Turner).

83. Trial Transcript, *State v. Patterson,* note 55, at pp. 292–94.

84. *New York Times,* April 5, 1933, p. 40.

85. *Decatur Daily,* April 4, 1933, p. 1.

86. *Birmingham Age Herald,* April 5, 1933, p. 5.

87. Trial Transcript, *State v. Patterson,* note 55, at p. 89 (testimony of Victoria Price).

88. *New York Times,* April 4, 1933, p. 10.

89. Trial Transcript, *State v. Patterson,* note 55, at p. 95.

90. If Price indeed appropriated the name Callie for "the boarding house lady" from reading *The Saturday Evening Post* her choice was ironic. Octavus Roy Cohen, who authored articles for *The Saturday Evening Post* as well as several books, used a black private investigator by the name of Florian Slappey as his protagonist in a number of his works. The stories featured exaggerated black dialect and Slappey as the bumbling although ultimately successful detective. Cohen was a native of South Carolina, where he briefly practiced law, and he also worked as a reporter for, among other newspapers, the *Birmingham Ledger.* To compound the irony, his stories were set in Birmingham, Alabama and Slappey was known as "the Black Beau Brummell of Birmingham." *See* "Archival Resources: Cohen, Octavus Roy," at http://www.bponline.org/Archives/collections/arts/cohenoctavusroy.asp (Web site consulted June 12, 2007); "Florian Slappey," at http://www.thrillingdetective.com/slappey.html (Web site consulted June 12, 2007).

91. Trial Transcript, *State v. Patterson,* note 55, at pp. 99–100.

92. Trial Transcript, *State v. Patterson,* note 55, at pp. 337–45 (testimony of George Chamlee).

93. Trial Transcript, *State v. Patterson,* note 55, at pp. 331–36 (testimony of Beatrice Maddox).

94. Trial Transcript, *State v. Patterson,* note 55, at pp. 76–81.

95. Trial Transcript, *State v. Patterson,* note 55, at pp. 72–73; see also ibid., at p. 329.

96. *Daily Worker,* April 4, 1933, p. 3.

97. Trial Transcript, *State v. Patterson,* note 55, at p. 126 (testimony of Victoria Price).

98. *Birmingham News,* April 3, 1933, p. 2; *Huntsville Times,* April 3, 1933, p. 2; *Birmingham Age Herald,* April 4, 1933, p. 2.

99. Trial Transcript, *State v. Patterson,* note 55, at p. 82–84 (testimony of Victoria Price).

100. Vorse, note 53, at p. 277.

101. Carter, note 3, at p. 210, quoting Robert Burns Eleazer correspondence to Will W. Alexander, Papers of the Southern Commission on Interracial Cooperation, April 17, 1933.

102. *New York Times,* April 6, 1933, p. 13.

103. *New York Times,* April 6, 1933, p. 13.

104. Trial Transcript, *State v. Patterson,* note 55, at pp. 398–401.

105. *New York Times,* April 5, 1933, p. 40.

106. Trial Transcript, *State v. Patterson,* note 55, at pp. 298–316 (testimony of Dallas Ramsey).

107. Trial Transcript, *State v. Patterson,* note 55, at pp. 633–51 (testimony of E.L. Lewis).

108. Trial Transcript, *State v. Patterson,* note 55, at pp. 325–30 (testimony of Norris Payne).

109. Trial Transcript, *State v. Patterson,* note 55, at pp. 331–45 (testimony of Beatrice Maddox and George W. Chamlee).

110. Trial Transcript, *State v. Patterson,* note 55, at pp. 346–59 (testimony of Willie Robertson [*sic*]).

111. Trial Transcript, *State v. Patterson,* note 55, at pp. 360–64 (testimony of Olin [*sic*] Montgomery).

112. *Daily Worker,* April 4, 1933, p. 4.

113. Trial Transcript, *State v. Patterson,* note 55, at p. 364 (testimony of Olin [*sic*] Montgomery).

114. Trial Transcript, *State v. Patterson,* note 55, at pp. 365–71 (testimony of Ozie Powell).

115. Trial Transcript, *State v. Patterson,* note 55, at pp. 371–97 (testimony of Ozie Powell).

116. Trial Transcript, *State v. Patterson*, note 55, at p. 393.

117. Trial Transcript, *State v. Patterson*, note 55, at pp. 402–21 (testimony of Andy Wright); Trial Transcript, *State v. Patterson*, note 55, at pp. 422–40 (testimony of Eugene Williams).

118. Trial Transcript, *State v. Patterson*, note 55, at p. 442 (testimony of Haywood Patterson).

119. Trial Transcript, *State v. Patterson*, note 55, at pp. 483–84 (testimony of Percy Ricks, a fireman on the train).

120. Trial Transcript, *State v. Patterson*, note 55, at pp. 443–47 (testimony of Haywood Patterson).

121. Transcript of Record, *Patterson v. Alabama*, 22 United States Supreme Court Records and Briefs, at pp. 37–38 (No. 99, Oct. Term 1932).

122. Trial Transcript, *State v. Patterson*, note 55, at p. 454 (testimony of Haywood Patterson).

123. Trial Transcript, *State v. Patterson*, note 55, at p. 462.

124. Trial Transcript, *State v. Patterson*, note 55, at p. 468.

125. *New York Times*, April 6, 1933, p. 13; *Daily Worker*, April 6, 1933, p. 1.

126. *Birmingham News*, April 5, 1933, p. 2.

127. *Birmingham Age Herald*, April 6, 1933, p. 2.

128. *Huntsville Daily Times*, April 6, 1933, p. 2.

129. *Birmingham News*, April 7, 1933, p. 2.

130. Trial Transcript, *State v. Patterson*, note 55, at pp. 530–42 (testimony of Lester Carter).

131. Trial Transcript, *State v. Patterson*, note 55, at pp. 545–46.

132. Trial Transcript, *State v. Patterson*, note 55, at p. 548.

133. Trial Transcript, *State v. Patterson*, note 55, at pp. 543–57 (testimony of Lester Carter).

134. Trial Transcript, *State v. Patterson*, note 55, at pp. 557–64 (testimony of Lester Carter).

135. Trial Transcript, *State v. Patterson*, note 55, at pp. 564–73 (testimony of Lester Carter).

136. *Huntsville Daily Times*, April 6, 1933, p. 2.

137. Trial Transcript, *State v. Patterson*, note 55, at p. 595 (testimony of Lester Carter).

138. Trial Transcript, *State v. Patterson*, note 55, at p. 609 (testimony of Lester Carter).

139. *Huntsville Daily Times*, April 6, 1933, p. 2.

140. Trial Transcript, *State v. Patterson*, note 55, at p. 630 (testimony of Lester Carter).

141. Trial Transcript, *State v. Patterson*, note 55, at pp. 633–53 (testimony of E.L. Lewis).

142. Trial Transcript, *State v. Patterson*, note 55, at p. 654.

143. *Birmingham Age Herald*, April 7, 1933, p. 1.

144. *New York Times*, April 7, 1933, p. 3.

145. *New York Times*, April 7, 1933, p. 3 .

146. *Birmingham News*, April 7, 1933, p. 2.

147. *Birmingham News*, April 7, 1933, pp. 1, 2.

148. *Huntsville Daily Times*, April 6, 1933, p. 1.

149. *New York Times*, April 7, 1933, p. 3.

150. Trial Transcript, *State v. Patterson*, note 55, at p. 662 (testimony of Ruby Bates).

151. *New York Times*, April 7, 1933, p. 3.

152. Trial Transcript, *State v. Patterson,* note 55, at pp. 666–67 (testimony of Ruby Bates).

153. Trial Transcript, *State v. Patterson,* note 55, at p. 671 (testimony of Ruby Bates).

154. Trial Transcript, *State v. Patterson,* note 55, at p. 673 (testimony of Ruby Bates).

155. Trial Transcript, *State v. Patterson,* note 55, at pp. 673–75 (testimony of Ruby Bates).

156. *Birmingham News,* April 7, 1933, p. 2; see Trial Transcript, *State v. Patterson,* note 55, at pp. 733–34.

157. *New York Times,* April 7, 1933, p. 3.

158. Trial Transcript, *State v. Patterson,* note 55, at p. 677 (testimony of Ruby Bates).

159. Trial Transcript, *State v. Patterson,* note 55, at pp. 678–746 (testimony of Ruby Bates).

160. *Huntsville Daily Times,* April 7, 1933, p. 4.

161. *Birmingham Age Herald,* April 7, 1933, pp. 1, 2.

162. *Birmingham News,* April 7, 1933, p. 2.

163. Trial Transcript, *State v. Patterson,* note 55, at pp. 750–59 (testimony of Dr. Carey Walker).

164. Trial Transcript, *State v. Patterson,* note 55, at pp. 760–68 (testimony of Dr. J.H. Hall).

165. Trial Transcript, *State v. Patterson,* note 55, at pp. 783–88 (testimony of Dr. J.H. Hall).

166. Trial Transcript, *State v. Patterson,* note 55, at pp. 794–800 (testimony of W.H. Hill).

167. Trial Transcript, *State v. Patterson,* note 55, at pp. 801–2, 803–7, 807–10 (testimony of Haywood Patterson, Ruby Bates, and Vertus Frost).

168. *Decatur Daily,* April 8, 1933, p. 6.

169. *New York Times,* April 8, 1933, p. 30.

170. *New York Times,* April 8, 1933, p. 30.

171. *Huntsville Daily Times,* April 7, 1933, p. 1.

172. *Decatur Daily,* April 8, 1933, p. 6.

173. Trial Transcript, *State v. Patterson,* note 55, at pp. 812–13.

174. *New York Times,* April 8, 1933, p. 30.

175. Trial Transcript, *State v. Patterson,* note 55, at p. 813.

176. *New York Times,* April 9, 1933, pp. 1, 16.

177. *Decatur Daily,* April 8, 1933, p. 6.

178. *Birmingham Age Herald,* April 8, 1933, p. 1.

179. *New York Times,* April 8, 1933, p. 30.

180. *Birmingham Age Herald,* April 8, 1933, p. 1.

181. *New York Times,* April 9, 1933, pp. 1, 16.

182. *New York Times,* April 8, 1933, p. 30.

183. *New York Times,* April 9, 1933, pp. 1, 16.

184. *Birmingham News,* April 8, 1933, p. 2.

185. *Decatur Daily,* April 8, 1933, p. 6.

186. *New York Times,* April 9, 1933, pp. 1, 16.

187. *Birmingham News,* April 8, 1933, p. 2.

188. *Decatur Daily,* April 8, 1933, p. 6.

189. *New York Times,* April 9, 1933, pp. 1, 16.

190. *New York Times,* April 9, 1933, pp. 1, 16.

191. *New York Times,* April 9, 1933, p. 16.

192. *Birmingham News,* April 8, 1933, p. 2.

193. *New York Times,* April 9, 1933, p. 16.

194. *Decatur Daily,* April 10, 1933, p. 1; *New York Times,* April 10, 1933, pp. 1, 2.

195. *New York Times,* April 10, 1933, p. 2.

196. *Birmingham Age Herald,* April 10, 1933, pp. 1, 3.

197. *Birmingham News,* April 10, 1933, pp. 1, 2.

198. *Daily Worker,* April 10, 1933, p. 1.

199. *New York Times,* April 11, 1933, pp. 1, 11.

200. *Birmingham News,* April 11, 1933, pp. 1, 2.

201. *Daily Worker,* April 13, 1933, p. 1; *New York Times,* April 12, 1933, p. 12; *New York Times,* April 13, 1933, p. 6.

202. Quoted in *Birmingham News,* April 16, 1933, p. 6.

203. *Huntsville Daily Times,* April 12, 1933, p. 4.

204. Quoted in *Birmingham News,* April 16, 1933, p. 6.

205. Quoted in *Birmingham News,* April 16, 1933, p. 6.

206. *New York Times,* April 10, 1933, p. 12.

207. *Time Magazine,* April 17, 1933, available at http://www.time.com/time/archive/printout/0.23657,847284,00.html.

208. *Decatur Daily,* April 15, 1933, p. 1.

209. *New York Times,* April 18, 1933, p. 3; *Birmingham News,* April 17, 1933, p. 1.

210. *Birmingham News,* April 17, 1933, pp. 1, 2.

211. *New York Times,* April 18, 1933, p. 3.

212. *Huntsville Times,* April 17, 1933, pp. 1, 3.

213. *Daily Worker,* April 18, 1933, p. 1.

214. *Huntsville Times,* April 17, 1933, pp. 1, 3.

215. *New York Times,* April 18, 1933, p. 3.

216. *New York Times,* May 6, 1933, p. 9.

217. *New York Times,* May 1, 1933, p. 18; ibid., May 7, 1933, p. 7; ibid., May 8, 1933, p. 4; ibid., May 29, 1933, p. 28; ibid., June 2, 1933, p. 20; *Decatur Daily,* May 6, 1933, p. 1; *Daily Worker,* April 18, 1933, pp. 1, 2; ibid., April 30, 1933, p. 1; ibid., May 3, 1933, p. 1; ibid., May 4, 1933, p. 1; ibid., May 9, 1933, p. 1; ibid., May 29, 1933, p. 1; June 2, 1933, p. 1.

218. *New York Times,* June 23, 1933, pp. 1, 11.

219. Decision on Motion for a New Trial, Judge Horton, June 22, 1933, available in Cornell Law School's microfilm collection, Scottsboro Cases. Judge Horton's opinion is reprinted in substantial part in Patterson and Conrad, note 28, at pp. 216–29.

220. Decision on Motion for a New Trial, note 218.

221. Decision on Motion for a New Trial, note 218.

222. Decision on Motion for a New Trial, note 218.

223. *New York Times,* June 23, 1933, pp. 1, 11.

224. *Daily Worker,* June 23, 1933, pp. 1, 3.

225. James Goodman, *Stories of Scottsboro* (New York: Vintage Books 1994), p. 209.

226. *Decatur Daily,* June 22, 1933, p. 1; *Huntsville Times,* June 22, 1933, pp. 1, 4; *Birmingham News,* June 22, 1933, pp. 1, 2.

227. *Birmingham News,* June 23, 1933, p. 4.

228. *Birmingham News,* June 22, 1933, p. 1.

229. *Daily Worker,* June 27, 1933, p. 1; Carter, note 3, at pp. 271–72; Linder, note 16, at 577.

230. *New York Times,* June 23, 1933, pp. 1, 11.

231. *Daily Worker,* April 14, 1933, p. 3.

232. "Judge Horton and the Scottsboro Boys," U.S.A. Home Video, 1976.

233. Linder, note 16, at 578–80.

234. Daniel T. Carter, "'Let Justice be Done': Public Passion and Judicial Courage in Modern Alabama," 28 *Cumberland Law Review* 553 (1997–1998): 561–62.

235. Linder, note 16, at 582.

236. Carter, note 234, at 561.

237. Linder, note 16, at 583.

CHAPTER 4

1. *New York Times,* July 26, 1933, p. 11.

2. *Daily Worker,* July 12, 1933, p. 2.

3. Haywood Patterson and Earl Conrad, *Scottsboro Boy* (New York: Bantam Books 1950), p. 41.

4. *New York Times,* October 29, 1933, p. E7, quoting *The Birmingham Post*; see also *New York Times,* October 20, 1933, p. 20; James Goodman, *Stories of Scottsboro* (New York: Vintage Books 1994), p. 209.

5. Goodman, note 4, at p. 215.

6. Hamilton Basso, "Five Days in Decatur," 77 *New Republic* 161 (December 20, 1933): 162. See *New York Times,* November 21, 1933, p. 14; *Birmingham News,* November 21, 1933, p. 1 (each displaying photograph of Judge Callahan).

7. Goodman, note 4, at pp. 209, 215.

8. *New York Times,* November 23, 1933, p. 6.

9. Trial Transcript, *State of Alabama v. Haywood Patterson,* p. 72, Decatur, Alabama, November, 1933, microfilm collection, Cornell Law School.

10. *Montgomery Advertiser,* November 27, 1933, pp. 1, 7.

11. Trial Transcript, *Alabama v. Patterson,* note 9, at pp. 88–89.

12. *Birmingham News,* November 20, 1933, p. 1.

13. *Birmingham News,* November 22, 1933, p. 2.

14. *New York Times,* November 21, 1933, p. 1.

15. *New York Times,* November 21, 1933, p. 1.

16. *Birmingham News,* November 20, 1933, pp. 1, 2; *Montgomery Advertiser,* November 21, 1933, pp. 1, 7.

17. Transcript of Record, *Clarence Norris v. Alabama,* pp. 168–272, United States Supreme Court (No. 534), October Term, 1934, microfilm collection, Cornell Law School.

18. Transcript of Record, *Norris v. Alabama,* note 17, at p. 183.

19. Transcript of Record, *Norris v. Alabama,* note 17, at p. 287.

20. Transcript of Record, *Norris v. Alabama,* note 17, at pp. 289–290.

21. Transcript of Record, *Norris v. Alabama,* note 17, at p. 311.

22. Transcript of Record, *Norris v. Alabama,* note 17, at p. 315.

23. Transcript of Record, *Norris v. Alabama,* note 17, at pp. 413–418.

24. *New York Times,* November 22, 1933, p. 42.

25. Transcript of Record, *Norris v. Alabama,* note 17, at p. 420.

26. Alabama Code § 8603 (1923).

27. Transcript of Record, *Norris v. Alabama,* note 17, at pp. 421–423.

28. Transcript of Record, *Norris v. Alabama,* note 17, at p. 429.

29. Transcript of Record, *Norris v. Alabama,* note 17, at pp. 430–473.

30. Transcript of Record, *Norris v. Alabama,* note 17, at p. 484.

31. Transcript of Record, *Norris v. Alabama,* note 17, at pp. 492–494.

32. Transcript of Record, *Norris v. Alabama,* note 17, at pp. 495–497.

33. *Daily Worker,* November 24, 1933, pp. 1, 6.

34. *Daily Worker,* November 22, 1933, p. 2.

35. Transcript of Record, *Norris v. Alabama,* note 17, at p. 48.

36. Transcript of Record, *Norris v. Alabama,* note 17, at p. 92 (emphasis added).

37. Transcript of Record, *Norris v. Alabama,* note 17, at pp. 93–95.

38. *New York Times,* March 29, 1933, p. 7.

39. Transcript of Record, *Norris v. Alabama,* note 17, at pp. 123–124.

40. Transcript of Record, *Norris v. Alabama,* note 17, at pp. 132–133.

41. *Decatur Daily,* March 28, 1933, p. 1.

42. *Decatur Daily,* November 23, 1933, pp. 1, 4; *New York Times,* November 24, 1933, p. 9.

43. Brief for Appellants, *State v. Patterson, State v. Norris,* pp. 51–52, Alabama Supreme Court (1934), microfilm collection, Cornell Law School.

44. *Montgomery Advertiser,* November 24, 1933, p. 1.

45. *New York Times,* November 24, 1933, p. 9.

46. *Birmingham News,* November 24, 1933, pp. 1, 2

47. Brief for Appellants, *State v. Patterson, State v. Norris,* note 43, at p. 53.

48. *New York Times,* November 24, 1933, p. 9.

49. *Decatur Daily* November 25, 1933, pp. 1, 4

50. *Montgomery Advertiser,* November 26, 1933, pp. 1, 6.

51. Transcript of Record, *Norris v. Alabama,* note 17, at pp. 165–166.

52. *Montgomery Advertiser,* November 27, 1933, p. 1.

53. *Huntsville Times,* November 27, 1933, pp. 1, 6; *New York Times,* November 27, 1933, p. 3.

54. *New York Times,* November 28, 1933, p. 11.

55. *New York Times,* November 28, 1933, p. 11.

56. Transcript of Record, *Haywood Patterson v. Alabama,* pp. 1–10, United States Supreme Court (No. 554), October Term, 1934, microfilm collection, Cornell Law School.

57. *New York Times,* November 28, 1933, p. 11.

58. Transcript of Record, *Patterson v. Alabama,* note 56, at p. 22.

59. Transcript of Record, *Patterson v. Alabama,* note 56, at pp. 55, 66.

60. Transcript of Record, *Patterson v. Alabama,* note 56, at p. 68.

61. Transcript of Record, *Patterson v. Alabama,* note 56, at p. 69.

62. Transcript of Record, *Patterson v. Alabama,* note 56, at p. 121.

63. Transcript of Record, *Patterson v. Alabama,* note 56, at pp. 15–16.

64. Transcript of Record, *Patterson v. Alabama,* note 56, at pp. 125–154, 191–207.

65. Transcript of Record, *Patterson v. Alabama,* note 56, at pp. 180–191.

66. Transcript of Record, *Patterson v. Alabama,* note 56, at pp. 166, 177.

67. Transcript of Record, *Patterson v. Alabama,* note 56, at p. 179.

68. Transcript of Record, *Patterson v. Alabama,* note 56, at pp. 442–464 (testimony of W.A. Sullivan and Elias M. Schwarzbart).

69. Transcript of Record, *Patterson v. Alabama,* note 56, at p. 180.

70. *Montgomery Advertiser,* November 29, 1933, pp. 1, 2.

71. *New York Times,* November 29, 1933, p. 4.

72. *Huntsville Times,* November 28, 1933, pp. 1, 6.

73. *Montgomery Advertiser,* November 29, 1933, pp. 1, 2.

74. *New York Times,* November 29, 1933, p. 4.

75. Transcript of Record, *Patterson v. Alabama,* note 56, at p. 211.

76. Transcript of Record, *Patterson v. Alabama,* note 56, at pp. 212–213.

77. *New York Times,* November 29, 1933, p. 4.

78. Transcript of Record, *Patterson v. Alabama,* note 56, at p. 222.

79. Transcript of Record, *Patterson v. Alabama,* note 56, at pp. 221–236.

80. Transcript of Record, *Patterson v. Alabama,* note 56, at pp. 241–242.

81. Transcript of Record, *Patterson v. Alabama,* note 56, at p. 255.

82. *Montgomery Advertiser,* November 29, 1933, pp. 1, 2.

83. *Daily Worker,* November 29, 1933, pp. 1, 2.

84. *Birmingham News,* November 29, 1933, pp. 1, 2.

85. *New York Times,* November 29, 1933, p. 4.

86. Transcript of Record, *Patterson v. Alabama,* note 56, at pp. 281–282.

87. Transcript of Record, *Patterson v. Alabama,* note 56, at pp. 284–294.

88. Transcript of Record, *Patterson v. Alabama,* note 56, at p. 308.

89. Transcript of Record, *Patterson v. Alabama,* note 56, at pp. 308–310; *Montgomery Advertiser,* November 29, 1933, pp. 1, 2.

90. Transcript of Record, *Patterson v. Alabama,* note 56, at p. 315.

91. Transcript of Record, *Patterson v. Alabama,* note 56, at p. 332.

92. *Birmingham News,* November 29, 1933, pp. 1, 2.

93. Transcript of Record, *Patterson v. Alabama,* note 56, at pp. 332–350.

94. *Birmingham News,* November 29, 1933, pp. 1, 2.

95. *New York Times,* November 29, 1933, p. 4.

96. *Birmingham News,* November 29, 1933, pp. 1, 2.

97. Transcript of Record, *Patterson v. Alabama,* note 56, at p. 357.

98. Transcript of Record, *Patterson v. Alabama,* note 56, at pp. 358–365.

99. Transcript of Record, *Patterson v. Alabama,* note 56, at pp. 365–369.

100. Transcript of Record, *Patterson v. Alabama,* note 56, at pp. 369–385.

101. *New York Times,* November 25, 1933, p. 4.

102. *Birmingham News,* November 25, 1933, p. 1.

103. *Huntsville Times,* November 26, 1933, pp. 1, 3.

104. *Montgomery Advertiser,* November 28, 1933, pp. 1, 3.

105. *Huntsville Times,* November 29, 1933, pp. 1, 8.

106. *Decatur Daily,* November 29, 1933, p. 1.

107. *Montgomery Advertiser,* November 30, 1933, pp. 1, 2.

108. *Huntsville Times,* November 29, 1933, pp. 1, 8.

109. *Birmingham News,* November 29, 1933, pp. 1, 2.

110. Transcript of Record, *Patterson v. Alabama,* note 56, at pp. 388–389.

111. *Decatur Daily,* November 29, 1933, pp. 1, 4.

112. *Montgomery Advertiser,* November 30, 1933, pp. 1, 2.

113. Transcript of Record, *Patterson v. Alabama,* note 56, at pp. 412–413.

114. *New York Times,* November 30, 1933, p. 40.

115. Transcript of Record, *Patterson v. Alabama,* note 56, at pp. 505–512.

116. *Birmingham News,* November 30, 1933, pp. 1, 2.

117. *New York Times,* November 30, 1933, p. 40.

118. *Chattanooga Times,* November 30, 1933, p. 2.

119. *Birmingham News,* November 30, 1933, pp. 1, 2.

120. *New York Times,* November 30, 1933, p. 40.

121. *Birmingham News,* November 30, 1933, pp. 1, 2.

122. *New York Times,* November 30, 1933, p. 40.

123. *Birmingham News,* November 30, 1933, pp. 1, 2.

124. *New York Times,* November 30, 1933, p. 40.

125. *Birmingham News,* November 30, 1933, pp. 1, 2.

126. *Birmingham News,* November 30, 1933, pp. 1, 2.

127. *Decatur Daily,* November 30, 1933, p. 1; *Montgomery Advertiser,* December 1, 1933, pp. 1, 10.

128. *New York Times,* December 1, 1933, p. 1.

129. Transcript of Record, *Patterson v. Alabama,* note 56, at p. 514.

130. *New York Times,* December 1, 1933, p. 1.

131. *Montgomery Advertiser,* December 1, 1933, pp. 1, 10.

132. *New York Times,* November 30, 1933, p. 40.

133. *New York Times,* December 1, 1933, pp. 1, 15.

134. *New York Times,* December 1, 1933, pp. 1, 15.

135. Transcript of Record, *Patterson v. Alabama,* note 56, at p. 518.

136. Transcript of Record, *Patterson v. Alabama,* note 56, at p. 524.

137. Transcript of Record, *Patterson v. Alabama,* note 56, at pp. 524, 526.

138. Transcript of Record, *Patterson v. Alabama,* note 56, at p. 526.

139. *New York Times,* December 1, 1933, p. 15 (reprinting text of Judge Callahan's charge to the jury).

140. Transcript of Record, *Patterson v. Alabama,* note 56, at pp. 534–535.

141. *New York Times,* December 1, 1933, p. 15.

142. Transcript of Record, *Patterson v. Alabama,* note 56, at pp. 535–536.

143. *Montgomery Advertiser,* December 1, 1933, p. 1.

144. Transcript of Record, *Norris v. Alabama,* note 17, at p. 498.

145. *Montgomery Advertiser,* December 2, 1933, pp. 1, 2.

146. *New York Times,* December 1, 1933, p. 1.

147. *Montgomery Advertiser,* December 2, 1933, p. 1.

148. *New York Times,* December 2, 1933, pp. 1, 6.

149. *Birmingham News,* December 2, 1933, pp. 1, 2.

150. *Montgomery Advertiser,* December 2, 1933, p. 1.

151. *Daily Worker,* December 2, 1933, p. 1.

152. *New York Times,* December 2, 1933, p. 1.

153. *New York Times,* December 2, 1933, pp. 1, 6.

154. *Daily Worker,* December 2, 1933, p. 1.

155. *New York Times,* December 3, 1933, p. 28.

156. *New York Times,* December 4, 1933, p. 1.

157. *Birmingham News,* December 2, 1933, p. 1.

158. Clarence Norris and Sybil D. Washington, *The Last of the Scottsboro Boys* (New York: G. P. Putnam's Sons 1979), p. 80.

159. *New York Times,* December 2, 1933, pp. 1, 6.

160. Transcript of Record, *Norris v. Alabama,* note 17, at p. 20.

161. Transcript of Record, *Norris v. Alabama,* note 17, at pp. 6, 10.

162. Transcript of Record, *Norris v. Alabama,* note 17, at p. 24.

163. Transcript of Record, *Norris v. Alabama,* note 17, at p. 40.

164. Transcript of Record, *Norris v. Alabama,* note 17, at p. 42.

165. *New York Times,* December 3, 1933, p. 28.

166. Transcript of Record, *Norris v. Alabama,* note 17, at pp. 143–144; Norris and Washington, note 158, at pp. 113–114.

167. Transcript of Record, *Norris v. Alabama,* note 17, at pp. 217–218.

168. Transcript of Record, *Norris v. Alabama,* note 17, at pp. 192–198; Norris and Washington, note 158, at pp. 120–126.

169. Transcript of Record, *Norris v. Alabama,* note 17, at pp. 198–206; Norris and Washington, note 158, at pp. 126–133.

170. *New York Times,* December 5, 1933, p. 9.

171. *New York Times,* December 3, 1933, p. 28.

172. *New York Times,* December 5, 1933, p. 9.

173. *Birmingham News,* December 4, 1933, p. 1.

174. *New York Times,* December 5, 1933, p. 9.

175. Transcript of Record, *Patterson v. Alabama,* note 56, at pp. 536–537.

176. *New York Times,* December 5, 1933, p. 9; *Montgomery Advertiser,* December 5, 1933, p. 1.

177. *New York Times,* December 3, 1933, p. 28.

178. Norris and Washington, note 158, at 142.

179. *New York Times,* December 6, 1933, p. 19.

180. *Montgomery Advertiser,* December 6, 1933, p. 1.

181. *Decatur Daily,* December 6, 1933, p. 1; *Birmingham News,* December 6, 1933, p. 1.

182. *Decatur Daily,* December 6, 1933, p. 1.

183. *New York Times,* December 7, 1933, p. 16.

184. Quentin Reynolds, *Courtroom: The Story of Samuel S. Leibowitz* (New York: Farrar, Straus and Company 1950), p. 285.

185. *Decatur Daily,* December 6, 1933, p. 1.

186. *New York Times,* December 7, 1933, p. 16; Reynolds, note 184, at p. 285.

187. *Montgomery Advertiser,* December 7, 1933, p. 1.

188. *New York Times,* December 7, 1933, p. 16.

189. *Daily Worker,* December 7, 1933, p. 1; *Daily Worker,* December 16, 1933, p. 2.

190. *New York Times,* December 8, 1933, p. 3; *New York Times,* December 12, 1933, p. 48.

191. *Montgomery Advertiser,* December 5, 1933, p. 4.

192. *Chattanooga Times,* December 8, 1933, p. 4, quoting *Memphis Commercial Appeal.*

193. *Decatur Daily,* December 7, 1933, p. 2.

194. *Decatur Daily,* December 8, 1933, p. 4.

195. *Decatur Daily,* December 9, 1933, p. 2.

196. Dan T. Carter, *Scottsboro: A Tragedy of the American South* (Baton Rouge, Louisiana: Louisiana State University Press, rev. ed. 1979), p. 303.

197. *Time Magazine Archive Article,* "RACES Conviction No. 3," December 11, 1933, http://www.time.com/time/archive/printout/0,23657,746468,00.html.

198. *Time Magazine Archive Article,* "New Plays in Manhattan," March 5, 1934, http://www.time.com/time/archive/printout/0,23657,747124,00.html.

199. *New York Times,* February 25, 1934, p. N1; *Decatur Daily,* February 24, 1934, p. 1.

200. Carter, note 196, at pp. 305–306.

201. *Decatur Daily,* May 26, 1934, pp. 1, 4.

202. Patterson and Conrad, note 3, at pp. 42–47.

203. *New York Times,* March 26, 1934, p. 3.

204. *New York Times,* April–8, 1934, p. 30.

205. Goodman, note 4, at pp. 235–238.

206. *New York Times,* May 14, 1934, p. 2; *Daily Worker,* May 14, 1934, pp. 1, 2.

207. *Patterson v. State,* 156 So.2d 567, 568 (Ala. 1934).

208. *Patterson v. State,* 156 So.2d 567, 570 (Ala. 1934).

209. *Norris v. State,* 156 So.2d 556, 558 (Ala. 1934).

210. *Norris v. State,* 156 So.2d 556, 560 (Ala. 1934).

211. *Norris v. State,* 156 So.2d 556, 561 (Ala. 1934).

212. *Norris v. State,* 156 So.2d 556, 562 (Ala. 1934).

213. *Norris v. State,* 156 So.2d 556, 563 (Ala. 1934).

214. *Norris v. State,* 156 So.2d 556, 563-567 (Ala. 1934).

215. *Norris v. State,* 156 So.2d 556, 567 (Ala. 1934).

216. *New York Times,* June 29, 1934, p. 9.

217. *New York Times,* July 10, 1934, p. 23; *New York Times,* August 28, 1934, p. 14; *Huntsville Times,* August 27, 1934, p. 1.

218. *Montgomery Advertiser,* October 3, 1934, pp. 1.

219. *Montgomery Advertiser,* October 2, 1934, pp. 1, 7; *Montgomery Advertiser,* October 3, 1934, pp. 1; *Montgomery Advertiser,* October 5, 1934, p. 1; *Montgomery Advertiser,* October 7, 1934, p. 1; *Birmingham News,* October 1, 1934, p. 1; *Birmingham News,* October 5, 1934, p. 32; *Jackson County Progressive Age,* October 4, 1934, p. 1; *New York Times,* October 4, 1934, p. 8; *New York Times,* October 7, 1934, p. 5.

220. Reynolds, note 184, at pp. 286–287; *Montgomery Advertiser,* October 4, 1934, pp. 1, 9; *New York Times,* October 4, 1934, p. 8.

221. *Daily Worker,* October 6, 1934, p. 1.

222. *Daily Worker,* October 12, 1934, p. 1.

223. *Daily Worker,* October 6, 1934, p. 1.

224. *Daily Worker,* October 6, 1934, pp. 1, 8.

225. *New York Times,* October 11, 1934, p. 11.

226. *Montgomery Advertiser,* October 5, 1934, pp. 1, 9.

227. *New York Times,* October 11, 1934, p. 11.

228. *New York Times,* October 13, 1934, p. 8; *Daily Worker,* October 13, 1934, pp. 1, 5 (reprinting letters); Carter, note 196, at pp. 313–314.

229. Reynolds, note 184, at p. 288.

230. *New York Times,* October 13, 1934, p. 8; *New York Times,* November 16, 1934, p. 18.

231. Carter, note 196, at p. 316.

232. *New York Times,* November 18, 1934, p. 29; *New York Times,* December 2, 1934, p. 26.

233. *New York Times,* January 8, 1935, p. 23.

234. Reynolds, note 184, at pp. 292–293.

235. The Supreme Court Historical Society, "History of the Court: Homes of the Court," http://www.supremecourthistory.org/02_history/subs_sites/02d.html.

236. Reynolds, note 184, at pp. 291–292; *New York Times,* February 16, 1935, p. 2.

237. Reynolds, note 184, at p. 294.

238. *New York Times,* February 16, 1935, p. 2; *New York Times,* February 19, 1935, p. 42.

239. *Decatur Daily,* April 1, 1935, p. 1; *Huntsville Times,* April 1, 1935, p. 1; *Birmingham News,* April 1, 1935 (alone among the three newspapers in using "Trial" instead of "Trials").

240. *Norris v. Alabama,* 294 U.S. 587, 589 (1935).

241. *Norris v. Alabama,* 294 U.S. 587, 593, n. 1 (1935).

242. *Norris v. Alabama,* 294 U.S. 587, 595–596 (1935).

243. *Norris v. Alabama,* 294 U.S. 587, 598–599 (1935).

244. *Patterson v. Alabama,* 294 U.S. 600, 602 (1935).

245. *Patterson v. Alabama,* 294 U.S. 600, 606–607 (1935).

246. *New York Times,* April 2, 1935, p. 15.

247. *Montgomery Advertiser,* April 2, 1935, pp. 1, 9.

248. *Birmingham News,* April 1, 1935, pp. 1, 2.

249. *New York Times,* April 2, 1935, p. 20.

250. *New York Times,* April 2, 1935, p. 15.

251. *Birmingham Age-Herald,* April 3, 1935, p. 6.

252. *Huntsville Times,* April 2, 1935, p. 4.

253. *Birmingham News,* April 2, 1935, p. 4.

254. *Montgomery Advertiser,* April 2, 1935, p. 4.

255. *Montgomery Advertiser,* April 2, 1935, p. 4.

256. *Montgomery Advertiser,* April 5, 1935, p. 1.

257. *Birmingham News,* April 5, 1935, pp. 1, 6.

258. *Birmingham News,* April 6, 1935, p. 4.

259. *Huntsville Times,* April 5, 1933, p. 4.

260. Quoted in *Birmingham News—Age-Herald,* April 7, 1935, p. 2.

261. *Montgomery Advertiser,* April 6, 1935, p. 4.

262. Quoted in *Birmingham News—Age-Herald,* April 7, 1935, p. 2.

263. *New York Times,* April 7, 1935, p. E8.

264. *New York Times,* April 7, 1935, p. E6.

265. *New York Times,* April 2, 1935, p. 15.

CHAPTER 5

1. *New York Times,* May 1, 1935, p. 6.

2. *Decatur Daily,* April 30, 1935, pp. 1, 2.

3. *Montgomery Advertiser,* May 2, 1935, p. 1.

4. *Decatur Daily,* May 1, 1935, p. 4.

5. *New York Times,* May 17, 1935, p. 6.

6. *New York Times,* August 23, 1935, p. 6.

7. *Huntsville Times,* September 22, 1935, pp. 1, 4.

8. *New York Times,* November 14, 1935, p. 1; *Huntsville Times,* November 13, 1935, pp. 1, 4; *Huntsville Times,* November 14, 1935, p. 1.

9. *Huntsville Times,* November 14, 1935, p. 1.

10. Clarence Norris and Sybil D. Washington, *The Last of the Scottsboro Boys* (New York: G.P. Putnam's Sons 1979), pp. 149–161.

11. *New York Times,* May 30, 1935, p. 20.

12. Dan T. Carter, *Scottsboro: A Tragedy of the American South* (Baton Rouge, Louisiana: Louisiana State University Press, rev. ed. 1979), p. 316.

13. Carter, note 12, at pp. 330–338.

14. *New York Times,* December 28, 1935, p. 32.

15. Allan K. Chalmers, *They Shall Be Free* (Garden City, New York: Doubleday & Co. 1951), pp. 45–53.

16. Carter, note 12, at pp. 338–340.

17. Chalmers, note 15, at p. 53.

18. *Huntsville Times,* January 6, 1936, pp. 1, 5.

19. *New York Times,* November 17, 1935, p. E7.

20. Transcript of Record, *State of Alabama v. Patterson et al.* p. 6, Alabama Supreme Court (1936), microfilm collection, Cornell Law School.

21. Transcript of Record, *State of Alabama v. Patterson et al.,* note 20, at pp. 12–41; *New York Times,* January 7, 1936, p. 18; *New York Times,* January 9, 1936, p. 11.

22. *Decatur Daily,* January 13, 1936, p. 1.

23. Transcript of Record, *State of Alabama v. Patterson et al.,* note 20, at p. 181.

24. Transcript of Record, *State of Alabama v. Patterson et al.,* note 20, at pp. 184–186.

25. *Huntsville Times,* January 20, 1936, pp. 1, 4.

26. *New York Times,* January 20, 1936, p. 40.

27. *Huntsville Times,* January 20, 1936, pp. 1, 4.

28. *New York Times,* January 21, 1936, p. 2.

29. *Decatur Daily,* January 21, 1936, p. 1.

30. Transcript of Record, *State of Alabama v. Patterson et al.,* note 20, at pp. 351–356.

31. *Montgomery Advertiser,* January 22, 1936, p. 1.

32. Transcript of Record, *State of Alabama v. Patterson et al.,* note 20, at pp. 364–365.

33. Transcript of Record, *State of Alabama v. Patterson et al.,* note 20, at pp. 494–495.

34. John Hammond, Jr., "The Trial of Haywood Patterson," *The New Republic* (February 12, 1936): 13–14.

35. Hammond, note 34, at 14.

36. *Montgomery Advertiser,* January 22, 1936, p. 1; Transcript of Record, *State of Alabama v. Patterson et al.,* note 20, at pp. 402–414.

37. Transcript of Record, *State of Alabama v. Patterson et al.,* note 20, at pp. 420–427.

38. Transcript of Record, *State of Alabama v. Patterson et al.,* note 20, at pp. 428–437.

39. Transcript of Record, *State of Alabama v. Patterson et al.,* note 20, at pp. 566–568.

40. *Birmingham News,* January 22, 1936, pp. 1, 2; Transcript of Record, *State of Alabama v. Patterson et al.,* note 20, at pp. 590–591.

41. Transcript of Record, *State of Alabama v. Patterson et al.,* note 20, at p. 596.

42. Transcript of Record, *State of Alabama v. Patterson et al.,* note 20, at p. 610.

43. *New York Times,* January 23, 1936, pp. 1, 7.

44. Transcript of Record, *State of Alabama v. Patterson et al.,* note 20, at pp. 638–640.

45. *New York Times,* January 23, 1936, pp. 1, 7.

46. Hammond, note 34, at 14.

47. *New York Times,* January 23, 1936, pp. 1, 7.

48. *Montgomery Advertiser,* January 23, 1936, pp. 1, 5.

49. *New York Times,* January 23, 1936, pp. 1, 7.

50. *New York Times,* January 23, 1936, pp. 1, 7; *Decatur Daily,* January 23, 1936, p. 1.

51. *New York Times,* January 23, 1936, p. 1.

52. Transcript of Record, *State of Alabama v. Patterson et al.,* note 20, at p. 705.

53. Transcript of Record, *State of Alabama v. Patterson et al.,* note 20, at p. 706.

54. Transcript of Record, *State of Alabama v. Patterson et al.,* note 20, at p. 714.

55. Transcript of Record, *State of Alabama v. Patterson et al.,* note 20, at p. 726.

56. *Decatur Daily,* January 24, 1936, p. 1; *Birmingham News,* January 24, 1936, p. 1.

57. Transcript of Record, *State of Alabama v. Patterson et al.,* note 20, at p. 737.

58. *Montgomery Advertiser,* January 24, 1936, p. 1.

59. *Birmingham News,* January 24, 1936, p. 1; *Decatur Daily,* January 24, 1936, p. 1.

60. *Birmingham Age Herald,* January 24, 1936, p. 4.

61. Hammond, note 34, at p. 14.

62. Chalmers, note 15, at p. 82.

63. *Montgomery Advertiser,* January 24, 1936, p. 1; *Decatur Daily,* January 24, 1936, pp. 1, 2.

64. *New York Times,* January 25, 1936, p. 14.

65. *New York Times,* January 24, 1936, p. 13.

66. *Montgomery Advertiser,* January 24, 1936, pp. 1, 2.

67. *Montgomery Advertiser,* January 24, 1936, p. 1; *Decatur Daily,* January 24, 1936, p. 1.

68. *Decatur Daily,* January 24, 1936, p. 1.

69. *Montgomery Advertiser,* January 24, 1936, p. 1. See also Haywood Patterson and Earl Conrad, *Scottsboro Boy* (New York: Bantam Books 1950), p. 52.

70. Carter, note 12, at pp. 347–348.

71. Hammond, note 34, at 14.

72. *Birmingham News,* January 26, 1936, pp. 1, 2.

73. *Decatur Daily,* January 26, 1936, pp. 1, 2.

74. *Montgomery Advertiser,* January 26, 1936, p. 7.

75. *Decatur Daily,* January 26, 1936, p. 2.

76. *Decatur Daily,* January 27, 1936, p. 1.

77. *Birmingham News,* January 25, 1936, pp. 1, 2.

78. *Birmingham News,* January 25, 1936, p. 4.

79. *Birmingham Age Herald,* January 25, 1936, p. 4.

80. *Montgomery Advertiser,* January 26, 1936, p. 4.

81. *Montgomery Advertiser,* January 28, 1936, p. 4.

82. *New York Times,* January 26, 1936, p. E12.

83. *Birmingham Age Herald,* January 25, 1936, pp. 1, 3.

84. *Birmingham News,* January 25, 1936, p. 1.

85. *Decatur Daily,* January 26, 1936, pp. 1, 2.

86. *Decatur Daily,* January 26, 1936, pp. 1, 2.

87. *Birmingham News,* January 25, 1936, pp. 1, 2.

88. *New York Times,* January 27, 1936, p. 7.

89. *Birmingham Age Herald,* January 25, 1936, pp. 1, 3.

90. *Birmingham Age Herald,* January 25, 1936, pp. 1, 3.

91. *New York Times,* January 26, 1936, p. 32.

92. *Montgomery Advertiser,* January 29, 1936, p. 1.

93. *Decatur Daily,* January 27, 1936, pp. 1, 2.

94. *Decatur Daily,* January 27, 1936, pp. 1, 2; *New York Times,* January 26, 1936, p. 32.

95. *Huntsville Times,* February 17, 1936, p. 1; *Huntsville Times,* February 21, 1936, p. 1.

96. *Decatur Daily,* February 5, 1936, p. 1.

97. *Birmingham News,* January 29, 1936, p. 1.

98. *New York Times,* January 30, 1936, p. 3.

99. James Goodman, *Stories of Scottsboro* (New York: Vintage Books 1994), pp. 268–274.

100. Hugh T. Murray, Jr., "Aspects of the Scottsboro Campaign," 35 *Science and Society*177 (1971): 185.

101. Langston Hughes, "Southern Gentlemen, White Prostitutes, Mill-Owners, and Negroes," 1 *Contempo* 1, December 1, 1931. Available at http://dc.lib.unc.edu/cdm4/item_viewer.php?CISOROOT=/vir_museum&CISOPTR=445 (Web site consulted April 18, 2007).

102. Lynn Barstis Williams, "Images of Scottsboro," 6 *Southern Cultures* 50 (2000): 61–62; *The Collected Poems of Langston Hughes,* eds. Arnold Rampersad and David Roessel (New York: Alfred A Knopf 1994), p. 143.

103. Williams, note 102, at 62–65; *The Collected Poems of Langston Hughes,* note 102, at p. 188.

104. Lin Shi Khan and Tony Perez, *Scottsboro, Alabama: A Story in Linoleum Cuts,* edited by Andrew H. Lee (New York: NYU Press, 1935/reprinted 2001).

105. John Wexley, *They Shall Not Die* (New York: Alfred A. Knopf 1934).

106. Hugh T. Murray, Jr., "Changing America and the Changing Image of Scottsboro," 38 *Phylon* 82 (1977): 84.

107. Williams, note 102, at 52, 65; Murray, note 106, at 85; Carol J. Oja, "Composer with a Conscience: Elie Siegmeister in Profile," 6 *American Music* 158 (1988): 167–168.

108. Daniel W. Pfaff, "The Press and The Scottsboro Rape Cases, 1931–32," 1 *Journalism History* 72 (1974): 73.

109. Chalmers, note 15, at p. 50.

110. Carter, note 12, at pp. 351–356.

111. Carter, note 12, at p. 353; Chalmers, note 15, at pp. 64–68.

112. Carter, note 12, at pp. 357-358; Goodman, note 99, at pp. 288–289.

113. *New York Times,* June 12, 1936, p. 9.

114. Carter, note 12, at pp. 361–362.

115. *New York Times,* December 10, 1936, p. 17.

116. Quentin Reynolds, *Courtroom: The Story of Samuel S. Leibowitz* (New York: Farrar, Straus and Company 1950), p. 304.

117. Carter, note 12, at pp. 363–365; Goodman, note 99, at pp. 289–292; Reynolds, note 116, at pp. 304–306; Chalmers, note 15, at pp. 91–99.

118. *Birmingham News,* May 18, 1937, p. 1; *New York Times,* May 18, 1937, p. 23.

119. *Birmingham News,* May 18, 1937, pp. 1, 9.

120. *New York Times,* May 18, 1937, p. 23.

121. *Birmingham News,* May 19, 1937, p. 6.

122. *Birmingham News,* May 25, 1937, p. 1.

123. *New York Times,* May 23, 1937, p. 65.

124. *Birmingham News,* May 26, 1937, p. 12.

125. *Montgomery Advertiser,* June 12, 1937, p. 4; *New York Times,* June 20, 1937, p. 62; Carter, note 12, at pp. 365–366; Goodman, note 99, at pp. 299–300.

126. *State v. Patterson,* 234 Ala. 342, 175 So. 371 (1937).

127. *New York Times,* June 15, 1937, p. 3.

128. *Decatur Daily,* July 5, 1937, p. 1.

129. *Decatur Daily,* July 8, 1937, p. 1; *Decatur Daily,* July 6, 1937, p. 1; *New York Times,* July 7, 1937, p. 11.

130. *Birmingham Age-Herald,* July 13, 1937, p. 1.

131. *New York Times,* July 14, 1937, p. 3.

132. *Chattanooga Daily Times,* July 14, 1937, p. 7; *Birmingham News,* July 13, 1937, p. 6.

133. *Birmingham News,* July 13, 1937, p. 6.

134. *Birmingham Age-Herald,* July 14, 1937, p. 1.

135. *New York Times,* July 14, 1937, p. 3.

136. *Birmingham News,* July 13, 1937, p. 6.

137. *Huntsville Times,* July 15, 1937, pp. 1, 4.

138. *State v. Norris,* 182 So. 69, 70 (Ala. 1938).

139. *Birmingham News,* July 14, 1937, p. 1.

140. *Decatur Daily,* July 14, 1937, p. 1.

141. *Birmingham Age-Herald,* July 15, 1937, p. 1.

142. *Huntsville Times,* July 15, 1937, pp. 1, 4.

143. *New York Times,* July 15, 1937, p. 11.

144. *Birmingham Age-Herald,* July 15, 1937, p. 1.

145. *New York Times,* July 15, 1937, p. 11.

146. *State v. Norris,* 182 So. 69, 71 (Ala. 1938).

147. *New York Times,* July 15, 1937, p. 11.

148. *Huntsville Times,* July 15, 1937, pp. 1, 4; *New York Times,* July 16, 1937, pp. 1, 6.

149. *Decatur Daily,* July 16, 1937, p. 1.

150. Chalmers, note 15, at pp. 103–104.

151. *Birmingham News,* July 16, 1937, p. 1.

152. *New York Times,* July 18, 1937, p. 8.

153. *New York Times,* July 18, 1937, p. E7.

154. Morris Shapiro, "Behind the Scenes at Scottsboro," 145 *The Nation* 170 (August 14, 1937): 171.

155. *Birmingham News,* July 19, 1937, p. 1.

156. *New York Times,* July 20, 1937, pp. 1, 24.

157. *Decatur Daily,* July 19, 1937, p. 1.

158. *Birmingham Age-Herald,* July 21, 1937, p. 1; *Birmingham Age-Herald,* July 22, 1937, p. 1.

159. *New York Times,* July 23, 1937, p. 3.

160. *Birmingham Age-Herald,* July 23, 1937, p. 1.

161. *Chattanooga Times,* July 23, 1937, p. 1.

162. *Decatur Daily,* July 23, 1937, p. 1.

163. *New York Times,* July 24, 1937, p. 30.

164. *Decatur Daily,* July 23, 1937, pp. 1, 2.

165. *New York Times,* July 24, 1937, p. 30.

166. Appellants' Brief, *Norris v. Alabama, Andy Wright v. Alabama, Weems v. Alabama,* p. 11, Alabama Supreme Court (1938), microfilm collection, Cornell Law School.

167. *Decatur Daily,* July 24, 1937, pp. 1, 2.

168. *New York Times,* July 24, 1937, p. 30.

169. *New York Times,* July 25, 1937, pp. 1, 4.

170. *Decatur Daily,* July 26, 1937, pp. 1, 2.

171. *New York Times,* July 25, 1937, pp. 1, 4.

172. *Birmingham News,* July 26, 1937, p. 2.

173. *New York Times,* July 25, 1937, pp. 1, 4.

174. *Birmingham News,* July 25, 1937, p. 1.

175. *Birmingham Age-Herald,* July 26, 1937, p. 1.

176. *Chattanooga Times,* July 25, 1937, p. 1.

177. *Huntsville Times,* July 25, 1937, p. 4.

178. Quoted in *New York Times,* August 1, 1937, p. 59.

179. *Birmingham News,* July 25, 1937, p. 8.

180. *Birmingham Age-Herald,* July 27, 1937, p. 4.

181. *Chattanooga Times,* July 24, 1937, p. 6.

182. *Chattanooga Times,* July 25, 1937, p. 16.

183. *New York Times,* August 1, 1937, p. 59.

184. Shapiro, note 154, at 170–171.

185. Chalmers, note 15, at p. 102.

186. Scottsboro Defense Committee, "4 Free, 5 in Prison—on the Same Evidence," available athttp://archive.lib.msu.edu/AFS/dmc/radicalism/public/all/fourfreefive/ALN.pdf?CFID=2855963&CFTOKEN=36811961 (Web site consulted May 5, 2007).

187. Scottsboro Defense Committee, note 186, at pp. 5–7.

188. *Decatur Daily,* July 24, 1937, p. 1.

189. *New York Times,* July 25, 1937, pp. 1, 4.

190. *Birmingham News,* July 24, 1937, p. 1.

191. *Birmingham Age-Herald,* July 22, 1937, p. 1.

192. *Huntsville Times,* July 28, 1937, p. 1.

193. Andy Wright, "Plea from a Scottsboro Boy," 145 *The Nation* (August 7, 1937): 159–160.

194. *Decatur Daily,* July 26, 1937, p. 1.

195. *New York Times,* July 27, 1937, p. 9.

196. *New York Times,* August 16, 1937, p. 21; Carter, note 12, at pp. 384–385.

197. *Decatur Daily,* August 16, 1937, p. 1.

198. *New York Times,* July 30, 1937, p. 8.

199. Goodman, note 99, at pp. 312–313.

200. *Patterson v. Alabama,* 302 U.S. 733 (1937); *New York Times,* October 26, 1937, p. 1.

201. *New York Times,* October 31, 1937, p. 70.

202. Chalmers, note 15, at p. 113.

203. Chalmers, note 15, at p. 117.

204. *Wright v. State,* 236 Ala. 263, 182 So. 5 (1938); *Weems v. State,* 236 Ala. 261, 182 So. 3 (1938).

205. *Norris v. State,* 236 Ala. 281, 182 So. 69, 72 (1938).

206. *New York Times,* July 6, 1938, p. 1.

207. *New York Times,* August 17, 1938, p. 38; Chalmers, note 15, at pp. 121–22.

208. *New York Times,* August 18, 1938, p. 3.

209. Chalmers, note 15, at p. 122.

210. *New York Times,* October 12, 1938, p. 34.

211. Chalmers, note 15, at pp. 123–126.

212. Goodman, note 99, at p. 323.

213. Carter, note 12, at p. 390.

214. Chalmers, note 15, at pp. 126–144; Carter, note 12, at pp. 391–393; Goodman, note 99, at pp. 323–326.

215. *New York Times,* November 16, 1938, p. 3.

216. Chalmers, note 15, at p. 150.

217. Scottsboro Defense Committee, *Scottsboro: A Record of a Broken Promise* (undated), p. 3. Available athttp://archive.lib.msu.edu/AFS/dmc/radicalism/public/all/scottsbororecordbroken/ALT.pdf?CFID=2855963&CFTOKEN=36811961 (Web site consulted May 7, 2007).

218. Chalmers, note 15, at pp. 151–154.

219. Chalmers, note 15, at p. 151; Goodman, note 99, at p. 329; Carter, note 12, at pp. 397–398.

220. *New York Times,* January 26, 1936, p. E12.

221. Chalmers, note 15, at p. 172.

222. Carter, note 12, at pp. 403–406; Chalmers, note 15, at pp. 171–193.

223. Carter, note 12, at pp. 407–410; Goodman, note 99, at pp. 313, 368–369; Norris and Washington, note 10, at pp. 180–181; Patterson and Conrad, note 69, at pp. 59–126.

224. Goodman, note 99, at pp. 370–372; Carter, note 12, at p. 411.

225. *New York Times,* January 8, 1944, p. 14; *New York Times,* June 10, 1950, p. 34; Goodman, note 99, at pp. 369–373.

226. *New York Times,* July 12, 1951, p. 26; *New York Times,* July–28, 1951, p. 6; *New York Times,* February 14, 1952, p. 28; *New York Times,* February 22, 1952, p. 13; Goodman, note 99, at pp. 373–375.

227. Norris and Washington, note 10, at p. 198; *New York Times,* January 8, 1944, p. 14; Goodman, note 99, at pp. 370–372.

228. Norris and Washington, note 10, at p. 200; Goodman, note 99, at p. 372; *New York Times,* September 28, 1944, p. 14.

229. Norris and Washington, note 10, at pp. 207–215; *New York Times,* September 27, 1946, p. 21.

230. Goodman, note 99, at p. 378.

231. Patterson and Conrad, note 69, at p. 208; ibid., at pp. 195–207; *New York Times,* July 21, 1948, p. 16.

232. *New York Times,* June 28, 1950, p. 22.

233. *Time,* "Long Journey," July 10, 1950. Available at http://www.time.com/time/archive/printout/0,23657,805459,00.html. Web site consulted March 10, 2006.

234. *New York Times,* July 13, 1950, p. 23; *New York Times,* July 14, 1950, p. 20.

235. *New York Times,* December 19, 1950, p. 32.

236. *New York Times,* September 25, 1951, p. 43; Goodman, note 99, at p. 381; Carter, note 12, at p. 414.

237. *New York Times,* August 26, 1952, p. 14.

238. *New York Times,* August 1, 1940, p. 19.

239. Goodman, note 99, at pp. 356–361; Carter, note 12, at pp. 400–402.

240. *New York Times,* July 14, 1942, p. 13; *Time,* "People," July 20, 1942. Available at http://www.time.com/time/archive/printout/0,23657,796036,00.html. Web site consulted March 10, 2006.

241. Goodman, note 99, at pp. 360–361; Carter, note 12, at pp. 399–400.

242. Chalmers, note 15, at pp. 118–119; *New York Times,* August 17, 1938, p. 38; Goodman, note 99, at p. 339; Carter, note 12, at p. 399.

243. Goodman, note 99, at pp. 356, 384; Carter, note 12, at pp. 399–400, 414; *New York Times,* August 17, 1938, p. 38.

244. *Time,* "Milestones," January 23, 1978. Available at http://www.time.com/time/archive/printout/0,23657,919327,00.html, Web site consulted March 10, 2006.

245. Norris and Washington, note 10, at p. 217; Quentin Reynolds, *Courtroom: The Story of Samuel S. Leibowitz* (New York: Farrar, Straus and Company 1950), p. 365.

246. Norris and Washington, note 10, at p. 228.

247. Norris and Washington, note 10, at p. 231.

248. Alabama Code § 15-22-27 (a).

249. Norris and Washington, note 10, at pp. 233–236, 273–276.

250. *New York Times,* April 22, 1976, p. 48.

251. Norris and Washington, note 10, at pp. 236, 235, 278–281; "Justice, at Last, for 'Scottsboro Boy'?" *The Crisis* 310 (November 1976); "Justice in Alabama?" *The Crisis* 311 (November 1976).

252. Norris and Washington, note 10, at pp. 277, 236–239.

253. *New York Times,* October 26, 1976, p. 1.

254. *New York Times,* November 30, 1976, p. 18.

255. *New York Times,* January 26, 1989, p. 21.

CHAPTER 6

1. *New York Times,* March 30, 1973, p. 42; "Milestones," *Time,* January 23, 1978, available at http://www.time.com/time/archive/printout/0,23657,919327,00.html, Web site consulted March 10, 2006; "Biographies of Key Figures in 'The Scottsboro Boys' Trials—Ruby Bates, Victoria Price" available at http://www.law.umkc.edu/faculty/projects/FTrials/scottsboro/SB_BBates.html, http://www.law.umkc.edu/faculty/projects/FTrials/scottsboro/SB_BPric.html, Web site consulted February 6, 2004.

2. *New York Times,* March 24, 1969, p. 25.

3. Hugh T. Murray, Jr., "Changing America and the Changing Image of Scottsboro," 38 *Phylon* 82 (1977).

4. Dan T. Carter, *Scottsboro: A Tragedy of the American South* (Baton Rouge, Louisiana: Louisiana State University Press 1969/rev. ed. 1979).

5. *New York Times,* April 22, 1976, p. 48.

6. Carter, note 4, at p. 417.

7. Carroll Van West, "Perpetuating the Myth of America: Scottsboro and its Interpreters," 80 *South Atlantic Quarterly* 36 (1981): 45.

8. Carter, note 4, at pp. 421–423.

9. Carter, note 4, at pp. 428–454; James Goodman, *Stories of Scottsboro* (New York: Vintage Books 1994), p. 388.

10. Carter, note 4, at pp. 454–459.

11. *Street v. National Broadcasting Co.,* 645 F.2d 1227 (6th Cir. 1981), *cert. granted,* 454 U.S. 815 (1981), *cert. dismissed,* 454 U.S. 1095 (1981); *New York Times,* December 9, 1981, p. 16; Thomas D. Long, "Public Figures and the Passage of Time: Scottsboro Revisited in Street v. National Broadcasting Co.," 34 *Stanford Law Review* 901 n. 11 (1982): 903.

12. James Haskins, *The Scottsboro Boys* (New York: Henry Holt & Co. 1994); Gerald Horne, *Powell v. Alabama: The Scottsboro Boys and American Justice* (London: Franklin Watts 1997); Lita Sorensen, *The Scottsboro Trials: A Primary Source Account* (New York: Rosen Publishing Group 2003).

13. See Steven Lubet, "Reconstructing Atticus Finch," 97 *Michigan Law Review* 1399 (1999); Claudia Johnson, "Without Tradition and Within Reason: Judge Horton and Atticus Finch in Court," 45 *Alabama Law Review* 483 (1994).

14. I. Bennett Capers, "The Trial of Bigger Thomas: Race, Gender, and Trespass," 31 *New York University Review of Law and Social Change* 1 (2006): 18–19.

15. *Coker v. Georgia,* 433 U.S. 584 (1977). The rape victim in *Coker* was an adult. It is presently unclear whether *Coker's* prohibition against the death penalty for rape applies when the victim is a child.

16. *Thompson v. Oklahoma,* 487 U.S. 815 (1988); *Roper v. Simmons,* 543 U.S. 851 (2005).

17. Wayne Myers, *Roper v. Simmons*: The Collision of National Consensus and Proportionality Review," 96 *Journal of Criminal Law & Criminology* 947 n. 321 (2006): 993.

18. Felix Frankfurter, *Of Law and Men* (Hamden, Connecticut: Archon Books 1956), p. 81.

19. Stephen B. Bright and Patrick J. Keenan, "Judges and the Politics of Death: Deciding Between the Bill of Rights and the Next Election in Capital Cases," 75 *Boston University Law Review* 759 (1995); *Harris v. Alabama,* 513 U.S. 504, 521–522 (1995) (Stevens, J., dissenting).

20. Nicholas L. Georgakopoulos, "Judicial Reaction to Change: The California Supreme Court Around the 1986 Elections," 13 *Cornell Journal of Law & Public Policy* 405 (2004); John H. Culver and Chantel Boyens, "Political Cycles of Life and Death: Capital Punishment as Public Policy in California," 65 *Albany Law Review* 991 (2002); Gerald F. Uelmen, "Crocodiles in the Bathtub: Maintaining the Independence of State Supreme Courts in an Era of Judicial Politicization," 72 *Notre Dame Law Review* 1133 (1997).

21. *Stein v. New York,* 346 U.S. 156, 196 (1953).

22. Jack Greenberg and Jack Himmelstein, "Varieties of Attack on the Death Penalty," 15 *Crime & Delinquency* 112 (1969).

23. *Brown v. Mississippi,* 297 U.S. 278, 284 (1936).

24. Richard C. Cortner, *A "Scottsboro" Case in Mississippi: The Supreme Court and Brown v. Mississippi* (Jackson, Mississippi: University Press of Mississippi).

25. Note, "Beyond *Batson*: Eliminating Gender-Based Peremptory Challenges," 105 *Harvard Law Review,* 1920 (1992): 1924–1925; Carole L. Hinchcliff, "American Women Jurors: A Selected Bibliography," 20 *Georgia Law Review* 299 (1986); *Taylor v. Louisiana,* 419 U.S. 522 (1975).

26. Julie A. Wright, "Using the Female Perspective in Prosecuting Rape Cases," 29 *Prosecutor* 19 (February 1995).

27. David P. Bryden and Sonja Lengnick, "Rape in the Criminal Justice System," 87 *Journal of Criminal Law & Criminology* 1194 (1997): 1282.

28. David C. Baldus, George Woodworth, David Zuckerman, Neil Alan Weiner and Barbara Broffitt, "Racial Discrimination and the Death Penalty in the Post-*Furman* Era: An Empirical and Legal Overview, with Recent Findings from Philadelphia," 83 *Cornell Law Review* 1638 (1998).

29. William J. Bowers, Marla Sandys and Thomas W. Brewer, "Crossing Racial Boundaries: A Closer Look at the Roots of Racial Bias in Capital Sentencing When the Defendant is Black and the Victim is White," 53 *DePaul Law Review* 1497 (2004); William J. Bowers,

Benjamin D. Steiner and Marla Sandys, "Death Sentencing in Black and White: An Empirical Analysis of the Role of Jurors' Race and Jury Racial Composition," 3 *University of Pennsylvania Journal of Constitutional Law* 171 (2001); David C. Baldus, George Woodworth, David Zuckerman, Neil Alan Weiner and Barbara Broffitt, "The Use of Peremptory Challenges in Capital Murder Trials: A Legal and Empirical Analysis," 3 *University of Pennsylvania Journal of Constitutional Law* 3 (2001).

30. Phoebe C. Ellsworth and Samuel R. Gross, "Hardening of the Attitudes: Americans' Views on the Death Penalty," 50 *Journal of Social Issues* 19 (1994): 21–22.

31. *Wainwright v. Witt,* 469 U.S. 412 (1985). *Compare Witherspoon v. Illinois,* 391 U.S. 510 (1968).

32. Michael Finch and Mark Ferraro, "The Empirical Challenge to Death-Qualified Juries: On Further Examination," 65 *Nebraska Law Review* 21 (1986): 44–50; *Lockhart v. McCree,* 476 U.S. 162, 201 (1986) (Marshall, J., dissenting).

33. *Swain v. Alabama,* 380 U.S. 202 (1965).

34. *Swain v. Alabama,* 380 U.S. 202, 224–227 (1965).

35. *Swain v. Alabama,* 380 U.S. 202, 222 (1965).

36. *Batson v. Kentucky,* 476 U.S. 79, 92 (1986).

37. See *Miller-El v. Dretke,* 545 U.S. 231 (2005); *Georgia v. McCollum,* 505 U.S. 42 (1992).

38. *Batson v. Kentucky,* 476 U.S. 79, 102–103 (1986) (Marshall, J., concurring); *Miller-El v. Dretke,* 545 U.S. 231, 266–269 (2005) (Breyer, J., concurring).

39. *McCleskey v. Kemp,* 481 U.S. 279 (1987).

40. John C. Jeffries, Jr., *Lewis F. Powell, Jr.* (New York: Charles Scribner's Sons 1994) p. 451.

41. See David C. Baldus and George Woodworth, "Race Discrimination and the Legitimacy of Capital Punishment: Reflections on the Interaction of Fact and Perception," 53 *DePaul Law Review* 1411 (2004); Scott W. Howe, "The Futile Quest for Racial Neutrality in Capital Selection and the Eighth Amendment Argument for Abolition Based on Unconscious Racial Discrimination," 45 *William & Mary Law Review* 2083 (2004).

42. Michelle J. Anderson, "From Chastity Requirement to Sexual License: Sexual Consent and a New Rape Shield Law," 70 *George Washington Law Review* 51 (2002); Susan Brownmiller, *Against Our Will: Men, Women, and Rape* (New York: Simon and Schuster 1975).

43. See Federal Rule of Evidence 412 (b)(1)(A).

44. Francis A. Gilligan, Edward J. Imwinkelried and Elizabeth F. Loftus, "The Theory of 'Unconscious Transference': The Latest Threat to the Shield Laws Protecting the Privacy of Victims of Sex Offenses," 38 *Boston College Law Review* 107 n. 207 (1996): 131.

45. Jonathan Kimmelman, "Risking Ethical Insolvency: A Survey of Trends in Criminal DNA Databanking," 28 *Journal of Law, Medicine and Ethics* 209 (2000): 214.

46. The Innocence Project, *200 Exonerated: Too Many Wrongfully Convicted* (New York: The Innocence Project 2007). Available at http://www.innocenceproject.org/200/ip_200.pdf. Web site consulted May 16, 2007.

47. Rodney Uphoff, "Convicting the Innocent: Aberration or Systemic Problem?" *Wisconsin Law Review* 739 (2006): 828.

48. Samuel R. Gross, Kristen Jacoby, Daniel J. Matheson, Nicholas Montgomery and Sujata Patil, "Exonerations in the United States 1989 through 2003," 95 *Journal of Criminal Law & Criminology* 523 (2005).

49. C. Ronald Huff, Ayre Rattner and Edward Sagarin, "Guilty Until Proved Innocent: Wrongful Conviction and Public Policy," 32 *Crime & Delinquency* 518 (1986): 523.

50. *Powell v. Alabama,* 287 U.S. 45, 49, 56, 57–58 (1932).

51. *Gideon v. Wainwright,* 372 U.S. 335 (1963).

52. See *Schriro v. Landrigan,* 127 S. Ct. 1933 (2007); *Rompilla v. Beard,* 545 U.S. 374 (2005); *Wiggins v. Smith,* 539 U.S. 510 (2003); *Strickland v. Washington,* 466 U.S. 668 (1984).

53. Kelly Green, "'There's Less in This Than Meets the Eye': Why *Wiggins* Doesn't Fix *Strickland* and What the Court Should Do Instead," 29 *Vermont Law Review* 647 (2005); Kenneth Williams, "Ensuring the Capital Defendant's Right to Competent Counsel: It's Time for Some Standards!" 51 *Wayne Law Review* 129 (2005); Stephen B. Bright, "Counsel for the Poor: The Death Sentence Not for the Worst Crime But for the Worst Lawyer," 103 *Yale Law Journal* 1835 (1994).

54. See *Mickens v. Taylor,* 535 U.S. 162 (2002); *Cuyler v. Sullivan,* 446 U.S. 335 (1980).

55. *Scottsboro Daily Sentinel,* January 27, 2004. Available at http://www.thedaily sentinel.com/story.lasso?wcd=323. Web site consulted February 17, 2004.

56. *Atlanta Journal-Constitution,* January 24, 2004, p. 1A.

57. *Atlanta Journal-Constitution,* January 24, 2004, p. 1A.

58. *Scottsboro Daily Sentinel,* January 27, 2004. Available at http://www.thedaily sentinel.com/story.lasso?wcd=323. Web site consulted February 17, 2004.

59. *Atlanta Journal-Constitution,* January 24, 2004, p. 1A.

Bibliography

BOOKS

Axon, Gordon V. *The Stock Market Crash of 1929* (New York: Mason & Lipscomb 1974).

Brownmiller, Susan. *Against Our Will: Men, Women, and Rape* (New York: Simon and Schuster 1975).

Carter, Dan T. *Scottsboro: A Tragedy of the American South* (Baton Rouge: Louisiana State University Press, rev. ed. 1979).

Cash, W. F. *The Mind of the South* (New York: Alfred A. Knopf 1970).

Chalmers, Allan K. *They Shall Be Free* (Garden City, New York: Doubleday & Co. 1951).

Cortner, Richard C. *A Mob Intent on Death: The NAACP and the Arkansas Riot Cases* (Middletown, Connecticut: Wesleyan University Press 1988).

———. *A "Scottsboro" Case in Mississippi: The Supreme Court and Brown v. Mississippi* (Jackson, Mississippi: University Press of Mississippi 1986).

Ericson, Richard V., Patricia M. Baranek, and Janet B. L. Chan. "Media and Markets," in *Crime and the Media,* ed. Richard V. Ericson (Brookfield, Vermont: Dartmouth Publishing Co. 1995), p. 3.

Frankfurter, Felix. *Of Law and Men* (Hamden, Connecticut: Archon Books 1956).

Goodman, James. *Stories of Scottsboro* (New York: Vintage Books 1994).

Haskins, James. *The Scottsboro Boys* (New York: Henry Holt & Co. 1994).

Holt, Thomas. "The Lonely Warrior: Ida B. Wells-Barnett," in *Black Leaders of the Twentieth Century,* eds. John Hope Franklin and August Meier (Urbana, IL: University of Illinois Press 1982), p. 39.

Horne, Gerald. *Powell v. Alabama: The Scottsboro Boys and American Justice* (London: Franklin Watts 1997).

Jeffries, John C., Jr. *Lewis F. Powell, Jr.* (New York: Charles Scribner's Sons 1994).

Khan, Lin Shi and Tony Perez. *Scottsboro, Alabama: A Story in Linoleum Cuts,* ed. Andrew H. Lee (New York: New York University Press 1935/repr. 2001).

Klarman, Michael J. "*Powell v. Alabama:* The Supreme Court Confronts 'Legal Lynchings'," in *Criminal Procedure Stories,* ed.. Carol S. Steiker (New York: Foundation Press 2006), p. 1.

Leibowitz, Robert. *The Defender: The Life and Career of Samuel S. Leibowitz 1893–1933* (Englewood Cliffs, New Jersey: Prentice-Hall 1981).

Morris, Norval. *Madness and the Criminal Law* (Chicago: The University of Chicago Press 1982).

Norris, Clarence and Sybil D. Washington. *The Last of the Scottsboro Boys* (New York: G.P. Putnam's Sons 1979).

Patterson, Haywood and Earl Conrad. *Scottsboro Boy* (New York: Bantam Books 1950).

Rampersad, Arnold and David Roessel, eds. *The Collected Poems of Langston Hughes* (New York: Alfred A. Knopf 1994).

Reynolds, Quentin. *Courtroom: The Story of Samuel S. Leibowitz* (New York: Farrar, Straus and Company 1950).

Sommerville, Diane Miller. *Rape and Race in the Nineteenth-Century South* (Chapel Hill: University of North Carolina Press 2004).

Sorensen, Lita. *The Scottsboro Trials: A Primary Source Account* (New York: Rosen Publishing Group 2003).

Surette, Ray. *Media, Crime, and Criminal Justice: Images and Realities* (Pacific Grove, California: Brooks/Cole Publishing Co. 1992).

Tolnay, Stewart A. and E.M. Beck. *A Festival of Violence: An Analysis of Southern Lynchings, 1882–1930* (Urbana, Illinois: University of Illinois Press 1995).

Vandiver, Margaret. *Lethal Punishment: Lynchings and Legal Executions in the South* (New Brunswick, New Jersey: Rutgers University Press 2006).

Wexley, John. *They Shall Not Die* (New York: Alfred A. Knopf 1934).

SCHOLARLY ARTICLES

Alexander, Raymond Pace. "The Upgrading of the Negro's Status by Supreme Court Decisions," 30 *Journal of Negro History* 117 (1945).

Anderson, Michelle J. "From Chastity Requirement to Sexual License: Sexual Consent and a New Rape Shield Law," 70 *George Washington Law Review* 51 (2002).

Baldus, David C. and George Woodworth. "Race Discrimination and the Legitimacy of Capital Punishment: Reflections on the Interaction of Fact and Perception," 53 *DePaul Law Review* 1411 (2004).

Baldus, David C., George Woodworth, David Zuckerman, Neil Alan Weiner, and Barbara Broffitt. "The Use of Peremptory Challenges in Capital Murder Trials: A Legal and Empirical Analysis," 3 *University of Pennsylvania Journal of Constitutional Law* 3 (2001).

———. "Racial Discrimination and the Death Penalty in the Post-*Furman* Era: An Empirical and Legal Overview, with Recent Findings from Philadelphia," 83 *Cornell Law Review* 1638 (1998).

Bardaglio, Peter W. "Rape and the Law in the Old South: 'Calculated to excite indignation in every heart,'" 60 *Journal of Southern History* 749 (1994).

Bates, Beth Tompkins. "A New Crowd Challenges the Agenda of the Old Guard in the NAACP, 1933–1941," 102 *American Historical Review* 340 (1997).

Bowers, William J., Marla Sandys, and Thomas W. Brewer. "Crossing Racial Boundaries: A Closer Look at the Roots of Racial Bias in Capital Sentencing When the Defendant is Black and the Victim is White," 53 *DePaul Law Review* 1497 (2004).

Bowers, William J., Benjamin D. Steiner, and Marla Sandys. "Death Sentencing in Black and White: An Empirical Analysis of the Role of Jurors' Race and Jury Racial Composition," 3 *University of Pennsylvania Journal of Constitutional Law* 171 (2001).

Bright, Stephen B. "Counsel for the Poor: The Death Sentence Not for the Worst Crime But for the Worst Lawyer," 103 *Yale Law Journal* 1835 (1994).

Bright, Stephen B. and Patrick J. Keenan. "Judges and the Politics of Death: Deciding Between the Bill of Rights and the Next Election in Capital Cases," 75 *Boston University Law Review* 759 (1995).

Bryden, David P. and Sonja Lengnick. "Rape in the Criminal Justice System," 87 *Journal of Criminal Law & Criminology* 1194 (1997).

Capers, I. Bennett. "The Trial of Bigger Thomas: Race, Gender, and Trespass," 31 *New York University Review of Law and Social Change* 1 (2006).

Carter, Daniel T. "'Let Justice be Done': Public Passion and Judicial Courage in Modern Alabama," 28 *Cumberland Law Review* 553 (1997–1998).

Culver, John H. and Chantel Boyens. "Political Cycles of Life and Death: Capital Punishment as Public Policy in California," 65 *Albany Law Review* 991 (2002).

Detweiler, Frederick G. "The Negro Press Today," 44 *American Journal of Sociology* 391 (1938).

Dorin, Dennis D. "Two Different Worlds: Criminologists, Justices and Racial Discrimination in the Imposition of Capital Punishment in Rape Cases," 72 *Journal of Criminal Law & Criminology* 1667 (1981).

Eberhardt, Jennifer L., Paul G. Davies, Valerie J. Purdie-Vaughns, and Sheri Lynn Johnson. "Looking Deathworthy: Perceived Stereotypicality of Black Defendants Predicts Capital-Sentencing Outcomes," 17 *Psychological Science* 383 (2006).

Ellsworth, Phoebe C. and Samuel R. Gross. "Hardening of the Attitudes: Americans' Views on the Death Penalty," 50 *Journal of Social Issues* 19 (1994).

Finch, Michael and Mark Ferraro. "The Empirical Challenge to Death-Qualified Juries: On Further Examination," 65 *Nebraska Law Review* 21 (1986).

Georgakopoulos, Nicholas L. "Judicial Reaction to Change: The California Supreme Court Around the 1986 Elections," 13 *Cornell Journal of Law & Public Policy* 405 (2004).

Gilligan, Francis A., Edward J. Imwinkelried, and Elizabeth F. Loftus. "The Theory of 'Unconscious Transference': The Latest Threat to the Shield Laws Protecting the Privacy of Victims of Sex Offenses," 38 *Boston College Law Review* 107 (1996).

Green, Kelly. "'There's Less in This Than Meets the Eye': Why *Wiggins* Doesn't Fix *Strickland* and What the Court Should Do Instead," 29 *Vermont Law Review* 647 (2005).

Greenberg, Jack and Jack Himmelstein. "Varieties of Attack on the Death Penalty," 15 *Crime & Delinquency* 112 (1969).

Gross, Samuel R., Kristen Jacoby, Daniel J. Matheson, Nicholas Montgomery, and Sujata Patil. "Exonerations in the United States 1989 Through 2003," 95 *Journal of Criminal Law & Criminology* 523 (2005).

Hinchcliff, Carole L. "American Women Jurors: A Selected Bibliography," 20 *Georgia Law Review* 299 (1986).

Howe, Scott W. "The Futile Quest for Racial Neutrality in Capital Selection and the Eighth Amendment Argument for Abolition Based on Unconscious Racial Discrimination," 45 *William & Mary Law Review* 2083 (2004).

Huff, C. Ronald, Ayre Rattner, and Edward Sagarin. "Guilty Until Proved Innocent: Wrongful Conviction and Public Policy," 32 *Crime & Delinquency* 518 (1986).

Johnson, Claudia. "Without Tradition and Within Reason: Judge Horton and Atticus Finch in Court," 45 *Alabama Law Review* 483 (1994).

Kimmelman, Jonathan. "Risking Ethical Insolvency: A Survey of Trends in Criminal DNA Databanking," 28 *Journal of Law, Medicine and Ethics* 209 (2000).

Klarman, Michael J. "The Racial Origins of Modern Criminal Procedure," 99 *Michigan Law Review* 48 (2000).

Linder, Douglas O. "Without Fear or Favor: Judge James Edwin Horton and the Trial of the 'Scottsboro Boys,'" 68 *University of Missouri at Kansas City Law Review* 549 (2000).

Long, Thomas D. "Public Figures and the Passage of Time: Scottsboro Revisited in *Street v. National Broadcasting Co.*," 34 *Stanford Law Review* 901 (1982).

Lubet, Steven. "Reconstructing Atticus Finch," 97 *Michigan Law Review* 1399 (1999).

Martin, Charles H. "The International Labor Defense and Black America," 26 *Labor History* 165 (1985).

Miller, James A., Susan D. Pennybacker, and Eve Rosenhaft. "Mother Ada Wright and the International Campaign to Free the Scottsboro Boys, 1931–1934," 106 *American Historical Review* 387 (2001).

Murray, Hugh T., Jr. "Changing America and the Changing Image of Scottsboro," 38 *Phylon* 82 (1977).

———. "Aspects of the Scottsboro Campaign," 35 *Science and Society* 177 (1971).

———. "The NAACP versus the Communist Party: The Scottsboro Rape Cases, 1931–1932," 28 *Phylon* 276 (1967).

Myers, Wayne. "*Roper v. Simmons*: The Collision of National Consensus and Proportionality Review," 96 *Journal of Criminal Law & Criminology* 947 (2006).

Note. "Beyond *Batson*: Eliminating Gender-Based Peremptory Challenges," 105 *Harvard Law Review* 1920 (1992).

Oja, Carol J. "Composer with a Conscience: Elie Siegmeister in Profile," 6 *American Music* 158 (1988).

Pfaff, Daniel. "The Press and the Scottsboro Rape Cases," 1 *Journalism History* 72 (1974).

Ross, Felecia G. Jones. "Mobilizing the Masses: The *Cleveland Call and Post* and the Scottsboro Incident," 84 *Journal of Negro History* 48 (1999).

Rossi, Faust. "The First Scottsboro Trials: A Legal Lynching," 29 *Cornell Law Forum* 1 (Winter 2002), online at http://www.lawschool.cornell.edu/pdfs/Winter2002Forum.pdf.

Sommerville, Diane Miller. "The Rape Myth in the Old South Reconsidered," 61 *Journal of Southern History* 481 (1995).

Uelmen, Gerald F. "Crocodiles in the Bathtub: Maintaining the Independence of State Supreme Courts in an Era of Judicial Politicization," 72 *Notre Dame Law Review* 1133 (1997).

Uphoff, Rodney. "Convicting the Innocent: Aberration or Systemic Problem?" 2006 *Wisconsin Law Review* 739 (2006).

West, Carroll Van. "Perpetuating the Myth of America: Scottsboro and its Interpreters," 80 *South Atlantic Quarterly* 36 (1981).

Williams, Kenneth. "Ensuring the Capital Defendant's Right to Competent Counsel: It's Time for Some Standards!" 51 *Wayne Law Review* 129 (2005).

Williams, Lynn Barstis. "Images of Scottsboro," 6 *Southern Cultures* 50 (2000).

Wolfgang, Marvin E. and Marc Riedel. "Race, Judicial Discretion, and the Death Penalty," 407 *Annals of the American Academy of Political and Social Science* 119 (1973).

Wright, Julie A. "Using the Female Perspective in Prosecuting Rape Cases," 29 *Prosecutor* 19 (Feb. 1995).

NEWSPAPERS AND PERIODICALS

Atlanta Journal-Constitution.
Birmingham Age Herald.
Birmingham News.
Chattanooga Times.
Daily Worker.
Decatur Daily.
Huntsville Times.
Jackson County Progressive Age.
Jackson County Sentinel.
Montgomery Advertiser.
New York Times.
Scottsboro Daily Sentinel.
Time Magazine.

COURT DECISIONS

Batson v. Kentucky, 476 U.S. 79 (1986).
Brown v. Mississippi, 297 U.S. 278 (1936).
Coker v. Georgia, 433 U.S. 584 (1977).
Cuyler v. Sullivan, 446 U.S. 335 (1980).
Georgia v. McCollum, 505 U.S. 42 (1992).
Gideon v. Wainwright, 372 U.S. 335 (1963).
Gitlow v. United States, 268 U.S. 652 (1925).
Harris v. Alabama, 513 U.S. 504 (1995).
Lockhart v. McCree, 476 U.S. 162 (1986).
McCleskey v. Kemp, 481 U.S. 279 (1987).
Mickens v. Taylor, 535 U.S. 162 (2002).
Miller-El v. Dretke, 545 U.S. 231 (2005).
Moore v. Dempsey, 261 U.S. 86 (1923).
Norris v. Alabama, 294 U.S. 587 (1935).
Norris v. State, 182 So. 69 (Ala. 1938).
Norris v. State, 156 So. 556 (Ala. 1934).
Patterson v. Alabama, 302 U.S. 733 (1937).
Patterson v. Alabama, 294 U.S. 600 (1935).
Patterson v. State, 156 So. 567 (Ala. 1934).
Patterson v. State, 141 So. 195 (Ala. 1932).
Powell v. Alabama, 287 U.S. 45 (1932).
Powell v. State, 141 So. 201 (Ala. 1932).
Rompilla v. Beard, 545 U.S. 374 (2005).

Roper v. Simmons, 543 U.S. 551 (2005).

Schriro v. Landrigan, 127 S. Ct. 1933 (2007).

State v. Norris, 182 So. 69 (Ala. 1938).

State v. Patterson, 175 So. 371 (Ala. 1937).

Stein v. New York, 346 U.S. 156 (1953).

Street v. National Broadcasting Co., 645 F.2d 1227 (6th Cir. 1981), *cert. granted,* 454 U.S. 815 (1981), *cert. dismissed,* 454 U.S. 1095 (1981).

Strickland v. Washington, 466 U.S. 668 (1984).

Swain v. Alabama, 380 U.S. 202 (1965).

Taylor v. Louisiana, 419 U.S. 522 (1975).

Thompson v. Oklahoma, 487 U.S. 815 (1988).

Wainwright v. Witt, 469 U.S. 412 (1985).

Weems v. State, 182 So. 3 (Ala. 1938).

Weems v. State, 141 So. 215 (Ala. 1932).

Whitney v. California, 269 U.S. 530 (1925).

Wiggins v. Smith, 539 U.S. 510 (2003).

Witherspoon v. Illinois, 391 U.S. 510 (1968).

Wright v. State, 182 So. 5 (Ala. 1938).

LEGAL RECORDS

Brief for Appellants, *Norris v. Alabama, Andy Wright v. Alabama, Weems v. Alabama,* Alabama Supreme Court (1938), microfilm collection, Cornell Law School.

Brief for Appellants, *State v. Patterson, State v. Norris,* Alabama Supreme Court (1934), microfilm collection, Cornell Law School.

Brief for Petitioners, *Powell et al. v. Alabama,* 22 United States Supreme Court Records and Briefs, Nos. 98, 99, 100, October Term 1932.

Brief for Respondent, *Powell et al. v. Alabama,* 22 United States Supreme Court Records and Briefs, Nos. 98, 99, 100, October Term 1932.

Decision on Motion for a New Trial, Judge Horton, June 22, 1933, microfilm collection, Cornell Law School.

Transcript of Record, *Norris v. Alabama,* United States Supreme Court (No. 534), October Term, 1934, microfilm collection, Cornell Law School.

Transcript of Record, *Patterson v. Alabama,* United States Supreme Court (No. 554), October Term, 1934, microfilm collection, Cornell Law School.

Transcript of Record, *Patterson v. Alabama,* Supreme Court of the United States, 22 United States Supreme Court Records and Briefs, No. 99, October Term 1932.

Transcript of Record, *Powell et al. v. Alabama,* Supreme Court of the United States, 22 United States Supreme Court Records and Briefs, No. 99, October Term 1932.

Transcript of Record, *State of Alabama v. Patterson et al.,* Alabama Supreme Court (1936), microfilm collection, Cornell Law School.

Transcript of Record, *Weems and Norris v. Alabama,* Supreme Court of the United States, 22 United States Supreme Court Records and Briefs, No. 100, October Term 1932.

Trial Transcript, *State of Alabama v. Haywood Patterson,* Decatur, Alabama, November 1933, microfilm collection, Cornell Law School.

Trial Transcript, *State of Alabama v. Haywood Patterson,* Decatur, Alabama, March-April, 1933, microfilm collection, Cornell Law School.

OTHER

American Experience. "Scottsboro: An American Tragedy," PBS online, at http://www.pbs.org/wgbh/amex/scottsboro/peopleevents.

"Archival Resources: Cohen, Octavus Roy," Birmingham Public Library Web site, at http://www.bplonline.org/Archives/collections/arts/cohenoctavusroy.asp.

Basso, Hamilton. "Five Days in Decatur," 77 *The New Republic* 161 (December 20, 1933).

Federal Rule of Evidence 412 (b)(1)(A).

"Florian Slappey," The Thrilling Detective Web site, at http://www.thrillingdetective.com/slappey.html.

Hammond, Jr., John. "The Trial of Haywood Patterson," *The New Republic* 13 (February 12, 1936).

Hughes, Langston. "Southern Gentlemen, White Prostitutes, Mill-Owners, and Negroes," 1 *Contempo* 1, December 1, 1931, at http://dc.lib.unc.edu/cdm4/item_viewer.php?CISOROOT=/vir_museum&CISOPTR=445.

The Innocence Project. *200 Exonerated: Too Many Wrongfully Convicted* (New York: The Innocence Project 2007), at http://www.innocenceproject.org/200/ip_200.pdf.

"Judge Horton and the Scottsboro Boys," U.S.A. Home Video (1976).

"Justice, at Last, for 'Scottsboro Boy'?" *The Crisis* 310 (November 1976).

"Justice in Alabama?" *The Crisis* 311 (November 1976).

Linder, Douglas O. "The Trials of 'The Scottsboro Boys,'" University of Missouri-Kansas City School of Law Web site, at http://www.law.umkc.edu/faculty/projects/FTrials/Scottsboro/SB_acct.html.

Ransdall, Hollace. *Report on the Scottsboro, Ala. Case* (May 27, 1931) (unpublished), reprinted on the University of Missouri-Kansas City School of Law Web site, at http://www.law.umkc.edu/faculty/projects/FTrials/scottsboro/SB_HRrep.html.

Scottsboro: An American Tragedy. PBS Home Video (2001).

Scottsboro Defense Committee. "4 Free, 5 in Prison—on the Same Evidence" (undated), available on the Michigan State University Web site, at http://archive.lib.msu.edu/AFS/dmc/radicalism/public/all/fourfreefive/ALN.pdf?CFID=2855963&CFTOKEN=36811961.

Scottsboro Defense Committee. *Scottsboro: A Record of a Broken Promise* (undated), available on the Michigan State University Web site, at http://archive.lib.msu.edu/AFS/dmc/radicalism/public/all/scottsbororecordbroken/ALT.pdf?CFID=2855963&CFTOKEN=36811961.

Shapiro, Morris. "Behind the Scenes at Scottsboro," 145 *The Nation* 170 (August 14, 1937).

Supreme Court Historical Society. "History of the Court: Homes of the Court," http://www.supremecourthistory.org/02_history/subs_sites/02_d.html.

Vorse, Mary Heaton. "The Scottsboro Trial," 74 *The New Republic* 276 (April 19, 1933).

Wilson, Edmund. "The Freight-Car Case," 68 *The New Republic* 38 (August 26, 1931).

Wright, Andy. "Plea from a Scottsboro Boy," 145 *The Nation* 159 (August 7, 1937).

Index

Note: The terms "first," "second," etc. next to some case names denote the trial of the defendant named. These are county, and not appellate, trials.

About the Author

JAMES R. ACKER is Distinguished Teaching Professor at the School of Criminal Justice, University at Albany. He is the author of *Wounds that Do Not Bind: Victim-Based Perspectives on the Death Penalty, Two Voices on the Legal Rights of America's Youth, Criminal Procedure: A Contemporary Perspective,* and other books, as well as numerous articles and book chapters.